Nazis at the Watercooler

# NAZIS AT THE WATERCOOLER

War Criminals in Postwar
German Government Agencies

Terrence C. Petty

**Potomac Books**
An imprint of the University of Nebraska Press

© 2023 by Terrence C. Petty

Acknowledgments for the use of copyrighted material appear on pages xvii–xviii, which constitute an extension of the copyright page.

All rights reserved. Potomac Books is an imprint of the University of Nebraska Press.
Manufactured in the United States of America.

Library of Congress Cataloging-in-Publication Data
Names: Petty, Terrence C., author.
Title: Nazis at the watercooler: war criminals in postwar German government agencies / Terrence C. Petty.
Other titles: War criminals in postwar German government agencies
Description: Lincoln: Potomac Books, an imprint of the University of Nebraska Press, [2024] | Includes bibliographical references and index.
Identifiers: LCCN 2024018194
ISBN 9781640125698 (hardback)
ISBN 9781640126398 (epub)
ISBN 9781640126404 (pdf)
Subjects: LCSH: Germany (West)—Officials and employees—History. | Civil Service—Selection and appointment—Germany (West)—History. | War criminals—Germany (West)—History. | Intelligence service—Germany (West)—History. | Ex-Nazis—Germany (West)—History. |
Germany—Politics and government—1945-1990. | Germany—History—1945-1955. | Denazification. | United States. Central Intelligence Agency. | Cold War. | BISAC: HISTORY / Wars & Conflicts / World War II / General | HISTORY / Modern / 20th Century / Holocaust
Classification: LCC DD259.4 .P48 2024 | DDC 943.087/5—dc23/eng/20240425
LC record available at https://lccn.loc.gov/2024018194

Designed and set in Lyon Text by Lacey Losh.

In memory of journalist Peter Wyden and historian Elizabeth Sumner, mentors and cherished friends who whispered their guidance as I sat at my laptop and wrote this book

*Every now and again collective memory needs to be refreshed. Myths survive because memory fails or becomes selective.*
—Moshe Zimmermann, Israeli Holocaust historian


*History, or, to be more precise, the history we Germans have repeatedly mucked up, is a clogged toilet. We flush and flush, but the shit keeps rising.*
—The narrator in *Crabwalk*, a novel by Günter Grass

# Contents

| | |
|---|---|
| LIST OF ILLUSTRATIONS | xi |
| PREFACE | xiii |
| ACKNOWLEDGMENTS | xvii |
| INTRODUCTION | xix |

### Part 1. American Culpability

| | |
|---|---|
| 1. Beginnings | 3 |
| 2. The Chameleon | 11 |
| 3. Gold Watch for a War Criminal | 25 |
| 4. Fickle Friends | 37 |
| 5. Secret Agent 9610 | 47 |
| 6. A Talk on the Terrace | 65 |

### Part 2. Second Guilt

| | |
|---|---|
| 7. Toppling the Wall of Silence | 77 |
| 8. The Reckoning | 87 |
| 9. Elusive Perpetrators | 91 |
| 10. Killers Welcome | 111 |
| 11. The Rosenburg File | 127 |
| 12. A Burial in Chile | 149 |
| 13. A Tainted Democracy? | 181 |
| 14. Redemption | 209 |
| 15. Squandered Opportunities | 235 |
| Epilogue | 247 |
| NOTES | 255 |
| BIBLIOGRAPHY | 269 |
| INDEX | 271 |

# Illustrations

1. CIA memo pertaining to Hans Globke, September 15, 1954 — 22
2. CIA memo on the Eichmann Case, March 28, 1961 — 23
3. CIA memo about Theo Saevecke's background, August 6, 1951 — 34
4. Theo Saevecke's letter informing the CIA he had been offered a job with the Bundeskriminalamt, April 3, 1952 — 35
5. CIA document showing the agenda for Erich Wenger and Richard Meier's planned trip to Washington DC, February 6, 1963 — 44
6. CIA memo about Erich Wenger and Richard Meier on their Washington DC visit, June 5, 1963 — 45
7. CIA progress report on Paul Dickopf, May 25, 1948 — 61
8. CIA memo about Paul Dickopf, December 30, 1968 — 62
9. CIA cable about Paul Dickopf, September 20, 1973 — 63

*Photographs following page 148*

10. Konrad Adenauer and Hans Globke in Rome, September 1963
11. Fritz Bauer
12. Adolf Eichmann at his trial in Jerusalem, July 3, 1961
13. Richard Gehlen leaving a Munich cemetery, April 7, 1972
14. Walter Rauff after his arrest in Milan, April 1945
15. The Villa Rosenburg in Bonn

# Preface

With its palaces and villas perched on the banks of the Rhine River, with its riverside esplanades, its bustling market square where vendors shout out prices for the day's fresh produce, with its resplendent rococo city hall, green parks, and an easygoing pace, Bonn is a charming little city. But there's a dark chapter of its past that's unlikely to appear on any tourism websites.

During the Cold War, when it was the seat of the federal government, Bonn was crawling with government bureaucrats who had previously been loyal servants of a despotic regime that subjugated a continent through warfare and mass murder. They were there from 1949 through the 1990s—employed at government ministries and agencies that conducted the business of the Federal Republic of Germany. They had swapped Nazi uniforms for suits, Hitler salutes for handshakes. Many of these bureaucrats had probably been minor cogs in the Third Reich machinery. But among them were men who were complicit in the Holocaust, in the expropriation of Jewish property, in cleansing Poland to make way for "Aryans," and in the administration of other Nazi policies in occupied lands.

It wasn't just Bonn that was infested with former Nazis; so were the nation's domestic intelligence service downriver from the capital in Cologne, its foreign intelligence service in the Bavarian town of Pullach, and its federal law enforcement agency in Wiesbaden as well as state and local agencies across West Germany. Postwar security agencies became safe harbors for the worst of the worse—men who had belonged to mobile killing units, known as Einsatzgruppen, and their subunits, Einsatzkommandos, that had executed civilians en masse on the eastern front.

During the Cold War, occasionally a German journalist would uncover the hidden Nazi past of a government official. Government leaders typically dealt with such scandals by accusing the East German Communists of leaking fake documents as part of their endless propaganda campaigns against West Germany and by transferring the tainted civil servant to some job where they would be invisible to the public.

Even into the twenty-first century, no one had any real idea of the depth and breadth of the infestation by former Nazis or of the seriousness of whatever misdeeds these bureaucrats had done in their pasts. This is because for six decades German government agencies never bothered to launch comprehensive, methodical investigations into their postwar hiring practices. Germans knew that former Nazis had been hired for government jobs, but there was little desire to dig into the matter. A self-willed collective amnesia among Germans protected Nazi-tainted government officials from a true reckoning with their past. As another Cold War journalist and friend Peter Gehrig put it: "The student movement and the left had a hard time convincing people looking for a Ford to replace their Beetle and wanting to fly to Turkey instead of driving to Rimini for vacation that there are more important things in life."[1]

I worked and lived in Bonn from 1987 to 1997. During my whole time there, public and official discussions about former Nazis working in government offices were rare. I had a membership in the Bonn American Embassy Club, a perk that came with my position as the Associated Press's chief correspondent in the capital city. Having an Embassy Club card granted access to an indoor swimming pool and an American-style restaurant that men couldn't enter without a sport jacket. The club and the pool were located within the American community, which looked more like a Middle America suburb than a German neighborhood. The community consisted of shoebox-shaped buildings where American families lived in modest apartments, a baseball diamond, an elementary school and a high school, and a shopping center with a café, movie theater, dry cleaner, video store, hair salon, barbershop, post exchange, and bookstore—pretty much everything to meet the needs of Americans who didn't want to take the trouble of trying to get to know their host city.

Germans, by and large, avoided the Americans' shopping center—it was too tacky for most, excepting the Bonn police officers who were drawn to the café's big hamburgers, which the officers ate with fork and knife rather than with their hands. But access to the fancy restaurant and to the swimming pool carried an exclusivity that, despite the steep annual fees, appealed to many German government officials, retired and otherwise. I used the lap pool a lot. Among the German regulars were elderly people who had retired from government service. As I swam my laps, I would wonder to myself about my elderly pool mates and about other German government retirees I'd encounter. What did they do during the war? While researching this book, I came to the realization that most of them must have been loyal servants of the Third Reich. The reason: after West Germany's founding in 1949, preference was given to experienced men and women for civil service jobs. War criminals were supposed to be excluded. But because government agencies never bothered to create effective candidate vetting systems and often simply chose to ignore strong signs of criminal misdeeds, it was not at all unusual for someone who by all rights should have been put on trial to instead be given a government job. This happened not just at the federal level but also at the state and municipal levels. As a result, civil servants whose dark pasts had been found out were rarely prosecuted. Nearly a whole generation of German government officials with Nazi pasts was never brought to account.

In 2005 Foreign Minister Joschka Fischer commissioned an inquiry into the Nazi pasts of postwar German diplomats, and the findings were published five years later. That project was followed by similar investigations by not just every major federal agency but also state and municipal offices across Germany. While these studies have brought a greater understanding of the Nazi taint within the postwar civil service, they did not result in criminal investigations. Bringing charges was not the purpose of the inquiries.

Soon after the founding of the West German state, Chancellor Konrad Adenauer declared that "this sniffing around for Nazis has to stop."

And that's precisely what happened.

It is a mindset that opened the doors of the postwar German civil service to men who had served with murder squads that massacred Jews and other civilians on the eastern front, to bureaucrats complicit in deporting Jews to death camps, to administrators sent to occupied territories to implement the Nazis' brutal policies, to judges and prosecutors responsible for death sentences for the slightest of offenses, and to rail managers involved in sending trainloads of the doomed to Auschwitz and other Nazi camps.

# Acknowledgments

Having grown up in the Champlain Valley, a region rich with sites from the French and Indian War, the Revolutionary War, and the War of 1812, a passion for history is in my bloodstream. So naturally I have deep respect for historians and the work they do. One of my greatest joys in researching this book was communicating with scholars and specialists who have blazed new trails in Cold War studies.

For their personal communications with me, whether by Zoom, Skype, phone, or email, I am grateful to German historians Frank Bösch, Norbert Frei, Klaus-Dietmar Henke, Patrick Wagner, Gerhard Sälter, Maren Richter, and Stefanie Palm and to law professor Christoph Safferling. My thanks also to Dieter Schenk for relating his fascinating life story, to journalist Ronen Steinke for his observations on the importance of Fritz Bauer, to documentary filmmaker Dirk Laabs for his insights into right-wing extremism in twenty-first-century Germany, and to cop culture expert Rafael Behr for his assessments of government moves to counter that extreme-right threat. My thanks also to Arthur Allen, a fellow veteran of AP coverage of Germany, for conversations we have had about the "great silence" during the Adenauer era.

I am especially grateful to American Holocaust historian Peter Hayes for encouraging my research, taking the time to read a draft of my manuscript, and for championing this book. Alan Steinweis, a historian of the Holocaust at the University of Vermont, my alma mater, has also been immensely supportive of my work.

Ulrich Renz, former chief editor of the AP's German Service—deserves special mention for giving me a deeper understanding of the Adenauer years with the personal story of his family. Uli's successor at the German Service, Peter Gehrig, was indispensable as a sounding board, for assistance in grasping complexities of the German legal and civil service systems and backstopping me on a number of text and quote translations to make sure nuances were not overlooked.

Bridget Barry, editor in chief at the University of Nebraska Press, and Thomas Swanson, former editor of Potomac Books, have my gratitude for embracing this project, as do their staff, who were a delight to work with in seeing it through to publication.

And of course my wife, Christina—my true north—deserves my most profound thanks, for the five decades she's stood by me, despite the stresses that come with being married to a journalist.

# Introduction

While researching this book, I wanted to get a sense of what it was like to have lived in Germany during the first postwar years. So I turned to an old friend and former Associated Press colleague, Ulrich Renz. Uli was eleven when American troops rolled into Giengen an der Brenz, a Swabian town that Renz, his brother, and their mother had fled to from air raids on Stuttgart. At that time his father was still in Stuttgart, doing odd jobs to get by. The father, Julius Renz, had been a Nazi administrator in occupied Poland. At war's end he knew he was going to be called before a denazification tribunal to have his wartime actions be judged and given a culpability classification. "He kept delaying this hearing, because he worried his time in Poland would come up. He feared he'd be arrested and deported to Poland to stand trial," Uli told me. On the denazification questionnaire, the father put down that from 1940 to 1945 he had worked for the Reichsnährstand, a government office that regulated food production. No mention of his work as an administrator in Nazi-occupied Poland. When the denazification tribunal finally questioned Julius Renz, "he was fully able to conceal his time in Poland," Uli said. Uli rebelled against his father. They seldom spoke, and the war years were an especially verboten topic. Uli dug into his father's past and found out about his membership in the Nazi Party and his administrative work in occupied Poland. Uli is convinced his father was a war criminal because of the nature of the duties that went with Julius's position.[1] Sadly, the broken relationship between Uli and his father was not out of the ordinary during those times. Generational conflicts of this sort were replicated across West Germany during the Cold War years.

This book is about the first decades of the Cold War. It is often called the "Adenauer era" because its politics were dominated by the first West German chancellor, Konrad Adenauer. But it could just as well be called the Era of the Great Silence because of a pervasive aversion among Germans of the wartime generation to talk about the Third Reich and its crimes.

I worked as an Associated Press correspondent in Germany from 1987 to 1997. I was fortunate to have been there when an exodus of East Germans and massive pro-democracy protests forced the opening of the Berlin Wall and when the two German states reunited. When I returned to the States, I couldn't get Germany out of my head. So as I performed my stateside duties as an editor, I carved out time to occasionally write about German topics.

In 2016 I began tracking the work of independent historians hired by German government ministries and agencies to examine the Nazi taint of the postwar civil service. This struck me as an incredibly important development, a historic one. I began reading the published findings of inquiries that had already been completed, starting with *Das Amt und die Vergangenheit: Deutsche Diplomaten im Dritten Reich und in der Bundesrepublik* (*The Office and the Past: German Diplomats in the Third Reich and the Federal Republic*), the controversial 2010 book about the German Foreign Office. That was followed by published studies of Adenauer era hiring practices at the Bundeskriminalamt (Federal Criminal Police Office), the Justice Ministry, the domestic and foreign intelligence services, the Federal Prosecutor's Office, and others.

Many of the historians were surprised by what they discovered: the depth and breadth of Nazi infestation in government agencies was worse than they had imagined. Given access to government documents long kept under lock and key, the researchers were also able to piece together networks of Nazis who had helped each other land postwar jobs, shed light on self-exculpation tactics used to cover up dark pasts, and expose how wartime perpetrators were given preference for government jobs over victims and anti-Nazi resisters.

Silence about the Nazi past was shaken in the 1960s by the trial of Adolf Eichmann, the trials of former guards at Auschwitz, street protests by German university students, and the departure of the old political guard, in the person of Konrad Adenauer, and the arrival of younger and more progressive politicians, especially the dynamic Social Democrat Willy Brandt. Despite these changes, there was little interest—even into the 1990s—in digging into how many former Nazis were in government agencies, how they got there, and whether they had any influence on policymaking. In 1985 Holocaust survivor Ralph Giordano published *Die Zweite Schuld, oder Von der Last ein Deutscher zu Sein* (*Second Guilt, or The*

*Burden of Being a German*), in which he called out Germans for allowing former Nazis to return to influential positions. In 1987 attorney Ingo Müller published a book that looked specifically at Third Reich judges and prosecutors who were back at their jobs in the postwar years. Both books created backlashes. In 1997 historian Norbert Frei published a scholarly, groundbreaking book about Adenauer's policy of reintegrating the "old elites." But it took several more years for the first government agency—the Foreign Office—to examine the hiring practices that provided safe havens for bureaucrats who if they didn't have blood on their hands, had it on their consciences.

Why did it take so long? This is a question that was tackled by the *Historikerkommissionen*, the teams of scholars who were granted access to personnel files to find out just how extensive the Nazi infestation of government agencies was during the formative years of the Federal Republic.

Andreas Wirsching was coleader, along with fellow historian Frank Bösch, of a team of researchers who examined records of the federal Interior Ministry. During a 2016 conference of academicians involved in these new government-commissioned investigations, Wirsching offered some convincing explanations for government agencies' procrastination in putting their postwar beginnings under the microscope.[2] The explanations are not exactly flattering.

Even into the 1990s, Wirsching said, if a researcher went to an elderly town historian and sought documents about certain personalities, the pursuit might end with the researcher being shown the door. There was a sense of loyalty within the older generation toward their wartime peers. This could also be seen in the fact that for decades there were streets named after Germans who were key figures in both the Third Reich and the postwar Federal Republic. This loyalty, or admiration, began to change as the wartime generation was dying out.

The change started not with the political class but with major German corporations—including Daimler, Deutsche Bank, Volkswagen, BASF, Bayer, Dr. Oetker, and Bertelsmann—that commissioned studies of their complicity with the Nazi regime. These corporate self-examinations were driven by market considerations. According to Wirsching, it was important for German players on the global market to show the outside world that they had fully confronted their Third Reich complicity. Similarly, governmental agencies were compelled to commission examinations of the past. Findings of the studies by corporations and by the government serve as a sort of "seal of approval," Wirsching explained.

"The seal of approval, or certificate, reads: 'Evaluation of National Socialism and its consequences has been completed,'" Wirsching said. "The results are—to be blunt—almost secondary. The most important thing is that this evaluation has been carried out, to a certain degree as a purification of the cultures of the respective corporate or ministerial authority."

Another explanation that's been given for German government agencies' long delay in examining their links to Third Reich bureaucracies is an evolving view of what it means to be a Nazi "perpetrator." Up until the Auschwitz Trials of the 1960s decisively showed otherwise, large segments of the West German populace chose to put the blame for the Third Reich's crimes not on ordinary Germans but on Hitler, his inner circle, and the Schutzstaffel (SS), the Nazi's elite guard. This way of thinking actually became part of West German jurisprudence, and it shielded concentration camp guards and others from being charged with murder.

"Research has increasingly expanded the 'perpetrator concept' since the 1980s," Wirsching said on April 26, 2016, at the Fifth Rosenburg Symposium, part of a series of conferences organized by the Justice Ministry to discuss the work of the government-commissioned historians. "If today the talk is of the 'perpetrators of the NS [National Socialist] regime,' then then this no longer means just the NS [Nazi Party], the henchmen of the Holocaust or the desk-bound perpetrators."

This is undoubtedly true. However, if the German war generation hadn't been so determined to sweep crimes and guilt under the carpet, if prosecutors and judges had been more aggressive in pursuing the perpetrators, it wouldn't have taken so long to see that it wasn't just Nazi bigwigs who were culpable but also doctors, police officers, businessmen, humble bureaucrats, and other ordinary Germans, who were back on the job during the Adenauer years.

Another suppressive factor among West Germans was that being open to the possibility that incriminating documents were authentic and not fake meant running the risk of looking like one was in league with the East German Communists. This was a stigma that outlived the East German state, demonstrating that the West Germans' counterpropaganda strategy was far more effective than document leaks coming from the East.

Even though historians who conducted the government-funded studies were granted access to documents never before made public, including personnel records, assessing a government employee's degree of guilt for Nazi crimes can be difficult. The researchers set as their goal not just "the counting of Nazis" but determining what exactly they had done during the years of the Third Reich. But many a postwar civil servant was so successful at covering his Nazi era tracks—through omissions, obfuscations, outright lies, and self-deception—that determining his complicity can prove to be elusive, like trying to grasp a slippery bar of soap in a tub of water. This is a problem that German government officials created for themselves by waiting so long to air the dirty Nazi linen concealed within the dresser drawers of postwar government bureaucracy.

The self-examinations by German government agencies began a few years after the U.S. Central Intelligence Agency started declassifying its files on Nazi war criminals under a 1999 law. German officials had no other choice. While the declassified CIA documents drew media and public attention to war criminals who were hired and protected by American intelligence—such as Klaus Barbie, the "butcher of Lyon"—the files also contain details on Nazi perpetrators who worked for the Americans and then for postwar West German security agencies, men like Theodor Saevecke, an SS officer who during the war rounded up Jews in Tunisia for slave labor and committed atrocities in Italy. The CIA files provide a sort of fly-on-the-wall view of discussions between former Nazis and U.S. spooks as the Americans tried to shape West German security agencies into forms that would be useful for them. Especially interesting in the CIA files are documents showing American intelligence officials' grooming of a German military intelligence officer—Paul Dickopf—to draw up plans for a West German federal police agency, which became the Bundeskriminalamt. Declassified files show that Dickopf was actually a paid agent for the CIA into the 1970s, spying on his own masters for his American pals. With these sorts of details no longer hidden from the public after they were declassified, the Germans couldn't very well have kept their own files under seal.

It should be noted that before German government ministries and agencies commissioned inquiries into the postwar hiring of former Nazis, a number of German authors had been doing their own digging. I've already mentioned Ingo Müller's book on incriminated judges, Ralph Giordano's work on "Second Guilt," and Norbert Frei's trailblazing study of Adenauer's policy of reintegrating former Nazis. Frei, in fact, has written and spoken prolifically about Germany's twenty-first-century confrontation with the Nazi past. He was editor of and contributor to a 2001 book titled *Hitler's Eliten Nach 1945* (Hitler's Elites after 1945), a collection of essays about doctors, industrialists, businessmen, military officers, lawyers, and journalists who, opportunistically, carved out successful careers for themselves both in the Third Reich and in postwar Germany. The book is a companion volume to a six-part TV documentary series that drew a mass audience. Dieter Schenk, a former employee of the Bundeskriminalamt, exposed war criminals who had worked at the federal police agency in his own book *Auf dem rechten Auge blind: Die braunen Wurzeln des BKA* (Turning a Blind Eye to the Right: The Brown Roots of the BKA), published in 2001. The public's appetite for learning more about the flaws and failures of the Adenauer era has been fed by other recent works as well. They include a biography, published in English in 2020, by journalist Ronen Steinke about Fritz Bauer, a state prosecutor who was instrumental in the capture of Adolf Eichmann; and a page-turning, best-selling novel, *The Collini Case* (2013), by defense attorney Ferdinand von Schirach, whose peg is a 1968 federal law that allowed thousands of war criminals to go unpunished.[3] Von Schirach, by the way, is a grandson of the National Socialist youth leader Baldur von Schirach.

A note on the format of the narrative, in two sections, that follows. Largely based on declassified CIA files, part 1 explores Americans' cozy relations with Third Reich figures who rose to positions of authority in West German government agencies, often with the assistance—or at least the forbearance—of U.S. officials. While part 1 focuses on American influence on West German security agencies, part 2 broadens the scope, using the findings of the German *Historikerkommissionen*, and other sources, to examine the Nazi taint across the postwar federal bureaucracy.

Nazis at the Watercooler

# PART 1

American Culpability

# 1

# Beginnings

On a cold January day in 1951, in the Bavarian town Landsberg am Lech, a car donated by a local appliance store and mounted with a loudspeaker blasts out a call for residents to come to the main square for a protest scheduled in a couple of days. The cause of the townsfolk's anger is the pending execution of convicted Nazi war criminals held at the Americans' prison in Landsberg. As the appliance store car cruises along the streets of the picturesque little town on the River Lech, a voice blaring from the loudspeakers beckons the townsfolk to a rally to demand the "acts of inhumanity"—meaning the execution of convicted war criminals—be stopped.[1]

Alarm over the fate of twenty-eight condemned war criminals imprisoned at the U.S. government's War Criminal Prison No. 1 was raised when rumors circulated among politicians in Bonn that an execution date had been set for some of them: the tenth of January. A Bavarian member of the Bundestag, Gebhard Seelos, quickly began organizing a Landsberg demonstration to force the American occupiers to cancel the executions.

On January 7, 1951, four thousand people stood shoulder to shoulder on Landsberg's main square. Among them were federal, regional, and local politicians. Seelos fired them up by denouncing the postwar Nuremberg trials of Nazi officials as injustices against Germans, against humanity, and against Christianity. There was thunderous applause as Seelos called on the Americans to "cease this cruel game."

Landsberg was among the many places in Germany where Jews who had survived the Nazi camps were being fed and housed by Allied governments after making long treks following their liberation. About twenty-three thousand of them had passed through Landsberg since the end of the war. When the five hundred who remained heard about plans for the January 7 rally, they determined they must make their voices heard.

As Seelos spoke to the townspeople, shouts rang out from Holocaust survivors who had come to the main square to stage a counterprotest.

Shouting matches and fights erupted. From within the throngs of war criminal–supporting townspeople came shouts of "Juden Raus!"—"Jews Are Not Wanted!"

As the riot was occurring, the condemned prisoners were waiting to learn their fate. As it turned out, the American occupying authorities had not yet decided whether to show mercy to any of the condemned men—although pardons were being considered. Among them were Oswald Pohl, a Schutzstaffel officer who had been in charge of administering the Nazis' sprawling concentration camp system, and Major General Otto Ohlendorf, whose Einsatzgruppe D murdered ninety thousand Jewish children, women, and men in the Soviet Union. The Holocaust survivors were justifiably incensed about Germans rallying in support of the two war criminals. The confrontation on Landsberg's main square ended when police moved in and arrested not unruly townspeople but Holocaust survivors.

The Landsberg prison was fraught with symbolism. After Adolf Hitler's failed Beer Hall Putsch of 1923, he was transported to Landsberg to serve his prison term. Hitler served less than a year of his five-year sentence. After his release, Landsberg became a place of pilgrimage for Germans who saw him as the Fatherland's messiah. They'd visit the Landsberg cell where he wrote *Mein Kampf* and walk the grounds as they followed the Führer's footsteps. This was a hallowed site.

Convicted perpetrators from the American military's trials at Dachau and the international trials at Nuremberg were sent to Landsberg either to serve their sentences or to await execution. By 1951 some 250 Nazi war criminals had been hanged on the gallows in the prison courtyard.

West German calls for pardons of Nazi war criminals began soon after the Third Reich's defeat, coming from religious leaders, war veterans, politicians, industry leaders, and everyday Germans. There was a groundswell of German empathy for the tens of thousands of Hitler minions locked up inside prisons by the Americans and their partners in the occupation of western Germany—the British and the French. They were seen not as criminals but as victims of *Siegerjustiz*, or "victor's justice," their incarceration an unwanted reminder to Germans of their embrace of Hitler and the Third Reich. Moreover, the prisoners had only been following orders. The thought of going easy on Nazis was appalling to many Americans, including some in government. But it was clear that the West Germans—especially former military officers—would not acquiesce to joining the

Allies' mounting confrontation with the Soviet Union and its satellite nations without pardons and amnesties for the Nazi perpetrators locked up in the victors' jails.

The fate of the condemned prisoners was in the hands of John J. McCloy, the U.S. high commissioner for Germany. McCloy's headquarters were in Bonn's Petersberg Hotel, a posh aerie overlooking the Rhine River, where his British and French counterparts also had their offices. Soon after being appointed to the position in the fall of 1949, McCloy began considering pleas for lessened sentences and pardons for some of the incarcerated prisoners. The crimes of Ohlendorf, Pohl, and a handful of others at Landsberg were so heinous that McCloy decided their executions had to be carried out. They swung from the Landsberg gallows on June 7, 1951. The remainder of the prisoners were eventually granted early release.

Outbursts of German sympathy for convicted war criminals also surfaced in the British occupation zone. While the American military's prison for war criminals was in Landsberg, Nazi perpetrators convicted in the British zone were incarcerated in Werl, a town east of Dortmund. One of the convicts, Wilhelm Kappe, succeeded in escaping from the Werl prison in the fall of 1952. Kappe showed up in the East Frisian town of Aurich, where he had relatives. By chance Kappe ran into an old friend, Friedrich Ballin, on an Aurich street. Ballin later walked by a stand run by a fishmonger, Wilhelm Heidepeter, who was also chairman of the Social Democrats in the Aurich senate. The two men got to talking, and Ballin mentioned his conversation with Kappe. Heidepeter informed local police, who found Kappe and arrested him. Kappe was able to escape the local police lockup by jumping out a window.[2]

As the search resumed, Heidepeter's fellow citizens were enraged to learn that he had abetted British occupying authorities by turning in Kappe. When they went to his booth at the weekly market, they didn't go to check on the price of that day's catch. They went to show their disdain for the fishmonger, spitting on the cobblestones. Aurich citizens armed with clubs gathered in front of his house, smashed a window, and left a poster that read, "The traitor Heidepeter lives here." Even Heidepeter's colleagues in the Social Democratic Party turned against him, stripping him of his duties. Fearing for his life, Heidepeter left town. Kappe and another war criminal who had escaped with him, Hans Kuhn, were ultimately captured.

The German re-embrace of Nazis had begun soon after the Third Reich's defeat.

When Adolf Hitler fired a bullet from a Walther pistol into his brain on April 30, 1945, he cheated the wartime Allies of the satisfaction of putting him on trial. Propaganda minister Joseph Goebbels and ss chief Heinrich Himmler also killed themselves. Many other Nazi satraps ended their own lives: 53 of 554 army generals, 14 out of 98 air force generals, 11 of 53 admirals, several ss and police leaders, and 8 of 41 Nazi regional leaders.

For the prosecution of major war criminals who had not evaded capture, the International Military Tribunal in Nuremberg awaited. A total of twenty-four major Third Reich figures were indicted on charges of crimes against peace, war crimes, and crimes against humanity in a trial that began in November 1945 and lasted nearly a year. Nineteen defendants were convicted. Twelve were sentenced to death by hanging, three to life imprisonment, and the rest to prison terms ranging from ten to twenty years. Hermann Goering, the highest-ranking Nazi to be tried at Nuremberg, killed himself by ingesting cyanide the night before his scheduled execution.

Prosecutions of war criminals did not stop there. There were plenty more to be judged. The four victorious Allies—the United States, Britain, France, and the USSR—held their own tribunals, as did numerous countries that had been victimized by the Nazis. Some five thousand Germans were convicted by American, French, and British military courts, which handed down nearly seven hundred death sentences. Tens of thousands of Germans were tried by the Soviets. Many were given long prison sentences, and an unknown number were executed. Thousands more were tried in Poland, Holland, and other countries.[3]

All of the arrests, convictions, and sentences were in line with the original intent of the United States, Britain, France, and the USSR, the vanquishers of the Third Reich. Before the war's end, they were all in agreement that Germany had to be thoroughly cleansed of Nazism and perpetrators made to pay for their crimes. Germans were called before "denazification" panels to face grilling on their activities during the Third Reich and categorized according to the adjudged degree of complicity with the Nazi regime: "Major Offender," "Offender," "Lesser Offender," "Follower," or "Exonerated."

In the Soviet zone, the military occupiers were brutally efficient. Thousands of Germans who had held government jobs at all levels—from mayors to state leaders—were hauled off to former Nazi concentration camps that were repurposed to serve as internment camps for Germans. Illness and death were rampant. Some of the detainees were just nominal Nazis, but that didn't matter to the Soviets. As new government structures began to develop, German Communists who had resisted the Nazis and Third Reich victims were among those given preference for positions. Nonetheless, new research by German historians shows that even the East German regime didn't completely exclude former Nazis from government jobs. A 2018 study found that in the early years of the East German Ministry of the Interior, 14 percent of its managers were former members of the Nazi Party, 5 percent had been in the Sturmabteilung (the paramilitary wing of the Nazi Party), and 1 percent in the Schutzstaffel. Researchers of other East German government offices made similar findings. Still, former Nazis were by and large kept out of East German police and security agencies. And unlike West Germany, the Communist regime didn't just open the doors of bureaucracy to nearly anyone who wanted in.

In the Western zone, the occupiers caved to Germans' demands that what they saw as the unjustified persecution of the populace be stopped. Soon after West Germany's founding in 1949, politicians, leading clerics, lawyers, and Wehrmacht veterans began pressuring the United States, British, and French governments not just to end denazification but even to grant pardons to convicted war criminals.

West Germany's lawmaking parliamentary chamber, the Bundestag, wasted no time in taking matters into its own hands, passing an amnesty law that freed tens of thousands of perpetrators, including officials of the Sturmabteilung, the ss, and the Nazi Party who had detained victims and sent them to jails and concentration camps, killers, Nazi functionaries who had caused bodily harm, and thousands who had been charged with "crimes and misdemeanors in office." A second amnesty law was passed in 1954.

In 1951 the Bundestag overwhelmingly passed legislation that opened the doors to the rehiring of former Nazis at all levels of public service.[4] The intent of the legislation, which regulated implementation of a section of the West German constitution called Article 131, was to win popular support for democracy by making it possible for Third Reich civil servants who had lost their jobs with the Nazis' defeat—they numbered about 430,000—to apply to return to government work. Article 131 even stipulated that 20 percent of the positions in the West German government bureaucracy had to be filled by civil servants who had lost their jobs at the end of the war. There was no such quota for the hiring of civil servants who had been persecuted by the Nazis. There were Allied misgivings about Article 131, including among the Americans, but Chancellor Adenauer issued reassurances that war criminals would be kept out of public service. That's not the way things worked out.

As a new government bureaucracy was being born, West German officials did not bother to create across-the-board mechanisms to thoroughly research the backgrounds of job candidates. Half-hearted attempts were made to check a job candidate's actions during the Third Reich, and some effort was made to keep especially incriminated people out of top positions, at least during the early years. Those doing the hiring actually preferred civil servants who had worked for the Third Reich because of their professional experience. As a consequence, someone who had worked, say, for the Third Reich Justice Ministry would have a better of chance landing a position with the West German Justice Ministry than a candidate who had faced persecution by the Hitler regime or had fled into exile.

The vetting processes that did exist were flimsy, superficial, and easy to beat. *Persilscheine*—testaments written for job candidates by associates and former comrades—helped countless Germans evade serious scrutiny of their activities in the Third Reich. These "Persil Certificates" were named after a popular detergent—making a former Nazi's past just as clean as fresh laundry. It was also not at all unusual for candidates for West German government jobs to falsify their résumés or to omit compromising details. Old-boy networks within government ministries consisting of former Nazis with tainted pasts assisted their former Nazi comrades in landing public service jobs. They helped each other conceal their Third Reich crimes, often with the aid of superiors who discouraged the posing of probing questions. Rumors might float around a West German government office that someone working there had been involved in unpleasant business in occupied Poland or Ukraine, but everyone knew not to speak too loudly about it.

The purported intentions of Article 131 were to achieve social stability through integration and to encourage a commitment to democracy by the populace. But establishing a preference for experienced Third Reich civil servants—and consciously choosing not to look too deeply into job candidates' pasts—filled West German government offices with a disproportionate number of tainted bureaucrats.

At the Interior Ministry in the late 1950s, two-thirds of employees in the higher levels of civil service were former members of the Nazi Party. At the Justice Ministry, about half the senior employees had been card-carrying Nazis. The figure was an astonishing 80 percent at the Agriculture Ministry. It was unusual for former ss, Gestapo, and Sicherheitsdienst members to work at agencies that were not related to policing and security in West Germany. But the federal police agency and the foreign intelligence service were infested with men who had once belonged to murderous organizations. Across West Germany there was virtually no effort to recruit people for the civil service who had been persecuted by the Nazis. They were simply not wanted. And none of this could have come to pass without the forbearance—and in many cases the complicity—of the U.S. government.

# 2

# The Chameleon

On a craggy hill overlooking the Rhine River, so the legend goes, Siegfried slew a dragon and then bathed in its blood. One October day in 1950, across the river from that craggy hill, in the city of Bonn, a middle-aged man wearing gold-rimmed glasses, a dark overcoat, and a Homburg hat is leaving the Palais Schaumburg. Hans Globke has just finished a meeting inside the palace with his boss, Chancellor Konrad Adenauer. Walking along the Rhine esplanade, this man with a paunchy torso and thinning hair is no heroic figure, no Siegfried. Yet he is formidable. That was true when Globke served the Third Reich, and it is again true as he serves new masters.[1]

We can imagine Globke sliding into the back of a black Mercedes. As he is chauffeured along the west bank of the river, there is no singing to be heard from Rhine Maidens guarding gold at the bottom of the Rhine. No sounds so operatic fill the air. There's the engine murmur of the Mercedes, and inside his official government car, Globke shuffles through papers on his lap. The black sedan delivers Globke to a prearranged lunch with three American occupation officials, including a CIA chief of station. The three want to size up Globke. The trio of Americans had begun drinking before Globke's arrival. Nectar of the occupation gods. They are not concerned about Globke's past—his oath of allegiance to Adolf Hitler, his authorship of a 1936 guidebook for implementing the Nazis' notorious Nuremberg Race Laws, or his service as a high-ranking lawyer in the Third Reich until its defeat in 1945. No, the three are looking for reassurances that Adenauer is committed to going ahead with the rearmament of West Germany, to becoming a part of the Western bloc of nations opposing the Soviet Union and its satellite states. The night before Globke's meeting with the three Americans, the West German interior minister, Gustav Heinemann, resigned in protest of the rearmament plans. Now the three Americans listen closely as Globke recounts Heinemann's confrontation with Adenauer a half-day earlier. "Twice God has struck our weapons from our hands, and it would be a sin to take them up again," Heinemann told Adenauer, according to a memo by the CIA officer who attends the lunch meeting with Globke. Adenauer had responded that a government minister with such views is not welcome in his cabinet—music to the Americans' ears. It is more assurance of a pact in the making: the vanquished tribe whose emblem had been the swastika would join forces with the American conquerors to stand against the rival conquerors, represented by hammer and sickle.

The CIA officer is impressed with Globke's capacity for putting away one glass of wine after the next. Most importantly, he likes the way Globke thinks. "In appraising Globke's character as a result of the three-hour talk, we were forced to conclude that there is little in his makeup or beliefs that should upset the U.S. High Commission," the American intelligence officer wrote in the memo, which was declassified in 2006. In other words, Adenauer's right-hand man could be counted on to work to shape West German priorities to align with those of the U.S. High Commission, the agency overseeing America's occupation of the defeated land.

Just six years earlier, Hans Globke was one of the most influential lawyers working for the Nazi regime—duties he loyally carried out from the time of Hitler's rise to power in 1933. His office was at the Reich Interior Ministry, one of the Nazi bureaucracies that implemented and brutally enforced Hitler's policies.

An archival photo from 1941 shows Globke in a military-style uniform. He is giving the stiff-armed "Hitler salute," along with Reich interior minister Wilhelm Frick, who during the 1946 Nuremberg trials was convicted of war crimes and subsequently hanged. It is the kind of image that helped fuel East German propaganda campaigns against Globke and Adenauer's government.

A connection can be drawn between the respective destinies of Hans Globke and Mildred Fish-Harnack, the American academic who was active in the anti-Hitler resistance. During the Third Reich, perhaps a few hundred Germans belonged to a loose network of groups that were trying to thwart the Führer. Two of the most prominent circles were led by Luftwaffe officer Harro Schulze-Boysen and by Reich Economics Ministry employee Arvid Harnack and his wife, Mildred. Schulze-Boysen and the Harnacks were both found out by the Nazis and executed. A close friend of

Hans Globke, Herbert Engelsing, was active in both groups and was able to dodge the fate of Schulze-Boysen and the Harnacks. As incongruous as it may seem, these connections caused the CIA to wonder whether Globke was a Soviet sleeper agent.

Bear with me while I explain.

After Globke's release from an American internment camp in December 1945, he was hired by British occupation authorities as a consultant on legal and administrative matters. After a denazification court classified him as "exonerated," Globke was appointed city treasurer for Aachen. He made an unsuccessful run for mayor of Trier in 1948 and the following year was made vice president of the board of auditors for the state of North Rhine-Westphalia. Soon after Adenauer was elected chancellor of the new West German state, in 1949, he hired Globke as an official in the chancellery, eventually putting him in charge of overseeing hiring for federal ministries and agencies.

For the next five years, the Americans showed little concern about Globke. That changed in the fall of 1954. The CIA's files from that period contain a flurry of documents pertaining to Globke. Some are memos written in 1949 and 1950 by American authorities and placed in the CIA's files four and five years later.

Two of those early memos express alarm about Globke's service for the Hitler regime. One of them, dated October 25, 1949, came from someone with the High Commission on Germany, or HICOG. "The German Civil Service situation is complex and a source of worry to HICOG," it reads. "This is especially true in the apparent trend to appoint former Nazis who were kept out of bizonal [American-British] administration due to the political scrutiny of the personnel officer."[2] The memo singles out Globke.

A memo dated December 21, 1949, from the HICOG regional office in Frankfurt states that "a cursory review of the records indicates that Dr. Globke, First State Secretary with the Federal Chancellory, was a co-author on the officially sanctioned 'Commentary on German Racial Legislation' published in 1936 and dealing with the Nurnberg laws." The memo seems to have been written to make sure American authorities knew about Globke's work for the Third Reich.

Also placed in the CIA's files in September 1954 was a U.S. Army memo, dated January 18, 1950, that warned: "The reactionary attitude of the Bonn government is . . . undoubtedly influenced by the individuals who have managed to enter the high levels of the Federal administration. I would like to list here once more briefly some of the more objectionable individuals holding high Federal positions."[3]

At the top of the list: "Dr. Hans Globke, Personnel and Civil Service Advisor to Chancellor Adenauer, formerly Oberregierungsrat in the Reich Interior Ministry during the Hitler regime and author of the official commentary on the Nuernberg laws."[4]

Deeper reading of the CIA files from the fall of 1954 makes it clear that it's not Globke's work for the Third Reich that concerned the agency at that time but questions that had arisen about his avowed ties with the anti-Nazi resistance.

And where did those suspicions start? As it turns out, with a friend and colleague not just of the Americans but of Globke: West German foreign intelligence chief Reinhard Gehlen. This was at a time when Gehlen was gathering intelligence for what turned out to be a witch hunt: suspicions that the remnants of the anti-Nazi resistance had become sleeper agents for the Soviets.

CIA memos show the American spy agency was blindsided when Gehlen "expressed reservations" about Globke, according to a five-page memo written on October 1, 1954, by the CIA's liaison at Gehlen's headquarters in Bavaria. The CIA decided to review whatever files were available on Globke. Among the documents they found were testimonials written for Globke to help him pass the denazification process.

The author of the CIA memo was impressed by the testimonials, written by a Roman Catholic cardinal, other church officials, and "several well-known persons." Also in the pile of testimonials was a declaration written by Herbert Engelsing, which read, in part: "When we were involved in the active SCHULZE-BOYSEN anti-Nazi group (in connection with which most of our friends were hanged), he did everything possible to provide an alibi for us."[5]

Engelsing said Globke provided him with secrets from the Nazi Interior Ministry that Engelsing passed on to Schulze-Boysen and claimed that Globke was a behind-the-scenes and "most clever" participant in the failed attempt to kill Hitler on July 20, 1944. The CIA memo said "it is quite possible" that Globke did indeed provide Engelsing with information that helped him evade arrest because Globke would have had access to that kind of information in his position at the Nazi Interior Ministry.

There seems to be nothing in the CIA files after this memo to suggest that the Americans still worried that Globke might be a Soviet sleeper agent. At this time Globke was working closely with the CIA to coordinate intelligence matters, including holding discussions about the West German government taking over supervision of Gehlen's spy agency from the CIA, which occurred in 1956, when Gehlen's operation became the Bundesnachrichtendienst (Federal Intelligence Service.)

So who was Hans Globke? What did he believe in? Did he hate Jews? Was he happy that the Nazis had come to power? And if he was in reality a member of the anti-Hitler resistance, as he insisted after the war, why did he help the Nazis carry out their anti-Semitic and continent-conquering agenda?

Born on September 10, 1888, in Düsseldorf to an affluent Roman Catholic family, Globke was raised in the city of Aachen. He served in an artillery unit during World War I and after the war got a law degree. In 1922 he joined the Catholic Center Party. He soon entered the civil service, serving as a judge in Aachen's police court and then as city treasurer. He moved to Berlin in 1929 after being hired by the Prussian Ministry of the Interior. Even before Hitler's rise to power, in 1933, Globke used his position at the Prussian Interior Ministry to push Jewish citizens toward public ostracism, drafting a rule that made it difficult for Jews to change their last names to more German-sounding names.

When the Nazis took over Germany in January 1933, the Prussian Interior Ministry essentially became the Interior Ministry for the whole country. Globke rose quickly in the Nazi bureaucracy. As an attorney for the Third Reich, he helped draft laws that tightened Hitler's grip on power. He was also involved in Nazi legislation that stripped Jews of their rights and laid the foundation for the coming Holocaust. Globke and his boss at the Reich Interior Ministry, Wilhelm Stuckart, cowrote a commentary on the notorious 1935 Nuremberg Racial Laws. The legislation consisted of two statutes. Under one of them, the *Reichsbürgergesetz* (Reich Citizenship Law), Jews lost German citizenship. The second statute, the *Gesetz zum Schutze des Deutschen Blutes und der Deutschen Ehre*, or Law for the Protection of German Blood and German Honor, banned marriage or sexual relations between Jews and "nationals of German or related blood."

Globke and Stuckart wrote of the two statutes: "Their basic importance consists in the fact that they prevent, for all time, the penetration of further

Jewish blood into the German folk-body." In addition to writing that commentary, Globke helped draft a 1938 law intended to make it impossible for German Jews to try to conceal their Jewishness. Under this order, Jews were compelled to add *Israel* or *Sara* to their names. The legislation made it easier for the Nazis to identify and persecute Germany's Jewish citizens. Passports held by Jews would henceforth be stamped with a *J*.

Top Third Reich officials were impressed with Globke. In an April 25, 1938, letter recommending him for a promotion, Wilhelm Frick, the Reich interior minister, wrote, "Senior Government Counselor Globke is undoubtedly one of the most capable and efficient officials in my ministry."[6] Frick spoke of Globke's "proven loyalty and constant readiness for all work since the National Socialist Party came to power." In 1938 Globke was awarded a medal in recognition of his work to transfer the Nuremberg Race Laws to Austria. In 1941 Hitler awarded him with a "silver merit award for faithful service." Given his accomplishments in the service of the Third Reich, it would seem that choosing to portray oneself as an opponent of the Hitler regime would be a tricky task. But that would be underestimating Globke's skills.

After Globke's 1945 release from an American internment camp, he contacted people about writing testimonials that would help exonerate him during denazification proceedings. As noted earlier, Globke got statements of support from leading church authorities and from Germans who had been in some way involved in the anti-Hitler resistance. And this helped him land the job as Konrad Adenauer's right-hand man.

Make no mistake: Adenauer was anything but a Nazi. In fact, he was a victim of the Third Reich. Adenauer was lord mayor of Cologne when Hitler rose to power in 1933. He was swiftly stripped of his position and in 1944 was sent to a concentration camp. Rather than hold a grudge against his former tormentors, when Adenauer was elected chancellor of West Germany, in 1949, he had already formulated a strategy for building government agencies: hire bureaucrats with the most experience, even if that experience was in the service of the Third Reich. Adenauer had much in common with Globke. Both were Roman Catholic, natives of the Rhineland, and former members of the Catholic Center Party. The chancellor saw in Globke a skilled bureaucrat with potentially useful connections among other civil servants of the Third Reich. Adenauer may have also had cynical motives for choosing a badly tainted bureaucrat as his top aide. By shielding Globke against attacks for his past, the chancellor could rely on Globke's cast-iron loyalty and willingness to do anything for him—including, as we will see later, conspiring with the foreign intelligence chief to use dirty tricks against Adenauer's opponents to ensure his reelection, an abuse of power that German historian Klaus-Dietmar Henke has compared to Watergate but worse, since unlike Richard Nixon, Adenauer got away with it.

From the very start of the Adenauer administration, the chancellor faced repeated demands from opposition politicians that Globke be fired for his service to the Third Reich, but Adenauer never wavered in his support. As the chancellor said early in his first of four terms: "You can't throw out dirty water if you don't have fresh water."

Globke usually dodged questions about what he had done during the Nazi years. And when he spoke about them, he spoke defensively. The image he tried to create for himself was akin to the one we have of Oskar Schindler, the factory owner who helped his Jewish workers avoid the gas chambers. Globke's main arguments were that he kept working for the Nazis in order to do whatever he could to soften the impact of racist statutes on Jews; he personally helped a number of Jews avoid capture; he fed information from the Nazi Interior Ministry to the anti-fascist resistance; and he himself had been a member of the resistance.

In 1961, in speaking of the guidebook for implementation of the Nuremberg Race Laws, which he and Stuckart had written, he said: "I would not have written the commentary had I been able to foresee the later development of the 'Jewish Question.' Under the circumstances prevailing at the time, the commentary provided protection for many persons who were being discriminated against on racial grounds."[7]

Ten years earlier, the Central Council of Jews in Germany addressed Globke's claim: "It was, is, and remains the opinion of the Jewish community that every functionary of the Hitler Reich who, regardless of rank, actively participated in the creation, interpretation, and implementation of the Nazi racial laws and the resulting persecution measures violated the moral law and has damaged the moral foundations of human coexistence." What's more, the council said pointedly, it's news to them that "any commentary on the Nürnberg racial laws ever saved Jewish lives."[8]

While his work for the Third Reich was under attack, Globke would point out that he never belonged to the Nazi Party. What he chose not to mention was that he had applied for party membership in 1941 but was rejected because of his links to the Catholic Center Party. Globke also skipped over the fact that he had belonged to a number of Nazi-affiliated organizations. He sounded more like a person who was eager to ingratiate himself with the regime rather than distance himself from it.

German historians say it is true that Globke knew people in the resistance, that he likely did supply helpful information to them, and that he coached some Jews on how to get a Jewish blood classification that would mitigate the impact on them from Nazi statutes. But over the decades it was hard for Globke to escape suspicion that while he may have done some good deeds, his striving for advancement in the Nazi regime, the thoroughness with which he approached his job, plus the accolades and medals he received, all suggest that he believed in what he was doing. Globke's critics believe that after the war he set out to create a legend for himself and that he was abetted in this endeavor by friends and colleagues, some of whom may also have been trying to launder their own Third Reich activities.

During a four-hour-long dinner in Frankfurt in February 1961, the American consul, Wayland B. Waters, had a deep discussion with the prosecutor for Hesse state over matters surrounding the recent capture in Argentina by Mossad agents of Adolf Eichmann, the logistical planner of the Holocaust. The state prosecutor was Fritz Bauer, a German Jew who had survived the Holocaust by fleeing Germany. Bauer was also a member of the Social Democratic Party, Adenauer's hated political rivals.[9]

Bauer had created a political dustup in Germany by pushing allegations from a former Nazi administrator for occupied Greece, Max Merten, that Hans Globke was responsible for the deaths of ten thousand Greek Jews. By turning down a proposal that they be evacuated to Palestine by a Red Cross ship, Merten claimed, Globke allowed them instead to be sent to Auschwitz. Globke denied the allegations and filed a lawsuit against Merten.

During the dinner meeting, according to Waters's report to his superiors, Bauer said he "would continue to the bitter end to fight remaining vestiges of Nazism in West Germany, and particularly anyone believed connected with Nazi war crimes," including Globke. Bauer made clear throughout the conversation his animosity toward Globke. "A dirty shame that Globke continues to hold on to his key job as principal adviser to the Chancellor," Waters quoted Bauer as saying.

Bauer told Waters that "a man who had, by his own admission, written the commentaries on the Nürnberg racial decrees, who had been responsible for the infamy of the 'Jewish first names,'" and who had stayed as a top official at the Reich Interior Ministry "until the bitter end . . . should not, as a simple matter of principle and justice, occupy a position such as Globke has held in Bonn since 1949—even if he had, as Globke alleged, helped some Jews."

"On this," Waters wrote, "Bauer's conscience would give him no rest." Bauer told Waters that "Eichmann had revelations to make which could be somewhat damning to Globke," although Bauer "thought it was doubtful that he would in fact make them." Bauer appeared forthcoming and open in his conversation with Waters. But when the American asked Bauer what he knew about Eichmann's arrest, he "clammed-up completely."

There were reasons for his reticence. It was Bauer who had learned the whereabouts of Eichmann in Argentina. He did not trust West German officials with the information, fearing they might alert Eichmann that he had been discovered, so he turned to the Israelis instead. Bauer also kept the United States out of the loop.

Bauer was a rare kind of civil servant in West Germany: a man in pursuit of war criminals, instead of protecting or ignoring them. Bauer's mistrust of West German judicial authorities is understandable. Over the course of a dozen years, he had watched with dismay as German prosecutors and judges routinely dismissed cases against suspected war criminals.

One year before the dinner with the American consul, an Israeli agent entered Bauer's office in Frankfurt after hours, when no one was there, according to German journalist Ronen Steinke, who wrote a biography about Bauer.[10] The Israeli agent knew exactly what to look for, and he found it on the desk: a file containing a photo of a Nazi officer and documents emblazoned with SS insignias. The agent photographed the documents and left as stealthily as he had come. This was no burglary. It was an intended handoff, one coordinated with Bauer. Weeks later it would lead to the capture of the man in the SS uniform: Adolf Eichmann, the world's No. 1 fugitive war criminal. Bauer had learned through a contact that Eichmann was living in Argentina.

Declassified CIA files reflect nervousness that when Eichmann went to trial, he might have some damning revelations to make about West German officials, especially Hans Globke. The allegations by Max Merten were already creating headaches for Adenauer's government. Bonn was braced for more from the Eichmann trial. A report filed on March 28, 1961, by the CIA's Office of National Estimates describes the potential implications from the Eichmann trial.[11] "Israel," the report said, "is interested in seeing that the world does not forget what the Jews of Europe suffered under Hitler, and in underlining Israel's claims to be the moral heir and trustee of the victims." It was an open question, said the report, "how far the Israeli Government is prepared to go in avoiding or playing down aspects which might embarrass people or governments friendly to Israel—notably the West German government."

The report noted about West Germany: "The West Germans have followed the Eichmann case developments and the impending trial with growing apprehension, sometimes bordering on hysteria. The unarticulated though widely held concern among Germans is that Eichmann's relations might implicate West Germans now prominent in business, cultural, political and, above all, governmental life. They are concerned that the publicity resulting from the trial will give new impetus to what they regard as an already existing anti-German trend, both popular and official, in the Western world, particularly in the U.S. and UK."

In Wayland B. Waters's report to his superiors, the U.S. consul in Frankfurt mused about Bauer's apparent yet mysterious involvement in Eichmann's capture. "Fritz Bauer," Waters wrote, "played a still somewhat obscure role in connection with the apprehension" of Eichmann. "Since the arrival of Eichmann in Israel, Bauer has been traveling back and forth to Tel Aviv, and is perhaps one of the most knowledgeable personalities on the Eichmann case outside Israel." Waters speculated that Bauer might "be connected in some high-ranking capacity with the Israeli Intelligence Service in West Germany."

As it turned out, Globke was not called to testify at Eichmann's trial. In fact, Adenauer's top aide was mentioned only once during the whole proceeding. Having avoided the prospect of blockbuster secrets about Globke or other German officials coming out in court, Adenauer told Israeli prime minister David Ben-Gurion that he was "deeply impressed with the way Israel handled the Eichmann trial."

Globke was further let off the hook after Fritz Bauer's investigation of Max Merten's allegations against Adenauer's top aide was transferred to the chief prosecutor in Bonn, who dropped the case for a lack of evidence. New research suggests Adenauer had interfered in the case to get it out of Bauer's hands.[12]

Less than half a year after Eichmann was convicted and sentenced to be executed, West Germany and Israel reached agreement on a massive arms deal.[13] If Eichmann had dirt on Globke or any other West German officials, as the logistical planner of the Holocaust swung from Israeli gallows on June 1, 1962, his secrets died with him.

In 1963, after more than a dozen years as West German chancellor, Adenauer decided to retire. During recent years his administration had been rocked by scandals, some of them involving war criminals in the West German government, such as an official in Gehlen's spy service who was giving secrets to the KGB. Adenauer and Globke had been inseparable since the founding of the Federal Republic. And when the chancellor withdrew from politics, so did his top aide.

Globke and his wife, Augusta, had planned to spend their golden years in Switzerland. They had purchased land there and built a house overlooking Lake Geneva. But the regional parliament turned down Globke's request for residency permits. He was just too tainted for the Swiss. Instead of protesting the decision, Globke sold the property and stayed put in Bonn, where he died at age seventy-four on February 13, 1973.[14]

So, what are we to make of Hans Globke? How should he be judged by history? There is no doubt that Globke was an important functionary in the construction of Germany's postwar democracy. Does that service outweigh his work for the Third Reich, somehow make amends for it? There's a problem with this line of thinking. While twenty-first-century Germany is one of the world's most successful democracies, its first two postwar decades were marred by witch hunts against leftists and unconstitutional snooping on the populace by West Germany's foreign intelligence service. And Hans Globke, Adenauer's overseer of intelligence and national security, was at the center of these activities. In recent decades German historians investigating the postwar Nazi taint have sought to understand whether a lingering Nazi ideology among postwar civil servants had influenced the autocratic-like measures undertaken by the Adenauer administration.

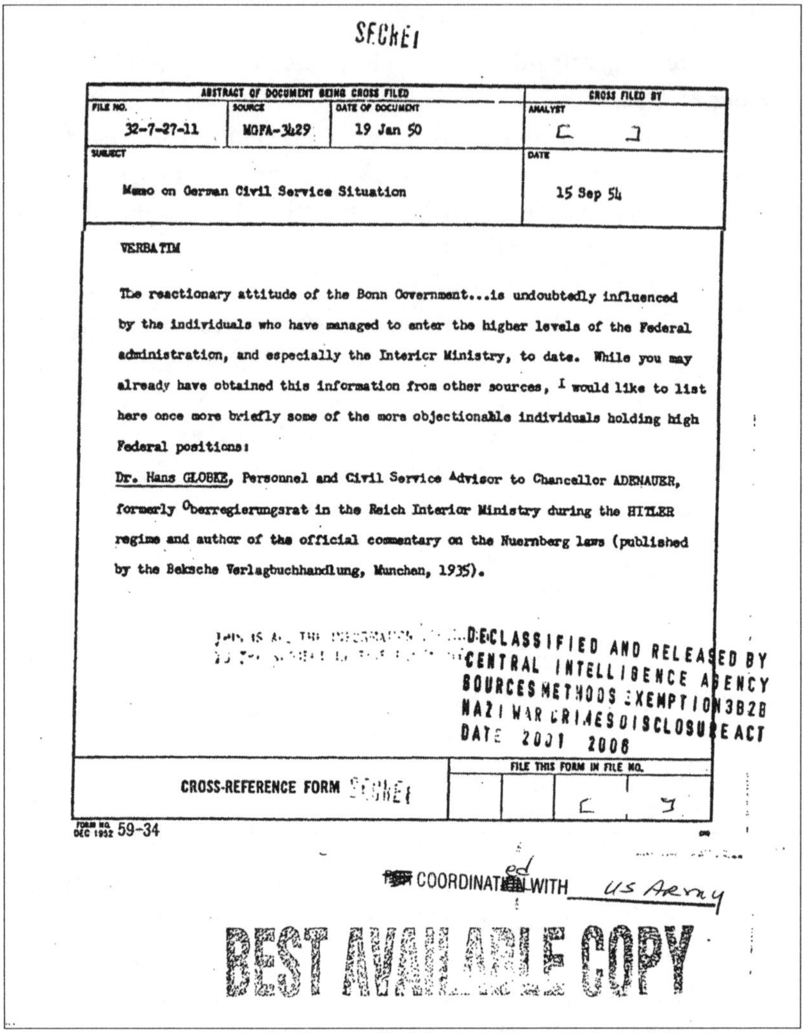

SECRET

| ABSTRACT OF DOCUMENT BEING CROSS FILED | | | CROSS FILED BY |
|---|---|---|---|
| FILE NO. 32-7-27-11 | SOURCE MOFA-3429 | DATE OF DOCUMENT 19 Jan 50 | ANALYST |
| SUBJECT Memo on German Civil Service Situation | | | DATE 15 Sep 54 |

VERBATIM

The reactionary attitude of the Bonn Government...is undoubtedly influenced by the individuals who have managed to enter the higher levels of the Federal administration, and especially the Interior Ministry, to date. While you may already have obtained this information from other sources, I would like to list here once more briefly some of the more objectionable individuals holding high Federal positions:

Dr. Hans GLOBKE, Personnel and Civil Service Advisor to Chancellor ADENAUER, formerly Oberregierungsrat in the Reich Interior Ministry during the HITLER regime and author of the official commentary on the Nuernberg laws (published by the Beksche Verlagbuchhandlung, Munchen, 1935).

DECLASSIFIED AND RELEASED BY
CENTRAL INTELLIGENCE AGENCY
SOURCES METHODS EXEMPTION 3B2B
NAZI WAR CRIMES DISCLOSURE ACT
DATE 2001 2006

CROSS-REFERENCE FORM SECRET | FILE THIS FORM IN FILE NO.

FORM NO. 59-34
DEC 1952

COORDINATED WITH US Army

BEST AVAILABLE COPY

**FIG. 1.** After the founding of the West German state in 1949, some American occupation authorities were alarmed by the return of Third Reich officials to positions of authority, as shown by this September 15, 1954, "Memo on German Civil Service Situation," pertaining to Hans Globke. But to win West Germany as an ally in the Cold War confrontation with the Soviet bloc, U.S. officials stood aside as the government of Chancellor Konrad Adenauer recruited former Nazis for key positions. Declassified document, CIA Reading Room.

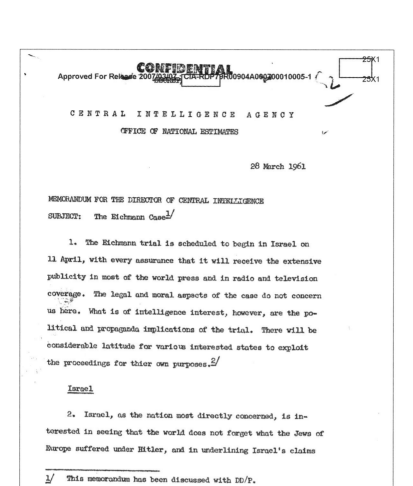

FIG. 2. After Israeli agents' 1960 capture of Adolf Eichmann in Argentina, West German officials were worried that Eichmann would implicate Hans Globke and others in Nazi crimes. In a six-page memorandum written in March 1961, the CIA's Office of National Estimates analyzed the potential political, strategic, and diplomatic ramifications of the Eichmann trial for Israel, Arab states, the Soviet bloc, and West Germany. As the memo observes, "The West Germans have followed the Eichmann case developments and the impending trial with growing apprehension, sometimes bordering on hysteria." Declassified document, CIA Electronic Reading Room.

# 3

# Gold Watch for a War Criminal

On a January day in 1952, in the skies between the once and future German capital, Berlin, and the new one, Bonn, a U.S. military aircraft ferried a Nazi war criminal to embark on a career with West Germany's equivalent of the FBI.[1] Since the defeat of the Third Reich, Theo Saevecke had worked as a covert agent for the U.S. Central Intelligence Agency. His specialty was recruiting informants inside Communist East Germany. But the CIA empathized with Saevecke's yearning to come out of the shadows. So the American spy agency enthusiastically endorsed his decision to accept a job offer with the German Federal Criminal Police Office, the Bundeskriminalamt, or BKA. His superiors at the CIA bought him a gold watch as a gesture of their respect and gratitude.

American intelligence knew about Saevecke's war crimes as an SS officer. They knew about the Jews in North Africa he had sent off to slave labor. They knew he had overseen the execution of Italian civilians. The Americans knew he was an unrepentant Nazi. A year before Saevecke joined the BKA, one of his CIA handlers wrote in a memo that the man "still hankers back after the days when the [Nazi] Party was in the saddle."[2] But none of this stopped the American spy agency from supporting Saevecke's pursuit of a position at the newly created BKA. From the perspective of the CIA, Saevecke's fervent anti-Communism trumped his Nazi past, not to mention the prospects for using him as a snoop on West German security services.

We remember the Cold War era for the spy games that were constantly being played between East and West. Theo Saevecke was a participant in this intrigue. But his significance is far greater than that. Saevecke is a symbol of the failure of the United States to prevent the postwar infestation of Germany's civil service by mass murderers, planners of the Holocaust, Nazi jurists, and others who had sworn fealty to Adolf Hitler and the Third Reich.

In 1930 Saevecke is on board a schooner plying the Atlantic, hauling saltpeter between Hamburg and Chile. A Hamburg native, Saevecke is drawn to the life of a seafarer. After attending secondary school, he joins the German Merchant Marine. A 1953 CIA memo written by Saevecke's case officer describes him as a "North German prototype—sturdy, tough, proud, reliable, with a salty sense of humor. He loves to collect all sorts of knick knacks connected with sail boats, and at heart will always remain a sailor."[3]

But Saevecke's sea adventures are cut short when he develops stomach ulcers. In 1934 he lands a job with the police department in Lübeck, another port city. Saevecke was already committed to the Nazi cause. He had joined the party seven years earlier, and while working for the Lübeck police department, he became a member of the Sturmabteilung, the Nazi paramilitary organization that terrorized Jews, Social Democrats, Communists, and other Hitler targets. Saevecke got a chance to advance his police career and his support of the Nazis when he transferred to Berlin, where he received training as a *Kriminalkommissar*, or detective superintendent. In Berlin, Saevecke drew praise from his superiors for his success in investigating arson and murder cases.

Shortly after nightfall on August 31, 1939, in a German town on the Polish border, men wearing Polish army uniforms launch an attack on the local radio station. These were not real Polish soldiers. They were German SS officers who had been ordered by Hitler to provide a pretext for an invasion of Poland. Prisoners from the Dachau concentration camp who are forced to accompany the SS men during the assault on the Gleiwitz radio station are shot dead wearing Polish military gear, to try to make it look convincing. At dawn on the following day, German tanks, infantrymen, bombers, and fighter planes launch a massive blitzkrieg attack on Poland, and Polish defenses are quickly overwhelmed. More than a million German troops are involved in the invasion. Among them are SS, Sicherheitdienst (Security Service [SD]), and Gestapo units. Their assignment: hunt and kill Polish Jews and intellectuals.

During the Nazis' invasion and bloody occupation of eastern lands, trained police officers were sent to do a lot of the follow-up killing. This freed up regular German troops to move onto the next conquest. The police officers, organized into mobile murder squads, rounded up and executed those victims the regular German troops never got to.

SS officer Theo Saevecke arrived in Poland ten days after the German invasion. He was attached to the Poznan office of the intelligence arm of the SS, the Sicherheitsdienst. After the war, Saevecke kept quiet about his actions there. Saevecke "has been most careful to avoid discussion or written mention of his activities for the SD on the Eastern front," states a memo written by a CIA officer on January 6, 1964.[4] This memo also reveals what Saevecke was trying to hide. An unnamed mole working for the CIA within Communist Poland's intelligence services met with the CIA official who wrote the memo on November 14, 1963; it is unclear where they met. In the declassified CIA memo, in place of the informant's name are empty brackets. Shortly after the German invasion, "[ ] found himself working as an office worker" in Ujazd, says the memo. German occupiers had taken over administration of the area. In late fall of 1939 "[ ]" was arrested and taken to a concentration camp, where inspections were conducted by a man identified by the double agent to his CIA handler as an SS officer whose name was pronounced "Sewecke," age thirty or so, with dark-blond hair and a well-built frame.

The Polish double agent told his CIA handler that he was then transferred to another camp, near Poznan, where he encountered the same SS officer. "Whenever one of the inmates was executed," he told the CIA officer, "a form notice would appear on the bulletin board with a check-mark in the square which designated death either by firing squad or hanging. These forms contained three signatures, one of which was often Saevecke's."

When dealing with double agents, of course, there is always a risk that the operative appears to be feeding genuine intelligence to an investigator but is in fact delivering disinformation. But there is nothing in the declassified CIA files to suggest the Americans were skeptical about the report by the Polish mole about Theo Saevecke. In any event, the Americans apparently kept these allegations to themselves because German officials never launched an investigation into Saevecke's two-year deployment in Poland. It is evidence of a war crime that was very clearly suppressed. But this should be no surprise. Throughout Saevecke's career at the BKA, the CIA was ready to help him cover up his wartime tracks.

In August 1940 Saevecke returned to Berlin, where he worked at the Reichskriminalpolizeiamt, Nazi Germany's central criminal investigation agency. He enrolled in classes at the Nazis' elite police academy, the Führerschule der Sicherheitspolizei (Leadership School for Security Police), in Berlin's Charlottenburg neighborhood. He followed that training up with a course at a police academy in Tivoli, Italy, run by the Italian government, Hitler's ally. He was given the SS rank of *Obersturmführer* (the equivalent of first lieutenant) in 1941, and the following year Saevecke was sent to Libya to serve as German SS intelligence and police liaison with Italian police units there.

Saevecke's destiny became intertwined with that of an SS officer who, after the defeat of the Third Reich, was one of the most wanted of fugitive war criminals: Walter Rauff. In late 1941, before the Nazis began sending Jews to their death at Auschwitz and other extermination camps, Rauff was head of a project that converted large trucks into mobile mass murder machines. Exhaust fumes from the vehicles were diverted into airtight containers on the back, asphyxiating up to 60 victims who had been crammed inside. These vehicles are believed to have killed nearly 100,000 people.

Having proven his talent for terror and murder, in 1942 Rauff was given a new assignment as head of an SS intelligence detachment that was being sent to North Africa. An Einsatzkommando led by Rauff rounded up some five-thousand Tunisian Jews for slave labor. Theo Saevecke was put in charge of implementing Rauff's orders.

After American and British troops chased the Germans out of North Africa in spring 1943, Saevecke fled with Rauff to Corsica. From there the two went to Milan, where they operated out of a headquarters set up in the Hotel Regina. The mission of the detachment of SS Security Service and Gestapo officers commanded by Rauff was to impose total German control over Milan, Turin, and Genoa and their surroundings through terrorizing the citizenry, killing partisans, arresting Allied agents, and rounding up Jews.

In the summer of 1944, a German SS officer named Kessels was traveling with two subordinates to a farmhouse outside the village of Corbetta to investigate reports that Italian partisans were storing arms there. The SS men were ambushed by about fifteen partisans, killing Kessels. The two other SS men returned to Milan and reported what had happened.

The transcript of 1947 interrogations by British officers of Saevecke and his subordinates describes what happened next.[5] Saevecke took ten SS men to Corbetta, found three partisans, and "personally gave orders to have them shot on the spot," according to the interrogation report. Saevecke ordered the farmhouse be set on fire. Ten other suspected partisans were arrested and taken to Milan.

The next day twenty SS men commanded by Rauff and Saevecke, along with one hundred members of an Italian fascist militia, showed up in Corbetta and encircled the village. All Italian males were ordered onto the public square. The SS, the Italian militiamen, and the village mayor "sorted out a number of victims to be shot," states the British interrogators' report. Five residents of Corbetta "were executed in public without more ado," and "the dwellings of the victims were all burned to the ground." Fifty more villagers were arrested and shipped off for forced labor.

During his interrogation by British intelligence, Saevecke justified "these repressive measures by the fact that several Germans had been killed in the neighborhood and many Italian Fascists had also been assassinated around Corbetta."

Both Rauff and Saevecke were arrested at the close of World War II. Rauff escaped custody and eventually made his way to South America, where he lived until his death in 1984. In 2011 historian Bodo Hechelheimer made the scandalous discovery while going through documents that while Rauff was a fugitive, he covertly worked as an informant for West German intelligence and was even brought back to his home country for training. Theo Saevecke's destiny was very different. His choice to offer himself as a Communist-hunting agent for American intelligence opened the doors for a career with the Bundeskriminalamt.

Saevecke was part of the CIA's "Cautery" chain of agents. A declassified CIA memo written by the agency's Karlsruhe chief of station in 1951 shows that while Saevecke's American friends saw him as a dyed-in-the-wool Nazi, they were impressed by his work for them. "No useful purpose is served by reasoning with him over the crimes perpetrated under the aegis of the Third Reich," the Karlsruhe station chief wrote. As for Saevecke's usefulness to the CIA, the chief vouched for the former Nazi: "[Saevecke's] performance as an intelligence operator has been outstanding."[6]

At the BKA, his new bosses were equally impressed. Saevecke's primary task was gathering intelligence on radical Leftist groups—the perfect fit for a man with a visceral hatred of the Left. But it didn't take long for Saevecke's Nazi past to catch up with him.

In a memo dated July 7, 1954, the CIA's office in Bonn informed agency director Allen Dulles that the West German Interior Ministry had opened an investigation of Saevecke. Allegations had emerged in Italy that Saevecke had participated in the rounding up of Jews in Tunisia for slave labor, the execution of Italian hostages while he was headquartered in Milan, and the mistreatment of prisoners in the city's San Vittore prison. Saevecke was suspended, pending an investigation.

Saevecke asked his CIA friends for whatever help they could provide. The Bonn chief said "no commitment" was made to Saevecke but that in "view [of] our interest in Cabanjo feel we should render whatever assistant [sic] we can. Request guidance."[7] "Cabanjo" was Saevecke's code name at that time.

In a memo dated July 12, 1954, Dulles's office told the CIA chiefs of station in Frankfurt and Bonn that if the agency found Saevecke's past "in any way defensible," it could pass on to the West German government documents that might help Saevecke. But the assistance was contingent on keeping the CIA out of the scandal that was brewing: "Meantime assure Cabanjo of our moral support but warn him that specific reference to KUBARK [cryptonym for the CIA] may queer whole plan."[8]

Dulles also offered Saevecke a potential lifeline: if he ended up getting "bounced" from the BKA, the CIA could arrange a job for him with "a private detective agency as insurance against Communist resurgence in future." Dulles didn't spell out exactly what he had in mind. In a CIA memo written the following year, the proposal was floated to hire Saevecke as a covert CIA agent full-time if he was forced out of the BKA.

The CIA was clearly nervous about where this might be headed. The agency was in contact with Saevecke's superiors at the BKA and with Saevecke himself. In a meeting with a CIA officer on July 14, 1954, Saevecke insisted he was innocent of the Italian allegations and handed the CIA officer a copy of a long statement he had given to Interior Ministry officials as his formal refutation. In the statement Saevecke argued that any actions he ordered or carried out were for the sole purpose of "safeguarding of the German Army in the rear area and the protection of the Italian population against the attacks of partisans."[9] He explained, "For the completion of these tasks I was authorized within my department in accordance with the general instruction to act on my own discretion." He rejected any responsibility for the execution of fifteen hostages in Milan, saying some "higher-ranking official which was not known to me" ordered an Italian military court to take retaliatory measures for partisan attacks, and the executions were carried out by Italian soldiers.

Saevecke maintained that when he had Jews in his area of authority rounded up, he was just following orders. "I could not at the time foresee the fate of the persecutees of which I only learned after the war," he claimed. He never ordered the mistreatment of prisoners at Milan's San Vittore prison, he insisted, though "that does not exclude the possibility that my subordinates have not always treated prisoners, i.e. assassins, with the consideration which in normal times would have been a matter of course."

There are at least two omissions in Saevecke's statement: Saevecke's wartime activities as an SS officer in Poland; and the executions in Corbetta. In 1954 American intelligence did not seem to know about the allegations of war crimes by Saevecke in Poland. As for Corbetta, the CIA intentionally tried to cover up the details.

A CIA memo dated August 5, 1954, cautioned: "Our possession of this report, which is still classified Secret, should not be discussed with German authorities, who would certainly want to see it. It would not do Herr SAEVECKE any good." There's a whiff of blackmail in the memo: "Evidently SAEVECKE admitted this [the Corbetta executions] to British interrogators, but as far as we can tell he has not been charged with it in the current investigation. It would be appropriate to discuss this incident with SAEVECKE and consider with him the advisability of suppressing the information. The usefulness of this lever in furthering our control over him is obvious."[10]

West German officials certainly had some knowledge about Saevecke's past. Up to this point, however, he had been able to escape any meaningful scrutiny by dodging full disclosure of his deeds as an SS officer, by insisting he had not personally been involved in war crimes or had just been following orders, and by taking advantage of the widespread German desire to forget about the past.

After a superficial investigation, one that dismissed Italian eyewitness testimony as unreliable and relied on records cherry-picked by the CIA, the West German government cleared Saevecke and allowed him to return to work in the spring of 1955.

That December, Saevecke's CIA contact at the U.S. Embassy in Bonn received a gushingly grateful letter from the reinstated BKA man. Saevecke wrote, in German: "With all my heart I wish you a blessed and happy holiday and for the coming year health, success, and many beautiful days. For both of us, I hope that we will continue to work together well and trustingly in the interests of our two peoples in the struggle for justice and dignity. I especially thank you for the trust that you have shown me in my difficult time. With kind regards, Your devoted Theo Saevecke." The CIA officer responded in German, with equally warm salutations: "Dear Herr Saevecke! Thank you very much for your Christmas greetings. For my part, I look forward to the continuation of our good cooperation in the common interest of our two services with confidence and joy. We are very pleased that certain personal misunderstandings could be cleared up for you. I wish you and your family all the best for the new year."[11]

Seven years later, Saevecke's Nazi misdeeds once again came back to haunt him. At about 9:30 p.m. on October 26, 1962, federal and local police raided the Hamburg editorial offices of *Der Spiegel* newsmagazine, seizing documents and arresting the magazine's lead editors. It was the first time since the Nazi years that the government had targeted the free press, and the nation was shocked. The magazine's alleged crime: publishing top secrets in an article about a NATO military exercise that had taken place called "Fallex 62." *Spiegel*'s article was a withering exposé of West Germany's lack of readiness for a Soviet-led invasion. West German prosecutors alleged that *Spiegel* had committed treason. Occupation of the newsmagazine's headquarters lasted a month. A federal court ultimately struck down the charges against *Spiegel*.

One of the main coordinators in the law enforcement operation against *Spiegel* was Theo Saevecke. His job at BKA would not normally have put him in a position of calling the shots on the raid of the magazine's offices. But he was filling in for his boss, who was traveling in a foreign country.

When it emerged that Saevecke had played a critical role in the scandal that was blowing up in the West German press, the CIA nervously monitored the situation. In December 1962 the agents noted that Saevecke was considering resigning because "he apparently realized that this [all the publicity] would most likely cause his SS past to be brought back into focus." That fear was justified. German TV produced an in-depth program about the BKA, and during an interview, BKA president Reinhard Dullien was asked whether any former SS officers had worked at the police agency. Dullien denied it. But it didn't take long for the West German news media to rediscover the SS pasts of numerous BKA officers, not just of Saevecke but of several of his comrades.

Hoping to get the press off its back, the BKA decided to transfer Saevecke and others to less visible positions. Saevecke was moved in February 1963 from the Bundeskriminalamt's high-profile Security Group in Bonn to BKA headquarters in Wiesbaden. The transfer failed to take the heat off Saevecke and the BKA. That spring Italian newspapers published earlier allegations about Saevecke's stint as an SS and Gestapo officer in Milan and added some new ones, such as setting up torture cells in a building adjacent to his Milan headquarters. The renewed scrutiny prompted another attempt by German officials to make Saevecke invisible, sending him to the Ahr Valley to act as security chief at a cavernous concrete bunker built into a hillside, about sixteen miles south of Bonn. To those who were aware of its existence, the bunker was known as "State Secret No. 1." It was here that West Germany's government would take refuge in the event of war with the Soviet bloc. And it was here that Saevecke would spend the remainder of his career as a government employee.

Among Saevecke's duties was preparing the bunker's participation in NATO exercises, during which West German government leaders would practice evacuating to State Secret No. 1. As West German chancellor Ludwig Erhard and other top government officials walked along the concrete-enforced corridors during a NATO preparedness drill in October 1966, the Nazi war criminal walked with them, according to German journalist Jörg Diester and historian Michaele Karle, who have written about the bunker and Saevecke's time working there.[12]

Saevecke was employed at the bunker until his retirement in 1971. If he thought that at this point nobody cared about his Third Reich crimes, he was mistaken. After fresh incriminating documents about Saevecke turned up in Italy in November 1997, prosecutors there began a new investigation on murder charges. Italian authorities demanded that Saevecke be handed over for trial, but he was protected from extradition as a German citizen. On June 9, 1999, the eighty-eight-year-old—dubbed in Italy the "Executioner of Milan"—was convicted in absentia of ordering the killing of Italian hostages and sentenced to life in prison. Saevecke died the following year. With the help of American intelligence and German government officials, he never served a single day in prison.

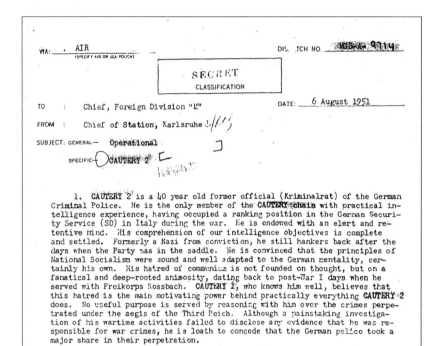

FIG. 3. At the start of the Cold War, it was not unusual for American and British occupying authorities to hire former Nazis as agents to gather intelligence on the Soviet bloc. One of them was Theo Saevecke, even though, as this memo states, "he still hankers back after the days when the [Nazi] Party was in the saddle." The memo also claims a "painstaking investigation of his wartime activities failed to disclose any evidence that he was responsible for war crimes." In point of fact, Saevecke had been involved in atrocities in Libya, Italy, and possibly Poland. Declassified document, August 5, 1951, CIA Electronic Reading Room.

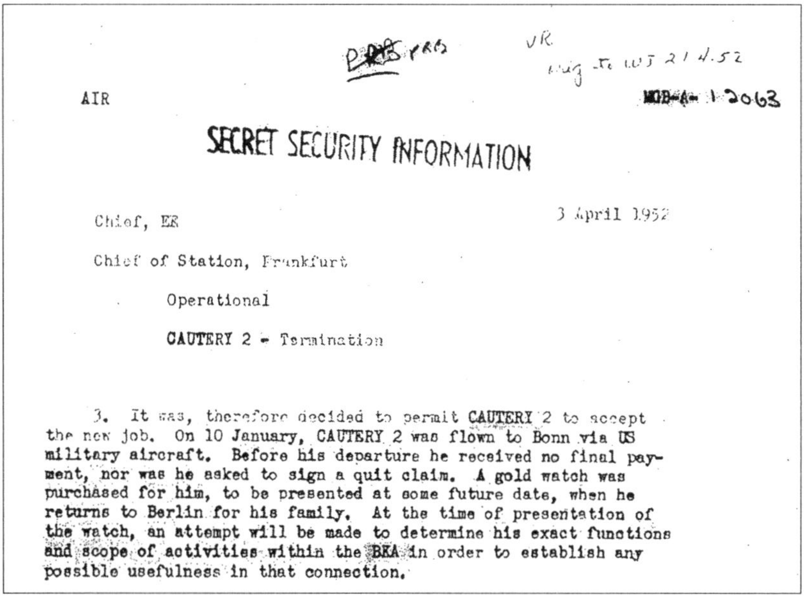

AIR

SECRET SECURITY INFORMATION

Chief, EE                                  3 April 1952

Chief of Station, Frankfurt

    Operational

    CAUTERY 2 - Termination

3. It was, therefore decided to permit CAUTERY 2 to accept the new job. On 10 January, CAUTERY 2 was flown to Bonn via US military aircraft. Before his departure he received no final payment, nor was he asked to sign a quit claim. A gold watch was purchased for him, to be presented at some future date, when he returns to Berlin for his family. At the time of presentation of the watch, an attempt will be made to determine his exact functions and scope of activities within the BKA in order to establish any possible usefulness in that connection.

FIG. 4. A number of former Nazis who had been spies for the U.S. government, including Theo Saevecke, went on to work for West German government agencies. In April 1952 Saevecke (code-named "Cautery 2") informed his CIA case officer he had been offered a job with the newly formed federal police agency, the Bundeskriminalamt. A U.S. military aircraft flew Saevecke from Berlin to Bonn to start his new job. The CIA case officer bought a gold watch for Saevecke, to show the agency's appreciation for his service. CIA Electronic Reading Room.

# 4

# Fickle Friends

In the first dozen years of the Cold War, Erich Wenger was a Commie-fighting superstar, at least in the eyes of his German superiors and his friends at the CIA. Built like a prize fighter, and with blond hair and piercing blue eyes, the six-foot-one-foot Wenger was an imposing figure, a perception accentuated by his habit of peremptorily placing his hands on his hips as he talked. Wenger's younger coworkers saw him as arrogant. His superiors saw him as the model counterintelligence officer.

In the spring of 1963, Wenger was preparing for his first visit ever to the CIA's headquarters at Langley, Virginia. Not one to show his emotions, he was nonetheless excited about the red-carpet treatment his CIA friends had planned for him, not just the briefings with America's top spooks but also the extracurricular treats that awaited him: tickets for a musical comedy and a baseball game in New York City, a rental car for sightseeing.

The CIA budgeted $4,250 for the visit by Wenger and a West German counterintelligence colleague, Richard Meier. Not a huge amount of money but enough to guarantee that the two Germans would enjoy themselves. Nonetheless, this was not a junket. This was serious business among spies. What American intelligence officials aimed to get out of it was intensified cooperation with West German counterintelligence against the Soviet bloc.[1]

CIA memos written in preparation for the visit by Wenger and Meier nearly salivate in anticipation of the potential espionage bonanza that was expected to come from expanding joint operations with the German domestic intelligence agency that employed them, the Federal Office for the Protection of the Constitution (Bundesamt für Verfassungsschutz, or BfV).

Wenger was head of the operations section of Department IV of the BfV. Department IV was, arguably, the most important arm of the BfV—carrying out counterintelligence operations against Eastern bloc spy agencies. Wenger ran double agents deep within enemy security agencies on the other side of the Iron Curtain.

In the run-up to the planned visit, a CIA officer wrote: "Wenger recognizes the seriousness of the Communist threat to which his country is exposed, and fully appreciates that only a united Western front under U.S. leadership can oppose this threat. Wenger has never expressed anything but pro-American sympathies to us, and we have always found him to be a most pleasant and cooperative liaison partner."[2]

The memo continued: "It is felt that the visit . . . will be to the mutual benefit of CIA and the BfV. During the past two years there has been a marked trend toward closer liaison between CIA and the BfV on matters of mutual concern in the CI/CE [counterintelligence/counterespionage] field, and the visit of Meier and Wenger is expected to accelerate this trend." The CIA had had its eye on Wenger for several years. In late 1956 Wenger was getting ready for a visit to West Berlin to meet with American intelligence officials. The CIA had obviously been keeping track of Wenger's counterintelligence successes. A CIA memo written in preparation for the talks noted, "There is no single person we would rather get next to in the BfV" than Wenger, adding, "we regard him as the standout case officer in the entire organization."

But the visit to the United States by Meier and Wenger planned for May 1963 was not to be. The CIA found out that a German investigative reporter—Peter Stähle—was on the trail of former SS members who had found refuge in the West German security services, and he'd dug up dirt on one in particular: former Gestapo officer Erich Wenger.

Revealing Wenger's wartime record threatened to drag the American spy agency into a West German political scandal that would embarrass U.S. officials. The CIA decided there was just one course of action: call off the two Germans' visit. The bad news was delivered personally to Wenger and Meier by a CIA officer who traveled to the BfV's headquarters in Cologne. The CIA officer gave some lame excuses: several CIA officials who were to participate in meetings with Wenger and Meier had fallen ill, and not only that, but "last minute changes in the travel plans" of other agency officials "necessitated their absence . . . during the critical period," according to a CIA memo.

Wenger didn't buy it, telling the CIA man that "there was little doubt in his mind that the trip was cancelled because of the danger of embarrassment to KUBARK [the CIA] resulting from his derogatory background."[3] In the last paragraph of the two-page memo, the CIA officer sounded an optimistic note that the whole thing would blow over. "As yet there has been no publicity on WENGER," the officer wrote, and "with the passage of time and the recession of public interest in other cases . . . we believe the likelihood of WENGER's case hitting the press will grow progressively remote."

The CIA officer could hardly have been more delusional. On August 27 the newsmagazine *Stern* published a blockbuster, written by Stähle. Stähle was threatened with a treason charge if he identified Wenger in his article, thus its title: "The Man with No Name." "The man with no name . . . voluntarily joined the Schutzstaffel in 1933. The young SS man embarked on the career of a police officer and during his training became a member of the Sicherheitsdienst," Stähle wrote. "The man with no name needn't feel lonely" in the BfV because, Stähle revealed, employed by the agency were a "shocking number of officials with SS, SD, and even Gestapo pasts." A follow-up by Stähle identified not only Wenger by name but also another former Gestapo member who had found refuge in the BfV, Johannes Strübing.

More than a dozen BfV officials were eventually unmasked as former members of the SS, the SD, or the Gestapo. A West German agreement with the Allies specifically barred former members of those Nazi agencies from employment with the Bundesamt für Verfassungsschutz. The BfV got around this prohibition by hiring them as freelancers. All used aliases and were paid through a secret account. The CIA knew all about it. A CIA memo written on September 9, 1963, reads: "In some cases this BfV practice was opposed by the Allies[;] in others it was tolerated."[4]

The BfV was also rocked by revelations that for years the agency had been illegally eavesdropping on German citizens, with the help of Allied intelligence. Ever since the defeat of the Third Reich, the Allies had been using occupation rights to wiretap anybody they wanted to and open their mail. The original purpose of these rights was to protect American, British, and French occupation troops from Germans who might want to take revenge for their country's defeat. West German government agencies were prohibited by the constitution from snooping on citizens' mail, telephone, and telex communications, but the BfV found a way around this restriction. The agency gave Allied officials the names of citizens it wished to have snooped on, and the occupiers would use their technology to do so. To many Germans, this invasion of privacy was a little too close to the practices of the Gestapo.

Fickle Friends

Erich Wenger's wartime record remains a little murky to this day. He was certainly no Adolf Eichmann or Klaus Barbie or Alois Brunner. Still, his known actions during the Third Reich should have kept him out of postwar government service, especially an agency like the BfV.

Born in East Prussia, as a young man Wenger had hoped to become a physician but was unable to get into medical school. As Hitler rose to power, Wenger lost no time in striking out on a different career path, joining the Nazi Party and the Sturmabteilung in 1932 and then the Sicherheitsdienst, or SD, the intelligence service of the SS. After training at the Charlottenburg police academy in Berlin, Wenger went to work as a criminal investigator at the Reichssicherheitshauptamt, the sprawling bureaucracy that oversaw policing in Nazi Germany and mass murder in the occupied lands. After the Nazis' conquest of France, Wenger was detailed to the German embassy in Paris, where he was in charge of the visa section. After fleeing Paris as Allied troops approached after the D-Day landings, Wenger joined a team of commandos fighting French partisans. He spent about eighteen months in British custody in Wuppertal, suspected of involvement in the execution of British paratroopers, but there wasn't enough evidence to pin it on him.[5]

After his release from British captivity in 1948, Wenger got busy reinventing himself. He was now using an alias, Eduard Wolters. He found work with a Christian aid agency, then with an insurance company, and then with the *Kölner Stadtanzeiger* newspaper.[6] He was hired by the BfV in September 1950 as a freelancer in the counterespionage department.

The scandal over the BfV's hiring of former Nazis like Wenger dragged on for months. Special parliamentary committees were convened. The Interior Ministry, which controlled the BfV, tried to defend itself by claiming there was no other choice but to hire Wenger and the others because it was hard to find candidates with the appropriate experience, that none of them had committed any serious misdeeds during the Third Reich, and through their postwar work they had all proven themselves to be champions of democracy, not a threat to it.

The whole thing finally blew over after the BfV used a mechanism that was frequently employed when a West German government agency was caught with incriminated former Nazis on its payroll: ship them off to another government office. For Erich Wenger it was the Federal Office of Administration, where he was put in charge of overseeing the maintenance of war veterans' graves.

Erich Wenger's downfall began with what many judge to be a war crime committed by British and American bombers. During the night of February 13, 1945, a formation of 244 British Lancaster bombers dropped incendiary explosives onto the city of Dresden, setting off firestorms that wreaked death and destruction. More Lancasters dropped their terrorizing loads just three hours later. The next day American B-17 Flying Fortresses dropped high explosives onto the smoldering city. Dresden burned for seven days, leaving a wasteland of rubble and charred corpses. Some twelve thousand buildings were destroyed. It's been estimated that twenty-five thousand to thirty-five thousand civilians died in the Dresden air raids, although the true number could have actually been far higher, due to an unknown number of refugees who had fled west to Dresden as the Soviet army advanced toward Germany. When there was no space left in cemeteries for victims, they were stacked onto one another on the market square and incinerated.

Dresden native Heinz Felfe was in the Netherlands when the firestorm swept through his native city, on duty with the Nazis' Sicherheitsdienst intelligence service. Felfe was captured by British forces at the war's end and was recruited to work for British intelligence, but he was cut loose when it was discovered he had tried to sell secrets.

Before Felfe was posted to the Netherlands in 1943, he was an intelligence officer in Berlin at the Reichssicherheitshauptamt (RSHA), the notorious Nazi terror apparatus. Felfe became buddies with another Dresden native and fellow RSHA employee, Hans Clemens.

Even though Felfe clearly had a flaky personality and could hardly be trusted with state secrets, he managed to stay in the game after he was dropped by British intelligence—first as an interrogator for the intelligence service of North Rhine–Westphalia state, then with the federal Ministry for All-German Affairs. It was while working for the federal ministry that he was contacted by his old friend and Nazi comrade Hans Clemens.

Clemens had switched sides. He was now working for the Komitet Gosudarstvennoy Bezopasnosti, or KGB. His Soviet handler, who went by the name "Max," was stationed at the KGB command in Dresden. Max's recruitment of Clemens was exquisitely planned. While Clemens was in a British POW camp, his wife, Gerda, had become a KGB agent.[7] Max sent Gerda to West Germany to deliver a message to her husband: that his Nazi past could at any moment result in him being accused of war crimes, but he could escape this danger by working for the KGB. It was unvarnished blackmail. Clemens traveled to Dresden in February 1950 to talk it over with Max. He told the KGB officer that he hated Americans because of the bombing of his native city. The wily Max then took Clemens on a tour of the bombed-out city. What I am giving you, Max essentially told Clemens, is the chance to exact revenge against the Americans. Return to West Germany and seek out your old Nazi comrades and talk them into spying for us on West Germany's foreign intelligence service, Max proposed to Clemens. The men also discussed Clemens's KGB pay, but it was the chance for retribution that seems to have sealed the deal.

Clemens had no trouble recruiting Felfe to work for the KGB, using the same arguments he had been told by Max. On a trip to Dresden, Felfe was given the same tour by Max that was given to Clemens. Both Felfe and Clemens succeeded in getting hired by the Gehlen Organization, the CIA-financed predecessor of West Germany's Bundesnachrichtendienst foreign intelligence service. Felfe's rise was meteoric. Reinhard Gehlen, head of the espionage organization, ultimately put Felfe in charge of the BND's counterintelligence operations against the Soviets. The KGB succeeded in solidifying Gehlen's trust in Felfe and expanding his access by providing him with information that the Soviets figured they could safely give up. The scheme had disastrous results not only for the BND but also for the CIA. After a tip from a Polish intelligence official to the CIA, on November 6, 1961, the BND arrested Felfe and Clemens. They were tried, convicted, and sentenced, respectively, to fourteen and nine years in prison.

Felfe exposed more than one hundred CIA officers, scores of BND agents, and counterintelligence operations run by the BND and the CIA against the Soviets. The CIA felt burned by the BND for its failure to realize that Felfe's SS past made him vulnerable to Soviet blackmail. Felfe's betrayal nearly destroyed the CIA's faith in West Germany's intelligence services. In February 1963 the chief of the CIA's Eastern Europe Division wrote a 120-page "damage assessment" report on the impact of Felfe's betrayal. "From June 1959 until his arrest on 6 November 1961," he wrote, "Heinz FELFE was the most knowledgeable of all BND officials on CIA operations against the Soviet targets in East and West Germany. As a result, the degree of compromise of operations, personnel and facilities in Germany has been very heavy."[8] With Wenger's Gestapo past exposed, the Americans could hardly continue to give him their unwavering support.

In 1963 allegations surfaced that the ss commando unit that Wenger led after fleeing the embassy in Paris had executed French civilians. Germany's Nazi-hunting agency embarked on a preliminary investigation and then handed the case over to the prosecutor's office in Cologne. But the investigation was abandoned in 1973 because of insufficient evidence. Wenger died later that year.

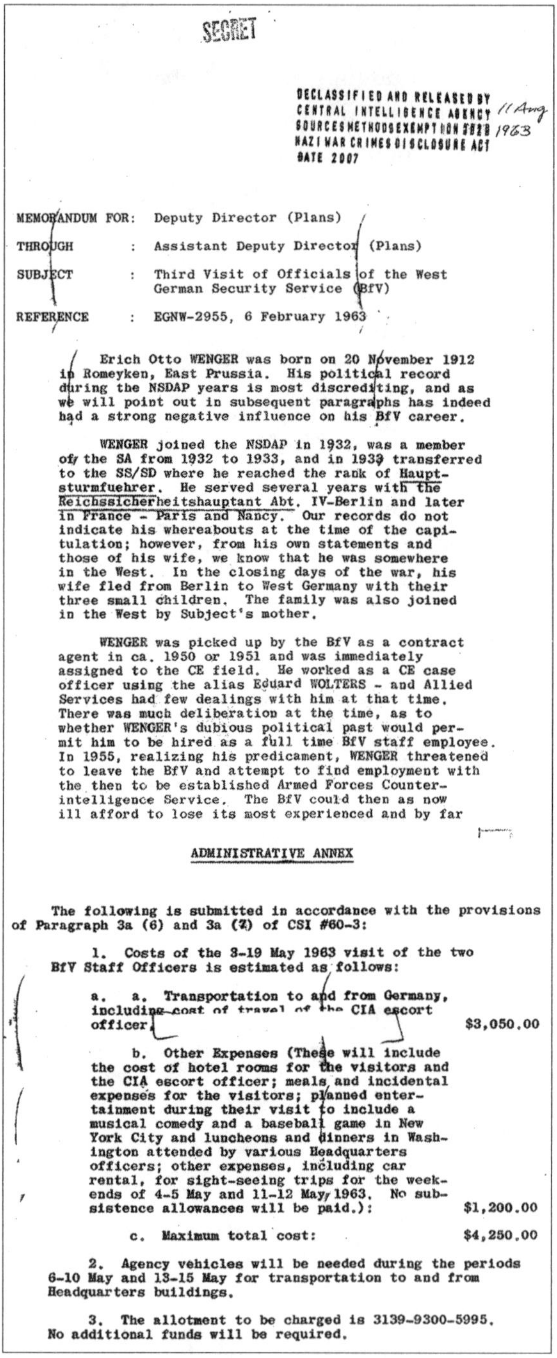

SECRET

DECLASSIFIED AND RELEASED BY
CENTRAL INTELLIGENCE AGENCY
SOURCES METHODS EXEMPTION 3B2B
NAZI WAR CRIMES DISCLOSURE ACT
DATE 2007

11 Aug 1963

MEMORANDUM FOR: Deputy Director (Plans)

THROUGH : Assistant Deputy Director (Plans)

SUBJECT : Third Visit of Officials of the West German Security Service (BfV)

REFERENCE : EGNW-2955, 6 February 1963

Erich Otto WENGER was born on 20 November 1912 in Romeyken, East Prussia. His political record during the NSDAP years is most discrediting, and as we will point out in subsequent paragraphs has indeed had a strong negative influence on his BfV career.

WENGER joined the NSDAP in 1932, was a member of the SA from 1932 to 1933, and in 1933 transferred to the SS/SD where he reached the rank of Hauptsturmfuehrer. He served several years with the Reichssicherheitshauptant Abt. IV-Berlin and later in France - Paris and Nancy. Our records do not indicate his whereabouts at the time of the capitulation; however, from his own statements and those of his wife, we know that he was somewhere in the West. In the closing days of the war, his wife fled from Berlin to West Germany with their three small children. The family was also joined in the West by Subject's mother.

WENGER was picked up by the BfV as a contract agent in ca. 1950 or 1951 and was immediately assigned to the CE field. He worked as a CE case officer using the alias Eduard WOLTERS - and Allied Services had few dealings with him at that time. There was much deliberation at the time, as to whether WENGER's dubious political past would permit him to be hired as a full time BfV staff employee. In 1955, realizing his predicament, WENGER threatened to leave the BfV and attempt to find employment with the then to be established Armed Forces Counterintelligence Service. The BfV could then as now ill afford to lose its most experienced and by far

ADMINISTRATIVE ANNEX

The following is submitted in accordance with the provisions of Paragraph 3a (6) and 3a (7) of CSI #60-3:

1. Costs of the 3-19 May 1963 visit of the two BfV Staff Officers is estimated as follows:

| | |
|---|---|
| a. a. Transportation to and from Germany, including cost of travel of the CIA escort officer | $3,050.00 |
| b. Other Expenses (These will include the cost of hotel rooms for the visitors and the CIA escort officer; meals and incidental expenses for the visitors; planned entertainment during their visit to include a musical comedy and a baseball game in New York City and luncheons and dinners in Washington attended by various Headquarters officers; other expenses, including car rental, for sight-seeing trips for the weekends of 4-5 May and 11-12 May 1963. No subsistence allowances will be paid.): | $1,200.00 |
| c. Maximum total cost: | $4,250.00 |

2. Agency vehicles will be needed during the periods 6-10 May and 13-15 May for transportation to and from Headquarters buildings.

3. The allotment to be charged is 3139-9300-5995. No additional funds will be required.

**FIG. 5.** Declassified CIA document showing the agenda for a planned 1963 visit to the agency by West German counterespionage expert Erich Wenger and a colleague, Richard Meier. On tap were not just meetings about spy wars with the Soviet bloc but also a baseball game and musical comedy in New York City as well as a rental car for sightseeing. The visit was scrubbed as a scandal brewed in West Germany over Wenger's Gestapo past. CIA Electronic Reading Room.

```
                                    CLASSIFICATION        DISPATCH SYMBOL AND NO.
      DISPATCH                        SECRET              EGNA-25875
TO    Chief, EE                                           HEADQUARTERS FILE NO.
INFO  Chief of Station, Germany                           32W 5 13/6

FROM                                                      DATE
      Chief of Base, Bonn                                 5 Jun 63
SUBJECT OPERATIONAL CARD LIAISON                          RE: "43-3" — (CHECK "X" ONE)
        Postponement of (MEIER/WENGER) Trip                   MARKED FOR INDEXING
                                                              NO INDEXING REQUIRED
ACTION REQUIRED                                               INDEXING CAN BE JUDGED
      See Para 5                                              BY QUALIFIED HQ. DESK ONLY
REFERENCE(S)
      REF:  Bonn-4582, 29 April 63

      1. We will summarize here the reactions of Dr. Richard MEIER and
   Erich WENGER to the postponement of their planned visit to PBPRIME in May 63.
   Reference reported that MEIER and WENGER, when first informed of the postpone-
   appeared to accept the reasons given, namely, illness of several key REMARK
   staffers and last minute changes in the travel plans of
   necessitated absence from Headquarters of other key staffers during the critical
   period. However, after some reflection both MEIER and WENGER developed some strong
   doubts, which they voiced to us a few days later, that this was the real reason for
   the postponement. Both of them commented, for example, that it was difficult for
   them to believe that the reason given was the real reason particularly because it
   was very similar to the explanation given for the postponement in the Autumn of
   1962.
```

**FIG. 6.** The CIA's chief of base in Bonn traveled to Cologne to tell Erich Wenger and Richard Meier that the 1963 Washington visit was being postponed. This declassified document shows the two West Germans were dubious about the CIA officer's story that the trip was being called off because some CIA staffers were ill or because of "last-minute changes" in travel plans. CIA Electronic Reading Room.

# 5

# Secret Agent 9610

It's a spring day in 1948. Agent 9610, a suave, blue-eyed German sporting a suit sits on a bench inside the waiting area of the train station at Limburg an der Lahn, a medieval market town with narrow streets, half-timbered houses, and a thirteenth-century cathedral. When three American intelligence officers arrive, Paul Dickopf shakes hands with each of them. The quartet sit down for a coffee and exchange pleasantries, then they get down to business. Dickopf is excited about the papers he is carrying in his briefcase to hand over to the intelligence officers. They were the German's nascent thoughts on the creation of a federal police force in the western region of occupied Germany. The three Americans thank Dickopf and return to Frankfurt.[1] In a series of confidential reports written over the next two years, their author, identified only as 9610, Dickopf provides his American handlers with his analyses of the law enforcement needs for the West German state that would soon be born and how a federal police force should be organized.

Dickopf's ideas did not come to him out of the clear blue sky. In his research Dieter Schenk, a BKA critic who in 2001 published a book, *Auf dem rechten Auge blind*, about tainted former Nazis in the Bundeskriminalamt, discovered similarities between Dickopf's vision of a West German federal police agency and the Nazis' Reichskriminalpolizeiamt (Reich Criminal Police Office), or RKPA.[2] Dickopf was well acquainted with the Nazis' police and intelligence operations because he had worked for them as an SS military intelligence officer during World War II. The Americans knew Dickopf's past, but that didn't matter. What did matter was that he was a staunch anti-Communist with a law enforcement background and was eager to please his American handlers. A CIA memo written on March 16, 1950, said about Dickopf: "He is obedient to our every wish, although he makes known his own views. Mentally brilliant, he is an excellent reporter and can be depended upon to keep us informed."[3]

This was not a one-way relationship, not by any stretch. What Dickopf was hoping to get from his American friends—and what they gave him—was their assistance in helping realize his ambition to rise to a position of power in West German security affairs. The partnership paid off in 1950, when Dickopf was hired by the West German Interior Ministry to work out the technical and operational details of a Bundeskriminalamt. He quickly climbed the civil service ladder. He was promoted to *Regierungskriminalrat* in the Interior Ministry in 1951, a year later was made a department head at the BKA, then was given another civil service promotion, appointed deputy president of the BKA in 1953, and in 1965 he rose to the BKA's top job: president.

During the gestation period preceding the birth of the BKA, Dickopf and American intelligence worked in tandem as midwives of sorts. The Americans used their clout as occupiers to steer Dickopf into consultations with German politicians and technocrats on German security matters, and Dickopf in the end won final legislative approval of much of his vision for the organization and operation of a West German federal law enforcement agency—the BKA. The partnership between Dickopf and American intelligence did not end there. Throughout his career at BKA, Dickopf maintained close contacts with the CIA. In a CIA memo from December 30, 1968, not declassified until 2007, a CIA officer wrote that he had met Dickopf—who was then BKA president—at his Wiesbaden home, where the German was paid "his salary for the month of December" and was also given a Christmas present.[4] Dickopf was serving as an agent for the CIA. The payments continued into 1971.

Dickopf's code name was "Caravel." When in early 1954 Dickopf informed his case officer he was contemplating moving on to a position with the International Criminal Police Organization in Paris, the CIA handler responded with alarm, writing in a memo: "From our point of view we would certainly lose our window into the German security scene and for this reason I will try to prevail on CARAVEL to stay in his current position." It's unclear whether it was the CIA that persuaded Dickopf to remain at the BKA, but remain he did.[5]

So just who was Paul Dickopf? He was a shape-shifter, a meister of manipulation, a charmer with the skills of a thespian, and a man with loyalties so slippery that in the 1940s he worked for the intelligence services of three nations: as a spy handler and mole with Nazi Germany's Abwehr military intelligence agency and, after his apparently faked desertion in 1943, as an informant for Switzerland and the United States.

Soon after Hitler became chancellor in 1933, Dickopf—then a law student at the University of Frankfurt—joined the Nazis' association of university students. He volunteered for a year of military service in 1934, and in 1937 he was hired by the detectives unit of Frankfurt police on a provisional basis and began the training needed to make it a permanent job. As the next step in his law enforcement career, Dickopf was accepted for admission into the Nazis' Security Police leadership school in Berlin for a six-month course of study. Before he matriculated, Dickopf was given the SS rank *Untersturmführer* (second lieutenant). Dickopf secured a position as a detective superintendent in Karlsruhe before being posted to the Abwehr office in Stuttgart in October 1939.

After Dickopf popped up in Switzerland in 1943 claiming to be a deserter, he went to great lengths to create a legend that portrayed him as an opponent of the Nazis since before Hitler came to power. He told Swiss and American authorities that the Gestapo had orders to hunt him down and kill him. He also claimed that the SS rank was not his choice—that it was automatically given to him as part of the Security Police leadership course. This was a fabrication, as shown by Dieter Schenk, who found documents demonstrating that Dickopf had gone through an application process to become a member of the SS. Dickopf was never a member of the Nazi Party. But Schenk found documents suggesting that Dickopf had continued collecting intelligence for the Germans after his supposed defection.

The life of Paul Dickopf was inextricably entwined with that of a Swiss man of similar skills and fluid loyalties, François Genoud, a Swiss Fascist and anti-Semite who simultaneously worked for German military intelligence and for the Swiss and without whom Dickopf could not have concocted the intricate legends and biographical obfuscations that made it possible for him to carve out a starring role for himself in West German security matters. As shown by Dieter Schenk's research, without Genoud, the American intelligence officers who wined and dined Paul Dickopf for three decades likely would never have met the German Abwehr officer.

In 1941 the Abwehr's headquarters in Berlin sent a cable to its Stuttgart office recommending that a Swiss national living near Stuttgart, Genoud, be considered as an agent to be sent into his home country to spy on enemy intelligence services working from there, including the U.S. Office of

Strategic Services (OSS), predecessor of the Central Intelligence Agency. Genoud was a promising recruit, the cable said, because of his membership in the National Front, an anti-Semitic party in Switzerland that modeled itself on Hitler's Nazi Party.[6] Genoud's apartment was like a temple dedicated to the Nazis, adorned with swastikas and a life-size portrait of Hitler. Dickopf made contact with Genoud, becoming his spy handler and beginning a relationship that lasted through Dickopf's three-decade-long connection and friendship with the CIA.

In June 1942 Dickopf received orders to travel to Berlin to meet with his superiors at Abwehr headquarters, or so he claimed in a biographical sketch requested of him by the OSS after he approached the agency in Switzerland with offers to provide it with German military intelligence. According to Dieter Schenk, even if this meeting did occur, as Dickopf claimed, it looks as though it was the start of an elaborate scheme by the Abwehr to infiltrate the OSS's office in Bern, Switzerland, which was run by Allen Dulles, master American spy and future director of the CIA. And François Genoud was a vital piece of the deception.

Dickopf's story to the OSS in early 1945 was that Abwehr headquarters had told him he would be infiltrated into Switzerland with a civilian alias—as an official working for the Reichsbahn at the German railroad agency's office in Zurich—with the covert mission of spying on the OSS and other foreign intelligence agencies and reporting back to his superiors. Dickopf claimed that he had become increasingly resistant to doing the bidding of the Third Reich and decided that he would switch his loyalties to the Allied cause. But according to Schenk, Dickopf's description to American intelligence of what happened between the 1942 meeting in Berlin and his acceptance by the OSS as an agent is so filled with inconsistencies, omissions, obfuscations, and extremely unlikely situations that the OSS must have known that Dickopf was being less than honest with the story about his ostensible defection.

According to the tale spun by Dickopf, he had traveled to Paris in August 1942 on orders of the Abwehr headquarters to receive training for his assignment in Switzerland. After three weeks in the French capital, Dickopf returned to Stuttgart. Dickopf told the Americans that what happened next was all part of his plan to flee Nazi Germany. In the biographical sketch written at the request of the OSS in February 1945, Dickopf said he told his Abwehr superiors in Stuttgart that while in Paris he came across an "important intelligence matter" that should be followed up on. The Stuttgart Abwehr office authorized Dickopf to return to Paris to dig into it, according to Dickopf's legend. Dickopf told American intelligence officers that he had recruited Genoud specifically to help him defect. Even though Genoud worked for the German Abwehr, he was also in the employ of the Swiss Security Service, the Sicherheitsdienst (SD). The plan, Dickopf told American intelligence, was that Genoud would help him escape to Switzerland and would introduce him to Swiss intelligence officers; Dickopf would then provide them with German military secrets and thus be guaranteed safe haven in Switzerland.

Dickopf stayed in Paris for a couple of months and in December moved on to Brussels, where Genoud had an apartment. Genoud would periodically travel to Switzerland to deliver reports to Swiss intelligence, mainly about the mood of the German populace and damage to German cities from Allied bombing runs. Dickopf claimed to the Americans that during this period he was planning his escape to Switzerland. According to his story, Dickopf decided the time had come when an Abwehr officer showed up in Brussels to find out what Dickopf was up to. Equipped with fake IDs and a story of facing imminent arrest for resisting orders, Dickopf crossed the border into Switzerland on July 17, 1943.[7]

During the war Switzerland was crawling with spies. The OSS launched operations into Nazi Germany from its base in Bern. The French, the British, the Russians, and the Germans also had intelligence operatives there. Although Switzerland was a neutral country, it used its own intelligence services to monitor what the spooks from other countries were up to. Genoud's relationship with the Swiss Security Service was a curious one. It is incontrovertible that Genoud worked for the Sicherheitsdienst at the same time he worked for the German Abwehr. Both the Abwehr and the Swiss SD knew he was a double agent. It's clear that Dickopf found Genoud useful for his own purposes. And it could well be that the SD chose to go along with the whole charade because having Genoud as one of its agents let the Swiss keep a close eye on what he was up to. In any event, it became clear after Dickopf's arrival in Lausanne in the summer of 1943 that the Swiss did not totally trust Genoud, which also raised suspicions about the German refugee now staying with Genoud at his apartment.

Swiss security officers and police descended upon Genoud's apartment on August 8, 1944. They arrested Genoud and his wife, Dickopf, and a

Lebanese businessman who had initially given Dickopf a place to stay after his arrival in Switzerland and jailed them in Bern. A variety of forged IDs were found in Dickopf's possession, bearing four different aliases. During his first day in custody, Dickopf wrote a seventeen-page biography that included his reasons for fleeing his homeland and that he was the one who had been providing Genoud with confidential German material to be handed over to Swiss intelligence.[8] Dickopf's interrogators were dubious.

Swiss files obtained by Dieter Schenk for his 2001 book include the transcript from Swiss investigators' questioning of Dickopf on August 23, 1944, a document showing the Swiss were finding it hard to swallow Dickopf's story. "Everything points to you still having contact with Germany," the interrogator told Dickopf, "and, even if you aren't working against Switzerland, you are working for a foreign country [meaning Germany] against a foreign state, and by doing this you are violating Switzerland's neutrality law."[9] Dickopf replied, "I deny this unequivocally."

The interrogator let slip that Swiss authorities suspected that Genoud himself was a Nazi spy, so Dickopf's relationship with him made the German's desertion story highly unlikely. "If, under the circumstances you described, you were truly anxious to flee to Switzerland for the sake of your own safety, by turning to Genoud you have at the very least turned to a person who may possibly be playing a double game," the Swiss interrogator told Dickopf. Dickopf responded, "I do not have this impression of Genoud [that he was a double agent] and he has my complete trust."

In a report written on August 28, 1944, the chief interrogator voiced suspicion that since Dickopf's arrival in Switzerland more than a year earlier, he had been spying for the Abwehr and using Genoud as a courier to deliver his reports back to Stuttgart. Swiss intelligence knew that Genoud had been in Stuttgart that June, which led them to believe he was still working for the Abwehr, even though his own spy handler, Dickopf, had supposedly defected to Switzerland. "It is inexplicable that following the supposed disappearance of Dickopf, German intelligence would continue to let Genoud do whatever he wants," the Swiss official wrote in his report on Dickopf.

Adding to the reasons for the Swiss to be suspicious about Dickopf were seized documents indicating that he had been sending expense reports to someone, possibly in the Abwehr. Dickopf made statements to Swiss officials about his financial situation and sources of income that seemed fishy. Also suspicious was the fact that after arriving in Switzerland, Dickopf did not bother to make connections with the tight-knit community of authentic German exiles who had fled the Nazis.

The final report on the interrogations of Dickopf stated that Swiss security officials were not able to prove that the German had fled his country for his own safety. It also said that "this man's training in espionage is extensive, and therefore allowing him to go unmonitored is dangerous for our country."

According to Dieter Schenk, Swiss records show that during the year prior to his arrest, Dickopf had been providing information to the Swiss Security Service officer who was Genoud's handler—a Captain Olivet—about the location of German troop units in Belgium and France; the organization of German Security Police, Gestapo, and Abwehr offices; and the morale of the German populace as the Allies racked up successes against the Third Reich.[10] This was anodyne material that was intended to secure Swiss intelligence's trust in Dickopf, at least in the view of Schenk. Whatever the value of Dickopf's information, it apparently drove a wedge between Swiss officials about whether the German could be trusted. The Swiss federal prosecutor's office recommended that Dickopf be given "benevolent treatment in view of his services" to Swiss intelligence. The Bern Police Department made clear that it did not believe Dickopf's claim that he was an opponent of the Nazis.

"It seems somewhat peculiar to me that a man who joined the criminal police in 1937, became an SS *Untersturmführer* in 1939, and then worked for three years in the *Abwehr* and was active in espionage, subsequently claims that he had never agreed with the German regime and had only participated [in the Nazi regime] purely because he felt forced to," wrote a Bern police official on December 5, 1944.[11]

Swiss officials decided to grant Dickopf refugee status but also to keep an eye on him. He was given an assigned residence—the Hotel Löwen in Worb, just outside Bern—and was told that if he wanted to leave Worb, he would need to get permission from the federal prosecutor's office. Dickopf had to pay for the costs of staying at the hotel.

Dickopf continued working as an informant for the Swiss but provided information the Swiss and the OSS already had from other sources, such as the throngs of Germans who were defecting or surrendering to save their own skins because it was obvious the war was lost, according to Schenk.

On January 24, 1945, Dickopf wrote a letter to Allen Dulles—the OSS chief in Bern—requesting a meeting. Included in the letter was a report written by Dickopf about the German intelligence services.[12] Dickopf's first personal contact with the OSS came just seven days later, when he met at the American Legation in Bern with Gero von Schulze-Gaevernitz, Dulles's assistant. It was the start not just of a working relationship but also of a mutual admiration friendship between American intelligence and Dickopf that lasted until his death.

CIA memos written in 1948 and 1949, though not declassified until 2007, show a shift in American views on how Dickopf's unique skills, ambition, and exuberance could best be exploited. Until then, Dickopf had been working with a fellow German—given the code name "07"—on developing agents in the Soviet-occupied eastern zone of Germany to spy for the Americans. The true identity of 07, a code name whose similarity to the fictional 007 is purely coincidental, has never been disclosed. While Dickopf was working with the Americans, he was simultaneously looking for a law enforcement job in the western zone, specifically in Hesse, his home state. But unlike his American friends, Hesse officials were put off by Dickopf's SS rank during the Third Reich and by his work for the Abwehr. Dickopf's contact with officials of the Greater Hesse State provisional government set up by the American military was arranged by von Schulze-Gaevernitz, Dulles's aide. On March 25, 1946, Dickopf met with Hesse interior minister Hans Venedey, who referred him to a Dr. Hamberger, the commander of Hesse's state police agency. The talks with Hamberger did not go well.

After one meeting Dickopf wrote: "Hamberger drew my attention to the fact that in the course of time I have to deal with hostility because anyone who is politically tainted will be attacked by the political parties. I therefore found it necessary to explain to Hamberger that I am in no way tainted and prefer not to waste time with him and myself if he insists on his erroneous opinion."[13]

In a follow-up meeting, Hamberger told Dickopf he had chosen someone else for the position of chief of detectives with Hesse police—a member of the Social Democratic Party, the strongest political force in Hesse. The decision incensed Dickopf, fueling the hostility he harbored, and often demonstrated, toward the leftist Social Democrats in the decades to come.

In February 1947 Dickopf submitted papers for "denazification," a necessary step to land a job as a civil servant in the Americans' occupation zone. Dickopf was exonerated the following year by the German court that examined his case, getting a considerable assist from Paul C. Blum, his handler at the American Legation in Bern. Blum wrote a glowing letter for Dickopf, saying the German "has been of very great service to me. His wide knowledge of German organization[s] and personalities has been invaluable; he is a trained member of the Kriminalpolizei and I have drawn extensively upon his experience for information on War Crimes and Criminals."[14] In *Auf dem rechten Auge blind* Dieter Schenk refuted Dickopf's claims that he provided anything of substance to the Americans. Schenk also listed the many "inaccuracies, omissions, or untruths" contained in the questionnaire submitted by Dickopf to the denazification court.

Contacts between Dickopf and American intelligence fell into abeyance for several months but resumed in early 1948. That spring CIA officers began filing monthly "progress reports" on their meetings with the man whose code name at that time was "Hathor." "Since contact was re-established with HATHOR about three months ago, the case officer has seen him approximately once a week," according to a CIA memo written on May 25, 1948.[15] "HATHOR's personal situation was greatly improved the first week in May when he finally achieved his denazification with flying colors."

Dickopf had become more valuable to the agency. "The successful completion of his denazification removes the last barrier to HATHOR's employment in the German police, and the only question remaining is that of placement in the office providing the greatest benefit both to us and to him," the memo states. In the CIA's next monthly progress report on Dickopf, written on July 31, 1948, the agency indicated more of its strategy for working with its newly reactivated agent: "HATHOR appears enthusiastic at the prospect of working with us in a police capacity to thwart Communist activity in the American zone."[16]

So that was the plan: assist Dickopf with getting hired by one of the German law enforcement agencies that were in the process of being set up and have him covertly gather information not on suspected Nazi war criminals but on Communists. The Americans by now were losing interest in pursuing Third Reich mass murderers, focusing instead on thwarting their new enemy: the Soviet Union and its satellite nations.

Whereas Dickopf had unsuccessfully sought a law enforcement job with Hesse state, he was now working with the CIA to get himself placed in an organization that would have a far more expansive reach—a law enforcement agency for the whole of occupied western Germany.

A memo written on December 23, 1948, spelled out the agency's strategy: "Our future plans for HATHOR depend largely on the steps now being taken by Allied authorities to permit the setting up of a tri-zonal criminal police office for Western Germany." But the same memo reveals the CIA's concerns about Dickopf. "HATHOR's financial situation has for some time given grounds for suspicion about his loyalty and orientation," it states. "He accepts no salary, has no job, and yet manages to live."[17]

When questioned about his finances, Dickopf told the CIA that money given to him by his father and father-in-law and the sale of antique books were helping him make ends meet. The CIA was apparently not totally satisfied with this explanation because the December 23 memo states that Dickopf had been asked to prepare a "detailed report on his past and present financial resources, including numbers of security certificates, and receipts from book sales."

The CIA seems to have suspected Dickopf was still working for the Swiss, and possibly for the French as well, but Dickopf denied it and agreed to take a lie detector test—which he apparently passed.

As the western occupation zone steered closer to creation of what would become the Bundeskriminalamt, American intelligence was putting former SS officer Paul Dickopf in the driver's seat. It was a choice that would ultimately open the BKA's doors to war criminals.

In 1949, when Dickopf was working with German and American officials on setting up a federal investigative agency, he learned that Chancellor Adenauer was adamantly opposed to hiring former SS and Gestapo officers for what would become the BKA, even if they had been exonerated during the denazification process. This view infuriated Dickopf, who maintained that excluding such experienced men would result in an "ominous splitting of the people" and to many Germans turning away from democratic ideas. What Dickopf failed to mention, no doubt intentionally so, was that beating the denazification process had become much easier since the job of scrutinizing former Reich members was transferred by American to German authorities in 1946. German denazification courts were prone to accepting former Nazis' descriptions of their Third Reich activities at face value.

Dickopf also maintained that during the Third Reich, police officers—like himself—were given SS ranks without their having asked for them. This was a fallacious argument. The fact of the matter was that police officers who held such ranks had filled out applications to be granted them. Dickopf himself had asked to join the SS, a fact that did not become known until decades later. But none of this mattered. The justification put forward by Dickopf was successfully put to use by subsequent BKA job candidates who had served in the SS.

Excluding former SS and Gestapo officers from the BKA would have disqualified most of the agency's job candidates at that time. So Dickopf campaigned for men who had once belonged to the Nazi elite. Dickopf's argument ultimately won out, opening the BKA to mass murderers. Dickopf handpicked some of the first employees at the BKA, knowing about their compromised pasts.

Dickopf saw as his two greatest nemeses communism and anyone out to diminish his powers. A third was a former prison located in the city of Ludwigsburg, not because of any danger he would ever wind up there but because of the threat it presented to tainted investigators at the BKA. In 1958 West Germany's first criminal agency dedicated specifically to tracking down Nazi war criminals began its work at offices inside the former prison. The agency, the Zentrale Stelle der Landesjustizverwaltungen zur Aufklärung nationalsozialistischer Verbrechen, is known in English as the Central Office of the State Justice Administrations for the Investigation of National Socialist Crimes, or simply the Central Office.

The birth of the Central Office was the result of a civil service case that drew attention to the widespread inclination of West German prosecutors and judges to avoid pursuing charges against war criminals. In 1955 a man named Bernd Fischer was hired as director of a refugee shelter near the city of Ulm, in southwestern Germany. As it turned out, he was covering up a murderous past. His real name was Bernhard Fischer-Schweder, and during the war he was the Nazi police chief in Memel, in occupied Lithuania. He was fired from his position at the refugee shelter when his past role became known. After he applied for another civil service job and was rejected, he filed a lawsuit with the local labor court. As his case was pending, a survivor of the Lithuania massacres saw a newspaper headline that read "SS Lieutenant Colonel Appeals for Reinstatement" and realized that the former Nazi trying to get back into the West German civil service had been involved in the killings in Lithuania. The survivor wrote to the newspaper, identifying Fischer-Schweder and providing details about a massacre of Lithuanian Jews that Fischer-Schweder had been involved in. Ulm's prosecutor had Fischer-Schweder arrested and began an investigation into the allegations. The prosecutor's findings resulted in the trial of Fischer-Schweder and nine others on charges of being accessories to the murder of more than five thousand Jewish men, women, and children as part of a Nazi killing unit called "Tilsit." The defendants were convicted but given light sentences, ranging from three to fifteen years. One substantial reason for the leniency shown the defendants was the widespread view in Germany then—one that prevailed into the 1960s—that it was only Adolf Hitler and his top functionaries who were actual war criminals and that those lower on the rung were just following orders.

Despite the light sentences, the Ulm trial brought the realization that there must have been many massacres like the one Fischer-Schweder had participated in that had yet to be investigated. In October 1958 the justice ministers of West Germany's states reached an agreement on the founding of an agency of government prosecutors whose sole job would be to pursue Nazi perpetrators. And thus was the Central Office born.

Paul Dickopf was deeply concerned about this newly minted team of Nazi hunters and with good reason. Prosecutors had already been digging into the pasts of a number of investigators at the BKA. An April 22, 1959, memo about a private meeting between Dickopf and his case officer reveals a side of Dickopf that took the CIA man by surprise. The conversation began with Dickopf bringing up revelations in *Der Spiegel* that the BKA's handwriting expert had forged his academic credentials to get the BKA job. Dickopf maintained that the magazine was distorting the facts. He then went on a tirade against journalists, complaining that "the press intimidates officialdom at every level and exercises a power that cannot be spoken of in terms of freedom of the press."

The author of the CIA memo reviewing Dickopf's remarks wrote, "This conversation interested the case officer more than its contents would normally merit, for the tone of voice was bitter and the statements were more candidly Right-Extremist than is usual with CARAVEL."[18] "Caravel" was the new cover name for Dickopf. In the meeting, according to the memo,

Dickopf "stated explicitly at one point that he favored legal repressive measures to discipline the press." The conversation then turned to the health of the aging Chancellor Adenauer, who might succeed him when he retired, and the wages of employees for police officers. Because of low pay and a German "disdain" for police, Dickopf said "the police and the BKA are having a very hard time attracting worthwhile people to the police service."

At that point the topic of the Nazi-hunting agency in Ludwigsburg, the Central Office, arose. It was broached by the CIA case officer, who was interested in learning more about the resignation of West Germany's minister for displaced persons, refugees, and war victims, Theodor Oberländer, over revelations about his own Nazi past.

The CIA officer asked Dickopf whether he thought Communist East Germany's Ministry for State Security might be feeding incriminating documents about West German officials to the Central Office "and even dictating who should be attacked." Dickopf then opened up about how the Ludwigsburg prosecutors were viewed at the BKA. The memo says, "CARAVEL stated 'between us only' that the Ludwigsburg Center was sarcastically known as the *Bundesstelle für Verfolgung von Kriminalbeamten*," which in English means "Federal Office for the Prosecution of Criminal Investigators."

Dickopf's subsequent comments show a man who was trying not to sound like he was a defender of war criminals, but at the same time he came up with a litany of criticisms of the Ludwigsburg office. He said it was a "repository of all kinds of true and notional derogatory information, much of which is undoubtedly fed in" by East German intelligence. Dickopf complained that the Ludwigsburg office "concerns itself mostly with former criminal police officers, and this not only hampers the operations of the BKA, but contributes to the black eye of the police."

In Dickopf's private meetings with his CIA handlers—be it in a car, over dinner, at home over a cognac, or with a bottle of Johnnie Walker Black Label scotch—his conversations were always businesslike, professional, on point. But an authoritarian side of Dickopf can be glimpsed in the CIA's declassified files. During one meeting, in 1964, Dickopf told a CIA officer that maybe it was not such a bad thing that habitual criminals had been sent to Nazi concentration camps because they came out "in good physical condition." During a meeting in 1968 in which Dickopf complained about the ineffectiveness of German investigative services, he put part of the blame on the Americans, griping about the "tremendous emphasis upon democratizing Germany after World War II and decentralizing the police forces."[19]

Despite the CIA's respect for Dickopf as a covert agent and CIA officers' friendship with this former SS officer, as president of the BKA, Dickopf struggled to keep up with the times. In the 1960s police forces were beginning to use newly developing electronic systems to sort through data kept on crimes and criminals. Dickopf preferred the old method of manually sifting through evidentiary documents. His antiquated approach ultimately cost him his job. He was forced into retirement in 1971. Still, Dickopf had many admirers in the larger world of policing, which led to him becoming the first German president of the International Criminal Police Organization, known as Interpol, in 1968.

The CIA's final memo about Dickopf was cabled from Germany to headquarters at Langley on September 20, 1973. It was brief but poignant: "Regret to report that Caravel, a staunch friend of the U.S. in general and of BKHERALD (one of the cryptonyms for the CIA) and its predecessor organizations in particular, died 19 Sept. 73." Soon thereafter, the street leading to the BKA's office in Meckenheim was named Paul Dickopf Strasse. The street sign remained there until 2012. By then the legend that Paul Dickopf had built for himself had collapsed. On June 25, 2012, about 140 people—BKA employees, local officials, and representatives of other federal agencies—gathered outside the Meckenheim office for a formal ceremony to rename the street.

"Naming of a street is always a symbolic act, showing a special appreciation for the role model function of the namesake. Having Paul Dickopf as the namesake for this street is no longer appropriate," the BKA said in a statement posted on its website.[20]

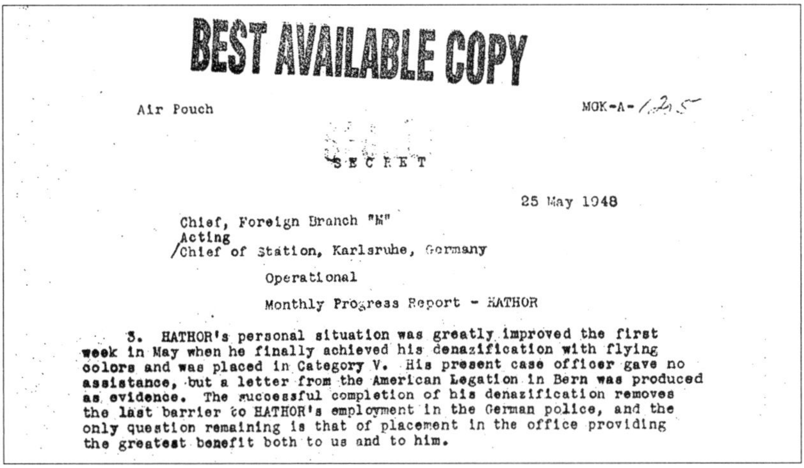

> BEST AVAILABLE COPY
>
> Air Pouch    MGK-A- /.2.5
>
> SECRET
>
> 25 May 1948
>
> Chief, Foreign Branch "M"
> Acting
> /Chief of Station, Karlsruhe, Germany
>
> Operational
>
> Monthly Progress Report - HATHOR
>
> 3. HATHOR's personal situation was greatly improved the first week in May when he finally achieved his denazification with flying colors and was placed in Category V. His present case officer gave no assistance, but a letter from the American Legation in Bern was produced as evidence. The successful completion of his denazification removes the last barrier to HATHOR's employment in the German police, and the only question remaining is that of placement in the office providing the greatest benefit both to us and to him.

FIG. 7. As U.S. intelligence agents groomed Paul Dickopf for a role in postwar German security, they wrote up monthly reports on their progress. In this report, from May 1948, a CIA station chief reveals the agency's strategy for making the best use of Dickopf, who at the time had the code name "Hathor." CIA Electronic Reading Room.

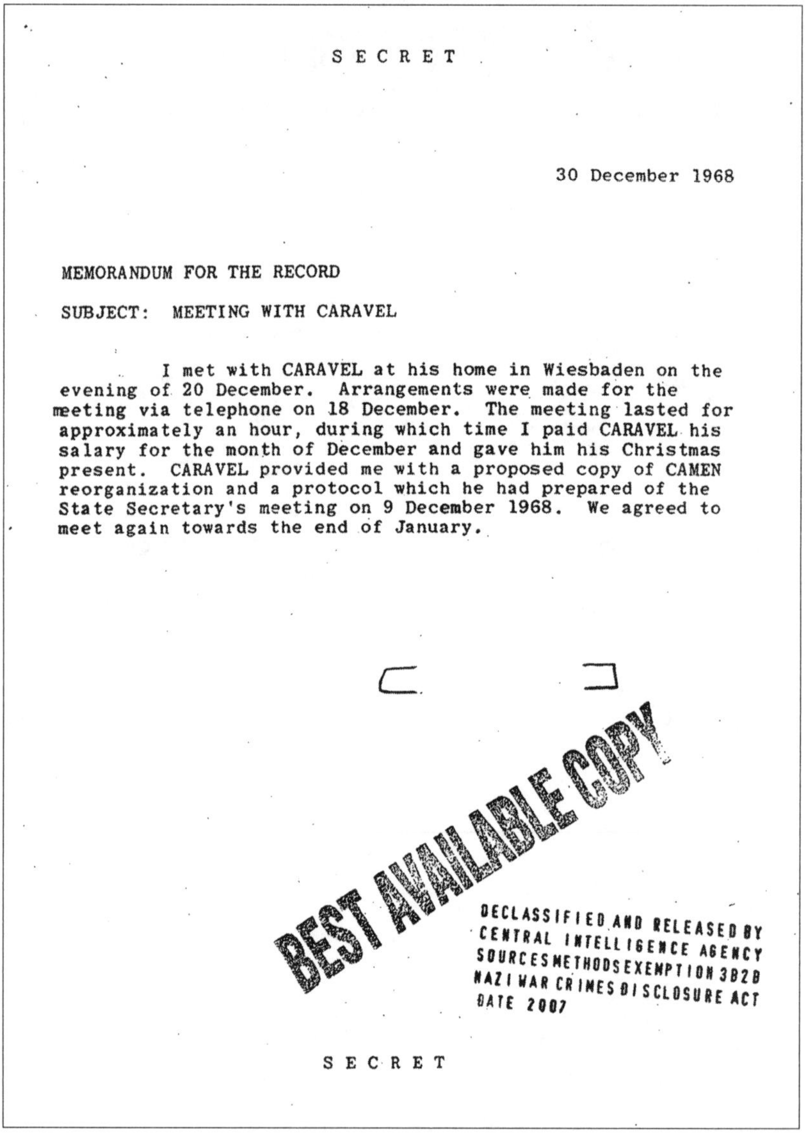

SECRET

30 December 1968

MEMORANDUM FOR THE RECORD

SUBJECT: MEETING WITH CARAVEL

    I met with CARAVEL at his home in Wiesbaden on the evening of 20 December. Arrangements were made for the meeting via telephone on 18 December. The meeting lasted for approximately an hour, during which time I paid CARAVEL his salary for the month of December and gave him his Christmas present. CARAVEL provided me with a proposed copy of CAMEN reorganization and a protocol which he had prepared of the State Secretary's meeting on 9 December 1968. We agreed to meet again towards the end of January.

[ ]

BEST AVAILABLE COPY

DECLASSIFIED AND RELEASED BY
CENTRAL INTELLIGENCE AGENCY
SOURCES METHODS EXEMPTION 3B2B
NAZI WAR CRIMES DISCLOSURE ACT
DATE 2007

SECRET

FIG. 8. This CIA memo, written in 1968, was not declassified until 2007. It shows that Paul Dickopf was a paid agent of the CIA. CIA Electronic Reading Room.

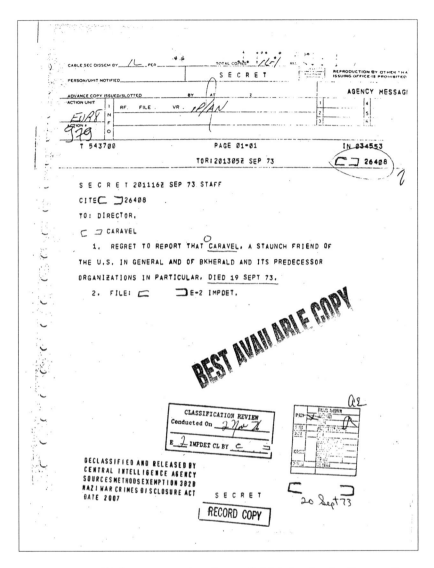

FIG. 9. A 1973 cable from a Europe-based CIA official, informing the director of the CIA that Paul Dickopf, code-named "Caravel," had passed away. CIA Electronic Reading Room.

# 6

# A Talk on the Terrace

U.S. Army captain John R. Boker Jr. climbed the stairs of a house on Bodenstedtstrasse in Wiesbaden, a spa city on the Rhine River. It was June 1945, weeks after Adolf Hitler killed himself in his Berlin bunker. Asleep on a bed inside the Wiesbaden house was General Reinhard Gehlen, who during the war was Hitler's chief of military intelligence for Nazi-occupied territories in eastern Europe and Russia.

"I'm sorry to disturb you, general," Boker told Gehlen, a small, fit man with protruding ears. The young American officer asked the forty-year-old Gehlen "to fix up and meet me on the terrace." "He came down and we sat together at a small table by ourselves in a corner of the terrace," Boker recalled in a 1952 report written at the request of the CIA.[1] "I told him that I was interested in talking about the Soviets because I understood that he had been the head of the German Military Intelligence Service dealing with them. He indicated he was very anxious to cooperate with the Americans." Boker learned that Gehlen's subordinates, at the general's instruction, had concealed files "between floors of remote foresters' lodges, had buried or otherwise cached."

Gehlen and his subordinates had surrendered to the Americans with a plan that promised not only to shield them from prying war crimes investigators but to reinvent their careers. Gehlen knew that his knowledge and the buried documents would be alluring to the Americans. They were his ticket to a return to power and influence. "By the middle of July 1945," Boker wrote, "we had succeeded in reconstituting General Gehlen's key members and staff, all of his important documents and were very much aware of the gold mine we'd found." This is an astonishing statement—that the U.S. military had successfully reconstituted a component of the just-defeated Third Reich. But ultimately, what was important for the Americans were not any atrocities that Gehlen's counterintelligence corps may have been involved in but the group's usefulness to U.S. intelligence.

Boker set out to persuade his superiors to build up Gehlen's corps into an espionage organization that would gather intelligence on the Soviets from a base in Germany. Boker asked Gehlen and his subordinates to use their files to write reports on Soviet military strength, which Boker would present to his superiors as an argument for the German general's value.

The commander of the American interrogation center in Wiesbaden was Colonel W. R. Philp. Boker arranged a "social evening" for Philp with the German captives at the "Generals' House," as the comfortable lodgings for Gehlen and his comrades was known. Bottles of wine were procured. Gehlen's group prepared a briefing on Soviet artillery tactics, a topic dear to the heart of Philp, who had been an artillery officer. Philp was won over by Gehlen and his officers. The decision was made to fly the German captives to Washington DC, along with their documents, to get full backing for reactivating Gehlen and his men—this time in the service of gathering intelligence on the Soviets.

Within the vast archives of declassified CIA documents on Nazi war criminals are numerous memos on social meetings between American officials—be they military officers, spies, or diplomats—and vanquished Germans who had something to offer. The memos reveal an astonishing solicitude toward the Germans, to the point of seeming fawning. Much wine was consumed, many dinners shared. While the memos contain substantive information, they also often show a fondness between the former enemies—the Germans are asked about their families, and the Germans do the same. Trips were arranged for Germans for briefings in Washington DC—sometimes including all-expenses-paid travel around the United States to see some of America's scenic wonders, for example, or for a baseball game or a Broadway show. More than seven decades after the defeat of the Third Reich, it may be hard to imagine having a warm conversation with former Nazis who had loyally and eagerly served Hitler. A determination to smash Nazism had driven Americans to go to Europe to fight and to die. But suddenly, the object of that hatred shifted, toward America's wartime Allies, the Soviets. And the old enemies, former Nazis, were wooed with dinner parties, fine cigars, and collegial embraces.

Still, in the initial days after Germany's defeat, there was skepticism about making deals with the former enemy, as Boker discovered as he and the Gehlen group arrived in the U.S. capital in August 1945. "There was considerable hostility to working with Germans in any way," Boker recalled in the report he wrote for the CIA in 1952.

Gehlen and his group were taken to an army interrogation center in Alexandria, Virginia. Their handler, Boker, became dismayed when he heard they were put into solitary cells at the center's prison compound and pleaded that they be removed from confinement and put to work producing reports on the Soviet military, as Boker had them do in Wiesbaden. Boker's request was granted.

Boker arranged for the head of the interrogation center—a Colonel Lovell—to have dinner with the Gehlen group. In the end American military authorities determined that Gehlen and his men could help fill a void in U.S. intelligence-gathering abilities in Europe. Gehlen was given the go-ahead to build a secret espionage organization in Germany, with the United States footing the bill and the U.S. Army supervising the new troupe of spies. Gehlen wasted little time. Covert field offices occupied by the U.S.-funded Gehlen Organization, as it was called, sprang up across western Germany, with its headquarters in Pullach, a town in Bavaria.

From the early years, the U.S. government's relationship with the Gehlen operation was akin to that of a foster agency seeking adoptive parents for an adolescent with a criminal record and persistent behavior problems. While the U.S. Army was excited about the possibilities for exploiting the Gehlen Organization—which was given the code name "Operation Rusty"—to thwart Communists, at the same time it failed to rein in what one U.S. intelligence memo called the organization's "free-wheeling" ways. Reluctant to cede control, Gehlen refused to provide his American overseers with the real names of his agents and informants or details of individual intelligence operations—a frustration for U.S. officials throughout the Cold War. Even though the U.S. Army's Counterintelligence Corps (CIC) was intended to be an ally, not a rival, of Operation Rusty, Gehlen's group competed with the Americans for the favors of informants by offering greater pecuniary compensation for their services. Higher-ups in the U.S. Army were eager to transfer supervision of Rusty to a civilian agency, such as the Central Intelligence Group (CIG) or the Strategic Services Unit (SSU). But these agencies balked because of the attendant headaches that would accompany trying to provide oversight of Operation Rusty. Finally, in 1949, the newly formed Central Intelligence Agency agreed to take on the task.[2]

The CIA encountered the same frustrations with the Gehlen group—which now had a new code name, "Zipper,"—as experienced by the U.S. Army. Gehlen refused to share operational details and the real names of his agents with the CIA. The American agency set up a liaison office on the same grounds in Pullach as Zipper's headquarters. So desperate were the Americans to learn the identities of Zipper's personnel that a camera was set up to photograph people entering and exiting the group's headquarters. The CIA was able to begin to figure out the true identities of Gehlen's operatives through this snooping on the recalcitrant German spy agency. At the same time, the CIA tried to exercise more control by insisting that Zipper scale back its operations—both to save money and to focus on projects that would yield useful results.

The Gehlen Organization quickly grew to four thousand employees. Most worked not at the Pullach headquarters but at the field offices, which had a great deal of autonomy, including over hiring. This arrangement had disastrous consequences. Groups of SS, Gestapo, and SD officers who had shared office space during the war were once again working together, recruited by their former Nazi superiors, who were now field office bosses. A number of the newly minted spooks were recruited while detained at U.S. POW camps. A Gehlen operative would drive into the camp, pick up an old comrade, and drive off to start a new career.

Otto Albrecht Alfred von Bolschwing's employment with the Gehlen Organization began in a different way. About a decade before Gehlen's talk on the terrace with Captain Boker, Bolschwing—a dapper German nobleman and adventurer—passed himself off as a monk while working undercover for Nazi intelligence in Nazareth, then under British control. Bolschwing changed disguises in Haifa, now posing as a German businessman. And since he was in the Middle East, Bolschwing thought he'd also go looking for a chest of money rumored to have been buried during the closing days of World War I. Bolschwing was quite the operator and something of a loose cannon. Unabashedly anti-Semitic, as made clear by his link later on with Adolf Eichmann, his penchant for meddling in diplomatic matters put him for a short time in alignment with Zionist dreams. While working for the Nazis' Sicherheitsdienst intelligence service in Palestine, Bolschwing hoped to get Arab tribal leaders to work with Jews in staging a revolt to end British control of the region. The British did not put up with this subterfuge, booting Bolschwing out of Palestine in 1936.[3]

Bolschwing is a sort of prototype of Nazi perpetrators who managed to reinvent themselves after the defeat of the Third Reich, through the use of obfuscation, omission of damning facts in their personal biographies, outright lying, and claims that while carrying out the Nazis' criminal policies, they were actually trying to work against the Hitler regime. Bolschwing covered all of these bases in the postwar years as he first went to work for Gehlen and then for the CIA. Also working in his favor was a callous indifference within the Gehlen Organization to an agent's Nazi past. Bolschwing's true colors were exposed by his duties when he got back to Berlin from the Middle East in 1936 and by his later association with Eichmann and with a fascist group in Romania that committed atrocities against Jews.

After his return to Berlin, Bolschwing was assigned to the Jewish Affairs Department, predecessor of the Holocaust planning office that came to be run by Eichmann. Bolschwing quickly impressed his superiors, drafting a document that proposed solving the "Jewish problem" by encouraging public violence toward Jews and chasing them out of the country.[4] "The most effective means is the anger of the people leading to excesses in order to take away the sense of security from the Jews," wrote Bolschwing.

Bolschwing's radical zeal was rewarded in 1940 with a posting to Bucharest, Romania, as a Sicherheitsdienst agent. The young Junker aristocrat became a sort of godfather to a virulently anti-Semitic political movement, the Iron Guard. During an abortive coup against the Romanian government in January 1941, members of the movement went on a rampage against Jews, torching their homes, throwing them out of buildings, and killing them in slaughterhouses. The Iron Guard revolt was encouraged and backed by Bolschwing, who harbored Iron Guard leader Horia Sima and his subordinates at the German Embassy compound and smuggled them to Germany. This was the start of a long relationship that in the postwar years brought members of the Iron Guard into the Gehlen Organization and then into the CIA.

While Bolschwing's protection and encouragement of the Iron Guard was approved by SS chief Heinrich Himmler, he ran afoul of the Foreign Office, which protested the SD's interference in foreign affairs. Bolschwing was brought back to Berlin, arrested, and held in confinement for several months. Bolschwing moved to Salzburg, Austria, in 1944. When U.S. Army troops rolled into the region in 1945, Bolschwing helped the Americans capture a number of Nazi officials.[5] Bolschwing's actions during this time period were classic behavior for Nazi perpetrators trying to distract from their own crimes. It worked for Bolschwing, as it worked for others. Passing himself off as a member of the anti-Hitler resistance, Bolschwing parlayed assistance to the GIs into jobs with the German and American intelligence services.

It was 1947. Gehlen and his newly hatched network of American-financed spies had grand ambitions. Headstrong and highly egotistical, Gehlen foresaw infiltrating his agents throughout Europe. Hiring Bolschwing was supposed to give Gehlen eyes and ears in the Balkans, especially in Romania. The Gehlen Organization was not Bolschwing's first choice for an employer in the intelligence field. He approached the American's Central Intelligence Group, the immediate predecessor of the CIA. The thought of recruiting Bolschwing wasn't exactly received with enthusiasm. A cable from CIG headquarters in Washington DC to the Vienna office stated, "Otto Albrecht Alfred Bolschwing is a shady character," and the CIG office in Heidelberg seconded that sentiment. This was enough to convince CIG's operations in Austria to stay away from Bolschwing.[6] Despite such misgivings, Bolschwing was able to persuade the CIA that his access to the Iron Guard and to sources in Austria made him a valuable asset, and he was hired in 1950.

Thus far, Bolschwing had escaped any serious scrutiny of his actions during World War II. When Austrian authorities asked their American counterparts for information on Bolschwing's past, some within U.S. intelligence went into full cover-up mode. Files on Nazi personnel were kept under guard by U.S. authorities at the Berlin Document Center (BDC). After the Austrians asked for files on Bolschwing, the CIA's base in Pullach asked the BDC to suppress the files—to essentially deny it possessed any files pertaining to Bolschwing.

Pullach's request landed on the desk of Peter Sichel, who was chief of the CIA's Berlin Base. Sichel was not one of those cowboy American spies who felt they could write the rules as they went along. He believed in setting and following certain standards in intelligence gathering. So, when he got the request from Pullach to bury the file on Bolschwing, it went against his professional and personal inclinations.

In his response to the CIA's Pullach Base, he wrote:

1. 1. We would like to draw your attention to some circumstances, which, in my opinion, make it unwise to have a negative file check on such persons as von Bolschwing [meaning it would be unwise to suppress Bolschwing's file].

2. 2. The File at the Berlin Documents Center as to Nazi membership and SS membership, as well as the SS personnel files, are so complete that it is unlikely that any person checked, who was a member of either of these two organizations would not be found in the files. On top of this the persons you are dealing with are so well known and their background so well publicized in the past that I do deem it improbable that you can protect them from their past history.

3. 3. At the end of the war, we tried to be very smart and changed the name of several members of the SD and the Abwehr in order to protect them from the German authorities and the occupation authorities. In most cases these persons were so well known that the change in name compromised them more than if they were to face a denazification court and face the judgment that would have been meted out to them. Since I regard it impossible to keep secret such associations, except in cases where a person was a clandestine agent of a given organization, I request you to reassess the advisability of withholding information available in the Berlin Documents Center.[7]

I made the acquaintance of Peter Sichel in 2022, just a few days before he turned one hundred. He did not specifically recall Bolschwing or writing that response to the CIA's office in Pullach. But he remembered very well his views then—and more than seven decades later—about giving government jobs to members of elite Nazi units like the SS and the SD. In an email exchange from his home in New York City, Sichel wrote: "Everyone knew of our strict principle not to engage former leading personalities of the Nazi Regime, being army or security police service. This was not necessarily the opinion of some other 'officers' largely working with Gehlen organization or OPC." OPC stands for the Office of Policy Coordination, which at the time planned and ran the CIA's covert operations.

Sichel, a Jew who had escaped Germany and joined the U.S. Army before getting involved in intelligence, made his views known to Richard Helms, who at the time was in charge of the CIA's operations in Germany. He later became director of the agency. Sichel told me in our email exchange: "I counseled Dick Helms, that we should not protect any former SS, SD, etc., officers, but let them go through the regular denazification process. If they were personally involved in War Crimes, they should be handled like everyone else."

Sichel was among those who had unsuccessfully lobbied against the CIA taking over supervision of the Gehlen Organization. "My reason," Sichel told me, was "no Eastern European or Russian would work with a German Intelligence Service. I also was against preserving what was, at best, a report mechanism which previously had served the German General Staff. I also disapproved of us financing the preservation of so many general staff officers, who later were the framework of the West German Army. I also warned that the Russians were likely to infiltrate Gehlen organization (was I ever right about that)." All the same, Sichel was not ready to disobey a direct order. "For the record," he told the CIA's Pullach Base, " I would like to state ... that we can withhold such information if desired."

While the Austrians never got hold of the war criminal files on Bolschwing, the CIA did. The documents raised numerous red flags, providing strong indicators that the man now working for the CIA was a war criminal and that he had, in fact, been an assistant to Eichmann. A CIA officer wrote about the decision to obscure the Nazi record of Otto Bolschwing, using his code name, "Unrest": "These files, of which we have a copy, show that UNREST became a member of the NSDAP [Nationalsozialistische Deutsche Arbeiterpartei, or National Socialist German Workers' Party] in 1932 with the number, 984212. He was a member of the SD *Hauptamt* and in 1940 was promoted to *Obersturmfuehrer*, in 1941 to *Hauptsturmfuehrer*."[8] The term SD *Hauptamt* is a reference to the headquarters in Berlin of the Sicherheitsdienst, the intelligence agency of the SS.

The memo repeats some self-serving claims that Bolschwing had written in a biography he provided to the CIA when he was hired, such as that "he held no real SS membership" and that he had only joined the Nazi Party when he was a businessman in Silesia because he hoped the local *Gauleiter* would help him get financial backing for a cement factory he wanted to build. "We believe that further explanation of UNREST's SD, SS, and NSDAP connections are in order and will request that he provide it," states the author of the memo. The CIA officer added, "We will later explore UNREST's reasons for keeping these files from the Austrians."

If the CIA ever did dig further into Bolschwing's Nazi activities, the agency never acted on the results. The agency's enthusiasm for Bolschwing as an operative did start to cool but apparently not because of damning information in his Nazi files. Bolschwing was not being as productive as Pullach Base had hoped. Instead of applying himself to expanding American intelligence operations in southern Europe, Bolschwing put more energy into writing what one CIA memo called "political and sociological studies, interesting from an historical and academic point of view, but not the type of material which will ensure continuance of his salary."[9]

The CIA transferred Bolschwing to Operations Base in Austria, where he succeeded in redeeming himself—so much so that when Bolschwing began talking about a desire to move to the United States, the Salzburg CIA chief became personally involved in trying to make that happen. In 1953 CIA headquarters approved bringing Bolschwing to the United States. Working with the Immigration and Naturalization Service on Bolschwing's behalf, the CIA mentioned his Nazi Party and Sicherheitsdienst membership but did not go into any detail. During this process the CIA checked with the files of the army's CIC and G-2 intelligence services for information on Bolschwing. Two documents named Bolschwing as a member of Adolf Eichmann's staff, with informants as the sources.

When Bolschwing was given a polygraph examination in September 1953, after twenty-two hours of questioning, the examiner brushed aside indications that Bolschwing was lying about his connection with Eichmann and other touchy matters. The examiner concluded that Bolschwing's responses were "not due to any deception but rather the fact that subject is unable to recall all the exact details behind all the activities that he has engaged in prior to the war and during the war, and therefore becomes emotionally disturbed by the thought that he might have forgotten some essential point."[10]

Despite resistance among immigration officials and a worry among some in American intelligence that details of Bolschwing's past could emerge, the CIA succeeded in procuring a visa for him. To prevent Austrian authorities from knowing that Otto Bolschwing had left the country, the CIA provided him with a fake identity: U.S. Army captain Albert D. Eisner. Bolschwing was given termination benefits, six months' pay, and free boarding passes for him and his family aboard the luxury liner SS *Andrea Doria* to sail from Genoa, Italy, to America.[11]

# PART 2

Second Guilt

# 7

# Toppling the Wall of Silence

One day in the spring of 1990, gathered around an enormous table inside the West German Foreign Office in Bonn, the top diplomats from the four nations that occupied postwar Germany as well as their counterparts from the two German states began a series of meetings that would change the face and course of Europe. The meeting, the first of four so-called Two Plus Four Power talks, was convened to begin negotiations on reaching an agreement on conditions to be met to allow German reunification. I covered the May 5 meeting for the Associated Press. I didn't think of it then, but I can't help thinking of it now: how many of the American, British, French, Soviet, West German, and East German diplomats knew about the former Nazi perpetrators who, during the first three decades of the postwar era, had sat in the same room, walked the same halls, where this conference was occurring? I have to assume that Soviet foreign minister Eduard Shevardnadze, for one, knew incriminating details about the former Hitler helpers who had once worked in this building and at embassies abroad. After all, it was the Soviets' East German allies who had spent much of the Cold War years embarrassing West German officials by leaking documents about the Nazi pasts of hundreds of West German civil servants. But the participants convened the Two Plus Four talks to put the Cold War behind them, not to open old wounds.

On September 12 in Moscow, as the six nations met one last time to ink a treaty that cleared the way for German unification, all sides were jubilant about the start of a new era. It was from this pact that a New Europe was born. At first elation over reunification crowded out any prospective reflection on the dark aspects of West Germany's origins, and then it was the daunting, unforeseen economic, political, and social challenges that came with annexing the formerly Communist state to the capitalist West.

The years after German unification offered the perfect opportunity to finally attend to some unfinished business: firmly confronting West Germany's embrace of Nazi war criminals in the early postwar years. Doing so would no longer be seen as handing a propaganda victory to communism, since the Communists had lost. But rather than using this moment to clear the air of old allegations and suspicions of war criminals in the employ of West German government agencies, German officials chose to maintain their silence. It took a reformed Marxist street fighter to kick down that wall of silence.

A high school dropout and the son of a butcher, Joschka Fischer was involved in the German student movement in the 1960s in Stuttgart and later in Frankfurt am Main. While working at a left-wing bookstore, he began attending university lectures organized by revolutionaries. He joined the group Revolutionärer Kampf (Revolutionary Struggle), participating in street battles with police. As terror attacks by the Red Army Faction raged in the 1970s, Fischer renounced violence and joined the newly founded Greens Party. He was elected as a Greens delegate to the Bundestag in 1983 and was appointed environment minister for Hesse state in 1985. Even though Fischer had become part of the political establishment, he held onto his confrontational style. During a debate in the Bundestag, Fischer said to the chamber's vice president: "If I may say so, you are an asshole." As leader of the Greens' "Realos" (Realists) faction, which had frequent disputes with the fundamentalists "Fundis," Fischer succeeded in bringing the party into the mainstream, steering it away from militant left-wing positions while never abandoning principles that made them distinctive among other parties, especially on the environment.

Fischer was catapulted into the highest levels of political power when the long-serving conservative chancellor Helmut Kohl lost to Social Democrat Gerhard Schröder in the 1998 federal election. The Social Democrats failed to win a Bundestag majority, so Schröder put together a coalition with the Greens. And he chose Joschka Fischer to be minister of foreign affairs, one of the most prestigious positions in the German government. Fischer handled his duties with skill, integrity, and diplomatic charm. But something of the street fighter came out in him once again when he learned in 2003 that the Foreign Office's in-house newsletter had published an obituary of a retired diplomat that glossed over his 1948 conviction by a Czech court for signing death warrants while he was a Prague-based Nazi prosecutor.

Incensed, Fischer banned all further publication by the in-house magazine of deceased Foreign Office officials who had served the Third Reich. Anger over Fischer's ban erupted a year later with the death of another retired diplomat, ninety-three-year-old Franz Krapf, who during the war had been a member of the Nazi Party and of the SS. With an obituary for Krapf disallowed in the Foreign Office's newsletter, more than 130 retired diplomats honored Krapf's service by signing a respectful obituary prominently displayed in the conservative newspaper the *Frankfurter Allgemeine Zeitung*. Fischer's response was to name a panel of independent historians to thoroughly examine not just German diplomats' crimes during the Third Reich but also details of the pasts of those who were able to land postwar jobs with the Foreign Office. Two Germans, an American, and an Israeli were appointed to lead the inquiry. All are internationally respected historians whose work had focused on the Third Reich years and the postwar era. They were assisted by a team of junior colleagues. In 2010 the historians released their findings in a nearly nine hundred–page tome titled *Das Amt und Die Vergangenheit: Deutsche Diplomaten im Dritten Reich und in der Bundesrepublik* (The Office and the Past: German Diplomats in the Third Reich and in the Federal Republic).

*Das Amt* was a sensation. Breathtaking sales of the book showed that Germans were hungry to know about the Nazi crimes of their country's postwar diplomats, how they were able to revive their careers and dodge being held accountable. Helping catapult the book to bestseller status was the fact that it was not written like a dry piece of history. The work is packed with damning details about the Nazi misdeeds of postwar diplomats. More than that, *Das Amt* exposed as a lie the contention—widespread among Germans—that diplomats during the Third Reich had formed a bastion of anti-Hitler resistance, acting behind the scenes to soften Nazi policies.

For non-Germans unfamiliar with the evolution of Germany's postwar democracy, one that is not exactly squeaky clean, among the most disturbing passages of *Das Amt* are those dealing with a now-defunct department of the Foreign Office that was called the Zentrale Rechtsschutzstelle (Central Legal Defense Agency), or ZRS. Created in 1950 putatively to provide legal assistance to German soldiers held captive in foreign lands, the ZRS went far beyond this stated mission and in a manner so nefarious that it seems incredible that the German government got away with it.

As France and other countries victimized by the Nazis hunted for German perpetrators to put them on trial, the Central Legal Defense Agency was actively helping them avoid arrest. It took the sleuthing of legendary Nazi hunter Simon Wiesenthal to blow the cover off the ZRS.

In early 1968 Wiesenthal learned of a newsletter, *Warndienst West* (Warning Service West), circulating among Austrian veterans with the names of comrades who were being sought by France for war crimes. Wiesenthal was able to track down the source: the Hamburg office of the German Red Cross.[1] Wiesenthal took the information to Adalbert Rückerl, head of the Central Office, the Nazi-hunting agency based in Ludwigsburg. It was clear to Wiesenthal and Rückerl that *Warndienst West* had been in operation for some time and that hundreds of German and Austrian perpetrators had been tipped off about arrest warrants for them. Among them was Alois Brunner, a notorious SS officer responsible for the deportation of more than 100,000 Jews to death camps. Brunner was able to escape justice by fleeing to Egypt in 1954 and then to Syria, where he died in 2001.

Wiesenthal did not believe that the German Red Cross would have undertaken this scheme on its own, that it must have been a cover for some other operators. And he was right. The arrest tip sheets were coming from the West German government—specifically, the ZRS. The scandal blew up in April 1968, when *Der Spiegel* magazine published an investigative piece containing more damning details about *Warndienst West* and how it operated. The ZRS would send lists of names of former SS and Sicherheitsdienst officers who were sought by foreign countries, mainly France, with the request that their whereabouts be determined so they could be warned about the arrest warrants against them. In its communications with the German Red Cross, the ZRS used language that tried to conceal that the perpetrators were serious war criminals, according to *Das Amt*.

Beginning with its founding in 1950, the ZRS was led by Hans Gawlik. During the Nazi regime, Gawlik served as a public prosecutor and later a judge in occupied Poland, punishing opponents of National Socialism. Like so many former servants of the Third Reich, Gawlik was able to finagle a new career for himself in postwar Germany. He was appointed as a defense attorney for Nazi bigwigs at the war crimes trial in Nuremberg.

Gawlik and his ZRS associate Karl Theodor Redenz were ordered to appear at the West German Justice Ministry to offer an explanation of their actions. The men were fiercely unrepentant. They contended that they were merely following the mandate given them by the law that created the ZRS, that the men on the warning lists were not war criminals but innocent soldiers, and that charges brought by France against the soldiers were factually inaccurate. Gawlik brazenly sent a letter to the Justice Ministry stating that Wiesenthal and Rückerl had damaged the reputation of the Foreign Office.[2]

The Justice Ministry got no assistance from the Foreign Office, overseer of the ZRS, which did not take action against Gawlik. The Bonn prosecutor's office chose not to bring any charges, and the investigation was suspended. The ZRS was disbanded in 1968, after Gawlik and Redenz retired.

As disturbing as it is to read *Das Amt*'s telling of the misdeeds of Hans Gawlik and the ZRS, the historians' greater service was to demolish a six-decade-old myth that the Third Reich Foreign Office was a stronghold of quiet resistance against Hitler and his murderous policies. This was a view widely held not just by diplomats but by Germans across the board. There were legends of brave German diplomats who had sought to soften the execution of Nazi policies, to save Jews, and were either participants in or supporters of conspiracies to assassinate Hitler. A 1979 pamphlet published by the Foreign Office, *Auswärtige Politik Heute* (Foreign Policy Today), expressed this canard in a pompous and self-righteous fashion. It asserted that the "Foreign Office offered tenacious and time-winning resistance to the plans of the Nazi power holders without being able to prevent the worst. The Office long remained non-political and was regarded by the National Socialists as a site of opposition."[3]

That was all a smokescreen. The authors of *Das Amt* chronicle carefully coordinated efforts to exonerate diplomats, cover up their Third Reich misdeeds, and resurrect their careers in postwar Germany, at the expense of actual victims of the Nazis who were snubbed for Foreign Office jobs because they did not have the right connections.

One of the architects of this system of whitewashing diplomats' pasts, according to *Das Amt*, was Herbert Blankenhorn, who worked at the German embassy in Washington DC from 1936 to 1939. Blankenhorn was among hundreds of German diplomats arrested by American and other

Allied soldiers as World War II came to a close. While in captivity, Blankenhorn wrote a report for the Americans with the title *The German Foreign Office under the Nazi Regime*. The report contended that the Nazis' No. 2 diplomat—Ernst von Weizsäcker—was in reality the leader of a group of about thirty diplomats who tried to thwart the National Socialists. Similar claims were made by two other captive German diplomats who wrote reports for the Americans and listed colleagues who supposedly opposed Hitler. The three documents were vague and provided no examples of specific activities taken by German diplomats against the Nazis.[4]

Weizsäcker and seven other senior former diplomats went before an American military tribunal in Nuremberg in November 1947 in what was called the "Ministries Case," on charges that included participating in the murder of Jews and Allied servicemen and conspiracy to wage aggressive war. As explained by the authors of *Das Amt*, the trial directly challenged the argument that German diplomats in the Third Reich were only "nominal" and not "real" Nazis and that they were motivated not by lockstep loyalty to the Nazi cause but by a sense of professional duty to one's country. There was honor to be seen in the Third Reich diplomatic corps, not blind fealty to Hitler, or so said the mythmakers. Behind the scenes Weizsäcker's defenders continued to busy themselves with trying to reinforce the image of the diplomatic corps as upstanding civil servants who had valiantly tried to thwart Hitler's maniacal schemes but, alas, failed.

Scion of a noble family, Weizsäcker was a complicated person. His father was minister president of the Kingdom of Württemberg. The son, Ernst, served as a naval officer aboard warships during World War I, earning the Iron Cross. He joined the Foreign Service two years after the war's end, stationed in Basel, then Copenhagen, Geneva, and Oslo. When Hitler came to power in 1933, Weizsäcker was Germany's ambassador to Norway. He joined the Nazi Party in 1938. Also that year he was made state secretary, the second-highest position in the Foreign Office. Weizsäcker and some like-minded diplomats opposed Hitler's march to war, not on humanitarian grounds but out of worry that Germany would lose. They did not want Hitler to be overthrown but hoped to steer him away from leading their beloved Fatherland into humiliating defeat.

When it came to the Nazis' deranged commitment to at first criminally marginalize and ultimately to wipe out European Jews, Weizsäcker not only stood by and let it happen but also expressed support for Third Reich policies. According to the authors of *Das Amt*, Weizsäcker once told the Swiss envoy in Paris that Jews had to leave Germany, "otherwise they are going surely sooner or later toward their complete annihilation," but he also stood in the way of increasing the flow of Jews from Germany.[5] As trains in Nazi-occupied countries began delivering doomed Jews to extermination camps, some German diplomats warned that the transports could have a negative effect on public opinion, according to *Das Amt*. But a memo presented to Weizsäcker for his approval about transports from France mirrors what the authors of *Das Amt* call "the tepid and feckless nature of these interventions." The memo that originally reached Weizsäcker's desk said the Foreign Office had "no reservations." Weizsäcker changed the wording to "no objections."

The myth-building backers of Weizsäcker, who was arrested in 1947, and others standing in the docket at Nuremberg attempted to pull a concealing curtain over the damning acts of the Third Reich diplomatic corps. In the end the tribunal convicted Weizsäcker and six of his diplomat comrades in 1949. He was sentenced to seven years in prison, a punishment reduced in the same year to five. With the intervention of the U.S. high commissioner for Germany, John J. McCloy, Weizsäcker was granted an early release in October 1950. He had served three years and three months, including time spent pending his trial. The others were given similar kid-glove treatment.

The mythmakers, the deniers, ultimately prevailed. Over the ensuing years, tainted diplomats came to dominate the Foreign Office as Germans became increasingly angry over war crimes prosecutions, seeing themselves as victims of Allied "victors' justice." Seeking to placate them, the U.S. government and its partners simply gave in, abandoning their insistence that no former Nazis be hired as diplomats.

The historians who wrote *Das Amt* point to the results of a parliamentary committee's 1951 review of Foreign Office personnel. Of 237 new recruits in the agency's Upper Service who were surveyed, almost half had belonged to the Nazi Party. Among 129 officials who had previously worked for the Nazis' Foreign Office, 69 percent of them had belonged to the Nazi Party. However, the most shocking figure in the report was the number of employees who had been persecuted by the Nazis: 9 percent of the new recruits; and 12 percent of the Third Reich veterans.[6] Hitler's victims were systematically shut out of postwar Germany's diplomatic corps, while perpetrators were embraced.

From 1950 to 1954 the Nazi taint spread even further within the Foreign Office. During that time the number of former Nazis in the Upper Service grew to 325. As pointed out by the authors of *Das Amt*, this figure represented a higher percentage of Nazis than in the Third Reich's diplomatic service in 1937. Although the need for experience was used as an excuse to hire Third Reich veterans, most of the former Nazis in the Upper Service in 1952 had not previously been diplomats. Among officials at the Foreign Office were high-level diplomats who had had a hand in the Holocaust. While the postwar Foreign Office welcomed Third Reich diplomats who were eager to resume their careers, *Das Amt* documents how those who had tried to thwart Hitler were treated relatively poorly, almost as if they had betrayed the Fatherland.

During the war Fritz Kolbe was an advisor to minister of foreign affairs Joachim von Ribbentrop and also a key aide to Karl Ritter, Ribbentrop's liaison with the German army. Two years before the war's end, Kolbe began covertly passing Nazi secrets to Allen Dulles, the Bern station chief of the Americans' spy agency, the Office of Strategic Services. Kolbe's work for Dulles got him barred from landing a job with the West German Foreign Office, at least partly out of concern that he might continue acting as an agent for the Americans.[7]

Also among the handful of true resisters was Wolfgang Gans Edler Herr zu Putlitz, who had served in the diplomatic service of the Weimar Republic and stayed on as a diplomat after the Nazi takeover in 1933. Putlitz joined the Nazi Party and was also a member of the SS. But his loyalty to the Nazis evaporated because of Hitler's war plans. While posted to the Netherlands during the war, Putlitz spied for British intelligence, providing German military secrets, such as troop deployment plans, to his control officer. After the Gestapo caught on to what Putlitz was up to, he escaped to England before he could be taken into custody. Nazi Germany tried him in absentia and sentenced him to death. After Putlitz's return to Germany, his desire for an appointment with the West German Foreign Office was rebuffed, according to *Das Amt*.

Over the past several decades, Germany has been praised for how it has confronted the Nazi past. But the publication of *Das Amt* in 2010 unsettled the impression, raising questions about how well that process has really gone. For about a week, reviewers bestowed accolades on the historians and their work. But the overwhelming expressions of admiration did not last. Conservative columnists, older historians, and retired diplomats joined forces to attack *Das Amt* on various grounds. They accused the book's authors of defaming the diplomatic service, focusing too much on the Holocaust and too little on anti-Nazi diplomats, getting facts wrong, and not coming up with any information that had not been known already. There were complaints that the four lead historians of *Das Amt* had used younger scholars to write chapters of the book and that these junior colleagues lacked the proper perspective. There were suggestions that the book's readability and its bestseller success showed that it was not a serious work of scholarship. One critic likened *Das Amt* to propaganda pamphlets published by Communist East Germany to discredit the West German government.

The four historians who were in charge of the research that underlies *Das Amt* fought back against the assaults on their integrity. In the fall of 2011, two of them, Norbert Frei and Peter Hayes, published a fourteen-page essay, written in English for an international audience, refuting "reckless" and "spurious" assaults on the integrity of their work. "In view of the extent of the misinformation about *Das Amt* that is currently in circulation, we especially welcome this opportunity to present the main findings of our work in English," Frei and Hayes wrote in the article, published in the bulletin of the German Historical Institute.[8]

Among the complaints about *Das Amt* was that documents the commission of historians had used for their conclusions were already known. Moshe Zimmermann, the Israeli historian on the commission, gave a response that made an intriguing observation about how myth had shouldered aside memory during the Cold War era. Zimmermann made specific reference to a 1941 request by Franz Rademacher, a Nazi Foreign Office expert on Jewish questions, to his bosses for reimbursement of travel expenses for a trip to Belgrade. On the form Rademacher gave as the reason for his visit "Liquidation of Jews in Belgrade."[9]

Critics of *Das Amt* pointed out that the document's existence had been known since 1952, when Rademacher was tried in West Germany for murders he had overseen in Serbia, a confrontation with justice that Rademacher was able to elude by fleeing to Syria while on bail. What the critics were missing, or choosing to ignore, Zimmermann wrote in a 2011 essay published in the *Israel Journal of Foreign Affairs*, was that the Rademacher expense form demonstrated that "the whole Foreign Ministry apparatus knew about the destruction of Jews and was participating in it. That is why this document left such a shocking impression on the German reader of 2010 and on the minister of foreign affairs."[10]

While historians might know such details, the broader public may not—especially since German authorities spent decades trying to avoid discussing them. "Every now and again collective memory needs to be refreshed," Zimmermann wrote. "Myths survive because memory fails or becomes selective. The fact that the Rademacher document became so prominent in public discussion in October 2010 proves that since the early 1950s it had disappeared from collective memory and public consciousness."

# The Reckoning

November 9 is a date soaked with symbolism in German history. On that day in 1938, Nazi storm troopers smashed synagogues and Jewish shops across the country, terrorizing and rounding up Jews in the pogrom known as Kristallnacht. Fifty-one years later on that day, thousands of East Germans poured through the Berlin Wall as the Communist regime that ruled there since 1949 began to topple.

These epochal events were on the minds of German parliamentarians as they gathered inside the restored Reichstag in Berlin on November 8, 2012, where they were to examine the question of postwar continuities from the Nazi past. The discussion quickly devolved into a verbal brawl that brought up right-wing extremism in twenty-first-century Germany, a decade of murders by the neo-Nazi gang called the National Socialist Underground (NSU), and accusations that German intelligence was still covering up its knowledge of Adolf Eichmann and other war criminals.

"Today, one day before November 9, we are conducting an important debate, one that is more relevant than ever," Jan Korte, a boyish-looking delegate from the party Die Linke, or The Left, told the delegates. "The 1950s and 1960s were characterized by silence and the massive return of perpetrators to office," Korte said. He challenged the idea that the formative years of the Federal Republic were a "success story," pointing out mild sentences for Nazi functionaries convicted of having killed civilians, failure to bring charges or even dismiss seriously tainted civil servants, and the influence of former Nazis on postwar lawmaking.

Conservative delegates of the Bundestag responded with indignation, charging that Korte and others on the Left were unjustly dragging the reputation of the West German state through the mud. Armin Schuster, with the governing Christian Democratic Union, said Korte's words were like propaganda dished out by the East German Communists during the Cold War. He suggested that Korte's zeal in attacking the West German republic came from the ideological lineage of Die Linke, which arose from the Party of Democratic Socialism, which was the direct descendant of the Communist party that ruled East Germany for four decades. Schuster pointed out that while East Germany had failed as a state, the West German republic—despite incriminated former Nazis in its bureaucracy—was the foundation for the successful unified German democracy that exists today. "A functioning democracy developed on one side of the Wall, while on the other side was just the opposite," said Schuster. Amid the ideological bickering, there was uniform support for the government-commissioned research that was already under way into the Nazi "continuities" among personnel in the postwar civil service.

Eleven months before this fractious Bundestag session, Chancellor Angela Merkel's government issued an eighty-five-page response to a parliamentary questionnaire that had been submitted by Die Linke. In the questionnaire the delegates with Die Linke assailed the failure of postwar government officials to keep war criminals out of government jobs. "Whereas the scope and intensity of the Federal Republic's dealings with the Nazi past are often internationally regarded as exemplary, the opposite is actually true for the beginnings of the Federal Republic's policies related to the past," reads the questionnaire by Die Linke. "Political decisions were taken in the early Federal Republic of Germany to enable [Nazi] followers and incriminated persons to return to public service, and also to reduce the sentences of Nazi war criminals, directly counteracting the Allies' initial demands for a comprehensive denazification."

The response by the federal government to Die Linke's questionnaire, while somewhat passive-aggressive, showed that it was officially on board with shining a light into the dark corners of German bureaucracy where incriminated former Nazis had lurked for decades. The government's response, prepared by the Interior Ministry, began: "More than 60 years after the creation of the Federal Republic of Germany and more than 65 years after the collapse of the Nazi dictatorship, it can be said that the National Socialist dictatorship is generally the best-researched period in 20th-century history."[1]

Nearly twenty-six thousand German-language works about National Socialism were published between the years 2000 and 2010 alone, according to the Interior Ministry, and "federal and state governments have consistently supported this work from the very beginning." Additionally, the government for decades had funded memorials, exhibits, and museums showing the brutality and criminality of the Third Reich. Most of all, the Interior Ministry declared, "The decisive response to the experience of 12 years of Nazi tyranny was creation of a free, democratic order, the permanent anchoring of democracy and the rule of law in the Federal Republic of Germany."

The Interior Ministry conceded that the matter of "personnel continuities"—the reemployment of Third Reich officials by West German government offices—had not been subjected to in-depth research until after the Cold War. The ministry also acknowledged that there was a high number of such officials in the West German civil service. But this should be no surprise, the government said, because West German government agencies had sought out people with strong administrative experience.

The government also asserted that "institutions of the federal government have no Nazi past, because these institutions didn't exist until the constituting of the Federal Republic in 1949." This is an ontological sleight of hand on the part of the Interior Ministry, sidestepping the fact that multitudes of bureaucrats were working in the postwar equivalents of the ministries that had employed them during the Third Reich.

As defensive and even evasive as this parliamentary document often seems, it reinforced the federal government's commitment to continue probing the Nazi taint in the postwar civil service. That commitment was strengthened even more one year later, when Chancellor Merkel's Christian Democratic Union and its Bavarian sister party, the Christian Social Union, formed a coalition government with the Left-leaning Social Democrats. In their coalition contract, the parties pledged to "advance the confrontation with the Nazi pasts of ministries and federal offices."

Since then, there has been a flurry of government-commissioned inquiries into the Nazi taint, examining the postwar hiring practices of virtually every federal government agency: the Foreign Office, the Interior Ministry, the Justice Ministry, the Federal Criminal Police Office, the Federal Office for the Protection of the Constitution, the Economics Ministry, the Finance Ministry, and the Transportation Ministry. Several inquiries were commissioned by Germany's most secretive agency, the Federal Intelligence Service. State and local governments followed suit, sanctioning their own inquiries into the depth and breadth of the Nazi taint inside postwar government offices, limning ever more detailed pictures of the kinds of bureaucrats who gathered around the office coffee machine to talk about the weather, how their favorite *Fussball* team was doing, their families, vacation plans, their pets, favorite TV shows—anything but their service to the Third Reich.

# 9

# Elusive Perpetrators

"I made the decision during high school to study law. If I wanted to carry out this plan, I had to comply with the demands of the state, at least as viewed from the outside."[1] This was among the assertions encountered by researchers Stefanie Palm and Irina Stange as they sifted through piles of job applications and other documents while investigating the Nazi taint within the West German Interior Ministry. Similar justifications for having worked for the Hitler regime turned up again and again and again as Palm and Stange methodically peeled away layers of obfuscations, omissions, and lies protecting the secrets of incriminated postwar civil servants.

Some claimed they had been coerced into joining the Nazi Party, or they became members because they were running out of money and needed a steady income. There were lots of other excuses and self-exculpations. They had worked for the Third Reich to try to protect Jews. They had thought they could soften the impact of Nazi rules by being on the inside. They had friends who were in the anti-Hitler resistance or were themselves active participants in the resistance, even in plots to assassinate Hitler. They may have looked like loyal Nazis on the outside, but in their hearts they hated Hitler. We have already seen how such rationalizations were put to use by Hans Globke, Adenauer's right-hand man. It was a strategy used by job applicants across the West German government and at every level of the civil service bureaucracy. And it was a strategy that was, more often than not, successful.

Palm and Stange were among researchers who in 2015 began working under historians Frank Bösch and Andreas Wirsching to develop a fuller understanding of hiring policies and practices not just of the West German Interior Ministry but also its East German counterpart. The findings of the team were published in 2018 in an 860-page book titled *Hüter der Ordnung: Die Innenministerien in Bonn und Ost-Berlin nach dem Nationalsozialismus*

(Guardian of Order: The Interior Ministries in Bonn and East Berlin after National Socialism).

Palm recalls the very first West German Interior Ministry official whose files she inspected. She had located them at the Federal Archives in Koblenz. At the Interior Ministry the official had portrayed himself as an administrative officer who had suffered discrimination in the Nazi state for having an "apolitical attitude." But as Palm dug further, locating more files in other archives across Germany, she found this portrayal was a charade. "These self-ascriptions developed deep cracks," Palm wrote to me in an email on June 24, 2022. This Interior Ministry official had, in fact, been involved in the persecution of Berlin Jews. "This behavior of concealing critical points in one's biography from the occupiers or future employers and at the same time emphasizing exculpatory moments of action was typical for a large number of BMI [West German Interior Ministry] officials," Palm said. "In the BMI's culture department alone, 43 percent [of the reviewed employees] had concealed incriminating elements of their biography or incorrectly stated the dates of entry in and exit from National Socialist organizations."

Even more disturbing was the disinterest among Interior Ministry officials about what, exactly, an employee's actions had been during the Third Reich. "There were no disciplinary measures for the people I examined. And there were no records of discussions with the personnel department," Palm said.

Bösch's and Wirsching's team of researchers also documented Adenauer's machinations, even before West Germany's founding in 1949, to make sure that top jobs in the government-to-be went to supporters of his conservative coalition. Even enemies of Hitler had to make way for Adenauer's political friends and allies, with the justification that they were more experienced, even if that experience had been accrued as Third Reich lackeys.

Otto Wels, leader of the Social Democrats, was not known to be a polished speaker. But he rose to the occasion when, on March 23, 1933, the Reichstag convened to vote on the Nazis' proposal to hand dictatorial powers to Hitler. More than five hundred parliamentary delegates—excluding just over one hundred leftists who had been arrested or were on the run— gathered inside Berlin's ornate Kroll Opera House. Directly across from the opera house stood the charred ruins of the Reichstag building, the delegates' traditional meeting place. Convening in the Reichstag building was made impossible by a February 27 arson attack that Hitler used as an excuse to begin stripping away constitutionally guaranteed rights, including the right to free speech. Hitler had set his sights on absolute power, and the parliamentary meeting on March 23 would grant it to him. The atmosphere inside the Kroll Opera House was thick with menace. Brown-shirted Sturmabteilung troops stood at the exits and lined the aisles. A huge swastika banner was hung directly behind the speakers' podium. In his address Hitler lied, stating his government would use the powers he was seeking "only insofar as they are essential for carrying out vitally necessary measures." Leaders of other parliamentary factions approached the podium, and their views fell into lockstep with those of the Nazis. Only Wels's Social Democrats dared to be defiant.

Wels kept his cool as Nazi Reichstag delegates heckled him. His words have reverberated through the generations because of their utter fearlessness. Threats against Wels were real. Numerous Social Democrat functionaries had been attacked and murdered since Hitler came to power on January 30, 1933. When Wels walked up to the podium, in his pocket was a cyanide capsule, to be used in case he was arrested and subjected to torture.

Wels told the delegates inside the Kroll Opera House: "In this historic hour, we Social Democrats solemnly profess our allegiance to the basic principles of humanity and justice, freedom and socialism. No Enabling Law gives you the right to annihilate ideas that are eternal and indestructible." Wels boldly continued: "Freedom and life can be taken from us, but not our honor."

Wels was under no illusion that his calls to rally around Germany's parliamentary democracy would change the minds of the other parties represented in the Reichstag. They had all signaled their readiness to bow to Hitler. After all of the ballots had been counted, the three-quarters supermajority was easily surpassed. A total of 444 delegates voted for handing dictatorial powers to Hitler. Only the 94 Social Democrats who were present voted against it. Wels's powerful speech inside the Kroll Opera House were the very last words spoken against Adolf Hitler among parliamentary delegates for the remainder of the Third Reich. A month after passage of the resolution granting Hitler authoritarian power, the Nazi regime banned the Social Democratic Party as an "enemy of the state and people." Thousands of Social Democrats, including Otto Wels, fled into exile.

With all of the suffering and repression experienced by the Social Democrats during the Third Reich—the unwarranted arrests, the acts of torture, the assassinations—you would think that in the new German democracy that was born in 1949, they'd be given prominent positions in the civil service. But that is not the way things worked out.

September 1939. Bedzin, Nazi-occupied Poland. An SS death squad terrorizes the town, where about half the population of fifty thousand is Jewish. Flamethrowers destroy the Great Synagogue. Jewish residents are shot indiscriminately on the street. Five hundred Jews die during the rampage, including children.[2]

The following July a German bureaucrat named Erich Kessler arrives in nearby Katowice, taking his place as the second-highest administrator in the occupied city. The job of an administrator has something of a harmless ring to it. But in German-occupied Poland, administrators were critical in carrying out the Nazi plan to cleanse communities of Poles and Jews to make way for German settlers.

Eight years later, after the downfall of the Third Reich, Erich Kessler is entrusted by Konrad Adenauer to put together a team to search for personnel for top government positions in the new West German republic. Kessler brings in former colleagues from the Nazi Interior Ministry to assist in making personnel choices: Hans Ritter von Lex, Kurt Jacobi, Otto Ehrensberger, and Hans Globke.[3]

How did it happen that this former servant of the Third Reich—a man who was among German administrators in occupied Poland as atrocities were being committed there—was able to reinvent himself in postwar Germany? Why wasn't an opponent of the Nazis, an exiled Social Democrat, for example, given this opportunity, rather than a lackey of the Hitler regime? Answers to questions like this are not transparent. But the investigative work by Frank Bösch and Andreas Wirsching and their team offers new insights.

Kessler was born in 1899 in Memel, an East Prussia port city that is now part of Lithuania. Kessler studied law at the University of Königsberg. After completing a court clerkship and working various jobs in the Königsberg area, he moved about five hundred miles west to the Ruhr Valley, to Recklinghausen, where he was hired as a consultant at police headquarters.[4] In 1933, the same year Kessler was appointed acting head of the Wuppertal police headquarters, he joined the National Socialists and soon thereafter the Sturmabteilung. He became a member of numerous other Nazi, or Nazi-related, organizations as well. Kessler returned to East Prussia in 1934, taking a job as deputy to the top administrator in Gumbinnen. In 1937 he was hired as an administrator in a borough of Hamburg.

Kessler's career as a bureaucrat in Nazi-occupied territories began in 1938, when he was appointed to the Nazi district administrative authority in German-occupied Czechoslovakia. The next stop along Kessler's journey as a bureaucrat in German-occupied lands was as a department head of civil administration in Lodz, Poland, and then to Katowice.[5]

In 1944 Kessler was called back to Berlin, where he was made a section leader at the Reich Interior Ministry. He was captured by American troops at the end of the war and sent to a POW camp in Ludwigsburg. After his release, Kessler was hired by British occupation authorities to help with legal and administrative matters. It was while working for the British that Kessler was contacted by Konrad Adenauer, who even before his election as West German chancellor was busy making plans for a new government, and he put Kessler in charge of starting the search for job candidates.[6]

Stefanie Palm and Irina Stange found no evidence that Kessler was directly involved in war crimes while posted in Katowice. But they point out that given his position of authority, and the fact that Katowice is only twenty-five miles from Auschwitz, he at least must have known about the atrocities being conducted. It defies credulity to think otherwise. A Nazi document shows that in January 1944, Kessler was present at conferences of German occupation authorities convened in Breslau by Heinrich Himmler, the man in charge of overall operations of the concentration camp system. It is not known what Kessler's involvement in the conferences was.[7]

After the war, Kessler made multiple self-exculpatory claims about his work as a Nazi-era administrator. He said that when he moved back to East Prussia in 1934, it was because of conflicts with Nazi functionaries in Wuppertal. Disagreements with Nazi officials also led to a 1936 dismissal that lasted for three months, he said. And like so many other former civil servants of the Third Reich, Kessler claimed to have been an accomplice in attempts to assassinate Hitler. Historians say it is true that Kessler did have conflicts with Nazi officials, and it is entirely possible that he had connections with members of the anti-Hitler resistance. But Bösch and

Wirsching's researchers found that Kessler was promoted after his return to the Reich Interior Ministry in Berlin, which raises questions about how much it really bothered him to be working for the Nazi murder machine.[8]

While helping lay the groundwork for the postwar civil service, Kessler made no secret of his preference for hiring Third Reich veterans for top government jobs. Kessler argued that the postwar predecessor of the West German government—the American- and British-supervised Bizonia—was incompetent because of that body's preference for hires who had not worked for the Third Reich. Even if Kessler's true feelings about having worked for the Nazi regime are difficult to decipher, the stress he placed on hiring veterans of the Nazi civil service was a decisive factor in allowing even seriously incriminated bureaucrats to restart their careers.

One of those seriously incriminated bureaucrats was Gerhard Scheffler, who landed a position in the West German Interior Ministry in 1950. Scheffler tried to hide his past misdeeds as an administrator in occupied Poland. But the research team led by Bösch and Wirsching revealed Scheffler's visceral hatred of Jews and of democracy and his complicity in the Nazis' barbaric "Germanization" of Poland.

Born in Breslau in 1894, Scheffler spent four years at the front during World War I, studied law, and joined the Prussian administrative service in 1924. Soon after Hitler came to power in 1933, Scheffler joined the new regime's Interior Ministry, assigned to the municipal department. In 1939 he was sent to Poznan as city commissioner and was given more authority when he was appointed mayor of the Nazi-occupied city.[9] A 1944 photograph of Scheffler taken in Poznan, when he was mayor, shows a man with thick glass frames, a severe countenance, and a swastika button on his lapel.

Until recently, much was unknown about Scheffler's actions during his years in Poznan. He had succeeded that well in covering up his tracks. Discovery of a multipage manuscript written by him in 1946, but never published, cast a light on his secrets.

The manuscript reveals that as mayor, Scheffler reported directly to Arthur Greiser, who was *Gauleiter* of the Wartheland district of occupied Poland and was just as ruthless in carrying out Nazi policy as the notorious Hans Frank, head of the neighboring General Government. The two men were key figures in organizing the Holocaust in Poland. Both were tried and executed after the war. According to Bösch and Wirsching, there can be no doubt that Scheffler himself was involved in the Nazis' murderous policies. Scheffler helped organize deportations and seizure of homes and belongings and also issued ordinances that banned speaking Polish in public spaces and imposed restrictions on what Poles could buy at grocery stores. He called East European Jews "misbegotten half-breeds of the worst racial kind." Scheffler wrote about associating with Greiser, Himmler, and other top Nazis and about attending a speech in which Himmler spoke openly about the mass murder of Jews.[10] At the end of the war, Scheffler and his staff fled to Berlin.

Although Scheffler expressed no remorse in the unpublished memoir for his work in Poznan, he acknowledged the potential trouble it could cause him if he were found out. He wrote that he had to be careful "not to attract attention" to himself. Scheffler knew he was on the Allies' most-wanted list because he was told so by a Reich Interior Ministry colleague, Kurt Jacobi. Scheffler acquired a fake ID, under the name Dr. Otto Jungfer, fled west into the British occupation zone, and went underground, getting support from family and friends.[11]

Scheffler reemerged as the Allies, facing unrelenting pressure from the German public, politicians, and church leaders, began winding down their pursuit of war criminals. With the assistance of an acquaintance from his time as a district administrator in Lower Saxony, Scheffler—still using the alias Otto Jungfer—was given a job with an insurance company in Thuringia. Scheffler eventually felt safe enough to drop the alias and to seek a civil service job in the newly born West German republic.[12]

Among Scheffler's friends and allies was Johannes Kunze, chairman of the parliamentary faction of Adenauer's Christian Democratic Union in the state parliament of North Rhine–Westphalia. Kunze was also a high-ranking official in an organization of German Protestants called the "Inner Mission." Kunze got his friend a job on the central committee of the organization.

If Scheffler wanted to get a civil service job, he was going to have to face a denazification panel. His hearings began in March 1949. A total of twenty-eight people spoke or wrote in his favor. Among them were former colleagues at the Nazi Ministry of the Interior, including Hans Globke.

The Allied-imposed denazification process, which judged people as Major Offenders (Category I), Offenders (Category II), Lesser Offenders (Category III), Followers (Category IV), and Exonerated (Category V), was required for every German civil servant who sought to return to a government job. Being classified as a "Follower" or "Exonerated" could be a ticket to a return to public service. Whether someone actually deserved those classifications was another matter. Cheating the denazification regulations was ridiculously easy, especially after the process was handed over to German tribunals. Critics jokingly called the German-run denazification panels "followers factories" and "exoneration factories" because of the many Category IV and Category V rulings they churned out.

*Persilscheine*—the letters of recommendation named after a laundry detergent—helped countless perpetrators win the best denazification categories. Testimonials from top government officials, high-level members of the clergy, and supposed former members of the anti-Hitler resistance held special cachet. Glowing words were written in *Persilscheine*. Otherwise, they'd be of no use to the person requesting them. They might contain truths while at the same time glossing over any time periods in a job candidate's past that could be incriminating. It was a circular system of whitewashing, with former Nazis crafting *Persilscheine* for one another.

In his book *Blind Eye to Murder*, British author Tom Bower memorably describes the ease with which Nazi perpetrators beat the denazification system as well as how corruption helped bring about its demise. Mayors and other municipal leaders conspired with denazification tribunals and with townsfolk to bury the misdeeds of local Nazis.

Among the stories Bower tells is that of a mayor of a quaint town in Bavaria who had gotten rich by using his authority and membership in the Nationalsozialistische Deutsche Arbeiterpartei for profiteering. When the mayor, Wilhelm Siebenlist, was brought before the local denazification panel—staffed by fellow Germans—fourteen witnesses were ready to speak in his favor, ten of them his employees. The panel deemed that "no activity in the National Socialist sense" could be proven, and he got off scot-free, according to Bower. The prosecutor, Horst Schütze, was himself a former member of the NSDAP. Not only that, Schütze had been jailed three times for embezzlement.[13]

Bower tells of the district commissioner in Uffenheim, another Bavarian town, who interfered with the work of the local denazification panel by ceasing to appoint members to it. The commissioner was a former member of the Sturmabteilung. According to Bower, the local priest told his parishioners not to speak with the prosecutor, a Jew who had survived Auschwitz.[14]

Those who had enriched themselves through buying up the "Aryanized" properties of Nazi victims seemingly had little to fear from the denazification panels run by Germans. Consider the case of Xavier Lang. Of the twenty-six hotels owned by Lang, fifteen were purchased after Hitler became chancellor. Lang, whose annual income was seven hundred thousand marks, was fined a mere two thousand marks for profiteering, Bower wrote.

American occupation authorities assigned special personnel to check up on the German-run denazification tribunals. Their reports back to their superiors were alarming, according to Bower, telling of panel members who were "systematically ignoring the law, accepting bribes and whitewashing defendants."[15]

Of the three occupiers in the Western zone, the Americans were the most zealous in the pursuit of denazification. The Morgenthau Plan—named after Secretary of the Treasury Henry Morgenthau—to reduce Germany to an essentially agrarian state was ultimately rejected because it was unworkable and might well have turned Germans against democracy. The American denazification process that evolved in stages was far less punitive but was nonetheless riddled with troubles. The scope of what the Americans had in mind was gargantuan: requiring all adult Germans to fill out surveys that contained 131 questions about their pasts, most importantly what they had done during the Third Reich. The process was an enormous burden and intensified the hostility among Germans against the Americans. In the face of pressure from German church authorities, politicians, and the public at large, American and British authorities turned over denazification to German panels in 1946.

The same tricks used by former servants of the Third Reich to beat the denazification process came in handy in their pursuit of government jobs. Exactly as with denazification, former employees of the Hitler regime got former comrades to writing glowing recommendations for them. The most important qualification for being offered a job was showing proficiency and reliability while working for one's previous employer—in this case, the Third Reich. Former comrades who had managed to land positions of authority in postwar Germany provided not only that assurance but also vouched for job candidates' assertions that they secretly disliked the

Nazi regime, that they were just doing their jobs and were apolitical, that they had friends in the resistance, and all the other justifications among the panoply of excuses offered by former Nazis.

As for Gerhard Scheffler, despite his personal involvement in the Nazis' ruthless occupation of Poland, a German denazification tribunal awarded him the Exonerated classification. In justifying the decision, the panel said that while carrying out his duties, he did so "not in the National Socialist sense" but as a person performing his administrative tasks. This was a form of self-exculpation, and a highly dubious one, that was frequently employed during the Adenauer era.

Scheffler's clearance by the denazification court was noticed by former colleagues who themselves had succeeded in starting new careers in the West German civil service. A few months later, Scheffler was given a job at the North Rhine-Westphalia Ministry for Social Affairs by Rudolf Amelunxen, head of the ministry. Upon Amelunxen's recommendation, Scheffler was offered a job at the federal Interior Ministry by its head, Gustav Heinemann, and went to work there in April 1950. Scheffler rose quickly within the ranks of the Interior Ministry.[16]

Scheffler, who died in 1977, was never held to account for his part in the "Germanization" of the Wartheland. What would have happened if Scheffler's 1946 memoir had been known before he was hired by the Interior Ministry? Would that have barred him from the civil service? Would he have tried to persuade ministry officials that he was a changed man? Would the Interior Ministry have hired him anyway, arguing that his administrative expertise was needed? These are questions that cannot be answered because Gerhard Scheffler managed to keep his secrets to himself and the Interior Ministry chose not to dig deeply into his past.

One last question about Gerhard Scheffler, one that can be asked about so many of the postwar bureaucrats who had once loyally served the Third Reich. As a department head at the West German Interior Ministry, Scheffler helped draft a new social welfare law.[17] This was an important contribution to building the foundation of a democratic state. Imagine a set of scales. Let's put Scheffler's service to West Germany on one end of the scale and his involvement in the Nazis' extermination policies on the other. Can there be any argument that the latter would far outweigh the former? But does this mean that Scheffler's work for the West German nation is zeroed out by the Nazi past? It is a thorny question and one with no easy answers.

Like Gerhard Scheffler, Friedrich Rippich served as an administrator in the German-occupied region of Poland called "Wartheland" by the Nazi regime. It was this connection that got Rippich his position in the West German Interior Ministry. And as with Scheffler, the Interior Ministry did not bother to look too deeply into his service for the Hitler regime.

During the postwar years, Rippich tried to claim that his Third Reich record showed that he was against Nazi policies, that he did not volunteer for the SS, and that his career as an administrator had hit obstacles because of his religious beliefs. But files reviewed by the team of researchers led by Frank Bösch and Andreas Wirsching paint a different picture.

At age twenty-four, Rippich joined the NSDAP soon after Hitler came to power in 1933 and was named a district commissioner. Rippich also joined the SS. He was assigned to the Reich Interior Ministry in Berlin in 1937. After the German invasion of Poland, Rippich was promoted to *Sturmbahnführer*, an SS rank equivalent to major, and was sent to Sieradz, Poland, to serve as a district administrator.[18]

Several weeks after the Nazi blitzkrieg into Poland, Arthur Greiser—who was to be appointed governor of the Wartheland—declared it was his objective to turn the annexed land into a "model Gau of the Greater German Empire," one that would provide food for Germans, provide protection against "Polish and Jewish invasion," and settle the region with "people who will later know the term 'Polish' as a 'historical memory.'" The German occupiers embarked on a brutal, systematic program of ethnic cleansing, forcing hundreds of thousands of Poles and Jews from their homes, deporting them to the General Government , and handing their property over to ethnic Germans. Civilian German administrators had extensive involvement in this "Aryanization" project.

After the war, Rippich claimed that he had been anti-Nazi and had been denied promotion to a higher SS rank because of his religious beliefs. He also claimed that the only reason he had an SS rank was because it came automatically with his appointment as a district administrator.[19] The latter argument was used by many former SS officers after the war. But it does not hold water, as pointed out by historians and researchers who have been examining Nazi taints in the postwar civil service.

Rippich vanished after the Nazi regime's defeat and surfaced again in Argentina, like many a Nazi functionary trying to escape prosecution. Apparently, he thought it was safe to return to West Germany because in

1953 he applied for a position with the Interior Ministry in Bonn. He was encouraged to do so by Gerhard Scheffler, Rippich's former colleague at the Nazis' Interior Ministry and fellow veteran of the "Aryanization" project in the Wartheland. Provisional employment was approved by Ritter von Lex, state secretary at the Interior Ministry. Lex was also a veteran of the Nazi Interior Ministry. This was an "old-boy network" whose members were highly effective not only in re-employing former comrades but also in helping them paper over their pasts. Rippich had a rapid rise at the Interior Ministry, getting promoted into the top tier of the civil service system. He retired in 1970, but his past came back to haunt him. In 1977 a Dortmund prosecutor opened an investigation into his actions in the Wartheland. A request was sent to the Berlin Document Center—the American-run repository of Nazi files—for information about Rippich. In the course of further proceedings, Rippich's first name was misspelled in paperwork, and no files were found under that name.[20] Rippich appears to have been rescued from prosecution by someone's typographical error. Rippich died in 1995. He was eighty-seven years old.

Postwar tactics used by former servants of the Third Reich—evasiveness, equivocation, and outright lying—can make it tricky to get to the bottom of the degree of their incrimination. The smokescreens are so thick that it is often difficult to make out the degree of a Nazi's nastiness. Consider Karl von Rumohr. Rumohr joined the Nazi Party in 1933. On his 1954 application for a position with the West German Interior Ministry, he said he became a Nazi so that "state administration would not be left to the radical elements."[21] It's a strange-sounding justification and on the face of it impossible to disprove. But digging further into his past gives us a clearer picture of what made Karl von Rumohr tick.

Rumohr was born in 1900 in Upper Silesia, which is now part of Poland. After fighting during World War I, he studied law and then embarked on a career in administration. He joined the Nazi Party in 1933, and that December he took office as an NSDAP district leader, a position he held until April 1935. From May 1936 to July 1938 he managed the party's district office in Iserlohn. Nazi correspondence about Rumohr during this period said he had the "full confidence of party officials." He was so highly thought of that in May 1939 he was appointed head of a district administrative office in occupied Czechoslovakia. The team of researchers led by Frank Bösch and Andreas Wirsching turned up a

September 1939 report, written by Rumohr himself, showing that he was directly involved in booting Czech Jews out of their homes and "Aryanizing" their businesses.[22]

In that report Rumohr referred to a "large action" involving state police concerning the "Jewish question." Rumohr told his superiors that he had "taken precautions so that companies that are not yet Aryanized and whose owners were deported would be transferred, to the extent an economic necessity exists." The background to this report is that in June of that year a directive was issued that Jews living in Nazi-occupied Czechoslovakia would only be allowed to continue to operate their businesses with the written permission of district administrators.

Rumohr apparently had some sort of run-in with the local commander of the Nazi Sicherheitsdienst, who in September 1939 wrote him up for having a "negative attitude" toward SS and police officials who were responsible for carrying out deportations. Rumohr had also registered his disapproval of the burning of a Jewish home for apprentices and of the mistreatment of Czech prisoners by German police. Still, none of this stood in the way of his Third Reich career. Two years later, Rumohr was called to Berlin to work in the Reich Ministry for the Occupied Eastern Territories, which supervised the civilian administration of lands conquered by German forces. He was made head of a department that was involved in drafting regulations for occupied territories, although what sort of influence he had on the regulations is not clear.[23]

In May 1942 Rumohr was assigned as an administrator in Breslau. It was here, according to a postwar sworn statement by Rumohr, that he came into contact with a circle of military officers and others who were plotting to assassinate Hitler and make peace with the Western Allies. Rumohr claimed that after Hitler escaped the July 20, 1944, attempt on his life, he was arrested by the Gestapo because his name was mentioned during an interrogation of assassination plotters. As punishment, according to Rumohr, he was forced into the Wehrmacht.[24]

He took odd jobs after the war. A denazification panel in 1947 cleared him of any culpability by classifying him as Exonerated. He was admitted to the German Civil Servants Association in 1949 and soon thereafter was hired by the West German Interior Ministry as a member of the founding staff. Rumohr might well have had to settle for some other kind of employment if it were not for the advocacy of Erich Kessler.

Like a number of other former Nazis, Rumohr applied himself to the task of creating a new republic from the ruins of the Third Reich. His diligence was rewarded in 1955, when he was named head of the Interior Ministry's Internal Affairs Office. It was pretty much clear sailing for Rumohr until 1962, when the opposition Social Democrats started raising questions about his past actions in occupied Czechoslovakia. The Interior Ministry launched an internal investigation. Documents that turned up during the probe showed that in the paperwork Rumohr submitted when he applied for the Interior Ministry job, he had concealed the fact that he had worked for the Reich Ministry for the Occupied Eastern Territories and omitted other details as well. During questioning, Rumohr flatly denied even an indirect participation in the deportation of Jews.[25] His bosses at the Interior Ministry ultimately decided there was "no reason to take action" against him. Rumohr fell ill the following year, retired in 1965, and died in 1967.

So what was Karl von Rumohr—committed Nazi or conflicted Nazi? As he performed his duties as a servant of the Third Reich, did he have doubts about what he was doing? It is clear that he strove to advance his career as a Nazi administrator and that he was complicit in stripping Czech Jews of their properties and assets, and because of his later job in Berlin, he must have at least known about the mass murder of Jews. There must have been a part of him that believed in the Nazi cause, at least to some degree. But could his conscience have prompted him to seek contact with the anti-Hitler resistance? This is entirely possible. But when he applied for work at the West German Interior Ministry, why did he omit crucial information? What more did he have to hide? And as he pursued his new career as an administrator in the West German government—a job in which he acquitted himself well—did he do so out of devotion to parliamentary democracy, or did he do it to try to bury his sins?

Unlike other high-level officials at the West German Interior Ministry, Maria Daelen had been an actual member of the anti-Hitler resistance. In fact, she was among just a very few people in the whole postwar government who very clearly had been opposed to the Nazi regime. Daelen's courageous past had been hiding in history's shadows for decades. It was rediscovered by Maren Richter, one of the researchers who worked with historians Frank Bösch and Andreas Wirsching in their probe of Nazi taints within the West German Interior Ministry.

In the project led by Bösch and Wirsching, researchers were assigned certain tasks. Maren Richter's brief was to probe the Nazi taint within the Interior Ministry's Health Department. The Health Department was unique within the ministry because it was the only one not dominated by lawyers; instead, it was staffed by doctors and other medical professionals who, like the lawyers, had previously practiced their profession under the Nazi regime. In delving into the staffing of the Health Department, the twenty-first-century historian Richter came upon the anti-Nazi Maria Daelen.

The infection of top levels of the postwar health service by former Nazis makes the story of Daelen all the more compelling, so much so that Richter decided to write a book about her, *"Aber ich habe mich nicht entmutigen lassen": Maria Daelen—Ärtztin und Gesundheitspolitikerin im 20. Jahrhundert* ("But I Didn't Allow Myself to Be Intimidated": Maria Daelen—Twentieth-Century Physician and Health Policymaker), published in 2019.

In a photo taken in June 1939, six years into Hitler's dictatorship, a young Maria Daelen is wearing sunglasses, a scarf, a headband, and a summer blouse while driving a two-seat Ford convertible. She was an emancipated woman, a career-driven physician, childless and single—the very antithesis of the Nazis' view of the model female.

Daelen was the daughter of Katharina von Kardorff-Oheimb, a champion of the women's movement and one of the first female delegates of the Reichstag. Daelen's father was Felix Daelen, a prosperous engineer in Germany's metal industry.[26] Maria Daelen had been drawn to medicine at least partly because it would provide a path for her to exert her independence.

As a young surgeon at Berlin's Westend Hospital and later at the Charité Hospital, Maria Daelen watched as the Nazis' racist policies forced the dismissal of Jewish colleagues. At least two leading doctors she knew died by suicide. In a letter to her mother soon after Hitler's takeover in 1933, Daelen gave voice to her disdain for the Hitler regime: "I find my thoughts and feelings in blatant opposition to today's Germany."[27]

Rather than flee Germany, she chose to stay and work within the system. She began her own private practice in 1938, specializing in internal medicine and radiology while also working at a women's clinic. From 1943 until the Third Reich's defeat, according to Maren Richter, Daelen was a volunteer specialist for pregnant women and infants at government-run health offices for Berlin's Charlottenburg and Spandau districts.

Daelen's expressions of anti-Hitler resistance took various forms.[28] Among Daelen's friends were prominent people in the Berlin arts scene, some of whom she helped evade conscription by providing them with forged medical certificates. Daelen's circle of friends included members of the anti-Hitler resistance, a number of whom would be arrested and executed. Among them was German diplomat Albrecht Graf von Bernstorff, who was involved in the failed plot to kill Hitler on July 20, 1944. Others were Abwehr general Hans Oster and businessman Otto Hübener. Another friend was Heinrich Graf von Lehndorff-Steinort, who was also arrested in the sweep of July 20 plotters. For several months after Lehndorff-Steinort's imprisonment, Daelen would bring him fruits and cigarettes. He was executed in September 1944.

Richter found Daelen's role in the anti-Nazi resistance as "hard to categorize," noting the letter Daelen had written to her mother in 1933 and her support for Jewish colleagues dismissed from their hospital jobs. "However, her subsequent support did not pursue a lofty vision with ethical and moral claims, as it was with the resisters of July 20. Rather, her drive seems to have come from sympathy for people close to her and the unconditional willingness to help," Richter wrote in her biography of Daelen.[29]

Daelen did not escape the notice of the Gestapo. According to Richter, during an interrogation in January 1945, a Gestapo officer demanded that she show proof of her "Aryan" heritage. Daelen cheekily replied she didn't need such proof because "I already look like [Joseph] Goebbel's dream." The same day, according to Richter, the Gestapo visited her clinic, and Daelen went into hiding. As the Red Army drew closer to Berlin, Daelen fled south to the American-occupied sector.[30]

Daelen quickly established a friendly and professional relationship with the occupying Americans. She put her medical skills to work at an internment camp. In 1946 she was hired by the Interior Ministry for Hesse state to develop policies on nutrition, infant and maternal care, and the prevention of tuberculosis. Two years later, she was chosen as a participant in a German-American cultural exchange program. According to Maren Richter, Daelen was the sole woman among six German doctors to fly to the United States to visit hospitals, universities, and public health offices in order to develop ideas for improving and expanding their country's health services.

When Daelen was hired by the federal Interior Ministry in 1953 to work in the Health Department, she found herself among familiar faces, some of whom were incriminated former Nazis. They, too, could thank the Americans for help in restoring their careers. The victorious Allies had given high priority to restoring health services to prevent disease, so most doctors were allowed to continue practicing. The Interior Ministry's disinterest in probing the backgrounds of job candidates, including those in the medical profession, led to the hiring of a number of men with dubious backgrounds. Some of the top officials at the Health Department had held jobs in Nazi-occupied Poland. Maren Richter uncovered Interior Ministry personnel files in which job applicants had cleansed their biographies of anything incriminating.

In October 1945 a U.S. military court convicted seven defendants being tried for deaths at the Hadamar Euthanasia Center, where thousands of mentally disabled patients had been killed by gassing and narcotic overdoses. At the Nuremberg Doctors' Trial that began in December 1946 and ended eight months later, sixteen Nazi officials were convicted of involvement in the euthanasia program to murder the mentally ill. But with public demands to end war crimes trials and denazification, the vast majority of those complicit in forced sterilizations, cruel medical experiments, and the murder of mentally ill children and others with disabilities were able to resume their careers. Some even rose to prominence. They wrote for medical periodicals, published papers, and were invited to conferences, and dozens were consulted by officials in the Adenauer government on federal health matters.

These are the kinds of medical professionals with whom Maria Daelen would have had contact in her position at the federal Interior Ministry. What did she think of these incriminated physicians? Did she shun them? Did she try to avoid contact? Did she confront them about their Nazi pasts? The answer, it appears, is no.

During the Third Reich, pediatrician Werner Catel was a consultant to the Nazi regime on the T-4 euthanasia program that murdered children who were deemed to be mentally ill or otherwise burdens on society. Nonetheless, in 1954 he was appointed professor of pediatrics at Kiel University. In a 1964 interview with *Der Spiegel* magazine, Catel tried to argue that killing mentally disabled children who showed no "mental impulses" was the humane thing to do.[31] The reporter asked: "How do you examine six- or eight-month-old children for mental impulses?" "There's a lot of evidence that can, but doesn't have to, provide information," Catel replied. "Whether the child reaches for the bottle, whether it smiles, what its reflex behavior is like."

Given the fact that some children are late developers, the *Der Spiegel* reporter asked Catel how it was possible to determine with certainty whether a child's mental disabilities might not improve. Catel responded: "Believe me, it is always possible to distinguish these soulless beings from the developing human." Catel said he was particularly concerned about the burdens placed on the parents of a seriously disabled child: "Every doctor who has to deal with incurable idiots in practice knows about the conflict situations in marriages, which can go as far as destruction. He knows the constant horror at the sight of the monsters."

Maria Daelen knew Catel well. In 1948 the two of them ran a program to inoculate people in Hesse state against tuberculosis. Later that year, together they described the program at a conference of the German Tuberculosis Society, according to Maren Richter. It is hard to believe that Daelen was not disgusted by Catel's views, but she certainly didn't let them stand in the way of working with him professionally. How is this to be explained?

Frank Bösch and Andreas Wirsching, the lead historians on the investigation into the Interior Ministry, offer some insights. In *Hüter der Ordnung*, the two scholars write about working relationships among officials at the Interior Ministry. They describe an atmosphere in which there was mutual agreement that there would be no discussion of Nazi pasts. They tell of an Interior Ministry official, Franz Herrmann, who in 1933 was fired by the Nazis from his position at the Justice Ministry and spent several months in various concentration camps because of his Jewish origins and because of his pronouncements against the Hitler regime. Herrmann survived the camps, emigrated to Chile, returned home after the war, and was hired by the Interior Ministry in 1952, where he seems to have had no problems working with former Nazis. Bösch and Wirsching wrote, "There are many indications that he worked well together with his colleagues, although they had careers under National Socialism in their past and he at least informally knew about it." The same can be said of Maria Daelen, whose "daily contact with former National Socialist doctors" showed no signs that she had had any conflicts with them, according to Bösch and Wirsching.[32]

We sometimes think of the "good Germans" who lived during the Third Reich. Was Maria Daelen one of them? There is much that is unknown about Daelen's thoughts and actions as a physician working within the system during the Nazi years. Local health offices were involved in Nazi racial policies by acting as screening agents for people to be sterilized and even murdered. Did Daelen do anything to intervene, or did she just keep quiet about it? We know that she was generally opposed to the Nazi regime. But what, specifically, did she think about the murder of children who were deemed unworthy of living? After the war, Daelen apparently chose to work collegially with former Nazis out of a sincere desire to improve health services for Germans. But was there something more to it? Did she choose to keep quiet, to immerse herself in her work, because dwelling on the past was too painful and she just wanted to move on? If that is the case, then Daelen was not so far from the vast number of Germans who chose silence during the Adenauer era.

# 10

## Killers Welcome

When Eduard Michael performed his daily duties as personnel manager at the Bundeskriminalamt, when he went home at night and ate dinner with his wife and later, as he fell asleep, did he see the frightened faces of Jewish men, women, and children as they boarded trains to a Nazi death camp? Did he have nightmares about the cattle cars that delivered forty thousand people from the Jewish ghetto in Częstochowa, Poland, to their demise? Or did Michael suppress memories of his years as Gestapo chief in Częstochowa? Was he able to simply erase them, to live unburdened of guilt or shame?

Dieter Schenk, an eighty-two-year-old German, posed these questions to an audience during a speech in Essen on a spring day in 2018. He told his listeners of his own employment with the federal police agency, the Bundeskriminalamt, in the late 1980s, of the whispers he would hear about senior investigators who had dark pasts that were never to be talked about. Schenk reported his findings from years of archival research: for about three decades after World War II, about two dozen of the BKA's top men had served with Nazi units that had committed war crimes, and they were never put on trial. In 2001 Schenk published the results of his research in a blockbuster exposé titled *Auf dem rechten Auge blind: Die braunen Wurzeln des BKA* (Turning a Blind Eye to the Right: The Brown Roots of the BKA).

"How was it possible that the Bundeskriminalamt was built up by former Nazi criminologists? And how was the BKA able to hide this fact?" Schenk asked the Essen audience. He then proceeded to tell the whole disturbing story of how the BKA became infested with police officers attached, during World War II, to Einsatzgruppe and Einsatzkommando mobile murder units that killed an estimated 1.3 million Jews in German-occupied territories. He told of the BKA appointing Eduard Michael as the agency's first personnel manager, of Michael's hiring of cops who had served in Einsatz units, of the BKA harboring and even promoting seriously incriminated former Nazis, of the agency finally addressing the problem in the 1960s but then, instead of making sure they were brought to justice, simply transferring them to other positions or forcing them into retirement.

Of all of the government agencies that welcomed former Nazis onto their staffs during the postwar years, there is none whose infestation is more disturbing than the Bundeskriminalamt (although the Federal Intelligence Service may rival the BKA for this dubious honor). Some of the enforcement of West German law had been handed over to men who were once part of the Nazi murder machine.

In 2011 the BKA released a 380-page book that detailed the findings of its own inquiry—conducted by independent historians—into the Nazi taint within the investigative agency into the 1970s. The BKA-commissioned book, titled *Schatten der Vergangenheit: Das BKA und seine Gründungsgeneration in der frühen Bundesrepublik* (Shadows of the Past: The BKA and Its Founding Generation in the Early Federal Republic), would have been shocking and scandalous if Dieter Schenk had not already revealed many of the agency's secrets in his 2001 book, in which he named BKA investigators who had been involved in Nazi war crimes, the ease with which they were able to get jobs at the agency, and how their secrets were guarded by their superiors. Still, the inquiry commissioned by the Federal Criminal Police Office is important because it drew from personnel files that had not been available to Schenk and from the CIA's Nazi war crimes files, which had not yet been declassified when Schenk published his book. The researchers also found that the infestation of the BKA by seriously incriminated cops was even worse than what Schenk had described. Of the forty-seven senior officials at the BKA in 1958, thirty-three had belonged to the SS.[1]

On December 14, 1959, detective chief inspector Heinrich Erlen was summoned to the office of the BKA's new personnel manager, Gerhard Oesterhelt.[2] Erlen was informed that the Frankfurt prosecutor's office was investigating him on suspicion of having participated in the mass execution of Jews in Lithuania, and he was arrested on the spot. Erlen had been hired by the BKA in October 1956. Four months later, he was granted the coveted status of civil servant, the equivalent of tenure for a professor. And now Erlen was being confronted with his past. Unlike Eduard Michael, Gerhard Oesterhelt had a clean record. In the middle of his studies for a legal career, Oesterhelt was drafted into the Wehrmacht in April 1941, captured by the Russians in the spring of 1945, and released four years later. He finished his law degree in 1953 and was hired by the

Berlin police department as an administrative lawyer. When Oesterhelt replaced Michael as the BKA's personnel manager, the agency officials who were hiding dark secrets suddenly lost their protector. And when new documents and witness testimony began to surface about misdeeds by German cops serving in the Einsatz units deployed in the occupied eastern territories, Oesterhelt did what should have been done by the BKA all along—dig into the pasts of the agency's officers. Erlen was the first to be forced to face the music. He was soon followed by a senior detective inspector identified by the historians who looked into the BKA's postwar hiring as "Otto Sch."

Like a number of BKA officials, Otto Sch.'s alleged crimes came to light because he was called as a witness in a trial against the SS leader of a mobile killing unit that had operated in the occupied eastern territories. Otto Sch. gave testimony in the trial of Erich Ehrlinger, who as commander oversaw massacres of Jews in the Baltic states and the USSR. As Otto Sch. was questioned about the actions of Einsatzkommando units, he ended up incriminating himself on the witness stand, and an investigation against him was begun.

Scrutiny was then cast upon two more BKA detectives who had served with an Einsatzkommando unit, identified by historians as "Gustav H." and "Konrad Z." In 1962 both men were called as witnesses in the 1962 murder trial of SS colonel Alfred Filbert. The two had served under Filbert in Einsatzkommando 9 of Einsatzgruppe B as Filbert carried out massacres of Jews in Belarus. Court testimony by Gustav H. and Konrad Z. resulted in disciplinary proceedings against them by the Federal Ministry of the Interior, the department overseeing the BKA.[3]

The BKA's belated housecleaning occurred amid growing public awareness about the involvement of German police officers who had been attached to Einsatz units that went on mass killing sprees in the occupied East. The mass murder convictions from the 1958 trial in Ulm of ten men who had belonged to the Einsatzkommando Tilsit revealed the complicity of German cops in these atrocities. It also intensified pressure on German prosecutors, and on government agencies, to ferret out such perpetrators and bring them to justice. German documents show that while the BKA showed reluctance to air its dirty laundry, it was unable to resist demands by the Federal Interior Ministry that it do so. The Interior Ministry ordered the BKA to make use of the Central Office, the Nazi-hunting agency in

Ludwigsburg, to locate incriminating documents it might have on BKA officers who had been deployed with the Einsatz units. Oesterhelt needed no pressure from his ultimate bosses at the Interior Ministry to crank up the heat on tainted BKA investigators. His efforts over the next few years marked a significant break from the agency's posture of resisting the search for war criminals within its ranks.[4] But as we will see, Oesterhelt's pursuit of tainted BKA investigators came to naught. Some were forced to take early retirement, while others were transferred to other government jobs. Government documents show that a solicitude on the part of German officials toward suspected war criminals within the BKA resulted in virtually no punishment, other than perhaps a denial of promotion. Acknowledging a tainted investigator's service to the BKA was by and large given priority over bringing them to account for their involvement in Nazi atrocities.

Gerhard Freitag was hired by the Bundeskriminalamt in 1957 and just a few months later was granted civil service status for life. The Interior Ministry had initially raised some questions about Freitag's mention in the application process that he had been deployed to "foreign assignments" at various "theaters of war." It also emerged that Freitag had been a member of the SS. According to the team of historians who examined the BKA's files, Eduard Michael stepped in to give Freitag a helping hand. The Federal Interior Ministry had planned to question Freitag. Instead, BKA personnel chief Michael had Freitag submit a written statement about his foreign deployments and membership in the Schutzstaffel. Parts of Freitag's statement sound like the classic "my dog ate my homework" excuse. First, Freitag said he had joined the SS only at the insistence of his boss when he worked at a bank in the 1930s. Second, Freitag said that in reality he was never a member of the SS because he had never received a Schutzstaffel ID card. The card was supposed to be provided to him in Munich, he said, but he never got it. And that is why he did not put down on his BKA application papers that he had been a member of the SS—because he was not one.[5] As cockamamie as this story is on its face, the Federal Ministry of Interior bought it.

Things were going well for Freitag. Nothing seemed to be standing in the way of his career. But German prosecutors' belated prosecution of Einsatz units for atrocities in the east brought out new revelations about Freitag's past. In 1962 Freitag was called as a witness in the trial of Einsatzkommando members who had carried out mass executions in the Riga region in 1941. As it turns out, for several months in 1941, Freitag had been the adjutant to Rudolf Batz, commander of the Riga-based Einsatzkommando 2 of Einsatzgruppe A. Within just a few months, starting in early July 1941, Einsatzgruppe A murdered thirty thousand Latvian Jews. On the witness stand, Freitag sought to portray himself as an adjutant who had little interest in the job and nothing to do with the murder of Jews. "I sat in Batz' antechamber and had virtually nothing to do. Not only that, I did not have a good relationship with him," Freitag testified. "As far as executions, especially of Jews, I know nothing about that, at least nothing specific. I only heard that the Latvians had tortured Jews and Communists."[6]

Of course, with all of the hustle and bustle that would have been happening at Batz's headquarters, with members of Einsatzkommando 2 returning from the killing fields and then heading out once again to execute more victims, with paperwork that surely would have crossed Freitag's desk, and with recounting of the day's mass murder, it is impossible that Freitag could not at least have detailed knowledge about the atrocities. His claim that he himself did not participate in the killings also lacks credibility. It is known that every member of an Einsatzkommando unit was expected to take part in an execution at least once. Nonetheless, Freitag was still able to dodge further scrutiny. This changed two years after his testimony. A meeting was held at the Federal Interior Ministry to discuss personnel at the Bundeskriminalamt. According to a note from that meeting, Freitag was one of six officials within the BKA whose foreign deployments during the war raised "considerable suspicions." Freitag was called to Oesterhelt's office to give a complete accounting of his actions with Einsatzkommando units. Two days after that, the head prosecutor at Hamburg state court informed the BKA that consideration was being given to bringing charges against Freitag. The Federal Interior Ministry also began its own inquiry into Freitag's Einsatzkommando deployments.

The Hamburg state prosecutor traveled to BKA headquarters in Wiesbaden to question Freitag, but Freitag refused to cooperate. The prosecutor was reluctant to bring charges against him because of a lack of hard evidence that Freitag had personally participated in mass killings. The prosecutor said in a letter to Oesterhelt that during Freitag's time with Einsatzkommando 2, "there is no doubt" that the unit "repeatedly" carried out executions of Jews, that Freitag must have known about the killings and "in all likelihood" participated "in at least one of the actions." The prosecutor said he was "convinced" that Freitag was lying about his innocence. The challenge, the prosecutor wrote, was finding incontrovertible evidence that Freitag was among the men of Rudolf Batz's Einsatzkommando 2 who fired at Latvian Jews as they were brought to open pits and executed.[7]

The Interior Ministry continued its own inquiry, but it, too, went nowhere. In a report written on January 10, 1966, the head of the internal investigation wrote that Freitag's insistence that he knew nothing about the execution of Jews was "completely unbelievable." But it was impossible to prove this because of a tacit agreement among members of the murder units not to make incriminating statements against one another. "It is extremely unlikely that a witness can be found to refute Freitag's statements," the investigator wrote.[8]

The Interior Ministry's investigation of Freitag dragged on for years. Freitag had been suspended from duty, pending the results of the internal inquiry, which was formally ended on April 6, 1970. After Freitag's reinstatement, he received two promotions. The BKA said Freitag had already suffered enough, that he should be burdened no longer with suspicions that had yet to be proved.[9] Freitag retired from government service on March 31, 1973. He died twenty-two years later, at age eighty-two.

Ludwig Erhard, West German chancellor after Adenauer's departure from politics, returned from an official trip to Italy in late January 1964. He was accompanied by his bodyguard, Ewald Peters, a specialist with the BKA's Security Group. Peters was arrested soon after the government plane touched down at the airport outside Bonn. Evidence had surfaced that Peters was involved in the mass execution of Jews by an Einsatzgruppe in southern Russia. While locked up in jail, the fifty-year-old Peters died by suicide.[10]

One day after Peters's suicide, a meeting was called at the Federal Interior Ministry to discuss the "personnel situation at the Bundeskriminalamt," according to the authors of *Schatten der Vergangenheit*. Oesterhelt, the BKA's personnel manager, was there. So were the ministry's counsel on personnel matters, Franz Kroppenstedt, as well as other high-ranking ministry officials. Oesterhelt and Kroppenstedt reported on what was known about tainted former Nazis within the BKA. A total of fifty-six BKA officials had been identified as having wartime pasts that needed scrutiny. At the meeting it was decided that some of the tainted investigators needed to be removed from office. Six former Gestapo men and five former SS officers were quietly transferred to other government agencies that spring.

Even before this decision was made, several BKA officers had been transferred because of their Nazi pasts. Among them was Theo Saevecke, whom we met in chapter 3. The BKA's spring-cleaning did not get rid of all of the agency's worrisome personnel—far from it. Internal investigations continued against the dozens who remained. Requests were sent to Ludwigsburg to check on documents stored there. A number of BKA officers were temporarily suspended, and prosecutors began criminal investigations against some of them. But for all of this belated scrutiny of the BKA's bad apples, not much came of it. Prosecutors abandoned criminal investigations. Likewise, the Interior Ministry and the BKA inevitably pulled the plug on their own disciplinary proceedings. Heinrich Erlen, Otto Sch., Konrad Z., and Gustav H. were among the tainted BKA investigators who were able to sail off into the sunset with their civil service pensions.

During the formative years of the BKA, Dr. Bernhard Niggemeyer had helped raise the agency's stature by organizing annual international conferences on policing themes. Niggemeyer had been working at the BKA since 1953. One decade earlier, he was a leader of units of the Geheime Feldpolizei (GFP), or Secret Field Police, an intelligence agency of the German military that was involved in the massacre of civilians on the eastern front.

Niggemeyer was questioned about the Geheime Feldpolizei by an official with the Hesse State Criminal Office in February 1960 and five years later by a judge. Niggemeyer's statements were evasive, self-serving. He sought to persuade his interlocutors that the GFP had not been involved in killing innocent civilians, that it had no connection with Einsatzkommando units that were, and that—despite his title, *Geheime Polizeidirector*—he had not had the authority to give orders to GFP units. He said he would receive reports from a dozen GFP units about their intelligence activities, which included identifying partisans, but that was the extent of it.

Niggemeyer's fairy tale of not even knowing about the massacre of innocent Jews on territory that was under the purview of his own GFP units was blown apart by the indefatigable BKA critic Dieter Schenk. Digging around in archives, Schenk turned up documents showing that units under Niggemeyer had been involved in atrocities and that Niggemeyer must at least have been aware of and sanctioned them. In 1964, Schenk wrote, the Ludwigsburg Nazi-hunting office conducted preliminary investigations into two GFP units: GFP 729 and GFP 707. Witnesses told the Ludwigsburg prosecutors that the two units had been involved in the murder of civilian men, women, and children, under the guise of hunting partisans. Schenk also found a 1944 report written by Niggemeyer himself about the actions of the GFP units overseen by him from April through September. The report tallies up the number of people arrested by those twelve GFP units (16,470), how many were executed (675), how many were shot dead while "trying to escape" or "in combat" (32), and how many were handed over to the Einsatzkommandos (1,047), which, Schenk writes, would likely have murdered the prisoners.[11]

Niggemeyer's claim that he had not had powers to issue orders was also taken apart by Schenk. In reports about the actions of GFP units, Niggemeyer had tried to impress his bosses by talking about "my own actions," saying that he had paid visits to all twelve of the GFP units under his purview, and by listing items on the agenda in his meetings with Geheime Feldpolizei squad leaders, including the "carrying out of executions."

While there was some investigatory sniffing around about whether Niggemeyer had been personally involved in war crimes, he showed consummate skill in constructing a protective shield around not just himself but others at the BKA who had served with GFP squads. On February 6, 1962, according to Dieter Schenk, investigators with North Rhine-Westphalia's State Criminal Office arrived at BKA's headquarters in Wiesbaden for a meeting with Oesterhelt, the agency's personnel chief. The North Rhine-Westphalia officials were investigating GFP 717, one of the GFP squads under Niggemeyer's purview. The North Rhine-Westphalia investigators had come to question not Niggemeyer but five former members of GFP 717 who were now employed by the BKA. Niggemeyer had anticipated the visit. Before they could question the five BKA officers, Niggemeyer told the visiting investigators that as far as he was concerned, what they were up to was an illegal fishing expedition. Niggemeyer also said the mission of the GFP units was "fighting bandits in the East," a common postwar excuse for committing atrocities against noncombatants. When the visiting investigators met with the five suspect BKA officials, it was obvious they had coordinated their statements, among themselves and probably with Niggemeyer. They said the primary mission of GFP 717 was intelligence gathering, that they had never worked with the Einsatzgruppen, and that they were not involved in the execution of Jews.[12] None of the five BKA officers questioned by the visiting investigators were ever charged. Neither was Niggemeyer, who retired in 1968 and died twenty years later.

Otto Martin threw himself completely into the Nazi cause. He joined the Sturmabteilung and the National Socialist Student Association on December 1, 1930, at age nineteen, and the Nazi Party on January 1, 1931. Unlike most other Nazis who landed jobs with the BKA after the war, Martin was not a cop. His interest was science, especially biology and botany. After earning a doctorate at the University of Tübingen, Martin went to work as a research assistant at the university's Botanical Institute. From January to March 1939 he was among researchers at the SS's think tank, called the Ahnenerbe (Ancestral Heritage).[13] The Ahnenerbe conducted pseudoscience, its mission to do research that promoted Germans' racial superiority. In April 1939 Martin joined the Security Police's Forensic Institute. He served as a soldier on the eastern front from April 1940 to April 1943 and returned to the Forensic Institute in Berlin.

His work and his attitude pleased the SS leadership. When he was promoted to SS major in 1943, his superiors said in a written commendation: "Dr. M. is a National Socialist through and through and can be described as exemplary." After the war Martin worked in the pharmaceutical industry, before he was hired by the BKA in March 1952 as a forensics specialist. Martin was among the former SS and Gestapo men transferred to other government jobs during the BKA's 1960s purges of tainted lawmen. Many of them were sent to the Federal Statistics Office, including Martin. What happened to Dr. Otto Martin after that is symbolic of the kid-glove treatment often given to postwar civil servants with incriminating pasts. In the early 1970s he was taken back by the BKA and promoted to the position of scientific director. He retired from government service in 1976. There was never any investigation into the work he did as a Nazi biologist and whether he might have committed war crimes.

In 2007 the Bundeskriminalamt did something extraordinary, something historic, something totally uncharacteristic. It invited academics, current and former employees of the BKA, the head of Germany's Sinti and Roma community, a Holocaust survivor, and others to a series of conferences to discuss the Nazi perpetrators who had found refuge at the BKA during the Adenauer era. If it were not for the fact that for seven decades German government agencies had tried to ignore the Nazi stain in the postwar civil service, this would not have seemed like a big deal. But it was, and it hit a raw nerve.

The three conferences were initiated by the Bundeskriminalamt's president at the time, Jörg Ziercke. They were held as historians commissioned by the Foreign Office were digging into that ministry's files and three years before the publication of *Das Amt*. At the opening symposium on August 8, 2007, Ziercke said the purpose of the three-meeting series was to examine whether a controversial theory about Germans' handling of the Nazi past applied to the BKA. The theory, put forth by Holocaust survivor Ralph Giordano, posits a "second guilt" among Germans. According to Giordano, Germans' "first guilt" was their embrace of Hitler. The second guilt was the war generation's postwar silence about the Third Reich and the return of Nazi perpetrators to positions of authority.[14]

"Ladies and gentlemen, perhaps some of you are wondering why after more than fifty-five years the BKA in 2007 is suddenly remembering its story," Ziercke said in a conference room at the agency's headquarters in Wiesbaden.[15] "Perhaps others among you are wondering why the BKA even considers it necessary to discuss our own history with regard to National Socialism." Ziercke addressed the issue forcefully. "There can be no end to remembering the National Socialist genocide in which police participated," he said, recalling police officers who had been involved in massacres on the eastern front, rounding up Jews for deportation, acting as guards at concentration camps and on transports to extermination camps, among other crimes.

The objective of the three conferences, Ziercke said, would be to shed light on the consequences of the BKA having hired severely incriminated former Nazis. This self-examination may have come late, Ziercke said, "but in my belief, not too late."

In his address, historian Patrick Wagner said that from the fall of 1933 until the end of the war, police officers in Germany were directly involved in deporting more than 100,000 people to concentration camps: 30,000 Sinti and Roma; and 80,000 people judged to be "asocials" and "professional criminals." The second group included homosexuals, prostitutes, homeless people, foster children, and people guilty of crimes as trivial as stealing chickens. These figures do not include all of the police who were deployed in the occupied countries and were involved in atrocities against civilians.

Wagner painted a chilling picture of cops making personal choices about whom to deport as they performed their everyday duties in German towns and cities: "Local police had the authority to send to concentration camps every human being whom they viewed as potentially dangerous, recalcitrant or just plain annoying."[16]

The ideological foundation for police officers' involvement in sending citizens to concentration and extermination camps was the Nazis' twisted campaign to protect the "Aryan" gene pool from being infected by people deemed inferior or undesirable. Many police officers involved in these crimes were hired by postwar police and security agencies. They included men who were top functionaries in the Nazis' murderous treatment of the Roma population. In Adenauer's Germany they resumed their careers in police units set up to investigate members of the minority. To keep an eye on the Roma, these special police squads even used documents that had been collected by the Nazis on the minority.

Racist ideology toward the Roma was carried by former Nazis into West German police precincts, Romani Rose, head of the Central Council of German Sinti and Roma, said at the Wiesbaden conference.[17] These views appeared in government-funded newspapers and newsletters published for the West German policing community.

Rose presented some excerpts: A 1950 guest commentary in the Frankfurt magazine *Polizeipraxis* (Police Practice), written by a police sergeant in Württemberg, contained the assertion that "Gypsies have so little concept of religion that to them God and the devil are one and the same. Their actions are always instinctive. As different as Gypsies are from other humans, they are similar to each other all across the globe. If you know a dozen of them, you know them all." And a commentary in the 1962 edition of the police newspaper *Kriminalistik* (Criminalistics) was similarly racist: "The group of people to be observed are Gypsy half-breeds with parents of German or Jewish blood, or combinations of these, so ultimately mixed people from three blood strains, which may show a negative concentration of genetic material (cunning, deviousness, brutality, drunkenness, suicidal tendencies, etc.)." These are words that were printed in an officially sanctioned police newspaper nearly two decades after the fall of the Third Reich. Rose said "the former perpetrators determined the image of our minority in society." Although about a half-million Roma were murdered by the Nazis, West Germany did not recognize the deaths as genocide until 1982.

As the BKA prepared each of the three conferences in 2007, tempers were simmering within some quarters of Germany's police establishment over the airing of the BKA's secrets. In the days before the first conference began, a caustic editorial appeared in the publication that went out to members of the national police union, the Gewerkschaft der Polizei (Union of Police), also known as the GdP. It was in response to the BKA's announcement about the upcoming conferences.

"Navel-Gazing 2007: Doesn't the BKA Have Anything Better to Do?" read the headline in the periodical *Deutsche Polizei* (German Police). As police budgets were being cut, "while the global fight against Islamic terrorism is raging . . . and sheer terror is supposedly already knocking on Germany's door," does the BKA "really have nothing better to do than occupy itself with hypothetical brown birth defects from two generations ago?" The editorial referred to academics, authors, and other participants who had signed up for the three conferences as "podium gladiators."[18]

The commentary, signed by the *Redaktion*, or editorial board, was followed by a boisterous debate that played out in the pages of *Deutsche Polizei* and in letters to the editor in German newspapers. *Deutsche Polizei* interviewed Siegfried Brugger, who had worked at the BKA from 1959 to 1985. "A quote from Konrad Adenauer comes to mind," Brugger told the union newspaper. "Looking back at the past only makes sense if it serves the future." Brugger questioned the value of looking back at the Bundeskriminalamt's secrets. "At this point, I have not heard a convincing argument, including from Jörg Ziercke, that makes this project—which was so grandly announced in the press—understandable," he said. "What results of such an analysis could serve the future? One thing is for sure: the results would not be enough to prevent a dictatorship as terrible as Adolf Hitler."[19]

But there were also supporters among BKA retirees of their former employer's move to comprehensively examine its ties to the Nazi past. The tone of the editorial in the police union newspaper, in particular, angered some of its readers. "Undisputedly, opinions can be divided as to whether and in what form we should deal with the 'brown' past of the BKA. But snooty writing like this is in no way appropriate to the topic," wrote Klaus Bayer of Berlin. And he had nothing but praise for Ziercke's decision to launch the project of self-examination: "For every union member, the issue of professional ethics and self-image as an employee of a police department must be central. And that includes coming to terms with history, not suppressing it."[20]

Jürgen Vorbeck, police union shop steward at the BKA, had complained that no one from labor was represented as the series of conferences began. When the participants convened for their third conference in October 2007, Vorbeck had a seat among the podium gladiators.

It was not that the police union objected to going though old files to examine the wartime actions of BKA employees with Nazi pasts, Vorbeck told the gathering. "We are all agreed that everything must be done to prevent such things from happening again. This includes a clear picture of the past." But the nature of the conferences, and press coverage of them, were placing an "intolerable blanket of suspicion on a whole generation of BKA employees who were hired in the 1950s and 1960s," Vorbeck argued. "Many older colleagues today see their life's work trampled in the dirt. Some are even saying they'll never step foot in the BKA again."[21]

The conferences were going over the same ground that other researchers had previously examined, according to Vorbeck, and allegations of incrimination were not being fact-checked. Also, researchers should be talking not just about police officers guilty of Nazi crimes but also police officers "who paid with their lives for resisting the unjust regime." Vorbeck complained that the BKA's successes in federal law enforcement were being overlooked. Stefan Vossschmidt, who in 2007 was a department head at BKA, took exception to Vorbeck's speech. "Colleague Vorbeck," he said. "I'm very sorry. I am a member of the Police Union, and will remain a member, but you have not spoken for me. And I personally believe you have not spoken for the majority of union members." In fact, said Vossschmidt, he'd like to see more digging into the BKA's origins.[22]

That was also the overall consensus of the organizers of the conferences and of their participants. So the decision was made to commission a team of independent historians and researchers to conduct a comprehensive, methodical inquiry into the BKA's beginnings. Its tasks: to dig further into the pasts of BKA employees hired during the founding years and examine whether their backgrounds had any deleterious effects on policies and actions of the agency. The BKA budgeted 322,000 euros for the project, with Patrick Wagner leading a group of historians, Imanuel Baumann, Herbert Reinke, and Andrej Stephan. Four years later, the research team completed its task and published its findings, in the 370-page *Schatten der Vergangenheit*.

For a moment let's move on from the BKA and from tainted former Nazis who were hired for postwar government jobs to a group of war criminals who did not get away with it and were brought to justice in the twenty-first century.

On November 6, 2018, ninety-four-year-old Johann Rehbogen had to be pushed into a Münster courthouse in a wheelchair for the start of his trial. In 1942 Rehbogen was an eighteen-year-old SS guard at the Stutthof concentration camp near Danzig, which is now the Polish city of Gdańsk. More than sixty thousand people were killed at Stutthof, where Rehbogen worked for two years. And now, more than seven decades later, Rehbogen was being charged with being an accessory to the murder of hundreds of the inmates. During the trial Rehbogen said he did not know about the camp's systematic killing and he had thought disease and the camp's miserable conditions were responsible for the deaths. "I am not a Nazi. I have never been one. Even in the little time I have left, I will never be one," Rehbogen told the court in a statement read by his attorney. The case against Rehbogen did not last long. His trial was suspended after heart and kidney problems sent him into the hospital. Just a few months later, the case was dropped.

Rushing to find the last living Nazi war criminals and bring them to trial, for the past several years German prosecutors have been employing a new strategy to get around decades-old legal restrictions that hindered prosecution of camp guards if they had not been directly involved in killing. Under the new approach, prosecutors would present evidence showing a suspect had been a cog in the Nazis' murder apparatus. The new strategy was first tested against John Demjanjuk, the Ohio steelworker and Ukrainian native who went on trial in Germany in 2009 on charges of being an accessory in the murder of twenty-eight thousand Jews at the Sobibor death camp in Poland. He was convicted in 2011 and sentenced to five years in prison. He was released pending appeal and died in a German nursing home in March 2012 at age ninety-one.

German prosecutors were encouraged by their success in prosecuting Demjanjuk. They scoured Nazi-era documents in search of other perpetrators who could be brought to trial using the same approach. A series of prosecutions ensued. After Demjanjuk the next to stand trial was ninety-three-year-old Oskar Gröning.

Like with the other new prosecutions, Gröning was charged with being an accessory to murder. In his case he was brought before a court of law for having served as the bookkeeper at Auschwitz. Gröning was a bank clerk in Lower Saxony before the war. He joined the Nazi SS in 1940 and was sent to Auschwitz two years later. As the death camp's accountant, Gröning was responsible for itemizing jewelry and other belongings of Nazi victims as they arrived, counting cash that was also taken from them, and sending the money to Berlin. At his trial in Lüneberg, Gröning said he had seen horrible things at Auschwitz, such as an SS man smashing a baby's head. Gröning said he felt guilt toward the Jewish people and asked for forgiveness. The geriatric former Nazi was convicted in July 2015 of being an accessory to mass murder and sentenced to four years in prison. Like Demjanjuk and Rehbogen, Gröning never served any time behind bars. He died in a hospital in March 2018.

And so it has gone during German prosecutors' pursuit of the last living war criminals. Time after time indictments have been drawn up and nonagenarian suspects arrested, only to have justice cheated by age and infirmity. Reinhold Hanning, an SS guard at Auschwitz, was convicted in 2016 of being an accessory in the murder of 170,000 people. He died a year later at age ninety-five, before he could begin his five-year sentence. The 2016 trial of ninety-five-year-old Hubert Zafke, accused of being an accessory to at least 3,681 murders at Auschwitz, was abandoned because dementia made him unfit to stand trial.

Let's return now to the war criminals of the BKA. The contrast between their treatment and that of the frail defendants of recent years could hardly be more stunning. Although Cold War prosecutors did begin investigations of some of the BKA men, they typically went nowhere. There is an imbalance here of a tragic nature. Tragic not because of the age-induced infirmities of the former concentration guards who were put on trial or because of the decades that elapsed before they were tracked down and brought into a court of law. During each of the twenty-first-century trials, whenever an elderly defendant has been well enough to appear in court, a reckoning has occurred. Survivors have confronted their perpetrators. Detailed accounts of the crimes have been aired. Some sort of justice has been served. That did not happen with tainted BKA officials and other former Nazis who served in postwar governments. The victims of Einsatzkommando and Geheime Feldpolizei units the BKA men had served with number in the tens of thousands. We do not know the full depth of their individual guilt because they were never brought to trial. The victims or victims' families never had the opportunity to confront them in a court of law.

# 11

# The Rosenburg File

Inside a turreted nineteenth-century Bonn villa that could pass for a Grimm brothers fairy-tale castle, finely dressed postwar government lawyers walked the corridors, carrying draft legislation for the newly born Federal Republic of Germany. During the war, before it became home for the Justice Ministry, the villa—called the Rosenburg—was used as a holiday retreat for civilian employees of Hitler's Luftwaffe. The Rosenburg is perched on a forested mountain called the Venusberg. The view from the Venusberg is epic, with the Rhine River below as it flows past Bonn on its castle-studded course from the Swiss Alps to the North Sea.

With West Germany's founding in 1949 and Bonn as the provisional capital, one of the earliest orders of business was finding buildings for all of the ministries and agencies. Because of extensive damage from Allied bombing, locating suitable digs was a challenge. The Justice Ministry was initially domiciled within a former police barracks, which was not only cramped but also failed to project the dignity due such an august government institution. So, when the Rosenburg became available, Thomas Dehler, the first justice minister, grabbed it before someone else could.[1]

West Germany's legal elite peopled this turreted villa, their law degrees from the most prestigious universities in the land. With all of the legal work that needed to be done to get the Federal Republic of Germany on a solid footing, it must have been an incredibly busy place. But among the discussions that would have taken place among the ministry lawyers and administrators, there was a topic that they would speak of only in whispers, if at all: their previous jobs, in the Third Reich.

For all of its grandeur, the Rosenburg was crawling with lawyers with incriminating pasts. In the late 1950s more than half of the Justice Ministry's senior personnel were former Nazis. This was not at all unusual for government agencies at the time because having been just a nominal Nazi was no obstacle to being offered a job. In fact, it would have improved your chances. But at the Bundesministerium der Justiz (BMJ)—the Federal Justice Ministry—as at other government agencies, senior officials' failure to look deeply into job candidates' pasts opened the doors to jurists whose service for the Third Reich went far beyond having possessed a Nazi membership card.

"When Walter Strauss took up his position in September 1949 as state secretary of the BMJ, a surprising message awaited him from the staff of the British High Commission." Thus reads a passage from *Die Akte Rosenburg* (The Rosenburg File), the 590-page findings published in 2016 of the inquiry by historian Manfred Görtemaker and law professor Christoph Safferling into the Nazi taint at the Justice Ministry.

The message, from British occupation authorities, concerned a boxcar parked at the Bonn freight yard. Inside the boxcar, said the message, were personnel files that had been kept by Nazi justice authorities. The British suggested the West German Justice Ministry might find the files useful to vet job candidates.[2] Also available to officials at the Justice Ministry, and to all government leaders, were Nazi personnel files kept at the U.S.-controlled Berlin Document Center. Despite this wealth of records, little use was made of them to keep incriminated former Nazis out of the civil service. Greater efforts were made toward protecting the secrets of tainted Justice Ministry officials.

In 1957 the Justice Ministry showed how far it was willing to go to shield its people from war crimes charges. A Greek delegation had flown to Bonn on September 20, 1952. Head of the group was Dr. Andreas Toussis, general state prosecutor. Toussis came with a list bearing the names of twenty-one Germans, all accused of involvement in the deportation of Greek Jews to death camps. Included on the list was "Dr. Mertin." It was a minor typo, or maybe a slip in the transliteration. But it was clear enough who it was: Dr. Max Merten, who had been hired by the Justice Ministry earlier that year. Merten was called into a meeting with Georg Peterson, chief of the ministry's criminal law department, and asked for an explanation. Two days later, Merten informed the Justice Ministry he was resigning "in his own interest and that of his family."[3]

The Justice Ministry had known that Merten had been a top administrator for the Nazi occupation of northern Greece starting in the summer of 1942. He admitted as much in a three-page biography he had submitted before he got the Justice Ministry job. He was helped by a claim he made in his curriculum vitae: that he had saved the lives of thirteen thousand

Thessalonian Jews. Merten also presented the certificate of his denazification proceedings, which categorized him as "Exonerated." This is the kind of scenario that occurred time and again in the recruiting of government workers in the formative years of the new German democracy. It was not that those doing the hiring were naive. They were following guidelines in place across government agencies that experience had top priority, without thinking too much about whether that experience may have been gained tormenting the natives of German-occupied countries.

If Justice Ministry officials had taken a close look at those Nazi files that were parked in a boxcar at the Bonn freight yard, they may have found at least some suggestions of what Merten actually did in northern Greece as head of the occupying German army's department of "Administration and Economy." But with Merten's resignation, this was nothing ministry officials had to fret over, or so it was thought.

After the war Merten set up a law practice in Berlin. One of his clients was a German who had previously lived in Greece and who had hired Merten to try to get restitution for property he had lost there. Merten prepared to make the trip to argue for his client. He was assured by German Foreign Office authorities that he need not fear arrest in Greece; the Greek government, he was told, to promote trade with West Germany and in hopes of being paid damages for the Nazi occupation, had suspended the pursuit of German war criminals. We can only imagine Merten's shock and dismay when, after his arrival in Greece on April 26, 1957, he was arrested. He spent two years in pretrial detention before he was brought before a special military court in Athens and was convicted and sentenced to twenty-five years. The West German Justice Ministry came to Merten's rescue. A high-ranking ministry official, Ernst Kanter, was dispatched to talk the Greeks into letting Merten go.

Before Merten's arrest, Athens and Bonn had been haggling over Germans wanted for war crimes in Greece. There was some classic horse trading happening in the background. With the prospects of getting war reparations from West Germany, Greece had suspended its pursuit of war criminals. Displeased that West Germany was not fulfilling a promise to pursue fugitive perpetrators, Greek legal authorities had resumed their investigation of Germans suspected of war crimes, Greece had informed West Germany about this change. But the word never reached Merten.

During the war Merten was head of a department of the German occupiers' operations in northern Greece that was involved in stripping Jews of their property and valuables before they were deported to their deaths. Between forty-five and fifty thousand Thessalonian Jews were sent to Auschwitz and Bergen-Belsen.

In Athens, Kanter held multiple meetings with Toussis, with Merten, and with a Greek attorney representing Merten. According to Safferling and Görtemaker, Kanter expressed the astonishing viewpoint that Merten's wartime position in Nazi-occupied northern Greece "had nothing to do with executions, deportations or the persecution of Jews."[4]

Kanter himself had a Nazi past. Up until the war's end, he was the top judge with German forces in Nazi-occupied Denmark and was responsible for the death sentences of more than one hundred Danish resistance fighters.[5] At the West German Justice Ministry, one of Kanter's responsibilities was reviewing accusations of Nazi complicity against former Nazi judges—a classic postwar example of a tainted bureaucrat being put in a position of covering for other tainted bureaucrats.

Details of Kanter's talks with Toussis are to this day unclear. But the emissary from the West German Justice Ministry was successful. Eight months after Mertens's conviction, he was transferred into the custody of the West Germans. After a few days of jail back in his homeland, Merten was released.

Safferling and Görtemaker point out the oddness of the Justice Ministry's rescue of Merten. "Dispatching a [Justice Ministry] department subhead to Greece to settle a case involving a staff member who had not worked for the ministry for five years is as remarkable as it is suspicious," they wrote in *Die Akte Rosenburg*.[6]

They posit two theories. The Justice Ministry may have seen intervening in Merten's case as a way into settling the overall issue of the pursuit of Germans suspected of war crimes in Greece. On the other hand, write Safferling and Görtemaker, West German officials may have worried that while in Greek custody, Merten might reveal Nazi-era secrets of colleagues in the Justice Ministry or other government offices. If that was the motive, it didn't work. This is the same Max Merten who a few years later made explosive allegations against Hans Globke.

Among the former servants of the Third Reich given second careers at the West German Justice Ministry was Franz Massfeller. Like many of his colleagues, Massfeller's assigned area of expertise at the ministry was the same as at the Nazis' Reich Ministry of Justice, in his case family law. Some of Massfeller's work as a lawyer for the Nazi regime was known, including a 1935 commentary he cowrote on one of the so-called Nuremberg laws that were intended to keep German blood "pure" by banning marriages and sexual relations with Jews. Massfeller's complicity in this racist piece of legislation did not disqualify him for a job in the postwar West German civil service: he was hired by the Justice Ministry in January 1950. Massfeller submitted a statement assuring his new bosses he was never a true supporter of the Nazi regime, along with letters from a member of Adenauer's party and from Adenauer's state secretary backing up that assertion. This was enough to satisfy the Justice Ministry, which in August 1951 promoted Massfeller to ministerial councillor and lifetime civil servant.[7]

Things were going fine for Massfeller until the Bund der Verfolgten des Nazi Regimes (Federation of Victims of the Nazi Regime) revealed that in 1942 he had been a participant in two follow-up meetings of the Wannsee conference that had decided the "Final Solution of the Jewish Question." The federation brought civil charges against Massfeller, accusing him of incitement to murder.

Justice minister Thomas Dehler had no choice but to demand that Massfeller respond to the allegations. But this became yet another instance of a former loyal servant of the Third Reich claiming he had actually tried to help Hitler's victims and his West German bosses professing to believe him. Massfeller asserted that at the Wannsee follow-up meetings, he had used "delaying tactics" to try to protect Jews. Massfeller named a contemporary witness who would back him up: Franz Schlegelberger, who had been Massfeller's superior at the Reich Justice Ministry. Schlegelberger was among the Nazi jurists tried at Nuremberg, convicted, and sentenced to lifelong imprisonment. But this hardly mattered. Leaders of the West German Justice Ministry were satisfied with Massfeller's explanation and didn't bother to dig any further.[8]

On the other side of the Iron Curtain, the Communist East German leadership and state media took great glee in embarrassing West Germany by disseminating damning Nazi documents in their possession since the fall of the Third Reich. Into the 1960s the East German Communists published incessant broadsides against judges, prosecutors, and others who had worked for the Nazis and now held high positions in West Germany. The brochures bore titles like "The Face of Terror of the Criminal Bonn State." West German officials had largely shrugged off these kinds of attacks, figuring they would be given little credibility given the source, the Communist East German regime. But now the West German news media began paying greater attention to the nasty things coming out of East Berlin, which contributed to Massfeller's downfall. After the East Germans made new accusations against Massfeller, he went into early retirement in 1964.

There were others at the Rosenburg like Massfeller who were implicated in the persecution of Jews and other crimes in the occupied territories. Their responses to revelations about their pasts were often absurd, sometimes comical. For example, Hermann Weitnauer, who during the Third Reich was involved in the administration of Nazi law in the East, asserted in 1964 that he couldn't remember participating in a Wannsee follow-up conference and other meetings concerning Jews in the eastern territories. After discovery of a February 18, 1942, Nazi document initialed by Weitnauer—one that defined how to determine who was a Jew in the eastern occupied territories—he announced in May 1965 that he was leaving the Justice Ministry to accept an appointment as a law professor at the University of Heidelberg.[9]

Despite East Germany's relentless release of Nazi-era documents, officials in the West German civil service were usually able to hold onto their jobs, with the protection of their bosses. For two decades Walter Roemer was one of the most influential officials in the West German Justice Ministry as head of the Public Law Department. Roemer had succeeded in landing this senior position despite the fact that as a Munich-based prosecutor during the Third Reich, he had signed off on the execution by guillotine not just of criminals but also of anti-Nazi political prisoners. When Roemer retired in August 1968, Justice Minister Gustav Heinemann thanked him for his service to the Federal Republic of Germany, for "taking a leading role in helping to rebuild a constitutional state."[10]

May 20, 1969, is a date that on the face of it has no historical significance. But it should be remembered as the day that thousands of Germans who were complicit in planning and carrying out the mass murder of Jews were suddenly let off the hook en masse. And the name that needs to be associated with this miscarriage of justice is Eduard Dreher, top criminal law expert at the West German Justice Ministry.

Dreher was involved in the drafting of a seemingly harmless 1968 law that contained within it, supposedly unbeknownst to all who were involved in crafting, reviewing, and passing it, what later was compared to a depth charge. And when it went off, as the result of a court ruling in the spring of 1969, it blew up prosecutions that were in the works across West Germany of former Nazis who had been involved in planning and carrying out the Holocaust. It is highly unlikely that Eduard Dreher knew Hermann Heinrich, who in the early 1940s was a member of the Nazi security police in Kraków, Poland. But they are eternally linked by that 1968 law, which in reality was a backdoor amnesty.

In March 1968 a Kiel court convicted Heinrich of being an accomplice to murder and sentenced him to six years in prison. Heinrich appealed the case to the Federal Court of Justice. On May 20, 1969, the high court issued an astonishing ruling: because of revisions to West Germany's criminal code, the statute of limitations for charges of being a wartime accomplice to murder had expired in 1960. Heinrich walked.

The justices acknowledged that Heinrich was among those who had shot and killed Jews, but what got him off scot-free was his claim that he was not motivated by prejudice, as noted in the court's ruling: "The accused knew that the victims were being killed purely out of racial prejudice. He did not share this base motive, however, but was merely obeying orders as a police officer and member of the SS, although he had come to realize that the orders were criminal."[11] Because of Heinrich's lack of a "base motive" while acting as an accomplice, the justices ruled, the maximum sentence he could face under revisions to the Criminal Code was fifteen years. The statute of limitations meant those fifteen years had already elapsed.

The consequences of the ruling were disastrous, going far beyond the case against Heinrich. The trial of Heinrich was the first planned by prosecutors for the atrocities of the Nazi agency that planned the Holocaust: the Reich Security Main Office, or RSHA. Federal prosecutors had been drawing up charges against hundreds of defendants in connection with the actions of the RSHA. Like Heinrich, they would have been charged with being accomplices to murder, but the ruling by the Federal Court of Justice meant that the statute of limitations against them had also expired. What would have been the largest series of war crimes trials in West Germany had been brought to a halt.[12]

The high court judges based their ruling on a law that had taken effect on October 1, 1968, and bore the headache-inducing name *Einführungsgesetz zum Ordnungswidrigkeitengesetz*, or, in English, the Law Accompanying Introduction of the Law on Administrative Offenses. Making life somewhat easier for those who needed to refer to it, the law is known by its German initials: EGOWiG. Without going into the complicated details, the legislation was essentially drafted for the purpose of easing penalties for small offenses, such as speeding or running a stop sign.

The section of EGOWiG that blew up all of those planned prosecutions pertained to accomplices. Under the original criminal code, accomplices could receive the same sentences as a main perpetrator. Under EGOWiG, defendants convicted of being accomplices had to be given lighter sentences: "If particular qualities, relationships, or circumstances which establish the criminal quality of the actor (particularly those of a personal nature) are lacking in the case of an accomplice to said crime, then his sentence is to be reduced and reckoned according to the rules governing an attempt at such a crime."[13]

EGOWiG says nothing about accused war criminals. But it ended up also benefiting them. Convicting a suspected war criminal was difficult because prosecutors had to show the defendant had a base motive. So perpetrators were generally accused of being accomplices instead.

Was EGOWiG designed to sabotage the war crimes' prosecutions? Like detectives in a crime series on Netflix, Christoph Safferling and Manfred Görtemaker set out to crack the case, chasing down Nazi records and interviewing aged witnesses. They started with Eduard Dreher's life story, his origins, how he got interested in the Nazis, and his career as a judge on one of the regime's Special Courts, where defendants were given the harshest of sentences for the slightest of crimes.

Dreher was born in Rockau, not far from Dresden. His father was a professor at the Dresden Art Academy. After his law studies, Eduard Dreher served as a law clerk in Dresden in 1933. Four years later, he joined the NSDAP. He was hired by the Justice Ministry of Saxony state and in 1938 was appointed state prosecutor. At his request Dreher was transferred to the Nazis' Special Court in Innsbruck, where he had visions of skiing on alpine slopes. After the collapse of the Third Reich, Dreher appeared before a denazification panel in Garmisch-Partenkirchen. He was classified as a mere "Follower," which meant he was cleared to resume his law career.

Dreher joined a law firm in Stuttgart. In 1951 he was hired by the federal Justice Ministry.

Dreher quickly proved his value to the Justice Ministry and rose to the top levels of the West German civil service. He was made head of a ministry department on criminal law and coordinator of a government committee that drafted legislation on criminal justice reforms. The justice minister, Thomas Dehler, had planned to elevate Dreher to a judgeship on the Federal Court of Justice. But that plan fell apart after the first of several revelations about Dreher's work as prosecutor on the Innsbruck Special Court.

In 1944 sixty-two-year-old Anton Rathgeber was brought before the Innsbruck Special Court for having plundered bombed-out buildings. Dreher brought charges against Rathgeber under the Third Reich's *Volksschädling* law. Roughly, under Nazi law, a *Volksschädling* was someone deemed a "human pest" or "harmful organism." It is a charge that was brought thousands of times in the Nazis' Special Courts. Dreher demanded the death sentence for Rathgeber, and it was carried out.[14]

After the West German Justice Ministry got this information from Austrian authorities, Dreher was brought before his superiors to explain himself. In his official response, written on November 6, 1959, Dreher argued that his use of the *Volksschädling* ordinance was not illegal because it was justified under Third Reich law. Dreher's immediate superior at the time was Josef Schafheutle, who himself had worked for the Nazis. Schafheutle agreed that Dreher had done nothing wrong. Dreher was let off the hook, but the whole affair torpedoed his shot at a federal judgeship.

It didn't take long for new accusations to rise to the surface. The allegation that emerged in 1962 concerned the trial by the Innsbruck Special Court of fifty-six-year-old Josef Knoflach, who had repeatedly sneaked into a farmhouse and stole bread, sugar, and bacon. Dreher argued for the death sentence for Knoflach, on grounds he had broken the Nazis' "habitual criminal" law. Once again, the Justice Ministry asked Austrian officials for whatever documents they had on the case, and Dreher was told to provide an explanation. And once again, the ministry determined that he had not done anything wrong.

Three years later, the *Frankfurter Rundschau* newspaper revealed Dreher's aggressive push for another death sentence for a trivial crime. Karoline Hauser was brought before the Innsbruck Special Court for having stolen ration cards, and she was charged with violating the Third Reich's War Economy Ordinance. Dreher insisted that she be executed for violating the *Volksschädling* law, but the judge thought this was going too far, and Hauser was given a fifteen-year prison sentence instead.[15]

After going through documents about these known incriminating cases, Safferling and Görtemaker wondered whether there might be more. They were astonished by what they found in Innsbruck: documentation of seventeen people who had gotten the death sentence because of Dreher's prosecution. "Apparently, it never occurred to anyone at the BMJ [Bundesministerium der Justiz, or Federal Justice Ministry] to look for further cases where they occurred," the pair of researchers wrote wryly in *Die Akte Rosenburg*.[16]

One of the cases concerned Maria Pircher, accused of stealing clothing from another woman's suitcase. In a trial that lasted less than two hours, Pircher was convicted of being a *Volksschädling*, a "recidivist thief," and a "dangerous habitual criminal." She was executed on February 18, 1944, in Munich. Another document uncovered by Safferling and Görtemaker showed that one of Dreher's colleagues at the West German Justice Ministry—Walter Roemer—had signed off on the death sentence when he was prosecutor at the Munich District Court. When Dreher was at the Justice Ministry, if his bosses were at all interested in what he had done on the Innsbruck Special Court, one of his fellow section chiefs—Roemer—knew about at least one of the unjust executions that had been carried out because of Dreher. But Roemer himself was already under the gun because of his own role in implementing Nazi law.

The seventeen files gave Safferling and Görtemaker important new leads. Another crucial discovery was a 1968 note written by one of Dreher's subordinates at the Justice Ministry, Hartmuth Horstkotte, about a conversation he had had with a federal judge, Rudolf Schmitt, at a conference in Nuremberg two weeks before EGOWiG took effect. Schmitt had spotted the "depth charge" lurking within the law. And he informed Horstkotte that there was a very real danger that it could result in Hermann Heinrich beating his conviction for crimes at the Kraków Ghetto. Horstkotte passed this information on to his immediate superior, who in turn informed Eduard Dreher. There was still time for the Justice Ministry to take action before EGOWiG took effect. But nothing was done.[17]

Given Dreher's powers in drafting legislation, his expertise in dealing with parliamentary committees, and the discovery of documents that had never before been reviewed, Safferling and Görtemaker came to the conclusion that Dreher had played a key role in slipping the depth charge into the EGOWiG. "Because of his position in the criminal law department of the BMJ, only Dreher ... had the means to influence the drafting of a law in such a way that the statute of limitations in the law ultimately no longer held," Safferling and Görtemaker wrote in *Die Akte Rosenburg*.[18]

With his tremendous legal acuity, it's almost impossible to believe that Dreher did not foresee the ramifications of EGOWiG for future war crimes prosecutions. He could have been driven by fear of criminal investigation for his ruthless prosecution at the Innsbruck Special Court of people who had committed minor offenses. "The allegations that were made against him because of his work at the Innsbruck Special Court not only represented a danger for him from a criminal point of view, but were also detrimental to his personal reputation and his official position," wrote Safferling and Görtemaker.

Still, it's hard to believe that it was only Judge Schmitt who had noticed the fatal flaw in EGOWiG. Before its passage, it had received extensive review from the best legal minds in the land: Justice Ministry officials, lawyers sitting on Bundestag committees, lawyer associations, and others. None of them spotted the depth charge in EGOWiG, or at least no one said so.

Dreher did not last much longer at the Justice Ministry. The political winds were changing. The Left-leaning Social Democrats and the conservative Christian Democrats joined together to form a Grand Coalition government in 1966. Elections in 1969 gave the Social Democrats the majority they needed to govern without the CDU. Civil servants with Nazi pasts were losing their clout. Eduard Dreher felt all of this, so he retired in 1969. He was never prosecuted for his misdeeds during the Third Reich and died in 1996 at age eighty-nine.

It's puzzling. Why would the West German Justice Ministry's very first chief, as well as his second-in-command, have allowed the saturation of the ministry's top positions with men tainted by their involvement in the Holocaust and other crimes, especially when those two leaders—Justice Minister Thomas Dehler and Secretary of State Walter Strauss—had lost loved ones to the Holocaust, had aided Jews, and had themselves been subjected to Nazi persecution?

Why would Dehler and Strauss both have recruited incriminated lawyers to work at the Rosenburg, and furthermore, why would they have taken steps to shield them from scrutiny? Wouldn't Dehler and Strauss have committed themselves to not rewarding the same sort of Nazi functionaries who were responsible for their own personal losses and torment during the Third Reich? These are questions that motivated Manfred Görtemaker and Christoph Safferling in their probe of the Justice Ministry's Nazi taint.

As a law student in Munich in the early 1920s, Thomas Dehler was a founding member of a student association that swore allegiance to the freshly born Weimar democracy. Later on, Dehler joined a paramilitary organization that was formed to defend the Weimar constitution from the onslaughts of extremist groups such as the Nazis. The danger Dehler exposed himself to with his pro-republic, pro-Jewish activism can hardly be overstated. Munich was the birthplace of the Nazi movement, and the city was crawling with young Nazis itching for a fight. Worked up by the speeches by Hitler, they attacked and threatened leftists and Jews at a quickening pace. Two days after Hitler's failed putsch in November 1923, the anti-Nazi *Münchener Post* reported that at least thirty-four attacks had been carried out by the National Socialists in Munich so far that year, not including Hitler's failed coup a couple days earlier. The newspaper said the number was just a sampling of Nazi violence throughout Bavaria during the first eleven months of 1923.

It's mere happenstance but still intriguing: Thomas Dehler passed his final law exams on November 9, 1923, the same day Hitler's revolt was put down by Bavarian state troopers.[19] Dehler then joined a Munich law firm. He married Irma Frank, whom he had been introduced to by mutual friends in liberal student circles. Irma Frank and Dehler's boss at the law firm, Siegfried Adler, were both Jewish. The Dehlers moved to Bamberg, his hometown, and he was offered a partnership in the law firm run by Josef Werner, who was also chairman of the local Jewish community. Dehler and his wife were prominent members of Bamberg society, including in Jewish circles. Dehler was deeply involved with the Deutsche Demokratische Partei (German Democratic Party).

After Hitler's ascension to power in January 1933, Dehler made his mark by representing clients who were being brought before the courts for political and racist reasons. Many of his clients were Jews, and the Nazis took note of this. Their virulently anti-Semitic newspaper, *Der Sturmer*, described Dehler as "an inferior character" and a "true comrade of the Jews."

Dehler's prominence in Bamberg society seems to have built a wall of protection around him.[20] He was even respected by Nazi prosecutors and judges whom he faced in court. But the so-called Nuremberg Race Laws increased the threat level against Dehler and his family. Under those laws Dehler's wife was considered a "full Jew" and their daughter a *Mischling*, or offspring of an "Aryan" and a Jew. The marriage between Thomas and Irma Dehler was permitted as a "privileged mixed (race) marriage." Still, in July 1938 Thomas and Irma Dehler were called before a judge, who ordered them to fill out questionnaires documenting their racial origins.

The Jews of Bamberg, and the Dehlers, were not spared the torment, terror, and violence of Kristallnacht, the nationwide assaults on Jews carried out November 9–10, 1938. Bamberg's synagogue burned that night, like other synagogues across Germany. A total of eighty-one Bamberg Jews were hauled off to the Dachau concentration camp. The Dehler house was searched. Thomas Dehler was arrested by the Gestapo, and during what he called an "agonizing interrogation," he was told to divorce his "Jewish wife" if he wanted to avoid being sent to Dachau.[21]

As incongruous as it may seem, the champion who stepped in to protect Dehler and his family was a local Nazi of high ranking, Friedrich Kuhn. Kuhn had taken part in Hitler's failed 1923 putsch and even received the coveted "Blood Order" medal awarded to veterans of the Nazi coup attempt. Kuhn was also a local attorney, but more importantly, he was a friend of Dehler from their student days.

Yet Dehler's connections could not keep him from military service. He was called up in 1938 and later served with a supply unit in Nazi-occupied Poland. Dehler was ultimately forced out of the Wehrmacht, "deemed unworthy of being in the military" because of his marriage to a Jewish woman, his past pro-Weimar political activism, his previous membership as a Freemason, and his defense of Jews before the courts.[22]

As the Dehlers watched Jewish friends and relatives disappear into the maw of the Holocaust, they of course worried that they, too, would be deported. They later learned that Irma Dehler's father had perished at Theresienstadt, Irma's sister had gone missing, and two cousins had died in Poland. As this was happening, Dehler was able to conceal from the

Gestapo that in the 1930s he and a group of friends would hold secret meetings to talk about their hatred of the Nazi regime. It was all talk, no action. The small group never became as serious about overtly opposing the Nazis as resistance groups that pursued plans to assassinate Hitler. According to researchers Görtemaker and Safferling, Dehler expressed regret about not having done more in a letter to another member of their circle written in January 1950: "At that time we should have fought with more hate and therefore with more passion and with more commitment to act."

In November 1944 Thomas Dehler was dragooned into forced labor with the Todt Organization. After about a month, he was able to return to Bamberg with the help of a doctor, who certified that his lifelong asthma made it impossible for him to perform hard labor. The Dehlers were spared any more uncertainty about their fates when American troops entered Bamberg on April 13, 1945.

After the war Thomas Dehler was able to quickly jump-start his career. Because of his legal expertise, the American occupiers asked him and a colleague to draw up ideas for reconstructing the justice system in their zone, according to Safferling and Görtemaker. Dehler's background helped get him appointed first as general prosecutor on the Bamberg Superior District Court and later, in June 1947, as the court's president. And then Dehler did something that on the face of it makes little sense. As personnel officer for the Bamberg Superior District Court, Dehler chose a Nazi prosecutor he had faced in court, Willi Geiger. By any definition of a mere "nominal Nazi," Geiger, who had joined the Sturmabteilung in 1933, would not fit it. Görtemaker and Safferling describe Geiger in *Die Akte Rosenburg*: "Geiger had been state prosecutor at the Bamberg Special Court during the Nazi era and had thus directly served the legal and political ideology of the Nazi regime. So he had a classic National Socialist career, was heavily incriminated, politically discredited and thus not suitable for the constitutional judiciary of democracy in the post-war period."[23]

Nonetheless, Thomas Dehler saw something not redemptive about Willi Geiger but useful. Dehler was focused on turning the Bamberg Superior District Court—which had jurisdiction over a wide swathe of Bavaria—into a competent, efficient judicial system. For Dehler, Geiger's legal and administrative skills outweighed his service for the Nazis, which included successfully arguing for several death sentences in the Bamberg Special Court.[24]

Like Dehler, Walter Strauss, the long-serving state secretary at the Justice Ministry, had faced persecution during the Third Reich and had to constantly worry for his safety and that of his family. As a nineteen-year-old in Berlin, Strauss was a messenger in a Prussian military unit that bloodily put down the revolt by the socialist Spartacus movement in 1919. His participation in the suppression of the Spartacists may have years later helped shield him from persecution and even death because of his Jewish origins. His conversion to Protestantism, his ability to cultivate friends and supporters within the Nazi bureaucracy and within the local police force, plus an incredible amount of luck also helped him escape the fate of six million murdered European Jews, who included his parents.

Strauss studied law at Freiburg, Heidelberg, and Munich universities and served as a law clerk with the Berlin public prosecutor's office. From May 1928 until April 1933, Strauss worked as a court assistant for the Reich Ministry of Economics. But it was a temporary appointment, and when it expired on April 30, 1933, three months after Hitler came to power, the Reich Justice Ministry said he was being forced into retirement, without a pension.

Strauss was able to eke out a living as an assistant at a law firm and as a legal consultant. It is unclear whether his Jewish origins had anything to do with the next turn in his life. On September 1, 1938, Strauss was hired by the travel agency Atlantic-Express. According to Görtemaker and Safferling, Strauss was made head of an Atlantic-Express department that booked berths for Jews fleeing Nazi Germany, work that he did for four years.

Strauss obviously had a guardian in the Nazi bureaucracy. Görtemaker and Safferling assume it had to have been Hans Globke. It is known that Strauss held a special permit from the Reich Interior Ministry for his job with Atlantic-Express. That permit more than likely came from Globke, because of his duties at the Interior Ministry on emigration, immigration, and racial matters.[25] This may well explain Strauss's unwavering loyalty toward Globke during the postwar era. While the permit allowed Strauss to arrange for Jews to leave Germany by ship, it may also have kept him safe from harm. Strauss had other protectors within the Nazi apparatus. They included cops in Wannsee—where Strauss lived—who would inform him about people in town who came to them to denounce Strauss. Strauss was even able to evade arrest by the Gestapo in 1940.[26] His parents—Hermann and Elsa Strauss—were not as lucky. In 1943 they were dragged off to Theresienstadt, where his father died of a heart attack a year later. His mother survived the camp, but a few weeks after Nazi Germany's defeat, she succumbed to an infection that had developed while she was at Theresienstadt.

In 1942, with the Holocaust under way, Strauss had to cease his activities as a ticket-booking agent to help Jews emigrate. He spent the last three years of the war employed at a Wannsee workshop that repaired military equipment, until Soviet troops rolled in on May 2, 1945.

As with Dehler, with all that Strauss went through under the Nazis, it is difficult to comprehend why he would help former Nazis launch postwar government careers. But he did. The research by Safferling and Görtemaker shows that during Strauss's long tenure as the No. 2 official at the West German Justice Ministry, he was personally involved in bringing incriminated former Nazis on board and fending off allegations against them.

Strauss and his wife moved west to Hesse state in 1946. Even before West Germany's founding, its states had already elected their own parliaments and had begun governing themselves, under the supervision of the Allies. Strauss was hired as state secretary for Hesse by Karl Geiler, the state's governor. In 1947 Strauss was named as a deputy director in the administration of Bizonia and later became head of Bizonia's legal department. When Strauss selected staff members for the legal department, he turned to bureaucrats he had known over the years.

With the attempted appointment of Rudolf Harmening as his deputy, Strauss displayed either a callous indifference to the incriminated backgrounds of postwar civil servants or a desire to just overlook German civil servants' complicity in supporting the Nazi regime.[27] Harmening was a member of the SS from 1939 until the Nazis' defeat in 1945, and toward the end of the war, he was on the staff of the SS Race and Settlement Main Office, which was involved in enforcing racist policies in the Nazi-occupied eastern territories. The appointment of Harmening as Strauss's deputy was strenuously objected to by Adolf Arndt, a Social Democrat who was chairman of Bizonia committees dealing with legal and civil service matters.

Strauss came to Harmening's defense, asserting that one could "of course have a different opinion about the expediency and correctness of using Dr. Harmening as deputy head of the authority" but that Arndt was being unfair in his personal attacks on Harmening. Strauss ultimately backed off, and the deputy job went to someone else.

Strauss and Dehler were among the seventy delegates chosen to represent their states in the Parliamentary Council, which was created to draft a constitution for a new democracy in western Germany. When the Federal Republic of Germany was officially founded in 1949 and Adenauer was elected chancellor, he chose Dehler to be justice minister, and Strauss was appointed state secretary.

Dehler and Strauss both recruited lawyers and bureaucrats who had worked for the Third Reich, always placing the technical efficiency of job candidates above their Nazi pasts. In the course of their research, Görtemaker and Safferling picked up on some specious, nearly surrealistic reasoning that must have made it easy for even seriously incriminated former civil servants of the Third Reich to get hired by the West German Justice Ministry.

In an October 1947 speech to Bizonia administrative personnel, Strauss said that each employee, "regardless of his political activity as a citizen," must "in his capacity as a civil servant keep to the good traditions of Prussian officialdom" and "use himself exclusively for the office." This suggests that in Strauss's view, civil servants of the Third Reich were apolitical. Görtemaker and Safferling questioned how Strauss could possibly believe this after twelve years of despotic rule in which civil servants implemented Nazi policies. "Could he simply overlook the years of Nazi dictatorship in which those elites, whose reinstatement was now being discussed, played a central role?" the researchers wrote.[28]

Strauss's view—and it was one that was held across the top levels of government in the formative years of the Federal Republic of Germany—provided justification for the hiring of Third Reich civil servants because, after all, they were not really Nazis but had just been carrying out their professional duties.

The idea that civil servants of the Third Reich were nonpolitical is one tributary of a broad river of denial and defensive delusion that coursed through West German society. It is akin to self-exculpatory claims that were made that members of the Wehrmacht did not commit war crimes, that German diplomats were a bastion of anti-Hitler resistance, and that police officers were automatically given SS ranks, without their permission. These were all legends that made it possible for many West German civil servants to distance themselves from the Third Reich and its crimes, to help them put bad memories into a closet where, hopefully, they would remain forever.

From April 2012 to March 2017, the German Justice Ministry organized nine conferences featuring lectures and panel discussions to discuss the ministry's employment of incriminated former Nazis. It was an approach similar to that of the BKA. Görtemaker and Safferling were at the conferences to explain the goals and findings of their research. The conferences produced some fascinating displays of soul-searching among the participants.

Some of the venues for these symposia were chosen for their historical significance. They included the Wannsee villa where Nazi officials plotted the Holocaust; a Berlin court where Roland Freisler, president of the Nazis' infamous People's Court, issued rulings that doomed real and perceived enemies of Hitler; and the Nuremberg court where major Nazi war criminals went on trial before an international military tribunal. In 2014 the Justice Ministry took this show of self-examination to New York City, where Görtemaker and Safferling presented their project to the Leo Baeck Institute.[29]

At the first conference, held on April 26, 2012, at the former People's Court in Berlin, among the featured speakers was Klaus Kinkel, a charismatic Swabian whose three decades of government service included the titles of vice chancellor, foreign minister, justice minister, secretary of state at the Justice Ministry, and chief of the Federal Intelligence Service. In his address Kinkel admitted that he had long been bothered by the fact that judges and prosecutors who had committed unjust acts during the Third Reich were able to resume their careers in the new West German state. "It always concerned me that of the dreadful judges from that time, not a single one was prosecuted," Kinkel said.[30]

During Kinkel's six years as foreign minister, ten years at the Justice Ministry, and three years as head of the Federal Intelligence Service, he never initiated any quest like the one undertaken by Görtemaker and Safferling and the other teams looking into government hiring practices during the Adenauer era. As the audience listened, Kinkel expressed regret that he had never commissioned such a study and pondered why.

After Joschka Fischer commissioned the Foreign Office inquiry, Kinkel said, "I actually asked myself why, in God's name, didn't I work harder in this area?" He mused about the possible reasons. For one thing, said Kinkel, he did not know of any incriminated civil servants during his leadership at the Foreign Office and Justice Ministry. For another, said Kinkel,

"If I remember correctly, I saw no purpose in once again digging into this history." Kinkel quickly added, "This was wrong."[31]

Left unsaid by Kinkel was the fact that there was zero chance that his boss during Kinkel's years in leadership—Chancellor Helmut Kohl—would have tolerated one of his ministers stirring up trouble by unmasking incriminated former Nazis in government. Like the fellow Christian Democrat whom he considered his political godfather, Konrad Adenauer, Kohl was not above pandering to far-right-wing voters. It was Kohl who in a 1985 visit to mark the fortieth anniversary of the Nazis' defeat infamously took U.S. president Ronald Reagan to a war cemetery whose fallen included members of the Waffen-SS. During Kohl's twelve years as chancellor—first of West Germany and then of reunited Germany—he frequently faced allegations of being too soft on the Far Right. Outbursts of neo-Nazi violence after Germany's 1990 reunification also triggered accusations of pandering to the Far Right. As asylum shelters burned, Kohl hesitated to take action while at the same time pushing for measures that would make it more difficult for refugees to enter Germany. Given all that, it would have been totally out of character for Kohl to sanction hunting for Nazis lurking within the civil service.

Nonetheless, Kinkel's remorse over not launching some kind of inquiry into tainted civil servants seemed to be heartfelt. Toward the end of his address, Kinkel told a personal story about his first year at the Justice Ministry, 1982, when he was appointed state secretary. Kinkel recalled a conversation with a colleague about the Nazi past and mentioned a local magistrate in Hechingen, the Swabian town where Kinkel grew up. The magistrate, Paul Reimers, had lived two houses away from the Kinkel family's home, and Kinkel knew him.

The Justice Ministry colleague asked Kinkel to wait while he looked through some documents, "then told me something that I didn't know." As it turned out, the magistrate next door had been an assistant judge under Freisler at the People's Court and had handed down nearly one hundred unjustified death sentences. "He was allowed back [into the judiciary]!" Kinkel said. "Horrible! Horrible!"

Justice did finally catch up with Reimers, in a fashion. The Berlin public prosecutor's office opened an investigation into Reimers in 1979. After a five-year investigation, Reimers was indicted for ninety-seven People's Court death sentences. The eighty-two-year-old was able to avoid trial by having a doctor attest that he was incapacitated. Reimers hanged himself in 1984.

During the Justice Ministry's traveling symposia on the Rosenburg project, a number of other political veterans spoke about the decades-long failure to come to terms with Nazi-tainted civil servants. The seventh conference was held in Bonn on November 30, 2016, shortly after the findings of Görtemaker and Safferling's research team were published in *Die Akte Rosenburg*.

At that time Hans-Jochen Vogel, a leftist warhorse of politics, was the oldest former justice minister of the Federal Republic of Germany. He held the position from 1974 to 1982. At age ninety Vogel was unable to personally attend the Bonn conference on the Rosenburg project, but he did appear by video. Like Kinkel, Vogel expressed regret that he had never thought to launch an inquiry into Third Reich veterans at the Justice Ministry, some of whom would have still been there during Vogel's tenure as minister.

Vogel recalled that during a commemoration in 1977, he spoke of justice officials' complicity in the crimes of the Third Reich and the justice system's failure to support the fragile Weimar democracy that preceded Nazi rule. He recalled a plaque on the Justice Ministry building in Bonn that read: "Justice exalts a people. In memory of all who have fallen victim to tyranny in the service of justice—as a warning to us."

Nonetheless, Vogel said, "I did not address the problems that we are discussing today, namely the mistakes made by the Federal Ministry of Justice after 1949 in dealing with its own past." He questioned his earlier inaction, saying: "Today I can no longer explain in detail why I behaved like this. . . . It probably had to do with the spirit of the times." Over the years Vogel wondered what he might have done had he been a civil servant during the Third Reich. "Are you certain that you would have resisted and put yourself in danger?" he would ask himself.

During his long career as a civil servant and member of the Social Democratic Party, Vogel did in fact repeatedly call on Germans to confront the Nazi past and was always a champion of human rights, minorities, and the downtrodden. In 1993 he cofounded Gegen Vergessen—Für Demokratie (Against Forgetting—For Democracy), which promotes democracy and tolerance and crusades against extremism. Still, said Vogel, "nothing changes the fact that I was a small part of the silence" that for decades covered up for tainted Nazis in the civil service, something he regretted. Vogel died four years after his video appearance at the Rosenburg symposium in Bonn.

What does it mean to be a Nazi "perpetrator"? And what standards should be used to judge the degree of someone's culpability? To non-Germans these may seem like unnecessary questions. Aren't there obvious distinctions between "bad guys" and "good guys"? Discussions at the Justice Department's conferences displayed a historical thicket that makes it difficult to come up with solid answers. But it is a thicket that had become ever harder to penetrate by German officials' decades-long reluctance to examine the matter, as witnesses died and documents were shredded because they were seen as unnecessary to hold onto.

There is a word that is commonly used in Germany to indicate someone with a Nazi past. That word is *Belastung*. It is a frustratingly vague term, difficult to corral. It literally means "burden," as in being "burdened" by a Nazi past. A less literal translation is "taint," or "incrimination." Someone who had belonged to the Nazi Party is considered at least nominally *belastet*, or "incriminated." But that is not to say they are guilty of anything. After all, Oskar Schindler was among the eight million Germans who held party membership cards. And it was not just Nazi Party members who were involved in Third Reich atrocities. In their research the scholars who studied government agencies' postwar hiring repeatedly stressed that their work was not about "counting Nazis." There was a need to go far deeper than that. Much more important were the actions of Third Reich functionaries, at whatever level of power they worked. But getting a solid grasp on the Third Reich actions of someone can be a challenge to historians, not to mention understanding, and judging, a perpetrator's motives.

It is impossible to know how many former Third Reich employees who applied for government jobs in the new West German state lied about what they did during the Third Reich or avoided specifics by saying vague things like they had served during the war. But German documents show that such deception happened with a great deal of regularity. Even if a West German government agency bothered to look more closely than usual at an employee's Nazi past, rarely was that person disciplined for hiding dark secrets.

At Safferling and Görtemaker's presentation of the Rosenburg project to the Leo Baeck Institute in New York, Safferling said that while looking at old personnel records, he was "deeply shocked by the enormity" of the Nazi stain within the postwar Justice Ministry and by the discovery of networks of incriminated officials who helped cover for one another. "On the other hand," he explained, "because I'm looking through these biographies, I'm on the edge of understanding these people. Because they all have their individual stories, and there's never a black and white. There are so many different shades of gray. This makes it very, very hard for us researchers."[32]

How do we in the twenty-first century judge the thousands of former loyal servants of the Third Reich who pitched in with the building of a successful democracy? Does constructive postwar service make amends for deeds committed under the Nazi regime?

FIG. 10. West German chancellor Konrad Adenauer, *left*, and his state secretary, Hans Globke, in Rome in 1963. Photo by picture-alliance/dpa/AP Images.

FIG. 11. Fritz Bauer, the West German prosecutor who helped Israeli intelligence agents track down Adolf Eichmann in Argentina and played an essential role in the 1963–65 Auschwitz Trials in Frankfurt, n.d. Photo by Manfred Rehm/picture-alliance/dpa/AP Images.

FIG. 12. Nazi war criminal Adolf Eichmann at his trial in Jerusalem in April 1961 on charges of having organized the murder of millions of Jews during World War II. AP Images.

FIG. 13. Richard Gehlen, West Germany's foreign intelligence chief, leaving a Munich cemetery in 1972 after the burial of a top World War II officer. AP Images / Dieter Endlicher.

**FIG. 14.** Walter Rauff, a top Nazi war criminal, after his 1945 arrest by American troops in Milan, Italy. Rauff escaped custody and fled with his family to Chile. Documents released by the German government in 2011 show that Rauff secretly worked for West Germany's Federal Intelligence Service in South America for four years. AP Images.

**FIG. 15.** The Villa Rosenburg in Bonn, home of the West German Justice Ministry from 1950 to 1973. Courtesy Gerd J. Nettersheim.

# 12

# A Burial in Chile

On a spring day in 1984, a brown coffin with golden handles was borne from a home in Santiago, Chile, and put into a hearse. The coffin was taken by motorcade to a Lutheran church. Police were there to check the identifications of mourners, while news photographers snapped photos. After the funeral service, four pallbearers loaded the coffin back into the hearse. At the cemetery relatives of the deceased and others solemnly stood over the freshly dug grave. The coffin was lowered by rope into the ground as a priest, speaking German, intoned a prayer.

At one end of the grave stood three elderly men. One of them, wearing a leather trench coat, lifted his arm into the oh-so-familiar salute and uttered: "Heil Hitler, Heil Rauff." His two companions followed his lead, giving the Nazi salute in honor of the fugitive war criminal, inventor of the mobile gas chamber, Walter Rauff.

Twenty-seven years later, Germany's foreign intelligence service did something completely out of character. It released documents—files that it had long kept hidden from the public—showing that the Nazi war criminal buried in Chilean soil had worked as an undercover agent for the German agency for four years. The September 23, 2011, release by the Bundesnachrichtendienst of its files on Rauff marked the start of the spy agency's public admission that for decades it had provided refuge and employment to Nazi perpetrators. The same year a team of historians was commissioned by the BND to dig into thousands of documents that had been declassified by the espionage service. This about-face by the BND was stunning. Even as other German agencies were finally opening up about the incriminated former Nazis who had worked for them, the BND had dragged its feet. Plans in 2006 to have a historian write a history of the BND unraveled because of restricted access to files.

Ultimately, there were two factors that gave the BND no other choice. The first was the CIA's declassification of files on Nazi war criminals. Those documents contain not just the names and identities of incriminated former Nazis who had worked for the Americans but also scores who had been hired by the West German government. With the dump of classified American files, many of the Nazi cats were already out of the bag. Additionally, as the number of German agencies coming clean about the tainted people who had been in their ranks—including the Bundeskriminalamt—grew, the BND could hardly hold out. Since the researchers began their work, their output has been prodigious. Within the course of a dozen years, the teams—called the Unabhängige Historikerkommission, or Commission of Independent Historians, also known as the UHK—published more than a dozen volumes describing the findings of their research. Before we examine those findings, it's useful to better understand the case of Walter Rauff, a suitable poster boy from the BND's roster of mass murderers, anti-Semites, arms dealers, black marketeers, and other assorted sleazebags.

Rauff was born on June 19, 1906, the son of a bank manager. He served in the German navy from 1924 to 1937 and, like his future SS subordinate Theo Saevecke, traveled the world. Rauff was given command of a minesweeper boat but was forced out of the navy over an adultery scandal, according to Martin Cüppers, a historian who published a book about Rauff in 2013. Rauff's hopes for a military career looked washed-up, according to Cüppers. His future was rescued by a high-ranking Nazi whom Rauff had met during a maritime maneuver, Dietrich von Jagow, an *Obergruppenführer*, or lieutenant general, with the Sturmabteilung. Jagow put Rauff in contact with Reinhard Heydrich, who offered him a job at the headquarters of the Sicherheitsdienst, the intelligence agency of the SS, in Berlin.[1]

Heydrich and Rauff hit it off right away, and soon the banker's son was on the road to becoming a key operative in Hitler's plans to conquer the continent and eliminate its Jews. In his new job, Rauff drew up mobilization plans for the Sicherheitsdienst and Sicherheitspolizei in the event of war. When German troops invaded Czechoslovakia in March 1939, he was serving with an SS Einsatzgruppe that participated in the assault. Rauff then returned to Berlin. After Germany's invasion of Poland on September 1, 1939, according to Cüppers, Rauff was included in secret meetings among SS leaders on matters such as eliminating Poland's elite and sending Jews to ghettos. After the start of Operation Barbarossa—Germany's invasion of the Soviet Union—in June 1941, Rauff took on an assignment that after the war placed him among the most sought-after Nazi fugitives.

As the Wehrmacht battled its way through Ukraine and the Baltics, SS Einsatzgruppe task forces cleaning up behind the regular troops went on murder sprees, rounding up Jews, forcing them to stand at open graves, and executing them. Reports made their way to Heydrich that not everyone in the Einsatzgruppen was psychologically able to handle these face-to-face mass murders. It created stress among some troops, potentially endangering morale. Heydrich turned to Rauff, who came up with a solution.[2]

Rauff worked with a Berlin chassis maker to convert heavy trucks into mobile gas chambers. The trucks resembled large moving vans. Victims—up to sixty at a time—were crammed into the airtight chamber on the back of the vehicle and driven to a burial site. When the van arrived at its destination, its human contents were dead of carbon monoxide, piped into the killing chamber by hoses from the vehicle's exhaust.

Rauff arranged a test of a prototype *Gaswagen*, as the vehicle was called, at the Sachsenhausen concentration camp north of Berlin in November 1941. SS officers and civilian engineers were on hand as thirty Soviet prisoners of war were shoved naked into the back of the prototype, according to Cüppers. The doors banged shut, and the vehicle headed toward the camp crematorium. There were desperate shouts as the victims understood what was happening to them. When the vehicle arrived at the crematorium, there was a brief waiting period before the doors were opened. The test run was a success. They were all dead. At least sixty of these mobile killing machines were ultimately produced and deployed with Heydrich's Einsatzgruppen. They murdered nearly 100,000 Jews.

Rauff's cold-blooded efficiency was rewarded with a new assignment: command of an SS task force whose mission would be the murder of Jews living in Palestine. Orders issued by SS commander Heinrich Himmler to Field Marshal Erwin Rommel's forces in Egypt gave Rauff carte blanche in dealing with local civilians. "It [Rauff's commando unit] is authorized to take executive measures toward the civilian population within the scope of its mandate and on its own responsibility."[3]

Martin Cüppers points out this language is virtually identical to language contained in orders concerning the use of Einsatzgruppen on the eastern front. In other words, Rauff's Einsatzkommando Egypt was being sent to export the annihilation of Jews that had been occurring in Poland and the USSR to the Middle East.

Use of Rauff's mobile task force for this mission was contingent upon Rommel's drive to take Cairo. But this plan fell apart with Rommel's defeat in October 1942 at El-Alamein (there are also indications that Rommel refused to go along with the plan to wipe out Jews in Egypt and Palestine).[4] As Rommel's forces retreated across the desert, Rauff and his task force left Athens, where they had been waiting, and returned to Berlin. After American and British forces landed in Morocco and Algeria, Rauff's Einsatzkommando was sent to join German forces that had retreated to Tunisia. Their assignment was to recruit Arabs as collaborators and carry out sabotage against the advancing Allies. But Rauff wanted to push it further than that. He set out to enslave and kill Tunisian Jews. He started by commandeering Jewish homes in Tunis for his quarters.[5] Rauff ordered the Jewish community to provide two thousand laborers immediately to be used to strengthen German fortifications on the front lines. When barely one hundred showed up at the collection point, he had them all kneel, drew his pistol, and threatened to shoot them. He and his SS men stormed the synagogue, with Rauff shouting, "Everyone outside, pig Jews!" Rauff yelled at three Jewish leaders, "I've already killed Jews in Poland and Russia, and I'll show you what you can expect from me."[6]

Some five thousand Tunisian Jews were forced to work for the Nazis. Money, jewelry, religious objects, and other valuables were taken from them. As was foreseen for the Jews of Palestine, Rauff wanted to implement the genocide that was occurring in the USSR in Tunisia as well. His plan was a mass deportation of Jews by ship to Italy and then by train to death camps in Poland. But according to Cüppers, the Wehrmacht said the ships were needed for delivering military supplies.

American and British forces liberated Tunis on May 7. Rauff and his men had already fled to Italy, where Rauff was given command of Sicherheitspolizei and Sicherheitsdienst personnel in Milan. He set up headquarters in the Hotel Regina, from which he organized terror operations in the region encompassing Milan, Turin, and Genoa. Rauff wasted little time in going after Jews. About three hundred were arrested in November and taken to San Vittore prison in Milan. In December they were taken by train to Auschwitz. Rauff kept hunting for Jews, ordering raids on hospitals, homes for the elderly, and private homes and placing a bounty on the heads of

Jews who were in hiding. By the end of 1943, Rauff had deported more than one thousand Jewish men, women, and children.[7] He was awarded medals for his service to the Nazi cause and promoted to *Standartenführer*, the SS equivalent of colonel.

Rauff was also busy with large-scale reprisals against Italian civilians for partisan attacks on German soldiers. After a partisan disguised as a German soldier set off a bomb in a movie theater for German soldiers in Genoa on May 15, 1944, fifty-nine Italian prisoners were dragged out of Marassi prison and taken by truck to Turchino Pass, where they were executed.[8] In August, Rauff ordered the execution of fifteen prisoners on Milan's Piazzale Loreto square.

The war ended for Rauff and his men on April 30, 1945, as Milan fell to Italian partisans. American troops entered the city, and Rauff and his men barricaded themselves inside the Hotel Regina. A young first lieutenant from Cleveland, Ohio, John Davis, approached the hotel and was escorted inside by SS men and led to Rauff, who was dressed in his SS commander's uniform and seemed unready to give up. After tense negotiations, Rauff handed over his pistol to Lieutenant Davis. The mass murderer and his staff were led out of the hotel.

Rauff was uncooperative under interrogation by the Americans. "His contempt and everlasting malice towards the Allies [are] but lightly concealed," said Lieutenant Colonel Stephen Spingarn, head of the army's Counterintelligence Corps. Rauff "is considered a menace if ever set free, and failing elimination, is recommended for life-long internment," said Spingarn.[9] But Rauff never even stood trial. He escaped the POW camp in Rimini in December 1946.

The "rat lines" that helped war criminals are legendary, operated by Nazis and assisted by Roman Catholic clergy. Walter Rauff himself operated one of these rat lines—along with a Syrian intelligence officer—and ultimately used it to make his own getaway out of Italy.

The Syrian intelligence officer Captain Akram Tabarr is a figure from the immediate postwar years whose allure for former SS officers like Rauff was that he offered a trifecta of enticements: a refuge from capture, employment, and prospects for new opportunities to act out their hatred of Jews. Syria and other Arab states were dealt an embarrassing defeat by Israel in 1948. The Syrian government began preparing for future battles with Israel by strengthening its military, including hiring former Nazis.

Tabarr was sent to Rome to look for takers. The Syrian hired Rauff to use his contacts to do the recruiting. According to Martin Cüppers, within just a few months, the pair had sent dozens of military and security advisors to Syria. Among them were the fugitive former commandant of the Sobibor and then Treblinka death camps, Franz Stangl, and his Sobibor deputy, Gustav Wagner.[10] Rauff and his family joined the two mass murderers in Syria soon after their escape.

Rauff had a high profile in Syria, where he was given the task of reorganizing Syrian intelligence along the lines of the Gestapo. According to Cüppers, Rauff was also apparently bodyguard for Syrian leader Husni al-Za'im. But Rauff's VIP treatment didn't last long. After al-Za'im's military dictatorship was overthrown in August 1949 by another Syrian military officer, Rauff was forced to flee.

After spending a couple of months in Italy, the Rauff family landed in Ecuador in December 1949 aboard the passenger ship *Conte Grande*. After some initial struggles, Rauff was hired by a Mercedes-Benz dealership. As he built contacts with other Germans in exile, Rauff was able to parlay his modest start into ever-more-lucrative jobs in the import-export sector with companies representing German manufacturers.[11]

In November 1958 Rauff received a letter out of the blue from an SS comrade, Wilhelm Beisner. Rauff and Beisner went back more than a decade. During the war Beisner was on the SS team led by Rauff that would have been sent to Palestine to kill Jews. He also served on Rauff's terror squad in Tunis. Now Beisner had a tantalizing offer for Rauff. Beisner said he was in contact with the West German intelligence service—the Bundesnachrichtendienst—and asked Rauff if he would be interested in working for the agency in South America. Rauff did not take a lot of time thinking about it. He leaped at the opportunity.[12]

Rauff was hired as a BND agent in October 1958 and given the code name "Enrico Gomez," according to the agency's declassified files. Rauff's task was to develop sources for the agency in Central and South America and to report on political and economic developments in the region. The BND was especially keen on getting intelligence about Cuba, where Fidel Castro and his Communist rebels were on the cusp of toppling military dictator Fulgencio Batista.

The BND had high hopes for Rauff. A declassified document from 1960 has details on a South American intelligence-gathering tour, with Rauff using the guise of a traveling salesman. On the itinerary are stops in Chile, Ecuador, Venezuela, Peru, and Cuba, with the primary goal being gathering information on the "domestic situation in Cuba" and the "increasing Sovietization of the Castro regime." A BND memo written about two months later documents Rauff's failure to get a visa to enter Cuba from the Cuban consulate in Caracas. Subsequent BND memos express doubts about the abilities of their man in Chile. There's a growing tone of impatience in these communications. One memo requests a "precise report about the results of the trip, as well as the contacts that were made." A long memo written in August 1961 shows the BND was at the end of its tether. "There are some very good sources in Chile," it reads, but Rauff "is not among them." A subsequent memo called Rauff an "extremely unreliable man."[13]

The BND flew Rauff back to Germany twice. The second time, in 1962, was to face the music for what a BND memo called "poor performance." His monthly pay was sliced in half—from two thousand to one thousand deutsche marks. Before he was sent back to South America, Rauff was offered a "last chance" by undertaking another intelligence-gathering trip in his region. The trip never happened. The BND dropped Rauff as an agent in October 1962.

Under intense international pressure, the West German government issued a warrant for Rauff's arrest. His name had come up in the Eichmann trial, naming him as the creator of the "gas vans," and also during an investigation in Hannover. Rauff was arrested in Santiago, Chile, on December 2, 1962. Declassified BND documents show that he had been tipped off about his impending arrest and that he destroyed all documents pertaining to his work for the West German intelligence agency.

Chile's supreme court ruled that Rauff could not be extradited to Germany because of Chile's fifteen-year statute of limitations for murder. The mass murderer was released from prison on April 26, 1963. The BND gave Rauff's family thirty-two hundred deutsche marks for attorney costs.

After General Augusto Pinochet toppled Chilean president Salvador Allende in a 1973 coup d'état, rumors swirled that Rauff had been appointed as an advisor to the new military dictatorship, even that he was chief of the Dirección Nacional de Inteligencia (DINA), the Chilean intelligence service. There was speculation that the Nazi war criminal was assisting in the torture and disappearance of opponents of Pinochet's regime.

Martin Cüppers, who developed an expertise on Rauff by going through every document he could dig up, including Rauff's letters to relatives, does not believe that the German war criminal was a full-fledged member of Pinochet's terror apparatus. Cüppers points out that Rauff lived nearly two thousand miles south of the capital, in Punta Arenas, and that the former SS officer was busy as manager of a crab cannery there. It is true that Rauff personally knew Pinochet and was a fervent believer in his murderous regime. It is also true that Rauff had good friends within the Chilean military. Cüppers imagines that Rauff occasionally gave advice to his pals in the Chilean military but says there is no evidence to indicate that the relationship went beyond that.

Cüppers paints the final years of Rauff as those of a man who, while in the process of drinking and chain-smoking himself to death, never expressed remorse for his crimes, continued to voice hatred for Jews, and ranted against war crimes trials that were occurring. When he learned that the U.S. television series *Holocaust* was shown on West German TV, Rauff wrote to a relative: "Poor federal citizens [West Germans] who are forced to watch such garbage."[14]

Rauff retired from the cannery factory in June 1978. He and his Chilean girlfriend moved to Santiago, where they moved into a house next to his son's, according to Cüppers. The war criminal began writing a memoir, dreaming of turning it into a bestseller but abandoned the endeavor. In 1979 he was visited by his former SS superior and fellow war criminal Karl Wolff. The two comrades spent days reminiscing nostalgically about the Nazi regime. When Rauff turned seventy-five, in 1982, he and his son got drunk and stayed up singing "Deutschland, Deutschland Über Alles" and favorite Nazi tunes such as the "Horst Wessel Song." Rauff wrote to a nephew living in West Germany that he was "convinced the world will one day be ruled by Jews and Communism."[15]

Rauff died of lung cancer on May 14, 1984. One month later, a BND officer typed a six-page review of the spy agency's relationship to Rauff, including such matters as how much he was paid (seventy thousand marks over four years), disappointment with his performance, his destruction of documents linking him to the BND after he was alerted to his pending arrest, and the Chilean supreme court's ruling that he was protected from extradition by the statute of limitations.

In the memo the BND official restates the charges contained in the West German warrant for Rauff's arrest: "He was accused ... of involvement in the construction and deployment of the so-called mobile gas chambers and thus of having contributed to the genocide of 90,000 Jews." The writer of the memo conceded that hiring Rauff was "certainly inexpedient and lacking in political instinct." But not because of the utter depravity of Rauff's war crimes. Not because there was no justice for Rauff's victims. The tiny bit of BND regret expressed in the memo boiled down to the fact that Rauff's past history made him a potential target for blackmail by Communist intelligence services. The memo stated that now was not the time to "philosophize" over ethnical matters surrounding Rauff and the spy agency's use of him. It took the BND another twenty-seven years before it confronted this matter head-on by releasing its files on Rauff.

After the BND's revelations about Rauff, work by historians commissioned to look into the BND's hiring practices have exposed a dark, pervasive underworld of West German intelligence agents who were former Nazis, what they did during the war, how they got their jobs at the BND, and a chumminess that carried over from the Nazi years. They were like frat brothers. Some would visit each other's families at their homes, take vacations together, and exchange letters. Two former Gestapo officials who were hired by the BND—Carl Schütz and Dietmar Lermen—came up with a plan to build a house together.[16]

If Third Reich veterans in some of the more staid West German government agencies were shy about discussing what they had done for the Nazi regime, when BND employees like these men got together over a beer, discretion—and operational security—went out the window.

A favorite off-duty hangout for some BND agents in the late 1950s was a bar in Cologne. We can imagine the scene. There's a lot of backslapping and handshaking as the former Gestapo men arrive. Cigarettes are lit. Rounds of Kölsch, the regional beer, are ordered. The men regale each other with tales about their heroic service to the Third Reich. They gossip about colleagues, swap tips on getting promotions. And they coach each other on what to tell nosy prosecutors who might come around with questions about what they did during the war—discussing cover stories and coordinating alibis.

Details like these are packed into a very thick 2022 book written by one of the historians who examined BND files, Gerhard Sälter. In the book, titled *NS-Kontinuitäten im BND* (Nazi Continuities in the BND), Sälter provides a long roster of members of the Gestapo, the Sicherheitsdienst, the Sicherheitspolizei, and the Hitlerjugend who managed to get hired by the foreign intelligence operation led by Reinhard Gehlen and supervised during the early postwar years by U.S. officials. He documents their duties during the Third Reich and the operations their units participated in; he writes about many of them going underground with false names after the war and how quite a few found work with the U.S. Army's CIC intelligence agency. Sälter describes their efforts to rebuild their lives, tells of the involvement of many of them in extreme-right-wing postwar organizations that glorified Nazi ideology, and of mutual assistance that included helping Nazi comrades evade justice. According to Sälter, at least thirty-three of the BND's employees had belonged to Einsatzgruppen and Einsatzkommandos, the task forces that were responsible for the deaths of more than a million of the six million Jews killed during the Holocaust. Sälter postulates that the use of incriminated men by the American-run Gehlen Organization, and the West German-run BND that it became in 1956, can be seen as an extension of the aggressive policies pursued by the Third Reich.

According to Sälter, Gehlen viewed himself as a kind of holy warrior, protecting Western Christian culture from the godless Soviets. Sälter found a 1949 memo written by Gehlen ahead of a meeting with Chancellor Adenauer. As the Third Reich neared its demise in 1945, Gehlen wrote, he asked himself "how the struggle to preserve Christian culture could be continued from the situation expected after the war."[17]

"You can almost read right over it. But Gehlen actually wrote that the fight should be 'continued,'" Sälter wrote in his 2022 book. "By doing that, Gehlen placed his activity in a line of continuity with the war of annihilation of the East, which he ennobled as one that was waged to preserve the Christian Western world." It was a worldview that made Gehlen an attractive partner for American intelligence. Gehlen's idea was to create an intelligence service that would use experienced personnel to "carry on the Third Reich's fight against 'Bolshevism,'" according to Sälter. "Personnel continuity with National Socialism in the BND was not an accidental development, but the result of consciously cultivated ideas of continuity."[18]

A memo in the BND files of a top agency official, Kurt Kohler, said of the organization's beginnings, "We were all Nazis then, and said so openly."

Among the BND documents reviewed by Sälter was a 1983 note by Roman Hönlinger, a former Sicherheitsdienst member and Abwehr officer who worked for Gehlen from 1946 to 1976. Hönlinger said of his BND colleagues: "The employees—almost all former combatants—saw their new jobs as a continuation of the war against the SU [Soviet Union] by other means. They feared the further advance of communism and were glad that the former opponent of the war [the United States] was willing to work against communism."[19]

Also in the BND files examined by Sälter are documents pertaining to the daughter of SS leader and Holocaust architect Heinrich Himmler. The daughter, Gudrun, worked as a BND secretary from 1959 until 1963 and was assigned the cover names "Hiller" and "Sievers." "The order to hire her came from Gehlen," according to Sälter.[20] Gehlen felt sympathy for the daughter of one of the most notorious war criminals in world history, so much so that he took steps to shield her.

During the workweek Heinrich Himmler's daughter typed up reports and performed other clerical duties for the CIA's most important partner in espionage. During her free time, she did charitable work for Nazi war criminals and hung out with fascists. Gudrun belonged to an organization called Stille Hilfe (Silent Assistance), which collected money to aid "convicts of war." Gudrun Himmler was a dutiful defender of her father. In 1960 she told a reporter that the memory of her father had been "defiled by the Jews" and she was duty-bound to change that. Gudrun Himmler left the BND in 1963, just as the Federal Prosecutor's Office had begun investigating her as a "danger to the state."[21]

While Reinhard Gehlen may have indeed seen himself as a crusader to protect the Christian West from the unwashed Bolsheviks, he was at the same time a champion for irredeemable Nazis. In 1955 having certain character traits could torpedo your chances of getting hired by Gehlen's spy agency, according to an official document examined by Gerhard Sälter:

> Marital discord
> Sexual bondage
> Homosexuality

Heavy debt

A passion for gambling

Alcoholism

Drug addiction

Boastfulness

A compulsion to present oneself as an important spy.[22]

There were other hurdles to hiring as well, such as having close relatives who lived in Communist East Germany, having spent long periods of time in the "Soviet Sphere of Influence," and having done previous work for another intelligence service, unless it was okayed by leadership of the Gehlen operation. Conspicuously absent from the checklist are questions that would raise a red flag about possible participation in a war crime or the exposure of BND agents to potential blackmail by the Soviets or their East German allies.

These hiring rules—which were bent for people the Gehlen Organization really wanted to have on board—show the agency's callous indifference toward whether its employees had been involved in the implementation of murderous Nazi policies. It is an indifference that began at the agency's birth, when it was under the putative supervision of the U.S. Army.

Before joining the SS, Ebrulf Zuber was active in various "völkisch" groups in Czechoslovakia's Sudetenland region, his homeland, that pressed for annexation by Nazi Germany. After annexation in 1938, Zuber committed himself even more deeply to the Nazi cause.[23] He took the SS officer training course and became a specialist at the Germanische Leitstelle, a branch of the SS Main Office in Berlin that recruited for the Waffen-SS in Oslo, Copenhagen, The Hague, and Brussels. Beginning in late 1944 and into 1945, he was with a Waffen-SS unit fighting the Soviets, first in the Soviet Union and then in the battle for Berlin. At some point Zuber also worked at a Sicherheitsdienst office in the Bohemian city of Reichenberg. After the Nazis' defeat, Zuber was first held in captivity by the Soviets and then by the Americans, at the U.S. Army's Camp Kornwestheim near Stuttgart.

A year after the war's end, another SS officer—Hermann Wondrak—was in the process of putting together a Gehlen Organization field office in Esslingen, called Dienststelle 120 (Office 120), whose task was to gather intelligence on the Soviet bloc. Wondrak worked quickly to fill positions at Dienststelle 120. His first hire was a secretary, Erika van Brieland, who had also been his secretary at the SD office in Reichenberg. His second hire was Erhard Marschner. Marschner was followed by three more from Wondrak's SD office in Reichenberg: Wilhelm Richter, Fritz Klein, and Gerhard Undeutsch. Ebrulf Zuber was next. As of September 1948, Dienststelle 120 had grown to fifteen employees. At least eight of them had previously worked for Wondrak at Reichenberg, according to Gerhard Sälter.

The hiring of Zuber by Gehlen's spy agency was his ticket out of the Kornwestheim internment camp. This was not at all uncommon during the first couple of years after the war. Allied approval was needed to release camp prisoners, but that was no problem because they were going to be put to work as anti-Communist intelligence agents. An employee from the Gehlen Organization would drive to an internment camp and pick up a new recruit. U.S. sentries would just wave them through.

Cabals of former members of the SS, Gestapo, and Sicherheitsdienst were formed in the camps that became candidate pools for Gehlen's field offices. Some had known each other through their work for the Third Reich, while others were total strangers, but what they had in common was a desire to avoid trial. The camps served as incubators for hatching ideas to accomplish that goal. Internees consulted with one another about what to tell denazification panels to get them a classification of "Exonerated" or "Follower." They followed what was happening at Allied trials of war criminals for ideas on what seemed to work to get someone off the hook—saying you were just following orders, for example. But when it came to getting hired by the Gehlen Organization, these sorts of attempts at exculpation were hardly needed. If you were desired, Gehlen's spy service would get you out. The army's own intelligence agency, the CIC, was also a potential source of a get-out-of-internment-free card.

The initial recommendation for hiring for the Gehlen Organization had to come from someone already working for the agency. The operative making the recommendation, who himself often had an incriminating past, had to personally know the potential recruit and was responsible for vouching for the candidate's reliability. Background checks were superficial, unsystematic, and inconsistent. Neighbors, friends, and relatives might have gotten a knock on the door and been asked what they thought of the person who was being considered for a job. Police records might have been checked. However, the thrust of the paltry screening that existed was not to determine whether recruits had done something horrible during the war but whether they could turn out to be double agents, which is why there was concern about whether a potential Gehlen Organization employee had close relatives in the Communist East. As demonstrated by the unmasking of Heinz Felfe, and scandals that preceded it, the effort to keep Communist spies out of Gehlen's espionage operation was an utter failure. Using the beginnings of Dienststelle 120 as an example, Sälter shows how chain recruiting and indifference to a candidate's war record opened the doors to war criminals.

After getting a start with Dienststelle 120, Zuber was put in charge of a large field office in Augsburg that oversaw a suboffice called "Divan." Operating out of West Berlin, Divan ran agents in the Communist East. Hired to run Divan in 1957 was Wolfgang Otto, a former member of the Waffen-SS.[24]

Even as a youth, Otto was an embodiment of Nazism. In 1938 he graduated from a prep school for future Nazi leaders. That year the young man joined up with an SS Death's Head regiment that was formed to guard prisoners at the Dachau concentration camp. Years later, after he was hired by the Gehlen Organization, Otto claimed that he had not been involved in the abuse of Dachau prisoners because his duty was to guard inmates at work sites outside the camp. This is a lame argument; inmates were also killed on work detail.

Otto was with German troops that rolled into and occupied the rest of Czechoslovakia in 1939. After Germany's invasion of Poland, SS Death's Head units and the elite SS-Verfügungstruppe (Dispositional Troops) were fused with a division of the Waffen-SS, and from that merger the SS Das Reich division was formed. Otto was with the division at a time when it was murdering Jews and other civilians but insisted he was not personally involved.

The Das Reich division was deployed to France early in 1944. Over the next few months the division massacred hundreds of French civilians: 99 in Tulle, 642 in Oradour-sur-Glane, more than 60 in Argenton-sur-Creuse. Otto was a staff officer with the division during these outrages; after the war he said he had no personal involvement in them. He also denied having anything to do with the massacre of American prisoners of war in Malmedy, Belgium, on December 17, 1944, although he conceded that he knew that soldiers with the Sixth SS Panzer Army had been ordered to take no prisoners.

Fearing arrest by the Americans because of the Malmedy massacre, Otto changed his name and went underground after the war. But that does not mean he was inactive—far from it. According to Sälter, Otto led an underground network that distributed forged documents and helped SS members flee to Spain. By recruiting former members of the SS and former leaders of the Hitler Youth, Otto's ambition was to build the largest underground network of Nazis in the American occupation zone. Klaus Barbie was also a part of this network. The CIC had been keeping an eye on Otto and decided he could be useful to them. So the army's intelligence agency brought him into its fold. Otto didn't work for the CIC for long. In 1950 he joined a parade of German war vets who went to Syria to offer their services as military advisors, and in 1956, four years after his return to Germany, he was hired by the Bundesnachrichtendienst.

When the BND finally decided in the early 1960s to scrutinize the pasts of employees who had served with the SS, the Sicherheitsdienst, and the Gestapo, Otto was one of those on the investigators' radar. Otto was dismissed from the agency on April 30, 1965, but it was not atrocities against civilians in the Soviet Union or France that prompted the agency to kick him out; it was romance.

Otto had fallen in love with one of his East German agents. They planned to marry, but she didn't want to sever contact with her relatives in the Communist East. When it was discovered that the woman had traveled to East Germany without first getting permission, BND leadership decided that Otto had become a security risk, and he was dismissed.[25]

Otto and Helmut Schreiber, Otto's deputy in the BND's Divan operation, had a lot in common. They had both committed themselves to the Nazi cause as teenagers, served with SS Death's Head and Waffen-SS units, fought on the eastern front and with divisions that committed atrocities in France. And both later insisted that they were not involved in war crimes.

But Schreiber managed to last longer in the BND than his boss. Despite being wanted in France for alleged war crimes and at least two investigations against him by German prosecutors on a potential charge of being an accomplice to murder, he made it through to retirement in 1980. As pressure mounted in West Germany in the late 1950s and early 1960s to weed out members of security services who had served with the SS, the SD, and the Gestapo, Schreiber was among those who succeeded in keeping his job through obfuscation and dancing around facts.

Schreiber had quit secondary school to take a paying job as a leader with the Hitler Youth. In 1938 he had four thousand young Nazis under his wing. He signed up with the Deutschland regiment, which was involved in killing Jews after the 1939 invasion of Poland. Schreiber, who at this point had achieved the rank of *Untersturmführer*, or second lieutenant, was made leader of the regiment's Second Company. According to the historian Sälter, it is not clear what exactly Schreiber did in Poland. But the researcher found documentation showing Schreiber's regiment had stolen food, livestock, and money from Polish farmers, who included Jews: 133 tons of grain, 300 tons of potatoes, more than 5,000 cows, 69 pigs, and 68,000 zlotys [the Polish currency]. Additionally, Sälter discovered, at least two Poles had been shot dead "for resisting." "These plundered farmers were left on the edge of starvation," Sälter noted.[26]

When the Einsatzgruppe B task force began its genocidal operations in the Soviet Union in 1941, Schreiber's company was among its units. Schreiber's superiors were pleased with his performance. He was given three promotions over a two-year period, achieving the rank of *Sturmbannführer* (major) in 1944 and earning a decoration for "outstanding bravery." Schreiber took part in the Battle of the Bulge and combat at Remagen Bridge. At the war's end, Schreiber was captured by American troops but escaped. He changed his name to avoid being caught again and sent to France, where he was wanted for war crimes.

Despite all of this, Schreiber was hired by the BND in 1957. As scrutiny of the SS, Gestapo, and Sicherheitsdienst units increased over the ensuing years, Schreiber pulled out all the stops to argue his innocence. He claimed not to have known about killings committed by his own men and changed stories on the dates of his deployments. He said that far from being involved in the killing of civilians in the Soviet Union, as a staff officer he had had so little to do that he was bored with his job and sought a transfer. He changed his story in 1963, when he was being questioned by a BND panel—called "Org. 85"—that was tasked with looking into the wartime pasts of employees. Schreiber told his inquisitors that he was disgusted by the atrocities committed by Einsatzgruppe B and that he had succeeded in getting himself and most of his company transferred out of it. Despite inconsistencies like this and tenacious indications that he had been involved in war crimes, Schreiber was ultimately allowed to keep his job.[27]

Unlike Ebrulf Zuber, Wolfgang Otto, and Helmut Schreiber, Martin Jonckheere did not land a position with the BND's Divan operation through the Nazi comrades' usual recruiting chains. Jonckheere could chalk up his good fortune to postwar jobs he held at two swanky hotels in West Berlin while trying to evade arrest in his Belgian homeland for collaborating with German occupiers.[28]

Jonckheere was born in Ostend, a Belgian port city. He joined the Flemish Nationalist Party in the 1920s and in 1939 became a member of the Vlamsche National Verbond, or Flemish National League, which collaborated with the Germans. Historian Sälter found documents indicating Jonckheere had worked for a unit of the Germans' Geheime Feldpolizei (Secret Field Police) in France and the Abwehr in Belgium. During the last eight months of the war, Jonckheere was an employee at the Reichssicherheitshauptamt (RSHA), the Reich Security Main Office, in Berlin.

With the Red Army occupying Berlin, Jonckheere obtained forged documents. Using the name Martin-Jacobus de Wilde, he worked as a translator at the Hotel Savoy and head of reception at the Kempinski, according to Sälter. Jonckheere was itching to get out of Russian-occupied Berlin and back into the intelligence game. In fact, while he was working at the hotels, he took it upon himself to do some personal work as a spook. He took note of foreign hotel guests, especially those who were en route to, or from, the Soviet bloc. He observed whether they displayed any telltale signs that they might be Communist agents. The lists of names he compiled turned out to come in handy.

One of the guests at the Kempinski in the summer of 1955 was German general Ludwig Crüwell. Jonckheere must have known that Crüwell had contact with Reinhard Gehlen because the Belgian asked the general for assistance in getting hired by the BND. Crüwell said he would see what he could do. Jonckheere had been convicted by a Belgian court of collaborating with the Nazis, but this didn't matter to the Bundesnachrichtendienst, which hired him in 1956. He was granted German citizenship in 1964 and retired from the agency in 1970.

Sälter examined documents showing that in the late 1950s and early 1960s, the BND tried to recruit SS generals and senior leaders of the RSHA, the sprawling Berlin-based terror bureaucracy.[29] A BND department head,

Kurt Weiss, wanted to expand the agency's international operations. A BND subordinate, Reinhard Goertz, said he knew some SS veterans who would be perfect for the job because they all had contacts in the Middle East or North Africa. BND leadership gave Goertz the go-ahead to approach them for recruitment.

One of the prospective candidates was Heinz Jost, chief of the RSHA's foreign intelligence department from 1939 to 1942 and after that commander of Einsatzgruppe A in the Baltics and Belarus. Jost was put on trial at Nuremberg for atrocities committed by Einsatzgruppe A, convicted, and sentenced to life in prison. He was released from the Americans' Landsberg prison in 1952 after his sentence was commuted.

Jost and Goertz, a former SS *Obersturmbannführer*, or lieutenant colonel, had known each other since the late twenties, according to Sälter's research. Jost became a real estate agent after his release from Landsberg and, according to what Goertz told the BND, had intelligence contacts in the Middle East. For reasons that are unclear, Jost was not hired by the intelligence service, but the former RSHA bigwig fed Goertz the names of others who had been at the top of the Nazi leadership chain who might be interested in working for the agency.

The evolving list of possible recruits put together by Goertz and a BND colleague was a roster of top SS officers who had been involved in Hitler's plans to wipe Jews off the European map and create *Lebensraum* for Germans. One was Hans Ehlich, an author of the Nazis' masterplan to kill, enslave, and expel Poles and Eastern Slavs so their lands could be resettled by Germans. Ehlich was convicted at Nuremberg and sentenced to twenty-one months but served no time because of time already spent in custody.

In the end the recruitment efforts came to naught, Sälter found. Goertz, who within the BND had the reputation of being a showboat, was just not very good at the task given to him. But there may have been another reason as well. The 1961 arrest of Heinz Felfe and Hans Clemens on charges of spying for the Soviets brought the BND under intense scrutiny. There was worry that there could be even more Soviet agents within the BND and that secrets had fallen into the hands of the enemy. Plus, the American partner's trust in Gehlen was at stake. It was not the best time to try to bring on board even more top Nazis.

Emil Augsburg, a former SS officer, was hired by Gehlen three years after war's end. In 1957, a year after the West German government assumed control of Gehlen's operation from the CIA and renamed it the Bundesnachrichtendienst, Augsburg asked to be given the status of civil service employee. Now that the Gehlen operation was the responsibility of the federal government, the Chancellor's Office was checking up on the backgrounds of BND employees—or at least going through the motions.[30]

To back up Augsburg's 1957 request that he be elevated to civil service status, he submitted an autobiography. He wrote down the fact that he had been a member of the Nazi Party and the SS, provided his SS rank, and said he had worked for the Wannsee Institute, a secret SS think tank. He omitted damning details—such as his deployments to Poland with the Sicherheitsdienst in 1939 and with Einsatzgruppe B in the USSR.

The Chancellor's Office followed up with more questions, such as what was the purpose of the Wannsee Institute, under what circumstances did Augsburg attain the SS rank of *Sturmbannführer*, and how was he able to rise so quickly within the SS? Files reviewed by historian Sälter showed that the BND's response to the Chancellor's Office amounted to a whitewash of Augsburg's Nazi career.

During three deployments to Poland, the BND said, Augsburg had been involved in trying to preserve Polish cultural objects, such as repairing war damage to Warsaw University and to Polish libraries. The BND mentioned that Augsburg had been a member of Franz Alfred Six's Vorkommando Moskau (Moscow Advance Command), which was part of Einsatzgruppe B in the Soviet Union, but it skipped over the fact that Six's unit had committed atrocities. What the BND told the Chancellor's Office was that the Vorkommando Moskau consisted of "researchers of the East" whose work when they captured Moscow would be "in the cultural field."

As for the Wannsee Institute, where Augsburg had been a senior staff member, the BND told the Chancellor's Office that the SS think tank had researched the "East's political, cultural, and economic conditions." Left out was the Wannsee Institute's role in gathering information that was used in the planning of the Nazis' extermination policies in the USSR.

The BND's response to the Chancellor's Office for more background included a testimonial from a convicted war criminal, Franz Alfred Six. As head of Department VII at the RSHA, Six had been Augsburg's boss during the war. He had also been chief of the Vorkommando Moskau. Augsburg, Six said in the sworn statement sent to the Chancellor's Office, was the "best-versed expert on questions about the East," meaning the

A Burial in Chile

Soviet Union. Six's praise echoed pronouncements he had made in 1938, when he called Augsburg an "unconditionally reliable National Socialist" whose work was valuable to the Nazi regime.

Six was convicted at Nuremberg of war crimes and sentenced to twenty years in prison. He was released in 1952, having served a little less than eight years. The BND's inclusion of praise about Augsburg by Six might seem tone-deaf. But these were times when the German populace largely saw the Nuremberg trials as unfair, as "victor's justice." Gehlen himself had voiced similar opinions, so a glowing review of Augsburg from Six was calculated to have a positive effect.

Even though it was becoming clear that Augsburg was seriously incriminated and was lying about it, the Chancellor's Office saw no reason to dig any further. In February 1958 he was promoted to the civil service status he so desired. When Augsburg reached his tenth anniversary of service with Gehlen's spy agency at the end of that year, the BND chief congratulated Augsburg and apologized for not being able to attend the ceremony to personally present the medal. But with scrutiny intensifying of BND employees who had been deployed with units that had committed mass murder in the East, the agency ultimately dumped Augsburg in 1966.

Documents examined by Sälter show that while the Adenauer administration had some concern about the Nazi taint within the BND, it was never enough to take consequential action. After authority over Gehlen's operations was transferred from the CIA to the federal government in 1956, the Chancellor's Office was given the power to reject BND candidates whom it found objectionable. Here, finally, was an opportunity to clean up the ranks of Gehlen's operation. But it was an opportunity that was passed up—partly because of a lack of will on the part of the Adenauer administration but also because Gehlen essentially had the Chancellor's Office wrapped around his finger. Gehlen succeeded in preventing an accurate assessment of his personnel through tactical means, such as arguing that the true identities of agents had to be kept secret in the interest of the nation's security and providing employee lists that concealed the depth of the infestation within the Bundesnachrichtendienst.

Historian Sälter examined BND files and discovered that before a meeting of a special parliamentary committee in 1958, Gehlen told Hans Globke—Adenauer's chief of staff—that there was simply no way the BND could do without former Gestapo men who had been hired by the spy agency. Gehlen argued that such men were also working at other West German security services and on police forces. "For certain special tasks, officials with this [Gestapo] experience cannot by replaced by anyone else. Only they bring the necessary qualifications," he said.[31]

Ten former Gestapo men were due to be granted civil service status, and Gehlen insisted that they be promoted because they had "proven themselves over the years, and the BND cannot treat them worse than they are treated by other agencies." Gehlen did not explain, however, what it was about the experience of Gestapo officers, loyal servants of a despotic regime, that made them invaluable to the BND, an agency formed to protect a democracy. Nor did he address why the BND had not bothered to train untainted young people for positions within his spy service rather than rely on Third Reich leftovers.

The parliamentary committee met on June 11, 1958. Each of the major political parties were represented, including the opposition Social Democrats. Gehlen and his top lieutenants were also there. The committee heard the agency's arguments that Gestapo officers were needed at the BND because of their experience and that the ten who were on the timeline for being made civil servants should be granted the status. What apparently did not come up at the meeting was exactly who the ten were. "Names, functions, and previous activities of the Gestapo officials were not specifically asked at this meeting," according to historian Sälter. Gehlen got his way. The committee greenlighted civil service status for all ten.

That year the CIA attempted to draw Gehlen's attention to the possibility of Soviet intelligence using blackmail against BND agents with damning pasts to become double agents. The CIA's worry was provoked by leaks by Soviet bloc intelligence services of documents about the Nazi pasts of West German judges and other functionaries. The Chancellor's Office essentially told the Americans to mind their own business—nothing to see here, nothing to worry about.[32] The employees in question had been "carefully checked both in terms of their political past and in terms of security concerns," State Secretary Reinhold Mercker advised Gehlen to tell the CIA, according to Sälter. It was not the only time the CIA voiced similar concerns.

The Chancellor's Office became more involved in the BND's personnel matters but was easily steered by Gehlen's determination to protect his people by insisting they were clean, a strategy that also served to prevent potential interlopers from weakening his grip on his espionage empire. This was all thrown to the wind after Reinhard Gehlen's favorite BND case officer was unmasked as a Communist agent—by a movie ticket bought at a Berlin cinema.

When Heinz Felfe traveled to West Berlin in February 1957 for what he said was a meeting with a source who had been feeding the BND secrets about the Soviets, he was accompanied by a CIA liaison officer. The two spooks from the allied services separated on arrival—Felfe to his hotel and the CIA officer to his.[33]

The CIA's Berlin Base received a frantic cable; Gehlen was worried about Felfe's safety and was requesting round-the-clock protection for him from the CIA. Before Felfe and the CIA officer split up, he told the American that he intended to go to a movie at 6:30 p.m. When the CIA man called Felfe's hotel at 8:30 p.m., he was told Felfe was not there. When the American tried the hotel again at 4:00 a.m., Felfe had still not returned.

Felfe called the CIA officer at about eight the next morning, inviting him to breakfast. The CIA man did not pry about what Felfe had been up to since he last saw him the previous day. But Felfe told him anyway, which increased the American's suspicion. Felfe said he had gone to the 6:30 p.m. movie, got something to eat, then went to another movie at 10:30 p.m. Felfe dug two movie tickets out of his pocket. The CIA man noticed something about one of the tickets: the stub was not torn off. Felfe was lying about the second movie. What's more, Felfe did not explain where he was when the CIA officer called Felfe's hotel at 4:00 a.m. The CIA man did not challenge Felfe about the gaping holes in his story, but he did write up a report for his superiors and suggested that Felfe be investigated.

The BND and the CIA should have seen this coming. Right after the war, Felfe had worked for British intelligence, but he was fired because he lied and because he exhibited highly suspicious behavior. The CIC had collected dirt on Felfe as well. Gehlen's chief of counterintelligence, Ludwig Albert, was also suspicious of Felfe. In 1954 KGB defector Petr Deryabin told the CIA about the existence of two KGB agents in the Gehlen Organization. Their cover names were "Paul" and "Peter." As it turned out, the two were Heinz Felfe and Hans Clemens.

In 1959 a Polish intelligence defector—Michal Goleniewski—provided information that led the CIA to identify Felfe and Clemens as Soviet moles. Among a BND group that visited CIA headquarters in September 1956, reported Goleniewski, were two KGB agents. CIA investigators focused on Felfe. The Americans put a wiretap on his Munich phone, and CIA agents followed him when he made trips out of town. The BND was not immediately told about these efforts. That is how little the CIA trusted the security of its West German partners. After Goleniewski had safely been brought to the United States, Gehlen in February 1961 was told about the Americans' surveillance of his man. The CIA and the BND then worked together to monitor Felfe. By intercepting phone calls, radio transmissions, and Felfe's mail correspondence with Clemens, the agencies acquired all the proof they needed that both were KGB agents.

Felfe was summoned to a meeting at BND headquarters on the morning of November 6, 1961, according to a declassified CIA report. After his arrival, the compound's gates were locked and its telephone lines were cut. Armed police entered the office of the senior BND official whom Felfe was meeting and served an arrest warrant. Felfe grabbed his wallet and tried to destroy a piece of paper that was in it: "There was a small scuffle; the officers retrieved the paper, subdued Felfe." The note turned out to be more damning evidence of Felfe's treason. Hans Clemens was arrested at his BND office in Cologne nearly simultaneously—just eight minutes later than Felfe.

As the specters in ragged concentration camp clothing exhumed putrid corpses from mass graves along the eastern front, they surely knew they would be next. SS men yelled at the prisoners to hurry up. Evidence of genocide had to disappear. The disinterred bodies were layered onto a wooden pyre, soaked with gas, and incinerated. Bone fragments were crushed and mixed in with soil. The area was leveled, plowed, and replanted. Prisoners who were forced to perform this grisly task were executed.

More than two decades later, in 1968, Fritz Zietlow, former leader of an SS unit that participated in this gruesome undertaking, stood trial in a Stuttgart court. He was accused of being an accessory to murdering hundreds of Jews and Soviet slave laborers. His sentence: two and a half years in prison. It took this long to get such a mild sentence for someone accused of a heinous crime because since 1948 his employer—Gehlen's intelligence service—had not bothered to dig into his past.

The Felfe scandal had a profound effect on the BND. It prompted Gehlen to create a small investigative unit to review the Third Reich actions of employees who had served in the SS, the Sicherheitsdienst, and the Gestapo.

Interviews were conducted, and documents were sought. The purpose of this exercise, however, was not to bring war criminals to justice. It was to weed out employees who might be subjected to double agent overtures from the Soviet bloc and also remove them as potential sources for future public scandals.

Fritz Zietlow was among 157 employees who, from 1963 to 1965, were subjected to review by the small investigative unit, called "Organizational Unit 85," also known as "85" or "Org. 85." Zietlow was one of nearly 70 employees whom the BND decided had to go. Of the employees dismissed by the BND as a result of reviews by Org. 85, Zietlow was a rare case of an agency employee going on trial for war crimes.

Even into the twenty-first century, Org. 85 was a state secret. Its work was not widely known until 2010, when veteran journalist Peter Carstens wrote a blockbuster piece for the *Frankfurter Allgemeine Zeitung*. Carstens told the story of the origins of Org. 85 and how it had operated. Carstens even tracked down the lead investigator of Org. 85, Hans-Henning Crone. Carstens told of BND employees from field offices across the country arriving by train in Munich, where Crome awaited them in a covert BND office. "Those summoned were asked to bring their personal papers, ID cards, and certificates of their previous activities in places like Lublin, Minsk, or Semlin," Carstens wrote.[34]

The work of Crome's investigative unit was one of the topics tackled by historians who in 2011 began digging into the BND's dirty secrets. The lead historian on Crome, Sabrina Nowack, in 2016 published findings of her research in a book titled *Sicherheitsrisiko NS-Belastung: Personalüberprüfungen im Bundesnachrichtendienst in den 1960-er Jahren* (Security Risk Nazi Incrimination: Personnel Screening in the Federal Intelligence Service in the 1960s).

Nowack's book and Gerhard Sälter's *NS-Kontinuitäten im BND* are companion volumes. While Sälter reveals the names, biographies, and crimes of Nazi perpetrators hired by the Gehlen Organization, the chain-recruiting networks that got them their jobs, and the subterfuge used by Gehlen to protect them, Nowack discloses details about the outcomes of Crome's investigation of 157 employees who were chosen for review. It is important to note that the 157 did not represent the whole potential pool of BND employees who may have incriminated pasts. Excluded from the review were former enlisted members of the Waffen-SS and the Wehrmacht, which also committed war crimes. Nowack demonstrates how employees' potential past war crimes were of such little concern to the BND that when Crome and his team began their work, they essentially had to define what it meant to be "incriminated" and what sort of incrimination warranted dismissal from Gehlen's spy service.

When Gehlen started up the intelligence service under the supposed supervision of the U.S. Army, its founding members were largely German General Staff officers. As field offices of the Gehlen Organization recruited case officers and agents to conduct espionage against the Soviet bloc, the intelligence service increasingly became a safe refuge for men who had served with state security services responsible for atrocities: the SS and its Sicherheitsdienst intelligence unit, the Gestapo, the Geheime Feldpolizei (Secret Field Police), and the Einsatzgruppen and the smaller Einsatzkommandos.

When the Felfe scandal forced Gehlen to finally look into his employees' pasts, a decision had to be made about who would be chosen for scrutiny. The 157 selected to be on the list of what the BND called a "special circle of people" included employees who had worked full-time for the Nazi Party; leaders of the SS; members of the SS Death's Head units, of the SS Verfügungstruppe division, and of the Sicherheitsdienst; and police units like the Gestapo and the Geheime Feldpolizei. Enlisted members of the Wehrmacht and even of the Waffen-SS were excused because of the mistaken view that ordinary soldiers on the front had not committed war crimes.[35]

Although BND employees included in this special circle of people feared for their jobs and worried that their pasts would be laid bare, they had little reason for concern about their financial well-being. As historian Sabrina Nowack has shown, the BND was prepared to do virtually anything to ensure their continued loyalty and to make sure they didn't resort to selling intelligence to Communist spy agencies. Final decisions were made by a special commission created to review Crome's recommendations, and then by Gehlen, but everyone involved was in line with making sure employment separations occurred as amicably and as quietly as possible. Of the BND employees who lost their jobs as a result of Crome's internal inquiry, about two dozen had served with Einsatzgruppe units, mostly on the eastern front. Almost all of them left the spy agency with generous severance packages, but not all without a fight. That included Fritz Zietlow.

Born in the West Prussian city of Schneidemühl (now Piła, Poland) in 1902, Zietlow was an early supporter of the Nazis. He joined the party in 1925 and began working for Nazi newspapers. At one point he was an editor at Joseph Goebbels's fanatical *Der Angriff* (The Attack). He joined the SS in 1930, three years before the Nazis' came to power, and the Sicherheitsdienst in 1937.

During Zietlow's denazification procedure after the war and in his application for work with Gehlen's organization, he omitted many of the most incriminating details about his Nazi career. This fact, however, does not exonerate the BND, which for more than a decade accepted Zietlow's story at face value and ignored red flags that should have triggered deep scrutiny. In their respective research, Nowack and Sälter lift the veil from that past.

Beginning in 1943, Zietlow was deployed with Einsatzgruppe C, the SS task force that murdered 118,000 Jews in Ukraine, including 33,771 in the September 1941 massacre at Babi Yar. From 1943 to 1944, according to Nowack's research, Zietlow was leader of Sonderkommando 1005b, the SS unit that tried to destroy evidence of genocide by forcing prisoners to dig up murdered Jewish victims from mass graves and burn them on wooden pyres. Zietlow's last deployment before war's end was with a subunit of Einsatzgruppe H in Slovakia.

Research by Crome and his investigative team turned up Zietlow's Einsatzgruppe deployments and his leadership of the corpse exhumation squad. Crome recommended that Zietlow be fired, according to Sabrina Nowack, and was backed up in that decision by the BND review commission. The BND offered Zietlow five thousand deutsche marks in severance pay, contingent upon him leaving service by June 30, 1967, the soonest he could be legally separated from the BND under West German labor law.[36] The reasons given were false statements Zietlow had made to the BND and the fact that a Stuttgart prosecutor had begun a preliminary investigation against him for crimes committed by the SS body exhumation squad. Zietlow fought the decision, arguing he was protected from dismissal until September 30, 1968. Zietlow eventually agreed to leave at the end of June 1967. But he continued to fight the BND, seeking to get an extension on when his separation took effect so that he could get more money from his former employer. After a Munich labor court rejected his appeal, Zietlow took his case up a notch, to the Bavarian state labor court. The Bavarian court also ruled against him.

The Stuttgart investigation against Zietlow smashed any legal pylons he was trying to use to support his battles with the Bundesnachrichtendienst. On December 11, 1967, the Stuttgart state prosecutor's office formally charged Zietlow and three other former members of Sonderkommando 1005b with murder. Fifteen months later, Zietlow was convicted of being an accessory to murder and sentenced to two and a half years in prison. He died in 1972.

Konrad Fiebig also proved difficult to dump from the spy agency's roster of employees, and it was largely because of West German labor law. During the war Fiebig had served with the SS, the Gestapo, as judge on a Nazi "special court," and with Einsatzkommando 9, a subunit of Einsatzgruppe B, which was responsible for massacres of Jews and other civilians in Belarus and Ukraine.

According to historian Sälter, Fiebig joined the SS in 1939 and the Nazi Party a year later. After dropping out of law school, he joined the Kripo, or Criminal Police, and was assigned to the Kripo office in Breslau. Like many a German police officer, during the war Fiebig served with an Einsatzgruppe unit in the USSR. In his case it was Einsatzkommando 9, of Einsatzgruppe B. Einsatzkommando 9 killed tens of thousands of Jews while dismantling ghettos. Fiebig received at least two SS promotions for his deployments and in September 1942 was given a medal for his "service in the east." On the occasion of his last promotion, to SS *Hauptsturmführer*, Fiebig was praised for showing "special hardness" while performing his duties, according to Gerhard Sälter. At the end of the war, Fiebig was working for the Hamburg criminal police office.

Fiebig was arrested and interned in 1947 but was classified as Exonerated during his denazification proceedings. As in tens of thousands of other cases, the German officials who questioned Fiebig chose not to dig too deeply into his past. In 1948 Fiebig was recruited for the Gehlen Organization by another veteran of Einsatzkommando operations, Hans Schumacher. Fiebig made no secret that he had served with an Einsatzkommando and with the criminal police office in Breslau but claimed he had just performed normal policing duties.

By the late 1950s the BND knew about atrocities committed by Einsatzkommando 9, but Fiebig still kept his job. Fiebig was taken into custody in May 1960 as he was being investigated for murders in Belarus. Instead of firing him, the BND put him on paid leave. Fiebig was put on trial in Berlin on charges of having murdered eleven thousand Belarus Jews as a leader of Einsatzkommando 9 and judge of one of the Third Reich's special courts. He was acquitted in 1962 because of a lack of evidence.

The BND commission that was reviewing the recommendations of Crome and his investigators wanted to get rid of Fiebig but feared running afoul of Article 131. The heat on Fiebig intensified in 1966, when Munich prosecutors began their own investigation into members of Einsatzkommando 9. In the meantime Crome and his investigators felt they were able to establish ironclad proof that Fiebig had made false statements to the BND about his past. Lying to the BND was good enough reason to fire him. Instead, the BND agreed to a severance package. Nearly two decades after joining Gehlen's spy service, Fiebig left the BND in October 1966 with a 16,650 deutsche mark buyout.[37]

Paul Helmut Winker left the spy service in 1966 with 35,000 deutsche marks to begin a taxi service. Although the former Gestapo member had seen action with an Einsatzgruppe operating in occupied Poland in the 1940s and Crome's investigators said there was "reasonable suspicion" that Winker had been involved in atrocities, the BND proposed a buyout, one that included a sweetener. "He was offered a severance payment of 25,000 DM to establish a taxi service," according to Novack. "Subsequently, the sum was raised to just under 35,000 DM to absorb taxes that would be incurred."[38]

The BND was shelling out so much money for buyouts that funds set aside for appeasing managed-out employees were rapidly depleted. According to Nowack, payment of 200,000 deutsche marks was earmarked for severance packages for the fiscal year 1965, and more than three-quarters of that sum had been spent by the end of April.[39]

Knowing that the BND wanted to settle these affairs amicably and out of court, employees tried to get the best deal they could. Being transferred to a federal government job where they would get the same pay and benefits was ideal. If that couldn't happen, the BND tried to help out in other ways. One possibility was finding employment in the private sector for a dismissed employee, but this strategy appears to have been largely unsuccessful. When the BND approached a major company about hiring two of its former employees, the firm had its own security department investigate their pasts. The company discovered that one of the employees was under investigation for suspected war crimes and the other had been questioned as a witness in various criminal probes. The company passed on both.[40]

Some people are just hard to please, like Dietmar Lermen. Lermen served with the Trier Gestapo from 1935 to 1938, with Einsatzgruppe VI in Poland from 1939 to 1940, and then he returned to Trier. This service did not bother the BND as much as the fact that Lermen was an acquaintance of Heinz Felfe, the double agent who had nearly destroyed the BND's reputation. It was known that Soviet agents had made various attempts at recruiting former Gestapo men who had served in Trier. So, according to Sabrina Nowack, there was concern that Lermen could become an easy target. The BND commission reviewing Crome's recommendations chose to offer him a six thousand–deutsche mark severance package. Lermen agreed to voluntarily leave the BND, so long as the agency found him a new job. At the same time, Lermen filed a complaint with the Munich labor court, where he demanded a government job with the same pay. The BND countered with three different severance package proposals, but Lermen chose to pursue the court case.

At this point Lermen had landed a job with the unemployment office in Bergisch Gladbach, but he complained that the pay was worse "than that of a bad cleaning lady."[41] The BND tried to get Lermen a position with the federal civil defense agency, which replied that hiring someone with a past like his would be a blot on the agency. As the BND continued its search for a decent government job for Lermen, the spy agency lost the case in labor court because it was unable to prove he had been personally involved in war crimes. Lermen and the BND ultimately reached a generous settlement agreement that included payment of his legal costs.

Another former Gestapo man, Gustav Grauer, was offered eighty-three hundred deutsche marks in severance pay plus assistance in finding work.[42] From 1941 to 1942 Grauer was deployed as deputy leader of Einsatzkommando 3, a subunit of Einsatzgruppe A, the mobile murder force of assassins that operated in the occupied Baltic states. During their research, Crome's investigators found that Einsatzkommando 3 had murdered at least 66,159 people, including up to 20,000 Jewish children. Crome did not believe Grauer's assertions that he had not murdered anyone. A decisive factor in the BND's settlement offer was the near-certainty that Heinz Felfe had told the KGB about Grauer's job as a case officer. Although Grauer was called as a witness in numerous war crimes trials, he himself was never charged.

Waldemar Menge, an SS officer, served with Einsatzgruppe B, which carried out atrocities in Belarus. He told Crone's team that as a radio operator, he had had no involvement in the killing of civilians. Crone found this hard to swallow, but the BND went easy on Menge. Menge had been working in a BND field office, not the headquarters in Pullach. He was allowed to stay where he was but with conditions. He was barred from advancements in his career and limited to nonsensitive duties but continued to collect his normal pay and benefits.[43] He retired in 1979.

Something similar happened with Reinhold Macke, a former Waffen-SS officer who was involved in battles on the eastern and western fronts, including the Ardennes offensive. The BND discovered that Macke was wanted in France on war crimes charges. The agency decided to keep him but made his employment conditional. He could not, for example, step foot on French soil. The BND seems to have believed they could keep Macke's true identity from their counterparts in French intelligence.[44]

Gerhard Warzecha, who during the war had been chief of an office in France controlling Nazi police and Sicherheitsdienst operatives in the Rouen area, was also allowed to stay with the BND. Crome's team of investigators strongly suspected him of war crimes and wanted him ousted, but the BND personnel department weighed in that his war injuries and his years of service with the agency might make it impossible to fire him. The BND decided to let him keep his job. Meanwhile, Crome's investigators continued to look into his past. Like with Macke, it was discovered that Warzecha was on a French list of wanted war criminals. Crome's people pressed to have Warzecha removed, but the BND leadership decided otherwise. Warzecha retired in November 1969.[45]

Concerning another BND employee, Georg Wilimzig, who during the war served with an Einsatzkommando unit in Poland, BND boss Gehlen wrote: "Under no circumstances will he be thrown out onto the street."[46] Crome's team considered Wilimzig severely incriminated, but believed his expressions of remorse—that he had undergone an "inner transformation." The BND commission reviewing Crome's recommendation considered Wilimzig's separation from the agency appropriate only if a good job could be found for him. Gehlen himself decided the matter. Wilimzig not only remained with the BND but was promoted in 1965. He retired in 1976.

Early retirement was one of the least-messy ways for the BND to shed employees whose service was no longer desired. It could be accomplished through threats of dismissal, financial enticements, or a combination of the two—or in the case of former SS officer Walter Otten, a note written by a medical officer at the BND's behest. Crome's investigators had reason to suspect that while working at police offices in Münster and Bremen, Otten had been involved in the deportation of Jews to Minsk. They also believed that Soviet bloc intelligence services knew Otten's identity because he had been friends with Hans Clemens, Heinz Felfe's fellow KGB mole. After an Essen doctor certified that Otten was unfit to continue his duties, he retired in 1967.[47]

So what, exactly, did the BND accomplish through this exercise of weeding out—or at least sidelining—possible and known war criminals within its ranks? Or as historian Nowack puts it, was this a successful "self-cleansing"? Maybe it was a partial success. BND leadership did not have Crome's team conduct long interviews with 157 employees, cast a wide net for Nazi documents, and make recommendations on who should go and who should stay for the purpose of bringing incriminated employees to trial for their crimes. It was, essentially, an exercise in cleaning house to avert any more public scandals. The exposure of Heinz Felfe as a KGB mole rocked the BND, placing intense pressure on the spy agency to finally scrutinize those employees who might have something nasty to hide. But this was not a moral crusade to punish wrongdoers. Just the opposite. Those who lost their jobs received generous compensation and help in their search for new employment, and some incriminated employees were allowed to stay. What's more, most BND employees escaped scrutiny—and thus kept their jobs—because the investigations did not include all veterans of the Wehrmacht and the Waffen-SS. The results of the review were far from an accurate picture of the infestation of Nazi war criminals within the ranks of the most important intelligence ally of the U.S.-led NATO alliance in its Cold War confrontation with the Soviet bloc.

Nowack, however, sees something positive having come out of the work of Org. 85. "Although one cannot speak of a fundamental rethinking," Nowack admitted, there were some changes.[48] The Chancellor's Office kept a closer eye on personnel management at the BND. Former employees of the RSHA terror apparatus could not be hired without a thorough check of Nazi files to determine whether they had committed war crimes.

The BND's problem with former Nazis on its roster of employees was ultimately solved by human mortality. But even though they were gone by the 1990s, the agency continued to keep quiet about them. As humiliating as the Felfe scandal had been for the BND in the early 1960s and however disruptive the weeding out of tainted employees was for its operations, for another four decades the agency kept a lid on its essentially indiscriminate hiring of former Nazis and providing them refuge.

# 13

# A Tainted Democracy?

During a special session of the Bundestag in September 1951, Chancellor Adenauer proclaimed Germany's obligation to make amends for Nazi atrocities against Jews. This was a promise that turned out to omit a multitude of other victims of Nazi persecution: people forcibly sterilized or murdered for being deemed subhuman, Roma who were sent to their deaths at Auschwitz and other camps, slave laborers, homosexuals, German soldiers convicted by military courts and often executed for acts as unthreatening to the Third Reich as being nice to a Jew. These were injustices that stayed uncorrected for three and four decades. Also during this time, West German law enforcement officials were aggressively cracking down on some of the same political opponents—Communists and leftists—who were persecuted by the Nazis. And Adenauer's foreign intelligence chief, Reinhard Gehlen, was abusing the powers of his agency by spying on the chancellor's rivals and perceived enemies, at Adenauer's behest.

As German historians early in this century began peeling away layers of secrecy surrounding the postwar hiring practices of government agencies, as they discovered that the infestation of government offices by former Nazis with seriously compromised backgrounds was worse than had been previously imagined, at the same time many of them said that despite this blight, the republic's constitutional guardrails protected democracy from harm. But at what cost?

As a twenty-year-old German sailor in occupied France, Ludwig Baumann went with some navy pals to a movie theater, where they watched a propaganda newsreel that showed Wehrmacht victories in Russia. Projected onto the screen were scenes of thousands of captured Russians, forced to spend the night outside in the freezing cold. Baumann said to his friend and fellow seaman Kurt Oldenburg: "We don't want to commit crimes like this. We don't want to kill humans. We just want to live."[1]

Baumann was stationed in Bordeaux, serving with a unit guarding the harbor. On June 3, 1942, he and Oldenburg broke into a German armory.

They took two pistols, two magazines, and nine boxes of ammo. French friends provided them with civilian clothing and drove them in a truck to the French border. The two German seamen planned to make their way to Morocco and then to the United States. But they were captured, taken back to Bordeaux, tried by a military tribunal, and sentenced to death.

Baumann spent the next ten months in a cell, bound hand and foot, tortured for refusing to disclose the identities of his French helpers. He watched the execution of other prisoners through a window, and every day he wondered whether he was next. Baumann was granted a reprieve from execution, his sentence commuted to twelve years' imprisonment. He was never told why. But his ordeal was to last through the war—and beyond.

In 1943 Baumann was shipped off to the Nazi concentration camp in Esterwegen, in northern Germany, and then to the Wehrmacht's prison complex at Torgau an der Elbe, south of Berlin. Many of the prisoners at Torgau were deserters like Baumann. Also among them were conscientious objectors, soldiers who had disobeyed orders, resistance fighters, Allied prisoners of war, as well as prisoners accused of sedition, espionage, and aiding real and perceived enemies, including Jews. Several hundred prisoners were executed at Torgau—by firing squad, hanging, or beheading. Many more died from abuse, hunger, and disease.

"Those who survived were forced into penal battalions," Baumann told a Cologne audience in 2009. He was referring to military units consisting of prisoners sent to the eastern front as Soviet forces began to turn the tide against the Germans. Wearing red triangle patches to set them apart from the regular troops, these "penal battalions" were hurled into the most perilous of assignments. "We were thrown into villages to provide cover for the chaotic German retreat. Most died. I myself was wounded" and taken to a field hospital, Baumann recalled in 2009. "There was a young man there. He didn't want to be sent back to the front. So he poured a whole bowl of boiling water over his body in the bathroom. I witnessed that because I was his lookout." Baumann recounted the dire situation facing prisoner soldiers: "We congratulated those who were in the penal battalion and were badly wounded, such as losing an arm or a leg, because maybe they could survive and go home after all. But very few of us survived."[2]

After the war Baumann made his way back to Hamburg, his hometown. To understand the sad route Baumann's life took even during peace, it is important to go back farther in time, to his youth. As a boy, Baumann was already an outsider. He struggled in school because of his dyslexia. And while other boys eagerly signed up for the Hitler Youth, young Baumann wanted nothing to do with them. Baumann's father, who ran a tobacco wholesaling company, would listen to Hitler on the radio. When Baumann heard Hitler demanding *Lebensraum* for Germans, he asked himself "what this meant for people [non-Germans] living in the East. Should they all be driven out or face something even worse?" Baumann told his 2009 audience in Cologne, "I had such thoughts very early."

When Baumann was drafted into the navy, his rebellious streak accompanied him. Desertion, it seems, was preordained. At the end of the war, Baumann was captured by Soviet troops, but they didn't hold him for very long. He returned to Hamburg around Christmastime. He was just twenty-four years old. Haunted by the torment and abuse he had suffered, to suppress the memories, he took to drinking. After his father died, in 1947, Baumann inherited the family tobacco wholesale business but lost it as he fell deeper into the abyss of alcoholism. "I had hit rock bottom," he once told an interviewer.

On a trip to Bremen, he met the woman, Waltraud, who would become his wife. Together, they had six children, But Waltraud died giving birth to the last one. Each week, Baumann told the *Hamburger Abendblatt* newspaper in 2013, he would ride his bike to the cemetery to visit his wife's grave.

As counterintuitive as it might seem, the end of Waltraud's life may have rescued Baumann. Now he had sole responsibility for raising their children. He gave up drinking and got steady work, first as a TV salesman and later at a youth welfare office. When he returned from the war, Baumann had hoped to be treated with respect for having shown his opposition to the Nazi regime with his act of desertion. But that was not to be. Instead, he was subjected to abuse. "We [deserters] were called cowards, criminals, convicts, and traitors," Baumann said. Even Baumann's own father treated him like a coward.[3]

Within the consciousness of many West Germans during those postwar years were two strands of thinking that were directly related to each other. While most of the populace wanted to forget the war, many West Germans also saw people like Ludwig Baumann not as heroes but as traitors who had turned their backs on their fellow soldiers and on the nation.

Baumann didn't shy away from voicing his anti-war views. He told the *Hamburger Abendblatt* about being beaten up by police officers and former soldiers. But at the same time, Baumann was beginning to see his purpose in life. He was not about to join the legions of Germans who were trying to bury the past. He would do just the opposite. Ludwig Baumann became part of the postwar pacifist movement. He would stand outside army bases or at the train station, handing out pamphlets to young men, exhorting them to dodge conscription. When 300,000 people massed in a Bonn park in 1981 to protest plans to station U.S. medium-range nuclear missiles in Western Europe, among the predominantly youthful activists was sixty-year-old Ludwig Baumann. He attended vigils for peace. He spoke out for the creation of memorials for World War II deserters, at first without a lot of success.

As Baumann became ever more involved in the peace movement, he made contact with deserters like himself. In 1990 he and thirty-seven others formed an association that fought loudly for the dignity of deserters and to have their convictions by Nazi military courts overturned. He was made chairman of the new organization, the Federal Association of Victims of Nazi Military Justice. "We were thirty-seven old men and one woman," Baumann told his Cologne audience in 2009.

Like Baumann, they had kept silent long enough. They were determined to win recognition that they were not traitors to the nation but were victims of Nazi injustice. Still, winning over hearts and minds could be difficult. In 1992 Baumann applied for compensation from a hardship fund for victims of Nazi persecution. The bureaucrat handling his application pointed out that Baumann's death sentence had been commuted to twelve years' imprisonment, which, the bureaucrat said, "does not seem especially hard and excessive."

Baumann became the national face of an energetic campaign by these aging victims of Nazi injustice to win legal rehabilitation of World War II deserters and conscientious objectors. He courted politicians and journalists, producing documents and arguments to buttress their case. At parliamentary committee meetings, Baumann impressed delegates with his persistence, his presence, and his personal story. His cause was given a considerable boost in 1998, when the Bundestag passed a law granting rehabilitation to some victims of Nazi courts. But for Baumann's group and its growing number of supporters, this measure did not go far enough. To officially clear their names, deserters had to go through a long and involved process of gathering documents and individually making their case for overturning their convictions. For Baumann this was further humiliation for victims of Nazi military courts. Now pushing eighty, Baumann went to work persuading politicians to correct the situation, which the Bundestag did in 2002 by passing legislation that overturned the Third Reich convictions of all deserters and conscientious objectors.

Still, Baumann's work was not done. Not included in the 2002 law were soldiers who had been convicted of treason by Nazi military courts. Resistance to rehabilitating convicted traitors was entrenched among conservative politicians and even among some Social Democrats. And this became Baumann's next crusade: persuading the German populace that these men deserved to be officially cleared of having betrayed their country. Baumann's group was helped in this endeavor by historians who were supportive of their cause. They included Manfred Messerschmidt, one of Germany's most respected military historians.

Although a great deal of attention had been paid to civilian courts of the Third Reich, such as the notorious Volksgerichtshof (People's Court) of Judge Roland Freisler and the Sondergerichte (Special Courts), for a long time the Nazi regime's military courts were often overlooked. But far more people had been condemned by these courts than all the others. A total of thirty thousand prisoners were sentenced to death by military courts, and about twenty thousand of those sentences had been carried out.

Even with the Social Democrats in power, pardoning soldiers convicted of treason was at first a hard sell. This was partly because of a historic change in attitude among Germans about self-imposed limits on the use of the military. Since the end of the war, German governments had avoided deploying troops to foreign countries. This policy changed with Chancellor Kohl's decision in 1995 to send German combat troops to join NATO's peace-enforcing mission in Bosnia and Germany's participation in the 1999 bombing of Yugoslavia by NATO warplanes during the Kosovo crisis. Over the ensuing years, Germany became ever bolder about joining NATO-led missions abroad, including to Afghanistan. While the United States and other allies welcomed the German military's emergence from something of a pacifist cocoon, the idea of rehabilitating soldiers convicted of treason during World War II raised concerns that doing so could jeopardize morale within the military.

The work of historians sympathetic to clearing the names of these victims of Nazi military courts proved essential to ultimately restoring their honor. The argument against rehabilitation ran along these lines: the soldiers who had refused to fight for Hitler had not only betrayed their country but had also endangered their comrades by providing assistance to the enemy. This was a way of thinking that had not faced much scrutiny for decades after the end of the war. It was challenged by two historians, Wolfram Wette and Detlef Vogel, who examined a sampling of Nazi documents on thirty-three treason trials.

"When we started our research . . . we . . . had misconceptions as to who these war traitors might actually be," Wette said in an interview with *Deutschlandfunk* in August 2009. "We were looking for war traitors, but what we found was something very different." Wette noted the wide range of charges considered treasonous by the Third Reich. "We found court-martial judgments in which the concept of war treason appeared but which were extremely diverse in terms of the wording of the criminal offense."[4]

What drew their attention were not Benedict Arnold–style traitors who had consciously betrayed their comrades by actively aiding and abetting the enemy but soldiers condemned to death for offenses that were a far cry from the usual understanding of treasonous acts. Wette and Vogel published their findings in the 2007 book *Das letzte Tabu—Militärjustiz und Kriegsverrat* (The Last Taboo: Military Justice and Wartime Treason). Their work showed that under the Nazis' 1934 law on treason, a soldier could be sentenced to death for virtually any objectional behavior.

Wette and Vogel told the story of Adolf Hermann Pogede, a forty-six-year-old corporal who was beheaded by guillotine in 1944 for giving tobacco to a Red Army POW and telling his newfound Russian friend that Hitler's war was doomed to failure. Wette and Vogel also told about how the discovery of a diary of another corporal, Josef Salz, resulted in his execution by firing squad in February 1944. According to the military tribunal that condemned him, Salz had expressed himself as a "friend of Jews and Bolsheviks" and had "viciously abused and slandered the German people, their leadership, and the Wehrmacht."[5] The military judges said they believed Salz had jotted down these opinions so that he could show his diary to the approaching Red Army as proof that he was an opponent of the Hitler regime and thereby avoid the fate of being sent to a Soviet internment camp.

Even though Baumann himself had been rehabilitated by the 2002 law, he became a leader of the crusade to win recognition for these last opponents of the Nazi regime. Baumann equated the victims with General Claus von Stauffenberg and the group of resisters who had tried to kill Hitler in July 1944. For many years after the war, Stauffenberg was seen as a traitor. But gradually, he and other anti-Hitler resisters were accepted as heroes. There is little difference between Stauffenberg and soldiers unjustly convicted of treason by Nazi courts, Baumann argued. Those condemned by the Nazi military courts had shown their opposition to the criminal Nazi regime in their own way.

Baumann told his Cologne audience in January 2009: "Until these convictions are overturned, we will not have clearly broken with our Nazi past."[6] A majority of members of the Bundestag agreed. In September 2009 they passed a law granting blanket rehabilitation of soldiers who had been convicted of treason by Nazi military courts. It was a posthumous victory for the estimated twenty thousand German soldiers who were executed upon the orders of military courts.

Victories like these for Baumann and other activists did not occur in a vacuum. They came at a time of growing recognition of the fact that even decades after the Nazis' defeat, there were whole groups of victims who had not been recognized by postwar governments. They also came at a time when German society was finally starting to have a nationwide discourse about the former Nazis who had been hired by West German government ministries and agencies.

Ludwig Baumann died on July 5, 2018. He was ninety-six. During his last decade of life, Baumann was treated with the respect that was denied him for so long. He visited schools to talk about his life, his experiences, and his pacifist views. To celebrate Baumann's ninetieth birthday, Bremen Mayor Jens Böhrnsen threw a party for him at City Hall. "We are here to honor a most extraordinary human," Böhrnsen told the two hundred guests, who rose from their seats in unison to show their admiration for this pacifist warrior. Baumann graciously accepted the accolades, all well deserved. But there was one proffered honor that he refused: a *Bundesverdienstkreuz* (Federal Order of Merit). Baumann could not accept a medal that had also been given to former Nazis by postwar governments. On Baumann's one hundredth birthday, in 2021, this man who for years had been treated like a pariah was posthumously remembered across the country for his courage and his tireless campaigns to win recognition for deserters and conscientious objectors. A park in Hamburg was named for Baumann, as was an auditorium at a Bremen cultural and conference center. A film was shown at a Bremen movie theater on Baumann's trials and triumphs. There were speeches and music at Hamburg's memorial to deserters and other victims of Nazi justice. Commemorations were held in other cities as well.

While it is hard not to be moved and even uplifted by the arc of Ludwig Baumann's life—the death sentence that had been pronounced upon him, torture in a prison cell, his long captivity, the decades of disdain and insults he had to endure after the war, his determination to get justice, and his ultimate triumph—the destiny of his tormenters cannot be overlooked. After the war judges and prosecutors who presided over Nazi military courts were spared prosecution. Many resumed their legal careers in the German democracy that replaced the vanquished Third Reich.

On a winter's day in the year 2017, the souls of 300,000 dead were evoked within Berlin's venerable Reichstag building. Present to remember them were Germany's political and judicial elite and invited guests, among them eighty students from fifteen countries.

A German actor with Down syndrome, Sebastian Urbanski, stood at the lectern to read from a 1943 letter written by a forty-one-year-old man confined at a psychiatric clinic, where patients like himself were dying every day. The letter was written by Ernst Putzki to his mother while at the psychiatric clinic at Weilmünster. A year later, he was taken to the Hadamar institute, more widely known than Weilmünster. About fifteen thousand people were killed at Hadamar, one of six main killing centers created by the Nazis to eradicate people with disabilities. Putzki died there on January 9, 1945.

To those assembled in the plenary hall of the Bundestag, Germany's seat of legislative power, the symbolism of Urbanski speaking the written words of Ernst Putzki could not be overlooked. If Urbanski had lived during the Third Reich, he would certainly have been among those murdered because of their disabilities and illnesses, deemed unworthy of living by the Nazis.

"It is September 3, 1943, and we have now been through four years of war," read Urbanski. "Your letter came on Sunday, August 22. I didn't get the gooseberries. The parcel which you told me you had sent finally arrived yesterday. It was probably brought on foot. Its contents—two pounds of apples and a mushy stinking mess of pureed pear—was consumed with ravenous hunger. My fellow candidates for death scrambled for a fistful of rotten stuff."

Putzki described in graphic detail the inhumane conditions at Weilmünster:

> The people here are starving, just skin and bone, and dying like flies. There are around thirty deaths a week. Their skeletal bodies are taken away to be buried. There are no coffins. The food consists of two slices of bread a day—with jam, sometimes with margarine, sometimes with nothing.
>
> The people become like animals; they eat anything they can snatch from others, even raw potato and fodder beet. Death from starvation is hard on our heels, and no one knows who will be next.
>
> Previously, the people here were killed more quickly and their bodies taken for burning at dawn. But this met with resistance from the locals, so now we are simply left to starve. We live in squalid rooms with no radio, newspaper, or books. There's nothing to occupy us. How I miss my handicrafts! We eat off broken crockery and have nothing but threadbare rags to wear. They don't keep the cold out. We last had a bath five weeks ago and don't know if we will be given a bath again this year.

Putzki ended his missive to his mother very simply: "Your Ernst."[7]

And just as simply, the actor with Down syndrome left his place behind the lectern, uttering not another word. The plenary hall of the Bundestag was left in a melancholy silence. Some struggled to keep back a tear.

Two other souls—both victims of the Nazis' obsession with protecting the German gene pool—were summoned before the audience in the Bundestag, bearing witness not only to the crimes committed against people like them but to the postwar decades that forgot them. "Lives have long memories," said Hartmut Traub, nephew of Benjamin Traub, murdered in Hadamar's gas chamber on March 13, 1941. "Sometimes, remembering takes courage and perseverance. Sometimes, remembering is an obligation—one which is imposed upon us by the desire for justice and truth in place of guilt and failure."[8]

For families of the mentally and physically disabled who were murdered by the Nazi regime, restoring their memory has been a difficult task. There are complicated psychological reasons for this. It was not unusual for relatives to be persuaded by Nazi doctors that killing a loved one afflicted with disease or disability would liberate that person and the family. Living with memories like this must have been nearly unbearable for many—so memories were suppressed. Forgetting the dead was a coping mechanism for the living.

Traub had had an "abstract awareness" about Beni Traub, he told the audience inside the Bundestag's plenary hall. He set out to restore memories of his uncle, to rescue him from obscurity. "I spent two years searching for traces of Benjamin: in photo albums, in diaries, in archives, in personal and public documents, and in conversations. At the end of this memory work, I had gathered experiences and insights, but also questions, about my family and about our country. It changed my life."

Hartmut Traub learned a great deal about his uncle. Beni Traub was Hartmut's father's youngest brother, born on November 25, 1914, in Mülheim an der Ruhr. He was musically gifted, friendly, and outgoing. His life took a downward turn after a 1931 accident while chopping wood with an axe, severing part of his finger. The teenager was traumatized. He suffered a breakdown and tried to take his own life. He also became prone to having emotional outbursts. The family sought the help of psychiatrists. Beni Traub was diagnosed with "juvenile schizophrenia" and taken to a mental asylum in Bedburg-Hau, near the Dutch border.

Soon after Hitler came to power in 1933, the Nazis' Law for the Prevention of Offspring with Hereditary Diseases was passed. Four years after that, a medical bureaucracy was created whose mission was to eradicate or sterilize those who were deemed an economic and genetic burden on the Fatherland—"useless eaters," they were called, and "burdensome existences." The killings were planned by staff working out of a villa at Tiergartenstrasse 4 in Berlin, and thus was the program called "T4." Clinics and mental institutions around Germany sent in filled-in questionnaires about patients. A T4 committee chose who would die. Benjamin Traub was put on a list of those to be murdered.

On March 13, 1940, recounted Hartmut Traub, his uncle was among about sixty male patients at Bedburg-Hau who were taken by train to Weilmünster, the same mental hospital Ernst Putzki was delivered to in 1943. "For one year to the day, Benjamin lived and worked at this institution, which was more like a foretaste of hell than a psychiatric hospital."

On March 13, 1941, Benjamin Traub and sixty-three other patients at Weilmünster were told they were being taken for an outing. Patients were so excited about this that they invited the director of Weilmünster to come along. Gray buses were waiting outside. The patients boarded the buses. About an hour later, they arrived at Hadamar, where, said Hartmut Traub, "everything has been prepared for the new arrivals." This would turn out to be just a normal working day for Hadamar staff: "A mass destruction routine—sixty patients every day. And it has been going on for months." Hartmut painted a vivid scene of his uncle's death at the hands of the Nazis. "The buses drive into the center's cavernous garage . . . the gates are shut behind them."

There is no escape for Benjamin Traub and his fellow patients: "From the garage, they are taken along a passageway, built specifically for this purpose, which leads them directly into the main building." As Hartmut Traub told of the crime committed against his uncle and the others on that day nearly eighty years earlier, everyone in the audience knew this story was going to end tragically. But in its telling, Benjamin Traub was in a way given new life. The patients are given an initial examination. They are told to undress and then given tranquilizers by a doctor. "Their patient records are checked; photos and notes are taken." Hartmut Traub paused, looking up from his written speech at the audience. "The usual institutional procedure, or so it seems." The purpose of this procedure is to produce "a fabricated diagnosis of a fatal illness for the death certificate that can be explained by the patient's records."

The patients are led by hospital staff to a small, white-tiled shower chamber in the cellar. "Benjamin finds himself crushed into a tiny space alongside sixty-three other naked men. The doors are locked behind them. What thoughts will have crossed their minds as they stood there, captive? Do they feel fear, or panic? What can they hear? What can they smell? Who are the people pressed in beside them?" There is a gas cylinder just outside the shower room. A Hadamar doctor opens the cylinder's valve, releasing carbon monoxide into the killing chamber. "Benjamin is overcome with nausea. He loses consciousness. A few minutes later, he and his sixty-three companions in suffering are dead." Their bodies are taken to a dissection room. Gold teeth are extracted from those who have them. Brains are removed from some, for "scientific study." The corpses are loaded into the incinerators of Hadamar's crematorium and destroyed.

The audience inside the Bundestag was then introduced to another victim of the Nazis' T4 program, yet another soul who for decades lingered in the purgatory of obscurity. Her name is Anna Lehnkering, and she died in the gas chamber at the T4 program's Grafeneck killing center in March 1940 at age twenty-four. Her story was related by her niece, Sigrid Falkenstein, who, like Hartmut Traub, devoted herself to restoring the memory of her aunt. "Until 2003, no one in our family ever talked about Anna," said Falkenstein, who published a book about her aunt. "This silence, I think, had a lot to do with shame."[9]

Falkenstein came across her aunt's name while reading an internet site about the T4 program. "When I confronted my father, Anna's younger brother, with this discovery, he struggled to find answers." And then, for the first time, the father spoke his deceased sister's name. Anna "was such a kind and gentle girl," he told Falkenstein. "She loved playing with us children." Anna "found learning difficult," he told his daughter. "Some time in the thirties, she was sent to an institution, and she died somewhere along the way, during the war."

That was about all that Falkenstein could get out of her father. She needed to know more about her aunt, so, like Hartmut Traub, she immersed herself in patient records and other documents. She learned that Anna Lehnkering was born in the Ruhr region in 1915 and that at age four or so her parents noticed that she was extremely anxious and timid. She was sent to a school for children with learning disabilities. A 1934 medical report, written after Anna was subjected to an "intelligence test," stated that she was a case of "congenital imbecility." Anna was sterilized without her consent. In 1936 she was sent to the mental hospital at Bedburg-Hau and later taken to the Grafeneck killing center. Anna's mother received a letter from the Grafeneck center about Anna's death. Falkenstein wonders what Anna's mother thought when she got the news. "Did she really believe—did she perhaps want to believe—that her daughter's death was indeed a 'release,' in view of her supposed 'severe and incurable disease,' as the letter claimed? I have no answers." The mother developed severe depression later in life. "Silence makes you sick," said Sigrid Falkenstein. "Talking about one's experiences can help."

The memorial in 2017 to neglected victims of the Third Reich was presided over by Norbert Lammert, who at the time was president of the Bundestag and a member of Konrad Adenauer's old party, the conservative

Christian Democratic Union. In his address to the assembly, Lammert was blunt in his criticism of how postwar Germany had dealt with the plight of those who were sterilized and murdered by the Nazis because of their disabilities and illnesses, calling out the "years of indifference in the scientific community, the media, and politics."[10] "It was 2007 before the German Bundestag proscribed the Nazi regime's Forced Sterilization Act," and it wasn't until 2011 that agreement had been reached on a memorial for the Third Reich's medical murder victims. That memorial, located at the site of the Berlin headquarters of the *Aktion* T4 mass murder program, opened in 2014.

By the close of this gut-wrenching 2017 memorial ceremony within the Reichstag building, it had become clear that even as the forgotten victims were being given their due, their dignity restored, there was something that would always be denied them. And it is something that will always evade Germans in their struggles to deal with the Nazi past. Just as occurred with Nazi justices and jurists and other civil servants of the Third Reich, most doctors and staff involved in *Aktion* T4 were never brought to trial. For those who were, according to Lammert, "proceedings frequently ended in acquittal due to the statute of limitations expiring or the accused being permanently unfit to face trial." And many of them were rewarded professionally. "Former perpetrators were promoted to university professors, awarded orders of merit, their deeds suppressed," Lammert said. As victims like Ernst Putzki, Benjamin Traub, and Anna Lehnkering faded into obscurity in postwar Germany, their tormenters were allowed to resume their careers.

On March 27, 1952, a stranger carrying a package approached a boy on a Munich street. He asked the boy if he would do him a favor and take the parcel to the post office. The boy said yes, but he became suspicious when he noticed to whom it was addressed: Chancellor Konrad Adenauer. The boy alerted police, who brought the package to police headquarters. An explosion ripped through the cellar as an attempt was made to open the parcel, killing a bomb disposal expert and injuring others.

Cases such as this were handled by the Federal Criminal Police Office's Bonn-based Security Group, an elite unit that investigated threats to the government. A special Security Group team was appointed to investigate the attempt to assassinate Adenauer. Named to lead the team was Josef Ochs, a senior official with the Security Group.

Suspicion immediately fell on Israeli terrorists. Was it vengeance for the Holocaust? Or was there something else at play? On April 1 a group calling itself the Organization of Jewish Partisans sent two letters to Paris news media claiming responsibility for the bomb. One of the letters was sent from Geneva, the other from Zurich.

The letters said, "The German people—who slaughtered six million Jews in cold blood, sliced women's throats, strangled children, buried old men alive—these people want to obtain the forgiveness of our people under the pretext that stolen goods will be partially replaced." The letter alluded to reparations talks that had begun among West Germany, Israel, and the Conference on Jewish Material Claims Against Germany. The suggestion in the letter was that no amount of money could make up for Germany's genocide against Jews.

As Ochs and his team collected evidence, they learned that a man who may have been connected with the attack had stayed with a Jewish businessman in Frankfurt. Security Group investigators, led by Theo Saevecke, paid a visit to the man at six thirty in the morning on a Sunday in April. They searched the residence and questioned the businessman—a Polish Jew—and his wife. In his report to Ochs, Saevecke said neither the search nor the questioning yielded anything that would solve the case. On that same day, a French newspaper reported that an Israeli citizen—Elieser Sudit—had been arrested in Paris in connection with the case and four others had been tossed out of France. Ochs packed his bags and left for the French capital.

Sudit was never charged with the Munich package bomb explosion. The Paris judge sentenced him to a few months in prison on a weapons possession charge, but no proof was found that he had anything to do with the bomb. As it turns out, he did. In 2006 the *Frankfurter Allgemeine Zeitung* newspaper ran an article about a 1994 memoir written by Sudit but never published. Sudit, who identified himself as a former member of the Irgun terror group, admitted he had constructed the parcel bomb, but he realized it would never make it to Adenauer and had intended just to draw international attention. He also claimed that Menachem Begin, a member of the Irgun in the 1950s and later prime minister of Israel, had instructed him to build the bomb. That is an intriguing account but apparently still unproven. More interesting, for our purposes, is the German who led the investigation—Josef Ochs—and his background. Ochs was one of those

BKA officials with a highly compromised Nazi past. The story of Ochs's investigation of the assassination attempt, and of his Nazi past, was told by historians in 2011 in their examination of the Nazi taint within the BKA.[11]

Born on March 31, 1905, in the Taunus hills outside Frankfurt, Ochs studied law and economics at Frankfurt, Munich, and Erlangen. He began his career in law enforcement in 1936 with the criminal police in Frankfurt and after a few weeks was transferred north to Düsseldorf. Ochs joined the Sturmabteilung in 1933, the Nazi Party in 1937, and a year later was given the rank of *Obersturmführer* (first lieutenant) in the SS. He belonged to a number of other organizations associated with the Nazi Party, including the Reichsbund der Deutschen Beamten (Reich Union of German Civil Servants). Here were all the signs of a man who had chosen to thoroughly immerse himself in the life of a Nazi official.

After Germany's invasion of Poland in the fall of 1939, Ochs was sent to the occupied country to set up an office of the Nazis' Kripo (short for Kriminalpolizei) police agency in the city of Torun. No proof has emerged that he was involved in the atrocities committed there. He was in Poland for just a couple of months and then was called to Berlin for an assignment with the Nazi agency in charge of coordinating law enforcement across Germany: the Reichskriminalpolizeiamt (Reich Criminal Police Office), or RKPA. Ochs belonged to an RKPA department that organized the harassment, abuse, and arrest of prostitutes, the homeless, people who were judged by the Nazis to be work shirkers, as well as Germany's Roma minority. An estimated half-million Roma were killed by the Nazis, many in concentration and death camps. Historians hired by the German government to dig into the BKA's files examined documents indicating that Ochs himself had been involved in these repressive measures. One document shows that in May 1940 Ochs was at a "collection camp" in Cologne, where he was involved in the "selection" of Roma to be deported to occupied Poland. Another document, a letter written by Ochs on August 9, 1940, and addressed to criminal police in Magdeburg, stated that a family of eight who were being held by Magdeburg police were recorded in the files as *Zigeuner* (Gypsies). According to the historians commissioned by the government, the couple and their six children were deported to Auschwitz. The oldest son died there. It is not clear what happened to the others.

Ochs returned to the criminal police office in Düsseldorf in 1943 and was transferred again to Magdeburg. The transfer seems to have been in retaliation for Ochs's refusal to leave the Catholic Church. Ochs was held in a British internment camp for three years after the Nazis' defeat and in 1951 was hired by a law enforcement agency set up in the British occupation zone that was the predecessor of the Bundeskriminalamt. That was Ochs's path to the national police agency of the new West German republic. Ochs's Third Reich experience was such that he was given a lot of authority at the BKA. So, when the BKA was given the assignment of investigating the apparent attempt to kill Adenauer, he was just the man for the job.

After visiting Paris, Ochs wrote a report for his superiors that, on multiple levels, suggests he had not shed Nazi-style thinking in his approach to fighting crime. He speculated that a "widespread international organization" was behind the attack, operating out of Zurich, Amsterdam, Paris, and Munich, which he called the "centers of Judaism in Europe." He said it was no surprise to him that French authorities had not arrested any of the possible suspects, since the head of the French domestic intelligence agency was himself "of the Mosaic faith."

Ochs also mused about possible measures to deter future attacks from the milieu that he suspected was involved in this one. "At this time, reprisals are the only path," he wrote. "It's been said . . . that Jewish business owners are providing support for the terrorists—some voluntary, others under threat—sometimes in the form of money, and sometimes in the form of giving them accommodations."[12]

Ochs also blamed "displaced persons"—survivors of the concentration and extermination camps—for a rise in crimes across West Germany. "[West] Germany makes it easier than any other country for DPs to conduct their lucrative trade. Millions are being made in illegal currency trading and smuggling," wrote Ochs, adding, "A significant part of the illegal trade with the East also lies in Jewish hands." He alleged, "Many Jewish DPs live under false names."[13]

Ochs urged that immigration laws be rewritten to make it easier for police to expel "burdensome foreigners who live from illegal trade and go out of their way to avoid honest work." Ochs even suggested "internment camps for asocial foreigners with unclear personal details," which, it's safe to assume, would include Jewish refugees, "in order to put an end to their activities that endanger the state."[14] Ochs's proposals were never implemented.

During the first couple of decades of the postwar era, authoritarian thinking died hard. Civil servants clung to stereotypes about some of the same people who had been persecuted and murdered during the Third Reich. The postwar treatment of Roma was especially egregious. In 1956 the Federal Court of Justice rejected compensation claims by Roma survivors of concentration camps in Nazi-occupied Poland because, as West Germany's highest court argued, "they tend ... to criminality, particularly to theft and deception, in many cases they lack the moral drive to respect the property of others, because—like primitive prehistoric men—they possess an unrestrained drive for occupation."

In 1953 Bavaria passed a law that singled out "travelers"—in other words, Roma—for limits on some of their basic rights, based on the view that they were a public menace. Representatives of the BKA and law officials from the West German states held a series of meetings in the 1950s to discuss ways to intensify measures against the Roma. Josef Ochs, as the BKA's specialist on the matter, attended the meetings, where he said there had to be a nationwide solution to what he called the "travelers' plague." Among suggestions discussed at the conferences were nationwide checks on streets and roads and at rest areas specifically to ferret out travelers whose driving licenses or registrations were not in order or those who were using vehicles to operate a business without the necessary permission from authorities. Today we would call this racial profiling. There was also discussion about making it more difficult to obtain itinerant trade licenses—another idea that specifically targeted Roma. These proposals were not adopted—but only because the individual states could not agree on turning over their power to monitor the Roma to federal authorities.[15] Some of these modes of thinking preceded the Nazis, such as repressive measures against the Roma. But it was the Nazis who turned persecution into murder.

Perhaps it should be no surprise that Third Reich veterans like Josef Ochs continued to harbor stereotypes about, for example, the Roma and "asocials," since these people were his quarry while he was working for the RKPA. The government-commissioned historians who examined the BKA's files make some interesting observations about what it must have been like for West Germany's freshly hired civil servants to make the transition from dictatorship to democracy. "When officials from the Federal Criminal Police Office like Ochs sat at their desks in the 1950s, they didn't start with a blank slate," the historians wrote in their 2011 findings, *Schatten der Vergangenheit*.

After the demise of the Third Reich, German cops were faced with starting their lives over from scratch. Many spent time in Allies' internment and prisoner of war camps. When they were released, they had to take whatever jobs they could get. Historians who have been digging into the Nazi taint of postwar government agencies, including those who studied the BKA, have come across indications of good-faith efforts to adapt to democratic ways (although not so much within the BND). After struggling to make a living during the first postwar years, the civil servants now had job security and were enjoying the fruits of West Germany's "economic miracle." They were given promotions in recognition of their work and pensions that ensured good lives during retirement. Experts seem unable to agree on how much of a threat former Nazis in the West German civil service may have posed to democracy. But there's something that should not be lost sight of: during this period of transition, as civil servants like Josef Ochs discovered the guardrails of democracy, legions of Third Reich victims, like the Roma and deserters, had to wait for official recognition of the injustices that they had suffered. Postwar amends were not for everyone.

On August 17, 1956, police raids occurred across West Germany that reminded their targets—Communists—of the bad old days. After five years of deliberation, the Federal Constitutional Court on this day banned the Communist Party. Communist offices were searched, party assets confiscated, stacks of propaganda hauled away. A total of thirty-three party functionaries were arrested. Others went into hiding. Some went into exile in East Germany.

Law enforcement actions against Communists and their sympathizers had begun years earlier. Telephones were tapped, peace demonstrators surveilled, mail sent from East Germany intercepted and opened. Adenauer's government justified all this by saying that the very existence of the Federal Republic was in danger because of the Communist threat, organized by East Berlin and by Moscow.

Up until 1968, 125,000 investigations had been conducted on the basis of the perceived Communist threat. Of that number, somewhere between six and seven thousand people were convicted and sentenced. So as amnestied Nazi war criminals were enjoying their freedom in West Germany, Communists and other leftists—who were the first victims of the Nazi regime—were once again waiting for a knock on the door. Cops who had once sworn allegiance to Hitler were among those who were busting "Bolshevists" in the democratic Federal Republic of Germany.

The start of the twenty-first century brought with it renewed scrutiny of the Red Scare of the 1950s and 1960s and of West German government agencies' dealings with leftist activists. When in 2008 the BKA commissioned four historians to examine "Nazi continuities" with the law enforcement agency, one of their missions was to research the BKA's role in countering the perceived Communist threat. One of their approaches was to examine weekly reports written in the 1950s and the 1960s by the BKA's Security Group, which investigated potential cases of treason and high treason. While the Security Group aggressively pursued the Far Left, much less attention was paid to the Far Right.[16]

"The Security Group apparently saw itself increasingly as an informal central office for the collection of evidence against Communists," the researchers wrote in *Schatten der Vergangenheit*. As an example, the researchers offered a 1955 report by the Security Group about a raid that had been conducted by police in Bonn of the laundry room of a house on Joachimstrasse, where "communist propaganda and training material of all kinds" were found.[17]

Another weekly report by the Security Group tells of an attempt by an official at the federal Postal Ministry, identified as "Dr. R.," to fire a female employee, identified as "K.F.," for having committed "various civil service offenses" because of a "left-wing attitude." Dr. R. had reached out to the Security Group for assistance, seeking reasons "to justify a dismissal" that would stand up under federal labor law, according to the weekly report. It is unknown whether K.F. ended up keeping her job.[18]

The Communist youth organization the Freie Deutsche Jugend (Free German Youth), or FDJ, was banned by the Adenauer government in 1951. In March 1953 the BKA's Security Group conducted a sweep of FDJ functionaries in an operation given the code name "convalescent leave." Security Group investigators raided fifty-one residences and business offices and arrested thirteen people. Among them was Josef Angenfort, who was the most important FDJ official in the Federal Republic. He was also a delegate in the North Rhine–Westphalia state parliament. The two Security Group investigators who brought Angenfort to the Duisburg police headquarters were both former SS officers. At police headquarters there was a scuffle when Angenfort protested that he had immunity from arrest because of his seat in the state parliament (which was technically true), refused to allow himself to be bodily searched, and tried to rip up a piece of paper with handwriting on it. One of the Security Group investigators said in a report, "We broke his resistance and secured the scraps of paper." As the historians who wrote in *Schatten der Vergangenheit* point out, the actions of the two Security Group investigators can hardly be compared with those of the Gestapo during the Third Reich, a parallel that was drawn by critics in the late 1950s and early 1960s as the wartime pasts of postwar law enforcement and intelligence officials emerged and exploded into scandals. Still, the BKA and other law enforcement agencies could probably have saved themselves a lot of aggravation—and avoided jibes about being just like the Gestapo—if they had not relied so heavily on mass murderers and other Nazi perpetrators. Incidentally, Angenfort was convicted of "preparation of a high treason enterprise" and sentenced to five years in prison, despite his immunity as a state parliamentarian.

The zeal with which investigations like this were pursued is also exemplified by the 1963 trial in Bremen of Willi Meyer-Buer who, before the KPD was banned, was a state chairman of the party. Meyer-Buer was running for a seat in the Bundestag. During the campaign Meyer-Buer did not conceal his continued belief in communism. It was up to the court to determine whether Meyer-Buer was taking orders from the banned KPD. Among the witnesses was a chief inspector with the BKA Security Group. He testified that he had been given the assignment of systematically analyzing the campaigns of thirty-four political candidates who had previously belonged to the KPD. He did this by comparing campaign themes of the thirty-four with the election program of the KPD before its banning. The main theme of fourteen of the candidates was "No votes for the CDU/CSU," meaning Adenauer's government. For eleven candidates the main theme was pacifist in nature—such as calling for disarmament. The BKA investigator said those campaign themes were assessed to be Communist propaganda. The defense attorney at the trial, Heinrich Hannover, asked the BKA man whether he had checked to see if the same demands and sentiments had been made by candidates of any other parties. The BKA man replied, "That was not our assignment."[19] Meyer-Buer was convicted of illegal political activity and sentenced to nine months in prison on probation.

Overreach was displayed in another 1953 anti-Communist roundup, this one given the code name "Aktion Vulkan" (Operation Volcano), led by the BKA's Theo Saevecke. About forty people were arrested in the raids that occurred across West Germany, based on documents provided by an undercover agent with the Bundesamt für Verfassungsschutz (Federal Office for Protection of the Constitution, the German domestic intelligence agency, also known as the BfV). The federal government boasted about the arrests and publicized the suspects' names. But as it turned out, much of the information provided by the BfV was wrong, and many of the cases were dropped. One of the suspects, who was apparently innocent of espionage, hanged himself in his cell. Admitting the mistake, the federal government paid nearly a half-million deutsche marks to those who were slandered.

Even though Saevecke was viewed as a dyed-in-the-wool Nazi even by his CIA handlers, the former SS officer filed a report with the BKA in which he complained that the Security Group's investigations seemed too similar to the ways of the Third Reich. He said the Security Group "should be spared" assignments that are done in haste, which he likened to "actions in areas of deployment during the war." Only those operations should be undertaken that "improve the reputation of the BKA, not damage it," Saevecke wrote.[20]

Given the wartime atrocities that Saevecke was involved in, these are remarkable comments. After all, this is the same man who during a BKA Christmas party gave a speech in which he unabashedly referred to himself as "an early National Socialist." While Saevecke may still have been harboring some authoritarian urges, his report seems to indicate a realization that he and other investigators would have to hold them in check under the new democratic system. Seven decades after former Nazis like Saevecke were able to jump-start their careers in the newly born Federal Republic of Germany, it is impossible to know what they were thinking—whether any of them actually did hope for a return of authoritarianism, for example. But it is not uncommon to sense from memos that survive from that era that many of these formerly loyal servants of the Third Reich must have come to the realization that they had no other choice but to adapt to the new order. There was this consolation for former Nazis: it was a new order that did not require a change in attitude toward communism.

With the Cold War over and the two German states reunited, demands were made by the Left that reparations be paid to Communists and others who had been locked up during the Red Scare. The demands were especially loud from Die Linke (The Left), the post-unification party that combined breakaway leftist members of the Social Democratic Party and the Party for Democratic Socialism, the reformist successor of the Leninist party that ruled East Germany for four decades.

Jan Korte, a leading member of Die Linke, addressed the Bundestag on December 1, 2006: "The exclusion of Communists from victim compensation payments may have corresponded to the legal logic of the Cold War. Maintaining them goes against today's principles and the moral understanding of many in this country. This is all the more depressing because the basis for the exclusion of claims for compensation were the verdicts of public prosecutors and judges who as perpetrators had conducted political trials under the Nazi regime and after 1949 were once again sitting in judgment of resistance fighters."[21] But the effort hit a brick wall. Politicians were not ready to place Communists who had been hunted and tormented by the Nazis on the same level as Jews and others who were granted compensation for the ordeals they had suffered during the Third Reich.

The point was also made that political repression by the ruling East German Communists was far harsher than legal actions taken against Communists in West Germany. It is a fair argument, but it dodges the fact that many of those arrested during West German officials' pursuit of Communists and other leftists had done little more than express viewpoints that were at odds with Adenauer's pro-Western policies.

Photos and TV footage of John F. Kennedy's June 1963 visit to West Berlin, when he gave his "Ich bin ein Berliner" address, speak tomes about West German politics at that time. With Kennedy are Chancellor Konrad Adenauer and the mayor of West Berlin, Willy Brandt. Kennedy and Brandt look fresh and vibrant. Standing together, chatting amiably, they embody the future. When Adenauer is next to them, he is out of place. At age eighty-seven, he is forty-one years older than Kennedy and thirty-eight years older than Brandt. He looks like, and is, the past.

Brandt, a Social Democrat, was chosen by his party to be its chancellor candidate at a conference in Hannover in November 1960. Carlo Schmid, a leading Social Democrat, spoke to the attendees: "With the unused energies of the younger generation, unused forces must go to work. That's why Willy Brandt has to become chancellor!" Before JFK traveled to Berlin, Brandt had already paid a visit to the new American president at the White House, in October 1962. The transatlantic journey was a huge publicity coup for Brandt. They were both good-looking and charismatic, had new ideas, and knew how to charm a crowd. And thus was born the perception among many that Willy Brandt was "Germany's Kennedy."

Adenauer and his Christian Democratic Union watched Brandt's rise with alarm. Adenauer had remained undefeated since he was elected chancellor in 1949. But the Social Democrats had become an existential threat. One of the weapons Adenauer used against Brandt was West Germany's foreign intelligence chief, Reinhard Gehlen.

Klaus-Dietmar Henke was one of the historians commissioned to investigate the Nazi taint of Gehlen's Bundesnachrichtendienst. Henke's final findings were published in 2022 in a book titled *Geheime Dienste: Die Politische Inlandsspionage des BND in der Ära Adenauer* (Secret Services: The BND's Political Domestic Espionage in the Adenauer Era). Henke examined documents that had been kept secret by the government for nearly seven decades. His conclusions caused a stir not just in Germany but internationally. The internal snooping by Gehlen's spies, and requested by Adenauer, was an abuse of power that was the equivalent of the dirty tricks of U.S. president Richard Nixon, Henke wrote. A West German Watergate. But unlike Nixon, Adenauer and Gehlen got away with it. "With the systematic investigation of the SPD leadership, he [Gehlen] gave Adenauer a powerful political weapon," Henke wrote.

Gehlen had an informant deep within the leadership of the Social Democratic Party. His name was Siegfried Ortloff. After returning from exile in Sweden, Ortloff was offered work with the SPD in Hannover and later with the party's national executive board in Bonn. Ortloff was a confidant of the SPD national chairman, Erich Ollenhauer. As secretary of the SPD executive, Ortloff participated in SPD leadership meetings and took notes on them. Ortloff's Bundesnachrichtendienst handler was Siegfried Ziegler, code-named "Dr. König." During the war Ziegler was an Abwehr officer in the Balkans. Like so many in West German security agencies, before going to work for Gehlen, Ziegler was an informant for the U.S. Army's CIC intelligence agency.

From his position inside the SPD's Bonn headquarters, dubbed "the barracks," Ortloff wrote reports for the BND about everything discussed at SPD leadership meetings and party conferences. The reports went to Ziegler, then to Gehlen, and then to the chancellor's office.

There was another central player in this arrangement: Adenauer's chief of staff, Hans Globke. Globke was Adenauer's liaison with the BND. Globke and Gehlen were equal partners in the decade-long conspiracy to thwart the SPD by collecting intelligence on the party. The BND sent Ortloff's reports to Globke, who assessed them, wrote notes on them, and initialed them before passing them on to Adenauer.

Some days the information flowing from the BND to Globke was like water surging through a fire hose. In the first month of 1958, according to Henke, the BND contacted Globke no fewer than thirty-one times. Ortloff filed at least five hundred confidential reports from his spying on the SPD: "Sometimes, 12 reports on a single day reached the Chancellery."[22]

This political espionage occurred during volatile times, with Germany on the razor's edge of the East-West confrontation and West German political parties fighting it out for the favor of a vulnerable populace that was still getting used to the ways of democracy. Adenauer was pushing for German rearmament and for making its armed forces part of the Western alliance facing off against the USSR, both of which happened. The Social Democrats were less gung ho about rearmament and favored a reunified and neutral Germany. The Red Scare created hurdles for the SPD, which it was trying to overcome by jettisoning its historic commitment to Marxism. Having a plant within the SPD executive gave Adenauer and Globke insights into ideological cracks within the rival party, providing valuable material to Adenauer's election strategists.

The SPD was not Gehlen's only target of domestic espionage. The spy chief had informants in place throughout society—inside not just political parties but also government agencies, trade unions, businesses, church organizations, academia, and science and among celebrities and journalists. Gehlen began building these networks while his intelligence organization was still under the supposed supervision of U.S. authorities, even before the founding of West Germany in 1949. Some worked voluntarily for Gehlen; some were paid. Gehlen's American overseers tolerated this internal snooping.

When the Americans handed over responsibility for the Gehlen operation to the West German government in 1956, Gehlen saw this as an opportunity to expand his domestic spying, according to Henke. Adenauer and Gehlen played up the Communist threat to sow mistrust of the Social Democrats. Both of them tried to plant the idea in the collective German consciousness that electing a Social Democrat chancellor would be the equivalent of opening the front door to Bolshevik wolves waiting just outside.

Speaking to the CDU leadership in 1956, Adenauer said that if the Social Democrats won the next federal election, West Germany would quickly become a "Soviet satellite state of some kind." And it would not stop there, Adenauer said: "We are alone the dam that can still protect Western Europe ... from the Communist flood."[23]

Throughout the Adenauer era, Gehlen's spy service seems to have been just as focused on keeping Adenauer in power as conducting foreign intelligence, if not more so. When Israeli prime minister David Ben-Gurion announced the arrest of Adolf Eichmann on May 23, 1960, the West German government was caught completely flat-footed. Alarmed about revelations that might be coming down the pike, Adenauer, Globke, and Gehlen were forced to scramble. A multiagency committee held meetings to discuss strategies for protecting Globke and other government officials who may have something to hide. The group decided they needed to go on the offensive and launched a series of covert operations.

Before his arrest, Eichmann gave interviews to a right-wing journalist in Buenos Aires. After Eichmann's capture, the BND scrambled to get transcripts of the interviews in case they contained damning information about Globke. Attempts to sell material to news publications were monitored scrupulously. BND agents and informants also probed the private and business relationships of Eichmann's two brothers, who lived in Salzburg, Vienna. BND agents pored over 3,500 pages of transcriptions of the Israelis' interrogation of Eichmann and 145 pages of Eichmann's handwritten notes. Henke wrote, "Adenauer and his head of chancellery [Globke] pulled out all the stops to ensure that the trial in Israel didn't escalate into a tribunal in which the West German state, as the legal successor to the Third Reich, was accused of being the country of the murderers of Jews."[24]

The BND hired an informant to spy on Reinhard Strecker, a young university student who caused a nationwide sensation with a traveling exhibit that identified West German judges and prosecutors who were complicit in crimes of the Third Reich. Strecker was about to publish a book about Globke's past, based on documents he had collected. The BND informant, a German journalist who used the pen name Michael Mansfeld, was a supposed friend of Strecker. In notes to his BND handler, Mansfeld made assessments about things like Strecker's fervor for digging up incriminating documents and his financial status while sprinkling in some personal observations about Strecker's appearance and character. "Wears a goatee and looks like a tuberculous existentialist," Mansfeld wrote. "He's starving, literally! Doesn't have outstanding people skills. A slightly psychopathic penchant for absolute truth and a bit of an instinct for prestige." Mansfeld also commented on Strecker's politics. "Good connections to Warsaw and Prague, where he gets his material," he wrote. "The man is politically immature, but undoubtedly not a Communist."[25]

Mansfeld told his handler he would let the BND know if Strecker succeeded in finding a publisher for the book. Officials from the BND, the Federal Office for the Protection of the Constitution, and important ministries met to discuss whether to stop publication. But the matter was taken care of when Strecker and the publisher agreed to withdraw the book after Globke got a lawyer and filed for a temporary injunction. The publisher feared financial losses from a prolonged court case.

The BND was so concerned about protecting Globke that it seemed ready to look into even the slightest threat to the state secretary's reputation. In early 1960 a Hanns J. Wiecher sent a letter to Globke, in which Herr Wiecher said he was ashamed to be a German because of Globke: "While the little ones hang, the big ones (to which you may well be counted!) hold high offices of state. Resign, Herr Globke. Get off the political scene, which is polluting itself with people like you."[26]

Globke gave the letter to BND, and an investigation was begun. A BND agent looked into what Herr Wiecher did for a living, his economic situation, and his relationship with his wife. The couple, the agent reported, lives in an "orderly and happy marriage. His wife is judged to be a neat and clean housewife." Herr Wiecher drives a white Ford Taurus, the agent noted. It is unclear whether the BND went any further in its probe of Herr Wiecher.

The West German Foreign Office was deployed to try to preemptively blunt whatever incriminating statements and evidence might emerge from the Eichmann trial. During a speech in Boston, the Bonn government's ambassador to the United States, Wilhelm Grewe, falsely claimed that West Germany had never wavered in its pursuit of war criminals and that there were no incriminated former Nazis in positions of leadership.[27]

On the other side of the Iron Curtain, the BND had an undercover agent who kept the West Germans apprised of the East German Communists' plans to exploit the Eichmann trial for propaganda purposes. East German revelations about the Nazi background of Theodor Oberländer, the

West German minister of expellees and refugees, were instrumental in forcing his resignation in 1960. Bonn was constantly worried about more dirt coming out about people in government, which was the purpose of the informant in East Berlin, who had the code name "Lena."

As Eichmann was awaiting trial in Israel, the BND, Adenauer, and Globke breathed a sigh of relief when they learned Eichmann said he did not know Globke. Eichmann remained silent about Globke up until his execution. This was a victory for Adenauer, Gehlen, and Globke. Still, the Adenauer era would soon come to an end. Public trust in the old man was being pummeled by a series of scandals in the early 1960s. These included the unmasking of the BND's Heinz Felfe as a Soviet spy, the discovery that West Germany's domestic intelligence service was wiretapping everyday citizens, the 1962 raid by the BKA on the offices of *Der Spiegel* magazine, and revelations that war criminals such as Theo Saevecke were working for the government. Rather than face another election, Adenauer resigned on October 11, 1963, ending a supremacy over West German politics that had lasted fourteen years. Hans Globke went with him.

In the view of historian Klaus-Dietmar Henke, Gehlen's spying on Adenauer's political opponents—with the active participation of Globke—was "incomparably more serious" than Watergate. Unlike with Nixon, the West German triumvirate's dirty tricks never cost them their jobs. What's more, the BND's decade of spying on Adenauer's critics and rivals actually yielded information that helped him stay in power. If you want to call it a conspiracy, it is one that was aided and abetted, although unwittingly, by East Germany's Communist regime. As the Communist East Germans launched document-based broadsides against West German officials who had served the Third Reich, Adenauer, Gehlen, and Globke wrapped themselves in West Germans' fear of Bolshevism as a protective cloak against their ideological enemies.

More than three decades after the end of the Cold War, it has become fairly clear that Gehlen's anti-Communist operations were largely a failure. Being on the front lines of the East-West confrontation, the BND was the most important intelligence agency within NATO. But the spy games it played against its Communist enemies were often marked by ineptitude. The way historian Henke sees it, Gehlen's greatest success was in an area where he should not have been meddling: domestic politics. "Since Reinhard Gehlen never thought of putting aside internal espionage in favor of his actual mission—foreign intelligence—his entire term in office was characterized by abuse of power, betrayal, and misconduct. The Gehlen system developed into a predominantly retarding factor in the development of West German democracy," Henke wrote.

It is easy to understand what Adenauer and Gehlen got out of this triangular conspiracy. Adenauer acquired dirt on his rivals, and Gehlen cemented his power by making his agency the indispensable source of the dirt. And Globke? Well, the full-court press to protect his reputation after the capture of Eichmann showed how useful it could be to be Adenauer's right-hand man.

# 14

# Redemption

The shock of anarchic white hair and horn-rimmed glasses. Fritz Bauer looked more like a rumpled professor than Hesse's state prosecutor as he addressed a TV camera in the early 1960s. His tone was earnest, his cadence measured. The elderly lawyer's creased face traced years of persecution as a Jew and a socialist.

"Today," began Bauer, sitting behind his office desk, "Germany is proud of its economic miracle. It's also proud to be the homeland of Goethe and Beethoven." But, he continued, "Germany is also the country of Hitler, Eichmann and their many henchmen and followers." Bauer's words were chosen to appeal to young Germans who as they matured were growing frustrated by the war generation's stubborn refusal to talk about the Third Reich. "I believe that the younger generation of Germany is prepared to learn about Germany's entire history, and the whole truth... something that their parents sometimes have difficulty confronting."

But surely, there also would have been many Germans who were thinking, or even saying out loud, why is this old Jew stirring things up? What right has a man who fled the Fatherland to lecture us who stayed behind? And quite likely, there would have been many West Germans who wished he would just go back to Denmark, his place of exile during the Nazi years, or emigrate to Israel, where he belonged.

Bauer's TV address is the opening scene in a 2015 feature film about his life, *Der Staat gegen Fritz Bauer* (The People v. Fritz Bauer), directed by Lars Kraume. Bauer for decades was an underappreciated figure, actually maligned among many Germans who viewed him as a traitor. What a turnround. Bauer is now idolized as a man who hunted for incriminated former Nazis at a time when government officials were trying to protect them, even to thwart Bauer's own investigations. His life has been told in movies, documentaries, and magazine and newspaper articles. In 2014 the German Justice Ministry inaugurated the Fritz Bauer Scholarship Prize for Human Rights and Contemporary History, five thousand euros awarded every other year to a young legal scholar whose work carries on Bauer's spirit.

How did Bauer go from pariah to national hero? Journalist Ronen Steinke, author of a well-received 2013 biography of Bauer, tells how he personally came to be an admirer. Before becoming a journalist, Steinke had studied law. The English-language edition of his book, published in 2020, is *Fritz Bauer: The Jewish Prosecutor Who Brought Eichmann and Auschwitz to Trial*.

"At the very beginning of my own law studies, I accidentally discovered the story that Fritz Bauer secretly gave the Mossad a tip about where Adolf Eichmann was hiding in Argentina," Steinke, who works for the newspaper *Süddeutsche Zeitung*, told me in an email. "At the time, Fritz Bauer knew that if he had gone through the regular bureaucratic process to apply for Adolf Eichmann's extradition from Argentina, it would have been hopeless. There were too many old Nazis in the German bureaucracy, and they would have definitely sabotaged this plan."

Steinke wrote admiringly of Bauer: "That was a very inspiring story for me: I was impressed by Fritz Bauer's courage and isolation. Fritz Bauer's willingness to follow his own ideals of justice. Back then, as a student in the early 2000s, I was amazed: there wasn't a single monograph dealing with Fritz Bauer's life. As a student, I was going through our law library and couldn't believe how little interest there seemed to have been in this courageous person."

In his book Steinke tells of another TV interview with Bauer, this one from 1967: "At the time of the interview, he was the most famous—and, if the number of threatening letters he received is anything to go by, the most hated—prosecutor in the country. A plot to kill him had recently been uncovered. The year before, two right-wing extremists had hatched a plan to assassinate Bauer, whom they regarded as the 'main culprit behind the trials against war criminals.'" In the TV interview, writes Steinke, Bauer related a memory from his childhood. As a first-grader, Bauer was beaten up by some other boys. One of them yelled at Bauer, "Your family killed Jesus."[1]

Bauer won renown in the mid-1960s not because of Eichmann's capture—his assistance to the Israelis was kept secret for years, for Bauer's own safety—but because of his orchestration of the 1963–65 trial of twenty-two officials of the Auschwitz extermination camp. As attorney general for Hesse state, Bauer organized the prosecution of the defendants in a fashion that showed it was not just murder that occurred at the extermination camp but industrialized slaughter. Bauer's prosecutors showed how the roles of each of the defendants fit into the machinery of this factory of genocide—from an SS officer responsible for handing out prison garb for newly arrived victims to monsters who tormented, tortured, and murdered even children. Bauer wanted the trial to serve as a history lesson—to confront his countrymen with the gruesome and grisly details, with eyewitness stories from survivors, as an admonishment to Germans to never let such atrocities happen again.

Bauer kept a 6.35 mm pistol in his apartment. He had good reason to fear for his life. Bauer would get threatening phone calls in the evening, but he tried to make light of them. According to Steinke, Bauer joked, "My Nazis still haven't grasped that I'm not in bed before midnight." During the Auschwitz trial, when Bauer left his apartment in the morning, he'd find posters with swastikas on the facade of the building. Bauer once said: "When I leave my office, I enter enemy territory." Threats against Bauer went back several years. The fact that he was a Jewish prosecutor in relentless pursuit of Nazi war criminals made him a prime target.

In the early morning hours of April 20, 1957—Hitler's sixty-sixth birthday—seventy-eight Jewish grave markers and a memorial were toppled at a cemetery in Salzgitter. The perpetrators left behind a straw doll, shackled, and the message "Germany Awake, Israel Die." A series of such desecrations had preceded this one. The Central Council of Jews in Germany demanded that the West German government finally take action, and anti-Nazi demonstrations spread across the country. A reward was offered by the federal government for help in tracking down the perpetrators, and a special commission was appointed to investigate. The commission, incidentally, included two BKA investigators who had been with Nazi mobile killing squads during the war.

Something happened during the investigation that was to have echoes five decades later. During a killing spree of immigrants from 2000 to 2006, law officials initially blamed other foreigners for the deaths, instead of homegrown neo-Nazis. As it turned out, those killings were committed by three young Germans who called themselves the National Socialist Underground. The very same mistake was made during the investigation of the 1957 cemetery desecration in Salzgitter. Law officials first suspected that Arabs were responsible and then floated the idea that the attacks had been carried out by Communist East German agents to try to discredit

West Germany as a fascist-riddled state. Another hypothesis was that the attacks were carried out by anti-Semites from Baltic countries. It took four years for West German investigators to finally track down the real culprits: three young Germans from the Salzgitter area. Their identities came to light by chance. The three men were overheard in a bar talking about founding a neo-Nazi organization.[2]

Investigators accused the three not just of damaging the Jewish gravestones but also of making plans to bomb the Bergen-Belsen concentration camp memorial. The trio had also put together a list of "traitors" to be "liquidated." Fritz Bauer was among those on the list. The three were convicted and sentenced in March 1962 by the Third Panel of the Federal Court of Justice. The ringleader, twenty-seven-year-old Günter Sonnemann, was sentenced to six years on charges of "cemetery desecration with seditious intent" and plotting to create a "secret, criminal organization with the intent of carrying out bombings." His two accomplices got lesser sentences.

Another plot to assassinate Bauer was uncovered four years later. In March 1966 threats were made by phone and a letter to the West German agency created in 1958 to track down Nazi perpetrators—the Ludwigsburg-based Central Office. Federal investigators discovered plans by two Germans and an American to attack the Central Office, a concentration camp memorial in Neuengamme, and Fritz Bauer. The two Germans were arrested. The American had returned to the United States. The perpetrators had acquired an arsenal of weapons, including a machine pistol, and had unsuccessfully tried to steal explosives from a quarry. During questioning the two suspects in custody made no secret of their neo-Nazi beliefs and of their hatred of Bauer as the main force pushing for war crimes trials. The three had scouted Bauer's Frankfurt apartment. The three, who had sworn on a swastika banner to dedicate themselves to Nazi ideals, had wanted to create a national crisis by carrying out attacks and hoped this would lead to a return to a fascist state.

After a three-day trial that began on November 7, 1966, the two Germans were convicted by the Federal Court of Justice of belonging to a criminal and anti-constitutional association and attempted grand larceny. The court's ruling had a mixed message. It was clear that the defendants' "ultimate goal was creation of an authoritarian state like the Third Reich" and they knew "this could only be accomplished by murder, bombings, and arson attacks." But the court said there was insufficient proof that the defendants' plans had progressed to the point where they were ready to commit violent acts. The two suspects got off lightly, each being sentenced to two years in prison. The court justified the lenient treatment by noting their young ages, their "shocking political immaturity," and their being under the influence of older right-wing extremists.[3]

Bauer's whole adult life was dedicated to fighting authoritarianism, defending human rights, and championing liberal reforms to German law. Born to a Jewish family in Stuttgart on July 16, 1903, Bauer attended a high school for boys and then began his studies in law. With nationalistic German fraternities barring Jews, he joined a Jewish fraternity, the Freie Wissenchaftliche Vereinigung, or Free Academic Union, which championed humanist ideals.

Bauer passed his law exams in 1925. He was appointed to a local court judgeship soon after getting his doctorate in 1927. Bauer had joined the Social Democratic Party and was chairman of the Stuttgart chapter of the Reichsbanner, a self-defense force that protected Social Democrats against attacks from extremists like the Nazis. A skilled orator, Bauer gave inspirational speeches in defense of the Weimar Republic even as its foundations began to crumble.

On March 23, 1933, two months after Hitler came to power, Bauer was arrested at his office. He was among the thousands of Social Democrats who had been swept up and sent to jails and concentration camps. Bauer was taken to Heuberg, a concentration camp south of Stuttgart, where he and other SPD leaders received brutal treatment. After eight months Bauer was among SPD and Communist Party functionaries transferred to a prison in Ulm. He was released in November 1933, apparently due to the influence of friends in the judiciary. But there was a price for freedom: Bauer was among eight Social Democrats jailed at Ulm who agreed to sign a declaration in which they pledged they were "unreservedly on the side of the Fatherland." Clearly, Bauer did not mean this. And it was a statement that did not free him from persecution. Like all German Jews, Bauer had been barred from the civil service. He could not return to his job in the judiciary or even work as a private attorney, so he took a job at his father's textile business. Bauer was monitored by the police and had to be constantly mindful of not doing something that would get him packed off to a concentration camp.

With the persecution and abuse of German Jews intensifying, Bauer decided it would be best to flee to Denmark, where his sister Margot and her husband had moved to. Before he left Germany, Bauer had been arrested in Stuttgart and jailed for a day. The police, according to biographer Ronen Steinke, had warned Bauer: "We're watching you. If we catch you involved in anything remotely resembling political subterfuge, we'll throw you back into the concentration camp."

While Bauer was out of the reach of the Nazi regime, he nonetheless faced hardships in Denmark, according to Steinke. Danish police harassed Bauer because of suspected homosexual activities. Bauer was not able to work as a lawyer because he did not have a Danish law degree. He tried to scrape together a living by writing for a newspaper for German exiles. After German troops marched into Denmark in 1940, Bauer and other anti-Nazi German exiles were rounded up and taken to a prison camp. He was released later that year. But as European Jews were being shipped off to extermination camps, Bauer went into hiding along with his parents, sister, and brother-in-law. They boarded a motorboat on the night of October 13, 1943, and fled to Sweden. He returned to Denmark after the Nazis' defeat in 1945 and to Germany four years later.

During the postwar era, Fritz Bauer scored a number of major judicial achievements, but it took decades for him to be granted the recognition that was his due. One act for which he deserved praise, of course, was his critical role in the capture of Adolf Eichmann. But there was one that had occurred a decade earlier, when Bauer was attorney general for Lower Saxony state, that is important because it challenged Nazi-era ideas of loyalty to the state and resistance to authority.

The 1952 court case in the city of Braunschweig focused on a former SS officer who was turned into a folk hero by the Nazis for rounding up resistance fighters involved in the failed attempt to assassinate Hitler at his Wolf's Lair eastern front headquarters on July 20, 1944. The SS major, Otto Ernst Remer, was commander of a battalion in Berlin. Word was spread by conspirators that Hitler had died from the bomb explosion. A general ordered Remer to seal off government buildings, but Remer realized this was part of the plot. Remer and his troops were involved in the capture of the plot leader, Claus von Stauffenberg, and others. The conspirators were either executed or sent to concentration camps. Remer, turned into a hero by Joseph Goebbels's propaganda machine, was promoted to major general and put in charge of a battalion responsible for Hitler's security.

Even after the Nazis' defeat, there were many Germans who viewed Remer as a patriotic figure who had valiantly leaped into action to defend the Reich against traitors who deserved the fate that was dealt them after their capture. In 1949 Remer and other former Third Reich functionaries founded a political party that was in essence the successor of the National Socialists—the Sozialistische Reichspartei (Socialist Reich Party), or SRP. In public appearances Remer boasted about his role in crushing the conspirators and called them "traitors to their country" who were "paid by foreign powers." The federal interior minister at the time, Robert Lehr, had himself been a part of the anti-Hitler resistance. Lehr took offense at Remer's verbal assaults on the July 20 conspirators and lodged a legal complaint, accusing Remer of defaming the resistance. When Bauer learned of Lehr's complaint, he decided to bring formal charges against Remer.

When Remer's trial began in the spring of 1952, Bauer's mission had less to do with punishing the former SS major than with demonstrating that the July 20 conspirators, and others in the anti-Hitler resistance, were just the opposite of traitors to the nation, that they were, in fact, patriots for having stood up against despotism. Bauer's prosecution of the case served not just to effectively argue this point in a West German courtroom but to force the whole country to reflect on the meaning of patriotism and to confront German servitude to an immoral regime. "The aim of this trial is not to sow discord, but rather to build bridges and foster reconciliation... by having a democratic, independent court answer the question 'Were the July 20 conspirators traitors?'" Bauer said. "It now falls to the prosecutors and judges of our constitutional democracy to unreservedly rehabilitate the heroes of July 20."[4]

While Bauer in the end failed to persuade the court that Remer had defamed the July 20 conspirators, the judges did rule that the former SS officer had insulted resistance fighters. Remer was sentenced to only three months in prison. But Bauer succeeded in a larger cause: provoking a public debate about the ethical correctness—even obligation—to oppose a dictatorial regime. While this was clearly an achievement for Bauer, it was not a complete one. It failed to alter widespread pressure for ending war crimes trials and for giving amnesty to those already in prison. And while Bauer made impassioned arguments for honoring, and not punishing, those who dared to challenge authoritarian rule, it took five decades before the German Bundestag overturned the convictions of thousands of German soldiers who had been executed during World War II for desertion and other offenses.

Bauer was once again in the international spotlight eleven years later, as the boss of Hesse state prosecutors in the 1963–65 Auschwitz trial. Bauer's involvement in the case had its beginnings with SS documents from Auschwitz that had been found by a Holocaust survivor, Emil Wulkan; the documents concerned the killing of prisoners who were trying to flee. Wulkan gave the documents to a journalist with the *Frankfurter Rundschau*, who in 1959 gave them to Bauer. "He [Bauer] instantly recognized how politically explosive these papers were," Ronen Steinke wrote in his biography.

A year earlier, another Auschwitz survivor, Adolf Rögner, had filed charges against one of Auschwitz's most sadistic killing specialists, Wilhelm Boger. Rögner's complaint went nowhere, which was par for the course within the West German judiciary of those times. But when Rögner contacted the International Auschwitz Committee, things started to happen. The committee collected addresses of Auschwitz survivors who could provide testimony about the death camp. Bauer and the Central Office in Ludwigsburg pursued investigative leads. Ultimately, investigators were able to track down fifteen hundred witnesses and identify hundreds of alleged Auschwitz war criminals. Investigators picked twenty-two defendants to stand trial, chosen to demonstrate the systematic nature of the terror, horror, sadism, and mass murder committed at Auschwitz.

After eighteen months of hearings, which included testimony from 360 witnesses, on August 19, 1965, the Frankfurt court delivered its verdicts. Six defendants were sentenced to life in prison by the Frankfurt court, while other sentences ranged from three to fourteen years. The trial had been a sensation. TV crews from across Europe and journalists from around the globe covered it. Bauer kept a low profile during the proceedings, but he was steering the prosecution behind the scenes.

In the view of Ronen Steinke, the Auschwitz trial was Fritz Bauer's greatest achievement. This may well be true. But whatever impact the trial may have had on West German jurisprudence was dwarfed by the legislative "depth charge" that detonated four years later: the law that put thousands of Holocaust perpetrators out of reach of prosecutors because their crimes, being accessories to murder, were suddenly outside the statute of limitations.

On the morning of July 1, 1968, Fritz Bauer's body was found in his bathtub. The medical examiner determined Bauer had taken a sedative before getting into the tub, and the autopsy showed he had a moderate blood alcohol content. He was sixty-four years old. Conspiracy theories proliferated, of course. But the coroner said there was no evidence of murder, nor was there conclusive evidence of suicide. There had been increasing concerns about Bauer's health. One of his employees, Johannes Warlo, told Ronen Steinke in an interview that his boss's meals "mainly consisted of black coffee and cigarettes." The result of the Auschwitz trial, it seems, did little to alleviate Bauer's concerns about what was happening around him. According to Steinke, Bauer wrote to a friend on January 31, 1967: "The strong aversion in this country to confronting the past is growing even stronger and taking an ominous turn." Bauer's single-minded determination to pursue war criminals and bring them to justice, while not paying attention to his health, may have been what snuffed out his life.

Journalists, lawyers, and locals were the usual patrons bending an elbow at a humble bar in Karlsruhe called Crocodile. The scribes and attorneys were in Karlsruhe because it was, and is, the host city of three of the most important judicial bodies in the land: the Federal Constitutional Court, the Federal Court of Justice, and the Office of the Federal Prosecutor. In November 1959 the provincial town was rattled by a spectacle set up in a backroom of the Crocodile: an exhibit of Nazi documents revealing the Third Reich pasts of judges and prosecutors who were able to resume their careers in the West German state. The Crocodile was chosen for the exhibit after Karlsruhe officials had turned down a request to use City Hall. Word about the exhibit spread across the country, drawing extensive press coverage. This was an incredibly audacious act—to force West Germans, who by and large were trying to bury the past, to come face to face with the Nazi taint that had seeped throughout the postwar judicial apparatus.

The creator of this public provocation was a twenty-nine-year-old student, Reinhard Strecker. Five years earlier, Strecker was living in Paris, a self-exile. He had turned his back on his German homeland soon after the war's end. "For me, the sound of the Third Reich is the trampling of hobnail boots storming up the stairs," Strecker told biographers Gottfried Oy and Christoph Schneider for a book published in 2013.[5] Strecker was referring to storm troopers who ransacked Jewish apartments in his family's building during Kristallnacht, November 9–10, 1938. The Nazis did not find the three families the non-Jewish Streckers were hiding. Strecker's father was a leading member of something called the Confessing Church, which at first attempted to resist the Nazis' views on Christianity. While the Streckers were not overtly persecuted, it was something they had to constantly worry about.

After the war the young Strecker watched with dismay as Nazis began returning to positions of influence. So he left. Strecker had planned to hitchhike to England, but he became smitten by the Bohemian lifestyle in Paris and stayed. Strecker later told Schneider and Oy that he and some friends ran an art gallery across from Notre Dame cathedral. People who walked in were offered a glass of wine. Strecker studied languages at the Sorbonne. He discovered a streetcorner where Spanish Republicans who had fought in the Spanish civil war and survived German concentration camps would meet and discuss politics. "They had a profound influence on me," Strecker told Oy and Schneider. "In Germany, ever since the *Kaiserreich*, anarchism was a disreputable matter, a sinister word. But this was actually my political direction."

Strecker's parents had moved from Berlin to Celle, where his father, a lawyer, had gotten a job with the district court. At his parents' urging, Strecker returned to Germany in 1954. But he was not about to settle down in Celle, which Strecker described to Oy and Schneider as a "deeply brown, ultra-reactionary city." It was Berlin that beckoned young Strecker. He enrolled at Berlin's Free University, earning a little bit of money as assistant to a professor. Strecker had already developed an interest in Nazi perpetrators and their crimes. He began compiling information and put it on index cards, but he was denied access to West German archives. At the risk of being accused of carrying out propaganda for Communist authorities, he collected documents archived in Czechoslovakia and Poland. "I was determined to stop the process that began under Konrad Adenauer," Strecker said in a 2019 interview with *Deutsche Welle*. "I wanted nothing to do with what was reemerging in Germany. All the Nazis that I had hated were now back in office."

Strecker linked up with the Sozialistischer Deutscher Studentenbund (Socialist German Student League), a German analogue of the American Students for a Democratic Society that was associated with the Social Democratic Party. At first Strecker and the SDS hoped to use Nazi documents to pressure the Bundestag to launch inquiries into Nazi judges, prosecutors, and medical professionals who had resumed their careers in West Germany. But thousands of signatures gathered by Strecker and the SDS and presented to the Bundestag fell on deaf ears. So Strecker and his associates decided to pull the documents together into an exhibit and take it on the road. The exhibit was called *Ungesühnte Nazijustiz* (Unpunished Nazi Jurists). It got a test run in May 1959 at a Frankfurt congress of the SDS and other groups of young socialists. Because it was mainly leftist students who attended the Frankfurt congress, exposure to Strecker's findings was limited. Strecker decided the next stop would be Karlsruhe, in part to get the attention of the federal public prosecutor, Max Güde. Preparations were made by the Karlsruhe branch of the SDS. The Karlruhe City Hall agreed to lease space for the *Ungesühnte Justiz* exhibit, but the contract was canceled by Karlsruhe's lord mayor, apparently because of pressure from the federal government. "So we took the exhibit to a bar in the Old City, the Crocodile," Strecker told Oy and Schneider.

What visitors saw at the Crocodile was not a slick exhibit put together by PR-savvy professionals. It consisted of loose-leaf binders containing photocopies of Nazi files of more than one hundred West German jurists who had loyally served the Third Reich. It was the contents of those documents—such as death sentences by judges now working in West Germany—that turned the exhibit into a sensation that echoed across Germany and beyond.

As hoped, *Ungesühnte Nazijustiz* did get the attention of federal prosecutor Güde. "Güde must have talked with journalists about the exhibit and what it was about. He called me on the telephone, invited me to his office, and asked me to bring some documents along," Strecker told Oy and Schneider. Strecker spent a couple of hours with Güde at his office. As the federal prosecutor looked over the documents, he told Strecker: "They're authentic, all authentic." This was important. Just as important was Güde's encouragement to Strecker to continue his pursuit.

Max Güde was an impressive and compelling Cold War figure. He also personifies an object lesson that demonstrates the unwisdom of rushing to judgment of a former Nazi simply because of his or her apparent unbroken service to the Third Reich. Güde had much in common with Thomas Dehler, West Germany's first justice minister. Like Dehler, Güde was a devout Catholic who during his university years in the 1920s was actively involved in defending the Weimar democracy.

Güde's wartime and postwar careers are examined in a 2021 study of the federal prosecutor's office into the 1970s, titled *Staatsschutz im Kalten Krieg* (Protection of the State during the Cold War). The six hundred-page study, based on archival records and interviews, was conducted by historian Friedrich Kiessling and law professor Christoph Safferling, who was also coauthor of *Die Akte Rosenburg*.

Güde was born 1902 in a Black Forest town near the French border. He studied law at Heidelberg and Bonn and was among the top scorers in his law exams. After his legal clerkship, Güde became a state prosecutor, and in 1932 a judge in Bruchsal, just north of Karlsruhe. In 1933, after complaining about the imprisonment of a Jewish Social Democrat, Güde was transferred to the backwater town of Wolfach, where he was the sole judge in the local court. Nazi judicial officials did not view Güde as a team player. He put in for at least two transfers to higher positions on more prominent courts, and in livelier towns, but was rejected both times for coming up short on political acceptability. Güde joined the Nazi Party, but that didn't get him out of Wolfach. A Nazi personnel memo from March 1939 said of Güde: "His ideological attitude leaves much to be desired."[6]

After the war Güde was cleared of any suspicion of war crimes, and he was allowed to be part of Allied efforts to build a new judicial system in the western zone. He was appointed to lead the newly created state prosecutor's office in Konstanz, and on October 1, 1950, he was one of the first prosecutors hired by the freshly minted federal prosecutor's office. Five years later, he succeeded Carlo Wiechmann as chief federal prosecutor. Like Fritz Bauer, Güde stood out among postwar prosecutors. "Güde was much more of a public figure than his predecessor. The new boss in Karlsruhe was also politically different. Under the conservative auspices of the Adenauer era, Max Güde was as liberal as one could well be as federal prosecutor general," wrote Kiessling and Safferling.

In his inaugural address as chief federal prosecutor, Güde stressed the importance of protecting the state but not at the expense of citizens' freedom. He spoke out against the "unconditional obedience" to authority "with which we allowed ourselves to be strangled" during the years of the Third Reich. "No one," he said, "can serve two masters, not even the state prosecutor."

Güde's tenure as West Germany's top prosecutor came to an end after five years, when he decided to run for a seat in the Bundestag, which he won. Güde was succeeded by Wolfgang Fränkel, a jurist who lasted just four months on the job because of disclosures about his ruthless imposition of the death penalty while serving as a top Nazi prosecutor in Leipzig.

Fränkel was the perfect choice to succeed Güde, or so insisted the powerful friends and allies who pushed for his appointment. Hired by the federal prosecutor's office in 1951, Fränkel had amassed a great deal of expertise. There is no doubt that Fränkel was a highly skilled jurist, but it was more than professional skill that took him to the top. Fränkel had influential champions within the federal judiciary, including Carl Kirchner, a federal judge who, not coincidentally, had been Fränkel's immediate superior within the Third Reich judicial system.

The Bundesrat—the upper parliamentary house composed of delegates from the German states—approved Fränkel's appointment as federal public prosecutor on March 12, 1962. It didn't take long for Fränkel to become the center of one of the most embarrassing Nazi-related scandals of the Cold War era. It began with the publication by Communist East German authorities of a 130-page booklet with the title *From the Reich Prosecutor's Office to the Federal Prosecutor's Office*, with the subtitle *Wolfgang Fränkel— The New Federal Prosecutor General*. On the cover of the booklet, presented at a press conference in East Berlin in June 1962, was a photo of Fränkel, plus a crudely drawn swastika. Inside the booklet was meticulous documentation of Fränkel's Nazi legal career.

In 1941 paperwork on the sentencing by the Magdeburg Special Court of a petty thief landed on Fränkel's desk at the Nazis' highest judicial body— the Reich Court—in Leipzig, where Fränkel was an assistant prosecutor.[7] The petty criminal, Walter Goedicke, had been sentenced to eight years in prison for stealing 275 chickens. Fränkel was aghast at the Magdeburg court's sentence—not because of its severity but because of what Fränkel saw as its leniency. In Fränkel's view Goedicke deserved nothing less than execution. He put together an argument for vacating the Magdeburg court's sentence and sending the case back to that court, with the strong suggestion that Goedicke be sentenced to death instead. Fränkel argued that Goedicke's theft of chickens was a violation of a wartime ordinance that punished those who disrupted the supply of goods to the German populace. Fränkel also complained that the Magdeburg court had failed to take into consideration a series of crimes committed by Goedicke before the pullet purloining. Goedicke, wrote Fränkel, was a "completely unworthy member of the peoples' community."

Fränkel's superiors signed off on the recommendation without comment. Fränkel argued his case before the Reich Court, which agreed with him and sent the matter back to the Magdeburg court for consideration of a new sentencing. The Magdeburg judges bent to the will of the Reich Court, calling Goedicke a "morally inferior and asocial person" who deserved to be "weeded out... for the protection of the German populace." Goedicke was executed on February 21, 1942.

Fränkel had wielded a dubious legal tool known as the *Nichtigkeitsbeschwerde*, which means "annulment appeal." Introduced by the Nazi Justice Ministry in 1940, the *Nichtigkeitsbeschwerde* made it possible for prosecutors to interfere with already settled court cases if they thought the trial court had been too soft on the defendant. The 130-page bombshell booklet published by East German authorities showed that Fränkel was a zealous wielder of the *Nichtigkeitsbeschwerde*.

Fränkel's use of the *Nichtigkeitsbeschwerde* was so fanatical that the Reich Court didn't always agree with him. The Special Court in Kiel sentenced a Polish man, Joseph Fuczak, to six years for masturbating in a pasture.[8] Fränkel filed a *Nichtigkeitsbeschwerde* against the Kiel court's sentence. Appearing before the Reich Court's Third Criminal Panel, Fränkel argued that Fuczak's "obscene act" was a danger to German children and could have created "unrest within the populace," so he deserved to die. The Third Criminal Panel disagreed, saying Fränkel's manner of pleasuring himself, although done in the open, did not actually harm anyone. So the six-year sentence for masturbation stood. Other instances were also cited in the East Germans' documentation of Fränkel's actions at the Reich Court.

Fränkel was camping with his family in Italy as outrage over the disclosures grew back in his homeland. When he returned, he was called to Bonn to explain himself to Justice Minister Wolfgang Stammberger. According to Safferling and Kiessling, Stammberger handed the damning 130-page brochure to Fränkel, who left the office to read it. With the look of a crushed man knowing his career was over, Fränkel returned to Stammberger's office within a couple of hours, confirmed the documents' authenticity, and offered to resign. He was immediately placed on leave, and a committee was appointed to make a recommendation on what to do about Fränkel. The committee came to the conclusion that he was politically and judicially unfit to keep his job, so he was fired.

Meanwhile, Reinhard Strecker had become a major German celebrity by showing the *Ungesühnte Nazijustiz* exhibit across the Federal Republic over a four-year period and even taking some of the documents to London to show to members of the lower house of Parliament. While Strecker cannot claim direct credit for the downfall of Wolfgang Fränkel—it was, after all, the East German Communists who arranged the East Berlin press conference where the toxic 130-page brochure was made public—Strecker's doggedness in drawing attention to tainted West German jurists certainly created a political climate that made it impossible for Fränkel to stay on the job as the top federal prosecutor. Strecker's activism also forced West German politicians to consider legislation to try to persuade tainted judges and prosecutors to leave on their own volition. The Bundestag passed legislation offering judges and prosecutors who had participated in the administration of criminal law up until the end of the war the opportunity to resign with a full pension.

Reinhard Strecker had suffered persistent government obstructionism, harassment, accusations of treason, and even threats during his campaign to expose seriously compromised jurists who were sitting on the West German judiciary. His successes can certainly be seen as a form of redemption. But in reality, his work had done little to dent West German government resistance to holding such people to account or the practice of covering up the Third Reich misdeeds of postwar civil servants. Although about 150 judges and public prosecutors took the Bundestag's offer of retirement with a full pension, hundreds more remained on the job. And although there were disciplinary and criminal investigations launched against Fränkel, they were all ultimately dropped. He died in 2010 at age 105. Right up to the end, Fränkel insisted he had done nothing wrong during his service to the Nazi regime—that the executions he took part in were appropriate and just because they were carried out during wartime under Nazi law. This is a viewpoint of judicial punishments during the Nazi years that carried sway among some conservatives right into the twenty-first century.

Ten years before the BKA's 2011 official acknowledgment that war criminals were among the agency's first generation of investigators, a BKA critic who had quit the agency published a shocking book that tore the masks off those very same tainted investigators. Dieter Schenk joined the BKA in 1981, but he resigned in 1989 because of cozy relationships his country had developed with authoritarian nations. While at the BKA, Schenk had strong suspicions that some of his older colleagues were hiding Nazi secrets. But no one ever talked about it. A man who is much more likely to start digging rather than walk away when he senses wrongdoing, Schenk set his mind on finding out what the BKA was trying to hide.[9]

To understand what motivates Dieter Schenk, it's illuminating to examine his wartime childhood. In September 1944 seven-year-old Dieter Schenk clutched his mother's hand as they approached a train that was boarding passengers at the depot in Sarrebourg, France. From the platform Else Schenk hoisted Dieter into the train car. Next came their two suitcases. And then Else Schenk got on board herself. As steam billowed from beneath its iron wheels, the locomotive bucked and shook, like a rodeo bull eager to burst out of the chute. Finally, the locomotive lurched forward. The train rolled through the Alsatian countryside, past tidy farms, cows in pastures, lonesome copses of trees standing in green meadows. It followed the Saare River for a while, before climbing into the Vosges Mountains. Dieter Schenk sat next to the window as the train made its way eastward. He could not stop thinking of his father, Heinz, a Gestapo officer, stationed in Sarrebourg. The Schenk family had lived there for two years, part of the German force occupying France. As American troops and their Allies battled their way deeper into the French interior after the D-Day landings in Normandy, families of the German troops were sent back to their homeland. Dieter wondered whether his father would have to fight, whether he would be killed or captured, whether Dieter would ever see him again.

During the night the train arrived at the Schenks' destination: Schenklengsfeld, a hamlet in rolling farmland south of Kassel. They were greeted by Dieter's aunt, Anni Martin, who lived with her own three children in a house on the grounds of a Schenklengsfeld sawmill. Anni's husband had gone missing in the Battle of Stalingrad. To protect Dieter's grandparents from bombing that had destroyed much of Kassel, Anni had given them refuge. The good-hearted Anni was now taking in Dieter and his mother as well.

A few days later, Dieter was riding his bike down a dirt road. He heard a thrumming sound in the sky. "In 1944-45 Allied squadrons flew at high altitudes in the steel-blue wintry sky, like glittering, silvery cranes," Schenk recalled in an address to the Schenklengsfeld municipal council in 2017. Very quickly came what sounded like claps of thunder. That evening "the horizon shone bloodred in the direction of Kassel," the target of the Allied bombing run.[10] The enemy rolled into Schenklengsfeld on the Saturday before Easter 1945—an American tank, preceded by a jeep. The Schenks by now had moved into other lodgings: two rooms in a farmhouse owned by Hans and Liese Wolf. "I'll never forget the picture: the long bent antenna of the jeep and a foreign language coming from the loudspeaker in the military vehicle. I was curious and strangely without fear. Hans Wolf had hoisted a sheet as a white flag on the roof. One of the neighbors did not like that," recalled Schenk in his 2017 talk to the Schenklengsfeld municipal council.

Four GIs dismounted from the jeep. They searched houses as well as stables and barns. Finding no German soldiers, the jeep and the tank headed for the next town. A bridge gave way when the tank tried to cross it. The tank clanked out of the water and onto the riverbank, continuing on its way.

A small unit of GIs remained in town for a few months. The Americans handed out chewing gum and candy to the children. Some local women did the soldiers' laundry and were reimbursed with coffee beans—hard to come by in the final years of the war. It was only later, as an adult, that Schenk discovered there were some in town who were complicit in the deportation of local Jews. There was still German resistance in the area. An American tank parked near a farmhouse fired a shell. Reverberation from the blast shattered a window. One day Dieter saw the charred wreckage of German army vehicles on the side of the road.

After the war's end, ten-year-old Dieter learned that his father had died in an American internment camp of a pulmonary embolism after an operation. Dieter and his mother had no source of income, but relatives and townspeople made sure they were provided for. Despite the hardships,

Dieter was able to experience some joys of boyhood. He was always riding a bike, dodging rainwater-filled potholes on the dirt road that led out of town. He played soccer with other boys, using a ball made of stitched-together scraps of cloth. The local mill was a favorite spot for kids to play hide-and-seek. Even in old age, the sound of running water turning the mill wheel was a constant in Dieter Schenk's memories.

There was much the boy did not understand. He had not been born when Hitler became chancellor in 1933. He was age two when Nazi storm troopers destroyed synagogues and Jewish-owned stores and beat Jews on German streets during the Kristallnacht pogroms of 1938. He was just a toddler when German troops invaded Poland, the start of World War II. And while living in Nazi-occupied France with his parents, he had no idea what exactly it was that his father did. After the war the boy was curious to know more about the Third Reich, but this was the start of a long era of silence about the Nazi regime.

Dieter developed a deep admiration for Hans Wolf, who had hoisted the white sheet when the GIs arrived. Wolf had a gentle nature. He took care of a three-legged deer that lived in his garden and kept thirty bee colonies. If one of the bees got wet, Wolf would put it under his cap so it could dry off. Hans Wolf was the soul of generosity. He asked for no rent from the destitute mother and son. These were childhood observations that would become guideposts for Dieter Schenk, memories that would remain in his brain for decades to come.

A new father figure entered Dieter's life in the 1950s, when his mother remarried. The stepfather was a racist and an unrepentant admirer of Hitler, poisonous qualities that were to have a profound impact on Schenk. "He [the stepfather] embodied everything I rejected," Schenk would say decades later. Dieter could hardly wait to leave home, despite his close bond with his mother. At age eighteen he applied for work as a police officer and was hired.

Dieter's choice of a career might seem odd. Here was a young man who hated authoritarianism and disliked uniforms, but he took a job in which he would be in a position to exercise force. Before he was a Gestapo officer, Heinz Schenk was just a regular cop in Germany. Perhaps Dieter's longing for his father—a desire to get closer to him, to try to understand him—subconsciously put young Schenk on a similar career path.

Dieter Schenk ditched his police officer uniform for plainclothes when he became a detective with the State Criminal Office in Hesse state. Frankfurt am Main, the big Hesse metropolis, in the 1960s had become a magnet for international crime gangs that inundated the city with cheap heroin. In the early 1970s Schenk attended a police leadership academy and was appointed chief of detectives in Giessen, another city in Hesse. Along these stages in his law enforcement career, Schenk was often alarmed by the heavy-handed measures taken by police agencies against leftists and a kid-glove approach often shown toward those on the Far Right.

In 1981 Schenk spotted announcements for job openings with the Bundeskriminalamt. He applied and was hired. Schenk ultimately landed one of the most desirable positions at the BKA: drawing up plans for the protection of West German embassies and their diplomats around the world. Over the next eight years, Schenk traveled to more than sixty nations. It did not take long for disillusionment to set in. These were Cold War years, a time when the United States and its Allies were competing with the Soviet bloc to limit each other's global influence by wooing unaligned nations, even those known for human rights violations. In Schenk's position as security specialist for West Germany's diplomatic service, he saw this occurring firsthand, and it made him recoil. He witnessed West German diplomats cultivating friendships with dictators who had their political opponents kidnapped and tortured. After returning from trips to such countries, Schenk would complain to his superiors about how people who just wanted their freedom were being treated like terrorists by despotic leaders, and he argued West Germany's leaders should not be tolerating this.

As part of his job, Schenk was required to write reports about his visits, focusing on strategies and tactics to protect West German embassies and their personnel. But Schenk's conscience demanded he also write about human rights violations he had witnessed or had been told about, such as the hanging of political prisoners by their thumbs. In one report Schenk wrote about the connections between police in a Central American country and death squads. While Schenk's report was going through the process of official approval, someone deleted sentences that would have offended the leadership of the Central American country. This was intolerable to Schenk. He resigned from the BKA in 1989.

While working at the Bundeskriminalamt, Schenk heard whispers about a clique of BKA investigators known as the "Charlottenburgers." Schenk knew that these were men who had graduated from the SS police academy in the Berlin neighborhood of Charlottenburg during the early years of the Third Reich. And he knew that they were closely associated with Paul Dickopf, architect of the federal police agency. But when Schenk asked questions at the BKA about the Charlottenburgers, he made little headway in discovering much about them. "They had great influence in the BKA," Schenk said in 2017. "But there was a mystery about them. Details were concealed, at least from me."[11] When Schenk quit the BKA, his curiosity about the Charlottenburgers stayed with him.

Among the myriad forces that were directing Schenk's course in life was his deceased father. Ever since adolescence, Schenk had wondered what his father had done as a Gestapo officer, but he feared he might discover the worst. Had he been involved in the deportation of French Jews to death camps, for example? It was with great trepidation that a few years before joining the BKA, Schenk traveled to Sarrebourg, France, to confront his father's past.

During the visit to Sarrebourg, Schenk's mind was put at ease. He turned up the findings of an investigation by French police into Heinz Schenk's activities as a Gestapo officer. Heinz held a Gestapo office job, was not active in the field, and was exonerated by the French of any wrongdoing. In 2016, seventy years after Heinz Schenk's death, Dieter Schenk wrote a letter to his two daughters and to his grandchildren about his father. He told them of the relief he felt from discovering that Heinz Schenk was not a war criminal. "From all that I know now, I do not need to blame my dad anymore," he wrote. In the letter he pondered whether Heinz Schenk would have tried to talk his son out of going into law enforcement and whether he would have agreed with Dieter's humanitarian-based reasons for resigning from the BKA.[12]

Dieter Schenk's hunger for the truth did not stop with his father. After leaving the BKA, he set his sights on pursuing nagging suspicions that Nazi war criminals had found refuge within the federal police agency and that government officials helped them cover their tracks. He wanted to know more about the Charlottenburgers. He asked the BKA for files on Dickopf but was rebuffed because of an embargo on them. But he persisted. Using archives in Germany, Switzerland, and Poland, among other sources, he was able to reveal the BKA's deep secret: that in the first three decades following the Nazis' defeat, the ranks of West Germany's federal police force were infested with men who during the Third Reich had served in police units that had committed massacres in the Baltics, Ukraine, Russia, and Poland. Schenk also demonstrated that American intelligence officials were complicit in fostering an environment within the BKA that permitted the hiring of such men and sometimes in trying to hide their pasts.

Schenk's findings were published in his 2001 bestseller, *Auf dem rechten Auge blind*, released by one of Germany's most esteemed publishing houses, Kiepenheuer & Witsch. Even though the BKA's shameful secrets were now out, it took another ten years for the German government to officially acknowledge the truth of Schenk's revelations. That came with the publication in 2011 of findings by independent historians commissioned by the BKA to investigate the agency's postwar hiring. Within the 390 pages of those meticulously documented and highly damning findings are a total of ninety-two references to Schenk and to his research.

The BKA-hired historians said about Schenk: "From the historian's point of view... Schenk's great merits are obvious, because it was only with his publishing that an awareness was created within the broad public (and even within the BKA) that the Federal Criminal Police Office was set up by criminalists who had served in the National Socialist apparatus of extermination." The results of Schenk's work, the historians wrote, "have in many ways laid the foundation for the research project from which this book arose."[13]

Among those rare Germans who dared to puncture the unspoken omerta that protected Nazi perpetrators in postwar government offices, Ralph Giordano stands out. It was Giordano, after all, who coined a term that got more Germans to talk about that Cold War infestation of the civil service, to finally confront it: "second guilt." It is a concept that continues to animate discussions about the postwar years, more than three decades after German reunification.

Son of a Jewish mother, Giordano and his family managed to escape the Holocaust by hiding out for three months in the rat-infested ruins of a Hamburg cellar. Six months after the war's end, the twenty-two-year-old Giordano was walking along a street in the bombed-out port city. A few paces ahead of him was a middle-age German man, accompanied by two women. Giordano overheard the man tell the two women, in a loud voice: "The Jews . . . they are to blame for everything." Overcome with rage, Giordano charged at the German, knocked him to the ground, and then used his fists, teeth, and fingernails to assault this man who had the gall to claim that Jews were responsible for Germany's humiliating defeat and for the postwar hardships that followed. The German man escaped further punishment by getting up and running away.

Giordano would tell the story of this 1945 altercation as a way of establishing his ethical right to call out the public and officialdom for what he saw as failures to fully come to terms with the Nazi past. As government-hired historians were digging into old files in their search for Nazi perpetrators among postwar government employees, Giordano was invited to conferences that were organized to discuss their progress and findings.

At one of the conferences, Giordano said: "We live in a land in which the greatest crime in history, which took millions and millions of victims, killed, it must be said, behind the front lines like insects, was followed by the greatest rehabilitation project for perpetrators the world has ever known. With very few exceptions, they not only escaped punishment but were also permitted to pursue their careers unhindered."[14] This was a point that Giordano had been making for two decades, at least since the 1987 publication of his book *Die zweite Schuld, oder Von der Last, Deutscher zu sein* (The Second Guilt, or On the Burden of Being German). There was no single person in Germany who had fought for so long and with such passion for German authorities to finally confront the Nazi taint during the Adenauer era.

Giordano's life, going back to his Hamburg boyhood, explains where this persistence came from. Giordano was ten years old in 1933, when Hitler came to power. He lived with his parents and two brothers in a house in Hamburg's Barmbek district. His father was a pianist, and his mother, who was of Jewish heritage, was a piano teacher. In postwar interviews Giordano said he had had a carefree childhood for the first decade of his life. He had close friends. He had a sense of belonging. This sense of well-being and belonging unraveled when his best friend, Heinemann, said to him one day, using his nickname: "Ralle, we're not going to play with you anymore. You're a Jew." In a postwar interview, Giordano said: "This was like an execution. The world stood still."

One by one, the hawsers that kept Giordano—like all Jews—moored to a stable and safe life in Germany were snapping. He was tormented at school and watched as his erstwhile friends joined the Hitler Youth. At age sixteen Giordano was hauled in for questioning by the Gestapo, after a friend reported him for making negative comments about the Nazi regime. During interrogation, which included torture, the Gestapo insisted Giordano sign a document saying that the anti-regime ideas came from his Jewish mother. He refused to do so, knowing that would be a death sentence for her.

Firestorms, explosions, and terror tore through Hamburg during the last week of July 1943, as formations of British and American bombers dropped their payloads onto the populace—the British at night and the Americans during the day. During the night of July 24, when the first raid occurred, twenty-year-old Ralph was at his family's apartment, working on what would become, after the war, a novel. The family took refuge in the cellar.

"The bombs howled down, and there was a gruesome noise. If you heard the noise, then that meant that the bomb was hitting someone else; the bombs that hit you were the ones you didn't hear ahead of time," Giordano said in a 2010 interview for the PBS *American Experience* program. "It continued without interruption. When at 2:00 a.m. I climbed out of the basement and into the street, the linden trees that lined the street—big trees that reached as high as the fourth floor—they were bending towards the south, because oxygen had been so depleted by the fire."[15]

The Barmbek district was spared during the initial raids. "And then came the night from the twenty-ninth to the thirtieth of July, a Thursday to a Friday, when it was Barmbek's turn," Giordano said in the PBS interview. "After two minutes it was clear that Barmbek was the intended target. Everything was crackling—the fire crackled—and we were together, my parents, three brothers, and my grandmother and grandfather on my mother's side."

They had fled to the basement, but they realized that with fire burning all around them, it was not safe there. They made their way toward the city park, hoping to find safety there. They crawled on their knees and bellies through scenes right out of hell. "Imagine: bombs that weigh tons exploding around you, an entire district in flames." The bombing stopped when they reached the park. They knew right away that there would be no house to return to—the home where the Giordanos had lived for twenty years. The family was able to get by, but as Jews were being deported to the East, perils were always near.

Lilly Giordano, the mother, was at first spared deportation because she was in a "mixed marriage." But that protection was ultimately taken away. On February 9, 1945, she was ordered by the Gestapo to go to an "assembly point" to await deportation. The Giordanos knew exactly what that meant—she was being shipped to an extermination camp. At age twenty-two Ralph Giordano took charge of preparations to save his mother. The family spent the last three months of the war in a cellar crawl space. A good friend of Ralph Giordano kept them supplied with food until the friend's arrest by the Gestapo. Conditions worsened for the family in the cellar. Hungry rats tried to gnaw them. The Giordanos were nearing starvation. But they were saved by the arrival of British troops on May 4, 1945.

With the danger over, Ralph Giordano had thoughts of revenge—assassinating those who had tormented his family. This impulse passed, but the anger was still there. As former Nazis returned to positions of power in West Germany, Giordano moved to the Communist East, where he worked as a journalist. But he became disillusioned by the repressions of Stalinism and returned to the West.

During postwar interviews, Giordano often mentioned that the Nazi regime had left him unrooted; it had stolen his sense of belonging. For six decades—until the end of his life—he sought to recover that sense of belonging, to somehow reconcile with a populace that had allowed World War II and the Holocaust to occur. The course that he found, or perhaps found him, was through writing and through a new media: television. He was hired by Norddeutscher Rundfunk, a Hamburg-based public television and radio broadcaster. Three years later, he became a documentary filmmaker for Westdeutscher Rundfunk, based in Cologne. He made more than one hundred documentaries, traveling to thirty-eight countries, on topics that depicted the dangers of authoritarianism. He finished the novel he had been working on during the firebombing of Hamburg. It was an autobiographical one, about a family—the Bertinis—and their Third Reich ordeal. The 1982 novel, *Die Bertinis*, was exactly what the German populace—or at least some segments of it—had been waiting for. People were moved by the description of Giordano's family and what they went through. He was invited to public events to read from the novel and to schools to speak as a witness to the crimes of the Third Reich.

Giordano drew both praise and wrath with the 1987 publication of *Die zweite Schuld, oder Von der Last, Deutscher zu sein*. It was an uncompromising broadside against Germans' postwar embrace of even the worst of Nazi war criminals, or, as he called it, "the great peace with the perpetrators." Giordano's thesis of there being a "second guilt" was so powerful, and so controversial, that when the Bundeskriminalamt decided in 2007 to finally examine its postwar Nazi taint, this was the focus from the very start.

After the research was completed, in April 2011 the BKA held a conference to discuss the findings. During a panel discussion, Giordano was asked if he was content with the results. "For a man with my biography, this is a great hour," said the eighty-eight-year-old with a mane of silver hair. "Finally, what I have fought for for decades has happened." Earlier in the conference, one of the participants called the BKA's reckoning with its hiring of Nazi perpetrators an act of reconciliation. During the panel discussion, Giordano took exception to this characterization: "I don't in any way see the work of the BKA as an act of reconciliation but as a reckoning that was long overdue."

Government-commissioned researchers had indeed cast a light on dark secrets lurking in the corners of postwar Germany. But something was missing, something consequential, something that had slipped away with the passage of time as Nazi-tainted government workers grew old, retired, and died without being held to account. The reckoning, said Giordano, "came late, very late." Worse than that, "The perpetrators got away with it." At a previous conference on Germany's coming to terms with the second guilt, Giordano showed up with his arm in a sling. "The injury occurred during a dream," he explained to the audience. "I lay immobilized on railroad tracks. A train was approaching—ever closer, ever larger, ever louder. Just ahead of the oncoming wheels, I threw myself onto the floor—and the result you see today." He explained, "The dream is an expression of the constant fear of violent death that dominated my life in those years."[16] Bad dreams ended for Ralph Giordano on December 10, 2014. He died that day, at age ninety-one.

# 15

# Squandered Opportunities

Kurt Oppler, a victim of the Nazi regime, was the perfect candidate for a top managerial position when West Germany was founded in 1949. He would have been, that is, if the Adenauer administration had not favored former bureaucrats of the Third Reich over those who had opposed it. Oppler had sterling credentials. A Socialist who was born to a Jewish family, Oppler fled Nazi Germany in 1938, a year after the regime stripped him of his right to practice law. When Oppler returned to Germany in 1946, he leaped into the efforts to construct a democracy from the wreckage of the Third Reich. He was appointed, with the blessing of American occupation authorities, ministerial director in the Justice Ministry of Hesse state.

Oppler's administrative skills were rated so highly that in 1947 he was made head of the personnel department for the Bizone, also called Bizonia, the governmental entity that was created by the Americans and the British and was the predecessor of the government of the Federal Republic of Germany.

With these qualifications, it should have been easy for Oppler to make the transition from his position with Bizonia to an equally important job in the new West German government. But there were elements in the Adenauer government who were working against Oppler, largely because of his push for liberal reforms of the civil service law, including placing limits on Third Reich bureaucrats for government jobs.

For three years Oppler had to wait as thousands of former civil servants of the Nazi regime were welcomed into the new federal ministries and agencies. After Oppler complained to state secretary Hans Ritter von Lex about his treatment, a top official in the Interior Ministry wrote in a memo that such delays are solely due to a lack of "personal and professional suitability." That note was written by Kurt Behnke, who during the Third Reich was a prosecutor on an administrative court that enforced Nazi ordinances that excluded Jews and other perceived enemies from the civil service and punished bureaucrats who deviated from the party line.

In a 1938 commentary on the Nazis' new code for civil servants, Behnke wrote: "The National Socialist state demands from its civil servants ... unconditional loyalty and allegiance" to the Hitler regime, both at work and when they're off-duty. Furthermore, Behnke wrote that civil servants should "limit dealings with Jews" in order to "ward off Jewish influence." Using Jewish doctors and doing business with "members of the Jewish race" are to be regarded as "a serious offense."[1]

During the formative years of the Federal Republic of Germany, Behnke, as head of the Interior Ministry's civil service legal department, was personally involved in crafting hiring policies for the postwar civil service. Which is why Kurt Oppler, who certainly had all the right stuff, was ultimately turned down for a top managerial job. Instead, he was offered the position of ambassador to Iceland. Packing Oppler off to Reykjavík removed a prominent threat to Behnke and others in the Adenauer administration.

The Oppler story is told in *Hüter der Ordnung* (Guardian of Order), the 2018 report of findings of the team of academics under historians Frank Bösch and Andreas Wirsching who examined the postwar hiring practices of the interior ministries of the two German states. The chapter dealing with Oppler documents in detail how bureaucrats who were untainted by service to the Nazi state were routinely sidelined for civil service jobs in favor of those who were.

Dominik Rigoll was the researcher on the Bösch-Wirsching team who examined the political calculations and wheeling and dealing that went into crafting legislation that implemented Article 131, that section of the West German constitution that cleared the way for Third Reich civil servants to return to government jobs. By 1953, of some fifty thousand federal government positions, nearly fifteen thousand were held by bureaucrats who had worked for the Nazi regime, a number that kept growing over the years. This does not include jobs in state and municipal government offices.

Rigoll dug into a constitutional companion to Article 131 that is often overlooked: Article 132. This section of the constitution was ultimately used as the legal foundation for favoring "131ers"—as the beneficiaries of Article 131 were called—over bureaucrats who had been hired by the Allies and by state governments immediately after the war. In his research Rigoll discovered that of 115 senior officials working for Bizonia, 91 had not been required to go through the denazification process because they had not been Nazi Party members or they were victims of Nazi persecution. Kurt Oppler would have been responsible for having such a clean roster of employees. And that may have contributed to his downfall. "Oppler was hated by many," says Rigoll, "probably not only because of his attempts to liberalize civil service law, but also because the employee profile of the Bizone showed the whole world" that former Nazis were not necessarily needed as administrators.[2]

Article 132 was drawn up to regulate what would happen with civil servants hired right after the war and before the founding of the West German state, and especially those who before 1945 lacked experience in their respective fields. These bureaucrats were known as *Quereinsteiger*, or "career changers." They were also called "45ers." According to Article 132, *Quereinsteigers* who were deemed to lack "personal or professional suitability for their office" could be forced to take early retirement, be placed in lesser jobs, or be put on a waiting list. Untainted civil servants and victims of Nazi persecution were supposed to be protected. But when government officials sat down to write guidelines for implementing Article 132, that protection was pretty much thrown out the window. In February 1950 the Interior Ministry unveiled a regulation that left it up to supervisors to decide whether a 45er was suitable to keep his or her job, regardless of whether that person had been a victim of Nazi persecution or had opposed the Hitler regime. The ordinance also stipulated that a civil servant's conduct during the Third Reich "should be disregarded for the purpose of assessing personal suitability" for a civil service job. And thus, says Rigoll: "Neither contributions [by a civil servant] to rebuild after 1945 nor suffering endured under National Socialism could ... protect against being ousted from public service."[3]

By the start of 1950, a total of 1,274 federal government employees had already been sent into early retirement, put on a waiting list, or forced to take lower-paying jobs, creating more space for veterans of the Third Reich. This does not include state and municipal employees who were dealt the same career setbacks.

So, how did the Western occupiers feel about this situation? They were initially dismayed, so much so that before the birth of the West German state they tried to impose a civil service law that would, among other things, require the dismissal of bureaucrats who were caught lying about their pasts. But ultimately the Allies backed off, fearful of creating a backlash among Germans and losing Adenauer as a strategic and military partner at the dawn of the Cold War.

Rigoll also examined ramifications of the so-called Adenauer Decree, another policy that ended up keeping victims of the Third Reich out of government jobs. The "decree" was a resolution approved by Adenauer's government on September 19, 1950, that barred from government employment anyone who belonged to organizations that were a threat to the "free democratic state order," who worked for such organizations, or who supported them "in some other way."

At a press conference Adenauer showed a list of the organizations whose members and supporters were not wanted for government service. At the top of the list was the German Communist Party, followed by nine affiliated organizations. Just two extreme-right-wing parties were named, and they were buried on the list.[4]

Included among the Communist-affiliated organizations was the Association of Victims of the Nazi Regime, also known by its German initials, VVN. With 200,000 members, the VVN represented resistance fighters and victims of Nazism in their efforts for compensation, support, and recognition. The Adenauer government saw the VVN as pawns of the Communist East German regime. The situation was not so black-and-white. It was not just Communists who belonged to the VVN but also Social Democrats, Free Democrats, and members of Adenauer's own Christian Democratic Union (CDU). What bound them in comradeship was their suffering under the Nazi regime. Soon after the Adenauer Decree was announced, members of the VVN sent letters to the government pleading that blanket judgments not be made about them. Dominik Rigoll read a number of those letters.[5]

Max Bleicher worked for the customs office in Friedrichshafen, on the shore of Lake Constance, in southern Germany. In his letter to Interior Minister Gustav Heinemann, Bleicher wrote that under the Nazis' system of racial classification, he was a half-Jew. And he said he was a Social Democrat, not a Communist. "I joined the VVN not as a Communist, but as someone who was politically persecuted and am fighting for the compensation that I am due," Bleicher wrote.

Another plea to Adenauer came from Gerhard Lüpkes, who wrote that the VVN was "the only organization" through which the persecuted "could assert their rights." Some of its members are "true heroes" who were "rightly honored . . . until recently."

Similar words were written by Bavarian attorney Otto Roth, "a Christian, member of the Lutheran Church and a democrat" who had fought against Hitler "from the day he took power" and as a consequence was banned from practicing law and sent to a concentration camp. It was simply wrong, Roth wrote, that victims of the Third Reich were being treated like this when "incriminated Nazis of all types have been given preferential employment in Bonn."

Johannes Marx, a member of Adenauer's CDU, wrote that he was "among the many thousands who . . . suffered from the despotism of the National Socialist regime." Marx complained that the decision to bar VVN members from public service was made without a true understanding of the organization. While it was true that Communists were a dominant presence, Marx wrote, this was so because they had been persecuted by the Nazis en masse. He proposed the government conduct a review of the VVN's work and then decide whether the organization was a real threat to democracy.

Pleas like these to the Adenauer administration apparently went unanswered, according to Dominik Rigoll. It is unclear how many VVN members were kicked out of public service. Adenauer had insisted that a stable democracy could not be built without reintegrating Germans who had been supporters of Hitler. He warned that alienating them could endanger the Federal Republic's "internal peace" and argued that there were far too few untainted Germans with the experience to competently carry out positions of authority in the public sector. Or as he put it, it makes no sense to throw out dirty water if that's all you have.[6]

But was the polluted well of former Nazis really the only source to draw from? Was it truly necessary to hire former members of the SS, the Sicherheitsdienst, and the Gestapo, men whose units were guilty of the mass murder of Jews and other noncombatants and bureaucrats who had been involved in administering racist and genocidal policies? Were there no other alternatives? What would have happened if the Adenauer administration had required government agencies to carry out thorough background checks of job candidates and if there had been earnest attempts to find untainted bureaucrats for postwar government positions?

"We know that at the beginning of the [West German] Justice Ministry there were only 29 employees at the leadership level," said historian Manfred Görtemaker, who along with criminal law professor Christoph Safferling led investigations of the Nazi taint at the Justice Ministry. "Weren't there 29 untainted lawyers in Germany?"[7]

The pool of potential alternative job candidates for government positions was not insignificant. Despite Jews' hardships in being accepted for immigration in other countries, more than 200,000 had managed to safely escape Nazi Germany—mainly settling in the United States, Great Britain, Palestine, and Central and South America. This does not include thousands of non-Jewish Germans who fled their homeland for political reasons. Among these victims and exiles were Germans who before the Nazi takeover held government jobs—at the local, state, and national levels.

Safferling, professor of criminal law at Friedrich-Alexander-Universität in Erlangen, has some thoughts on how and where the Adenauer administration could have gone looking for untainted Germans for public service jobs. "The first one, encourage immigrants to come back to Germany"— exiles like Fritz Bauer and Willy Brandt—Safferling told me in a Zoom call.

Many exiles did not want to return because they were viewed by much of the populace as having betrayed the Fatherland by leaving while their countrymen suffered through Allied bombing of their cities and then denazification. Instead of alienating the exiles, the Adenauer administration could have welcomed them home. "This is a big failure," Safferling said. "Adenauer should have politically encouraged people . . . to integrate them [exiles] into German society and treat them as what they were—victims of the system."

Untainted lawyers—exiles and those who remained in Germany during the war—would have been another possible pool of civil service candidates. "I'm thinking of those who did not work within the National Socialist administration, and maybe there were some who even tried to uphold fairness at trial, and to fight for the rights of the accused," Safferling said. "When you look at the first [West German] minister of justice, Thomas Dehler . . . he had a Jewish wife and he stood up and didn't get divorced. He had contacts with the Jewish community in Bamberg all through the [Nazi] years. There were more like him that could have been encouraged to join the [postwar] administration."

Safferling offered more thoughts on how the Adenauer administration could have found experienced civil servants with Nazi-free pasts. Choosing women, for example. "In 1933-35, women judges and lawyers were driven out of office, because women were supposed to stay at home and give birth to young soldiers," Safferling explained. "But you had highly educated women," including women "who studied law and had law degrees, even PhDs. Why didn't one encourage them to join? But nothing was done. Nothing."

The Adenauer administration could also have searched among younger people for untainted candidates for the postwar civil service—people who had, perhaps, begun to study law but didn't finish because they were sent off to war or to concentration camps. They would not have had the experience that authorities in the Adenauer administration insisted was necessary. But why not train them? "They're not as experienced. But you don't want these old minds. You want new minds, because you have a new democracy with new challenges, with new societal ideas. So bring in more young people at an earlier stage," said Safferling.

So why didn't any of this happen? What stood in the way? That was a question raised by historians commissioned to look into the Nazi taint of postwar government agencies. Part of the answer lies within the hierarchical, rigid, and complex nature of the German civil service, whose basic elements date back to the Kaiser era. It is a tradition that in the Adenauer era actually gave job credits to bureaucrats who had served the Third Reich, at the expense of those who had not.

An important term to know in understanding how the system works is *Beamtenlaufbahn*. It literally means "career in the civil service." But it has a heavier weight than that. The *Beamtenlaufbahn* code has multiple levels, from the entry level *Einfacher* Dienst (Basic Service) to *Höhererdienst* (Upper Service). The higher you go on the *Beamtenlaufbahn* ladder, the more education and training are required. After the war the Adenauer administration resisted pressure by the Western allies to liberalize the system. The American occupiers especially were skeptical of promises by Adenauer that the new West German civil service code would be "in the spirit" of the Allied-imposed Law No. 15, which included mechanisms to weed out civil service candidates who were caught lying about their pasts. Subsequent developments showed that the Americans were right. Applicants for postwar government jobs were judged by the amount of experience shown on their résumés—including their years working for the Third Reich. What that meant was that it was difficult for candidates who had not worked for the Third Reich to compete with those who had.

Adenauer had given promises to the Allies that efforts would be made to keep Nazi war criminals out of government service. Some attempts were made at the beginning, especially to keep them out of managerial jobs. But as the 1950s wore on and East-West tensions continued to escalate, any earnest attempts to weed out seriously incriminated former Nazis fell by the wayside. Had he so desired, Adenauer could have instructed government ministries and agencies to automatically reject former members of the Sicherheitsdienst, the SS, and the Gestapo who had served on the eastern front as well as bureaucrats who had held administrative jobs that implemented racial and genocidal policies in occupied territories. But he didn't.

I asked Gerhard Sälter, one of the historians who examined the Bundesnachrichtendienst files, whether it would have been possible to create an effective foreign intelligence service without employing tainted former Nazis. Sälter answered that I was looking at the matter from the wrong perspective: "In 1945, the men around Reinhard Gehlen had absolutely no intention of building an intelligence service for a democratic Germany. Their first aim was to avoid several years of internment and intensive questioning by offering their services to the Americans. In the medium term, they wanted to maintain the social status they had achieved in the Third Reich. And there were some who wanted to preserve the values and political concepts of National Socialism and adapt them more or less to the new system. Establishing an intelligence service allowed them to pursue these goals. In this respect, the emergence of the BND seems to me to be more of a coincidental product of these intentions and the conditions created by the Allies in which these men had to move."[8]

The kind of experience accumulated by former SS, Sicherheitsdienst, and Gestapo officers was not the sort of experience suitable for the foreign intelligence service of a democratic state, Sälter said. "The professional experience gained in the Third Reich was shaped by and saturated with the practices of the system of [Nazi] domination," he explained. "In this respect it would have been advisable to recruit personnel" who were committed to building a democracy.[9]

To keep war criminals out of the West German foreign intelligence service, the Americans would have had to put someone other than Gehlen in charge—someone who would take firm control of hiring from the very start and also be willing to let the Americans know the backgrounds of its agents. On the other hand, it should be remembered that U.S. intelligence also employed Nazi war criminals. The CIA and its predecessors were hardly the best role models for Gehlen's spy service.

A similar situation existed at the Bundeskriminalamt. Like Gehlen's operation, the BKA was initially founded under the auspices of American intelligence largely to counter what was perceived as an existential threat from the Soviet bloc. Patrick Wagner, one of the historians who conducted the government-commissioned study of the BKA, described the agency's priorities: "It must be said that from the late 1940s and early 1950s, authorities such as the BKA were looking for experienced specialists to combat Communist enemies of the state and spies—and this expertise was specifically possessed by those police officers who worked in similar fields for the NS [Nazi] state up to 1945." Wagner, a professor of history at the Martin Luther University Halle-Wittenberg, explained that "the alternative would have been to hire completely new non-police staff and accept that during the first few years there would have been staff with little relevant professional experience. Those responsible did not want that because they considered the Communist threat to be great and imminent."[10]

Norbert Frei, a professor of history at the University of Jena, is a leading expert on Adenauer's reintegration strategy. Frei was also one of the four historians who conducted the government-commissioned study of the Foreign Office's postwar Nazi taint. "Of course, there was no alternative to the reintegration of the functional elites [from the Nazi system]," Frei wrote in an email. The victorious Allies' original intention to start with a clean slate—through denazification, internment of tens of thousands of Germans, and war crimes trials—during the first three postwar years left a "social-psychological" mark that "should not be underestimated, in my view," Frei said.[11]

By the time the West German republic was created in 1949, Frei told me, "there was a widely shared societal demand and therefore the need for extensive reintegration."

I asked Frei whether it would have been possible for federal ministries and agencies to have more thoroughly scrutinized job candidates to keep the most heavily incriminated ones out of the postwar civil service. "Certainly, many things could have been done more 'thoroughly' in terms of cleansing policy, and a significant proportion of those affected should not have been reinstated for the functioning of the state and the political system, nor was it necessary to do so," Frei responded.

Christoph Safferling thinks along similar lines. "There was certainly a necessity to have some of the former elite continue to work. It would have been impossible to do completely without them," said Safferling. "So the question is, how many were taken on that shouldn't have been?" After looking through biographies of top personnel at the Justice Ministry in the first dozen postwar years, Safferling said in his view about 20 percent of them should have been excluded because they "had blood on their hands."[12]

Patrick Wagner agrees that West German ministries could have targeted the most seriously tainted for exclusion from government work. As far as the BKA is concerned, he said, "they should at least have kept out personnel of murder units, like the Einsatzgruppen," that committed mass slaughter in the occupied territories.[13]

Even the East German Communists realized that they could not totally do without experienced bureaucrats who had served the Third Reich. That was a surprise discovery by Frank Bösch and Andreas Wirsching. In the West German Interior Ministry in the late 1950s, up to 66 percent of the senior officials were former members of the Nazi Party. In the East German Ministry of the Interior in the early 1950s, the figure was as high as 14 percent. Still, this is a low percentage. According to Bösch and Wirsching, the East Germans were able to limit their reliance on Third Reich veterans by fast-tracking the training of administrative job candidates with no previous experience—in other words, non-Nazis—to get them to a level where they could competently do the work. "While Communists occupied the top management level of the Ministry of the Interior, freshly trained young employees—who because of their age were not incriminated—quickly took over the middle management level," Bösch and Wirsching wrote in *Guardian of Order*.

The East German government employees were working in the service of an authoritarian regime, while their West German counterparts were building a democracy. Nonetheless, the East Germans' successful training of inexperienced employees throws into question the West German obsession with filling government positions with former servants of the Third Reich.

The greatest obstacle to blocking an infestation of the West German civil service even by obvious war criminals was Konrad Adenauer himself. Adenauer set the course when he uttered the comment "This sniffing around for Nazis has to stop." Desperate to keep Adenauer on their side for the Cold War that was brewing, the Western Allies stood by as his government granted amnesties to thousands of war criminals, as lawyers at the Interior and Justice Ministries drafted legislation that shielded thousands more from prosecution and West German courts handed down rulings that judges and prosecutors who were responsible for the Third Reich persecution and execution of people convicted of even trivial crimes had legally done nothing wrong.

In the early postwar years, Germany was in a precarious and potentially volatile situation. Cities lay in ruins, and multitudes of Germans had been left homeless. People had to scrounge for something to eat, and homecoming soldiers had no work. For many Germans the idea of an authoritarian government still had its appeal. Adenauer's strategy for dealing with this threat was to bind the Federal Republic to the West while at the same time finding ways to get Germans committed to a new democratic system. Essentially, Adenauer was following a big-tent strategy, but it was a lopsided approach. As former Nazis were welcomed into the big tent, there was less room for leftists and even people who had been persecuted by the Nazi regime.

Adenauer's image took a beating as government-commissioned historians began publishing the findings of their research. For seven decades the Nazi taint of the postwar civil service had been lurking in the shadows. Its existence was generally known, but there had never been a commitment by government officials to systematically examine it. The work of the researchers cast new light on how Adenauer's kid-glove treatment of Third Reich bureaucrats had led to a worse infestation of the postwar civil service by former Nazis than had been imagined.

"Adenauer was a ruthless Machiavellian," said Klaus-Dietmar Henke, the historian who wrote about the collaboration by Adenauer, Hans Globke, and Reinhard Gehlen to spy on Adenauer's political rivals. "Machiavelli said that a ruler can't have morals to stay in power," Henke said.[14]

Adenauer's choice of Hans Globke as his right-hand man reflected the chancellor's approach to governing. "With his laws and commentary, Hans Globke was one of the most important persecutors of Jews. It is unimaginable today that such a man would be hired for a government job," Henke told me in a phone call. But by making Globke his state secretary, Adenauer was sending a signal throughout the government bureaucracy about hiring tainted bureaucrats: "If Globke is there, then it can't be so bad." Henke understood why Adenauer had hired Globke: "Morally, this was very controversial, but politically it was very cunning, if also reprehensible."[15]

Excited press coverage was given to the work of Henke, Bösch, Wagner, Safferling, and their colleagues as they released their findings. They grabbed headlines across the land. They were interviewed on TV. There was a sense that, finally, the government had come clean about a chapter of postwar history that had been cloaked in secrecy since the end of the war. But after the years of work that had gone into the research and the millions of euros that had been spent, it feels like something is missing. Something has slipped away and because of the passage of time is unrecoverable.

Eckart Conze, one of the historians commissioned to examine files of the Foreign Office, put his finger on it during one of the Justice Ministry's conferences to discuss the research projects: "If the Federal Republic stabilized itself as successfully as has been accepted, and if this success is linked to the blanket reintegration of incriminated Nazis and the acceptance of continuity, what was the price? How much did that cost in the history of the Federal Republic?" Conze asked. "Who paid this price?"[16]

The answer is legions, including relatives of the dead who were not given the chance to confront perpetrators in court, victims of Nazi policies who had to wait decades for compensation, leftists who were hounded by West German law authorities, and Social Democrats who were kept out of top government positions because of Adenauer's pathological hatred of them. And the winners were still the winners: all of those postwar government employees who were spared serious scrutiny of their Nazi pasts. It seems the "second guilt" that Ralph Giordano spoke of had not been washed away.

# Epilogue

Three decades after the last of the aging former Nazis ended their postwar careers in government—cleared their desks, walked down the corridor, out the door, and into retirement—a new breed of extremists was exposed in Germany's police stations and military barracks. In the twenty-first century cabals of former and current cops and soldiers, armed with deadly expertise, ammo, and guns, were using internet chat rooms to conspire against the state—under the noses of their superiors.

The seriousness of the threat didn't begin to come into focus until 2017, when a 7.65 mm semiautomatic pistol was found concealed in a bathroom at Vienna International Airport by a janitor. Police set a trap. Two weeks later, when Franco Albrecht came to retrieve the weapon, police arrested him. At the police station, Albrecht, a lieutenant in the German army, was fingerprinted and released. His prints were sent to German police, who discovered that Albrecht had another identity, a fake one, as a Syrian refugee. Albrecht was re-arrested by German police, charged with planning to use the handgun in a terrorist attack, possibly against a German politician, and planting the idea that it had been carried out by a Syrian immigrant—a false flag operation intended to provoke civil unrest.

Albrecht's arrest led investigators to an extreme-right-wing network of current and former police officers and soldiers who were secretly hoarding weapons and training for the day that social order in Germany—they called it "Day X"—would collapse and they would be called on to restore order. Arsenals of firearms, tens of thousands of rounds of ammunition, Nazi memorabilia, and lists of enemies were confiscated during police raids.[1]

Content found on the mobile phone of a thirty-two-year-old police officer in the city of Essen led authorities to another network—this one posting and sharing neo-Nazi propaganda in internet chat rooms. In September 2020 raids were conducted on police stations in Essen and the surrounding area, and twenty-nine officers were immediately suspended. Cell phones were confiscated, and some of the content found on the phones was exceedingly vile. It included memes of a refugee in a gas chamber and of the shooting of a Black man, rounds of ammunition arranged in the shape of a swastika, and photos of Hitler.

Similar chat groups and extreme-right-wing cops and soldiers were exposed in Berlin and elsewhere. It was a crisis that had been building up over the course of several years, with officials either not noticing it or shrugging it off as nothing to be too concerned about. When Franco Albrecht was attending officer training, he wrote a master's thesis that repeated Nazi tropes: Europe's racial purity was endangered by immigrants, and Jews sought global dominance. Albrecht was reprimanded and ordered to submit a new thesis. But that's as far as it went. He was not kicked out of the military. A sense of denial among German officials and within the public had allowed dangers from the extreme Right to metastasize.

Former servants of the Third Reich who continued their careers in postwar Germany never became a serious threat to democracy for a multitude of reasons, most of them having to do with basic human desires: wanting a good job, opportunities for advancement, creature comforts, a pension, and happiness. Their twenty-first-century analogues—cops and soldiers who had turned to the extreme Right—are of a different, and more dangerous, breed.

Soon after Albrecht's arrest, investigators questioned a military reservist, identified as "Horst S.," who told them about chat groups he had participated in, about secret weapons caches, discussions about preparing for civil war, and lists that had been collected of the names of leftist politicians that included their addresses and photos. These chat groups were spread across the country, Horst S. said, grouped, military style, into geographic zones. They were administered by a military man who went by "Hannibal." Horst S. gave investigators specifics on one of the chat groups, Nordkreuz, which means "Northern Cross."

The founder of Nordkreuz was Marko Gross, a former paratrooper with the Bundeswehr who in 1999 joined the criminal investigative agency for the state of Mecklenburg-Western Pomerania, in former East Germany. Gross was a cop with elite skills: a member of the state criminal investigators' SWAT team, a shooting instructor and police sniper. Gross was a regular at a shooting range where elite military units and police from across Germany trained. Nordkreuz had about thirty members, and many of them were frequent users of the shooting range. The federal prosecutor's office began investigating Nordkreuz in 2017 because of suspicions that members of the group had planned to kidnap and murder leftist politicians. That August federal police raided Gross's home and the residences of other members of the group. An arsenal of weapons and more than twenty-three thousand rounds of ammunition were seized. A second police raid, in June 2019, found more than thirty-one thousand rounds of ammo and an Uzi submachine gun. Gross was placed under arrest.

Federal investigators were also on the trail of Hannibal, the reputed administrator of four regional chat groups, and were able to identify him as Andre Schmitt, a sergeant in Germany's equivalent of the navy SEALs—called the KSK. Schmitt also was founder of an organization called Uniter, which helped former members of special forces find new jobs and offered self-defense and combat training to civilian clients. Schmitt told investigators the chats were merely intended for the sharing of information about security threats in Germany. The deeper investigators dug, however, the more troubling signs they found of an infestation of fascist thinking in the security services.

In the spring of 2020, police showed up at the home of Philipp S., a forty-five-year-old sergeant major in the KSK. They used a digger to take scoops of earth out of his garden. During their search of the grounds and the KSK man's house, investigators found an AK-47, a crossbow, explosives, thousands of rounds of ammo, an SS songbook, Nazi literature, and postcards with swastikas.

Three years earlier, the KSK unit that Philipp S. belonged to—Second Company—threw a farewell party for their company commander at a shooting range. The party entailed heavy drinking, an archery contest, an obstacle course, and a bizarre competition involving the tossing of a severed pig's head. A woman who was flown in as a "prize" for the winner of the contests later went to the police and to national TV news, alarmed by what she had witnessed: special forces troops listening to neo-Nazi rock music and making the stiff-armed "Hitler salute."

The Defense Ministry launched an internal investigation into right-wing extremism within the KSK. The Second Company—the one Philipp S. belonged to—had the highest number of suspected extremists and was disbanded in July 2020. The scandal also had serious repercussions for the German military's counterintelligence agency, the Bundesamt für den Militärischen Abschirmdienst (BAMAD), which is responsible for identifying extremists within the ranks. The director of BAMAD was dismissed in September 2020.

A very strange threat surfaced in 2022, one that harked back to imperial Germany and involved a prince from a centuries-old noble family, conspiratorial meetings in the prince's crenellated hunting lodge, and plans to topple the German government and install the prince as head of state.

In December 2022 police officers raided 150 homes across Germany, including the hunting lodge of seventy-one-year-old Prince Heinrich XIII of Reuss, and arrested about two dozen people, including the prince. Among the other suspects were active and former soldiers, a police officer, and a member of the far-right-wing Alternative for Germany, a party that in recent years has acquired considerable political clout. Another member of the House of Reuss, Heinrich XIV, said his kinsman had broken off ties with the family long ago. In an interview with the broadcasting station MDR, Heinrich XIV said of his relative, "I am afraid he is now a conspiracy theorist, a confused old man." But federal investigators did not take this alleged conspiracy as the fantasy of an elderly man with diminishing cognitive abilities.

The alleged coconspirators are associated with a movement, *Reichsbürger*, or "Citizens of the Reich," whose ideas are so out there that for years it was dismissed as a fringe network with little to no public appeal. Its members maintain that the Federal Republic of Germany doesn't actually exist as a sovereign state, that it is a concoction created by the victors of World War II. Members of the movement tend to be anti-Semitic, xenophobic, and wistful for the days of the imperial Reich.

As bizarre as the *Reichsbürger* movement may seem, its messages have resonated with a lot of people who were angry about lockdowns during the Coronavirus pandemic, rising energy and consumer prices, immigrants streaming into their country, and a belief that the federal government has too much power. Like in the United States, adherents of the movement talk about a "deep state" and conspiracy theories that are similar to those of the fringe group QAnon, which originated in 2017.

After decades of being accused of going easy on right-wing extremists, German officials began cracking down on them. In March 2022 federal interior minister Nancy Faeser announced a ten-point plan to combat right-wing extremism. Two months later, she presented the results of a review put together by the domestic intelligence agency of cases of right-wing extremism that had been reported within federal and state law authorities and in the military.

From July 2018 to June 2021, according to the review, there were 327 confirmed cases, a sliver of a total of 355,000 federal employees in those agencies. But the potential danger from within the armed services and police departments is magnified by the fact that these right-wing extremists are trained and armed and can network with each other. The extremists within the police and security services coordinate clandestinely with like-minded thinkers in the outside world. Of the 327 employees, 201 were discovered to have links with 765 far-right entities or activities: with radical groups, chat lines, specific individuals, and radical-right-wing events. "We will not let our democratic constitutional state be sabotaged from within by right-wing extremists," Faeser said in presenting the results of the review.

For a long time German law enforcement agencies had shrugged off crimes by right-wing extremists as "isolated cases." The idea that far-right-wing networks existed within the armed forces, security services, and police departments was dismissed as hysteria fanned by left-wing media and leftist politicians. But in a report issued in September 2020, the domestic intelligence agency marked an important course correction by warning that ignoring potential networks of right-wing extremists could imperil Germans' confidence in the nation's defenders of democracy.[2] Germany's sixteen states were taking it seriously. Each of them adopted new strategies to better vet recruits for police and security services, better monitor those already serving, and better reinforce democratic principles through training.

In July 2022 eight members of a SWAT team in the city of Münster were suspended after it was discovered that they had participated in an internet chat group in which extreme-right-wing content was exchanged. Münster is in North Rhine–Westphalia, where Essen is located, and the state with the largest number of reported extreme-right-wing cases among police. The president of the Münster police force, Alexandra Dorndorf, said intensified efforts to root out extremists had led to the suspension of the eight officers. "Since the incidents [in Essen], we at the police are fully alert and have a sharpened awareness," said Dorndorf. "We vigorously follow up on every sign of right-wing extremist tendencies." In the same month Franco Albrecht was convicted by a Frankfurt court of plotting a "serious act of violent subversion" and sentenced to five and a half years in prison.

But there were also setbacks. Marko Gross, the police sniper and Nordkreuz founder, was tried and convicted on weapons charges by a court in former East Germany and given a twenty-one-month suspended sentence. Critics said he should have been charged with terrorism and slapped with a stiff prison sentence.

The case against far-right-wing Essen police officers also had results that were less than encouraging. Although some were fired or disciplined, others were able to return to their jobs because of limitations under German law on prosecuting participants of private chat groups.

Rafael Behr, himself a former police officer, is a professor at the Hamburg police academy and an author of books and articles about cop culture. In his view steps that have been taken to combat right-wing extremism within police departments are mostly window dressing and don't get at the heart of the problem. "Above all, the 'measures' show one thing: the authorities and those responsible for politics are alarmed. And now they try to make the problem quickly disappear from the scene with some actions. Most of these activities do not even get at the core of an antidemocratic attitude but work on symptoms," Behr told me in an email message.[3]

Since neo-Nazi attacks on foreigners began soon after the two German states merged in 1990, German officials have been struggling to put out the flames of right-wing extremism. There have been dips and spikes in the violence over the years, but the militant Right is just as dangerous as it was three decades ago. From 2019 through 2021 right-wing extremists in Germany killed fourteen people, most of them with immigrant backgrounds.

There is a vast reservoir of right-wing extremists in Germany. In 2022 domestic intelligence authorities were keeping watch on nearly forty thousand right-wing radicals, some five thousand more than the previous year. The Radical Right is a growing force in politics and in society. Federal security authorities say extremists have been buying up homes and property in eastern and northern Germany, trying to carve immigrant-free *Lebensraum* for themselves and their like-minded comrades. The Alternative für Deutschland (AfD) political party has become a potential danger to be reckoned with. In the 2021 Bundestag election, the AfD won 83 of 736 seats. It is a dominant political force in states of the former Communist East and has found appeal in the West as well, going from being a fringe group to part of the political mainstream. Although the AfD is not classified as an extreme-right-wing organization, in 2022 a court in Cologne ruled there were sufficient indications of "anti-constitutional endeavors" within the party for the domestic intelligence service to place it under surveillance.[4] Two years earlier, intelligence officials classified a faction of the AfD—called Der Flügel, or "The Wing"—as a "right-wing extremist endeavor against the free democratic basic order."[5] The AfD has become a magnet for police, soldiers, and government officials with far-right-wing, anti-immigrant leanings. Of the AfD's 28,500 members, domestic intelligence officials say about 10,000 are extremists.[6]

As alarmist as this may sound, threats to German stability are probably greater in the twenty-first century than at any time since the volatile early postwar years, when the success of the newly launched Federal Republic was anything but a certainty.[7] And much of this danger is lurking within the German political system and bureaucracy.

Dirk Laabs is a German investigative journalist and documentary filmmaker who has covered extremism and terrorism since the turn of the twenty-first century. Laabs interviewed militants preparing for Day X as well as members of the security services who have been tracking them. In his assessment the danger from groups like Nordkreuz is not that the government might be overthrown but that there could be bloody terror attacks.

"They are trained soldiers. It's guys with guns," Laabs told me in a Zoom call. "They are capable of doing an Oklahoma-style attack in Germany," he said, referring to the 1995 truck bombing by two American white supremacists of a federal building in Oklahoma City that left 168 dead and nearly 700 injured.[8]

As I write, antidemocratic forces have gained strength in much of the developed world, including my homeland, the United States. There has probably been no greater peril to an established democracy than the attempt by former president Donald Trump and his acolytes to undo the 2020 election of Joe Biden as president. The storming of the U.S. Capitol on January 6, 2021, showed the danger from groups such as the Proud Boys and the Oath Keepers. But Europe is also grappling with challenges to the democratic order, with far-right-wing street protests sparked by COVID-19 regulations, waves of refugees from Syria and elsewhere, and rising inflation. Democracy is being tested in a number of European countries.

It would be wrong, then, to single out Germany for its seemingly eternal struggles with ideological and spiritual descendants of the Nazis. But this is Germans' burden. Whenever some authoritarian or far-right-wing populist appears on the world stage, parallels are inevitably made with the rise of Hitler. The crimes of the Nazis were so monstrous that Germans' embrace of Hitler have become the standard by which to measure threats to the public order all around the globe.

Germany is a bit like Sisyphus, struggling to push the boulder to the top of the hill. The weight of the boulder may lessen over time, as the effort chips away at the heavy rock, but it's hard to imagine it will ever disappear completely.

# Notes

**Preface**

1. Peter Gehrig was chief editor of the German Service of the Associated Press from 1990 to 2010.

**Introduction**

1. Ulrich Renz was chief editor of the German Service of the Associated Press until his retirement in 1990. He also worked for United Press International and German newspapers. He became a journalist because of a desire to learn about the Third Reich and the Nazis' crimes.
2. Wirsching made the remarks at the Justice Department symposium Die Rosenburg: Die frühe Bundesrepublik und die NS-Vergangenheit—Aufarbeiter-Kommissionen im Dialog, held at the Haus der Wannsee-Konferenz, Berlin, April 26, 2016.
3. Steinke's biography of Fritz Bauer was first published in German, *Fritz Bauer: oder Auschwitz vor Gericht* (Munich: Piper Verlag, 2013). Schirach's book first appeared in German under the title *Der Fall Collini* (Munich: Piper Verlag, 2011).

**1. Beginnings**

1. See Antisemitismus, "Juden raus!" *ZEIT ONLINE*, accessed March 14, 2024, https://www.zeit.de/thema/antisemitismus.
2. See Hier wohnt der Verräter, *Der Spiegel*, accessed March 14, 2024, https://www.spiegel.de/politik/hier-wohnt-der-verraeter-a-c07a8d32-0002-0001-0000-000021977917.
3. Manfred Görtemaker and Christoph Safferling, *Die Akte Rosenburg: Das Bundesministerium der Justiz und die Nazi Zeit* (Munich: Verlag C. H. Beck, 2016), 39.
4. The 1951 legislation was approved by all political parties, including Adenauer's chief rivals—the Social Democrats. Given the widespread desire to paper over the past, voting against the legislation would have been political suicide.

## 2. The Chameleon

All declassified CIA documents are available in the agency's Electronic Reading Room and are searchable using the agency's CIA Records Search Tool (CREST).

1. Report from CIA Karlsruhe chief of station on lunch meeting with Hans Globke, October 23, 1950, CREST: 519a6b24993294098d510bd6.
2. Cable from Frankfurt on HICOG's worries about the German civil service situation, October 25, 1949, CREST: 519a6b24993294098d510bd7.
3. Dispatch from Frankfurt pertaining to an army memo on the German Civil Service, September 15, 1954, CREST: 519a6b24993294098d510c1b.
4. Spellings in my text are as they appear in the CIA documents, which are in English and contain many spelling inconsistencies.
5. Operational report on "Causa" (Globke) from CIA chief of base at Pullach, October 1, 1954, CREST: 519a6b24993294098d510c1c.
6. Jürgen Bevers, *Der Mann Hinter Adenauer: Hans Globkes Aufstieg vom NS-Juristen zur Grauen Eminenz der Bonner Republik* (Berlin: Christoph Links Verlag, 2009), 40.
7. Press release from the West German Embassy in Washington DC, February 7, 1961, CREST: 519a6b24993294098d510bb5.
8. Bevers, *Der Mann Hinter Adenauer*, 108.
9. American consul in Frankfurt to the U.S. State Department, memo on conversation with Fritz Bauer, February 7, 1961, CREST: 519a6b24993294098d510bb5.
10. Ronen Steinke, *Fritz Bauer: The Jewish Prosecutor Who Brought Eichmann and Auschwitz to Trial* (Bloomington: Indiana University Press, 2020), 1–2.
11. Memo to the director of central intelligence from the Office on National Estimates on the Eichmann case, March 28, 1961, CREST: RDP79R00904A000700010005-1.
12. Bevers, *Der Mann Hinter Adenauer*, 170–71.
13. Bevers, *Der Mann Hinter Adenauer*, 201.
14. Bevers, *Der Mann Hinter Adenauer*, 206–7.

## 3. Gold Watch for a War Criminal

1. Operational report from CIA chief of station in Frankfurt on "Cautery 2" (Saevecke), April 3, 1952, CREST: 519bdecc993294098d514183.
2. Operational report on "Cautery 2" from CIA Karlsruhe chief of station, August 6, 1951, CREST: 519bdecc993294098d51418a.
3. Memo from chief of Berlin operational base to Bonn station chief on Saevecke's background, January 8, 1953, CREST: 519bdecc993294098d514174.
4. Dispatch from CIA chief for Eastern Europe on past suspicions Saevecke could be a hostile agent, January 14, 1964, CREST: 519bdecc993294098d514178.

5. Transcript of interrogations by British officers of Theo Saevecke and his subordinates, June 4, 1945, CREST: 519bdecc993294098d51417c.
6. Karlsruhe station chief's report on work for the CIA by "Cautery 2" (Saevecke), August 6, 1951, CREST: 519bdecc993294098d51418a.
7. Dispatch from Bonn CIA chief to CIA director, July 7, 1954, CREST: 519bdecc993294098d51416e.
8. Office of the director to CIA chiefs of station in Frankfurt and Bonn, memo, July 12, 1954, CREST: 519bdecc993294098d51419.
9. Cable from Bonn CIA chief to Frankfurt chief of mission with English translation of Saevecke's statement to the Interior Ministry, CREST: 519bdecc993294098d514196.
10. CIA memo on Saevecke's interrogation by British troops, August 5, 1954, CREST: 519bdecc993294098d514187.
11. Exchange of letters between Saevecke and an unidentified official at the American Embassy in Bonn, December 29, 1955, CREST: 519bdecc993294098d51417a.
12. Saevecke's work at "State Secret No. 1" is detailed on a website that collects and publishes archival information and new reporting about this and other bunkers built during the Cold War to provide refuge for government leaders during a national emergency. The article by journalist Jörg Diester, historian Michaela Karle, and others pertaining to "State Secret No. 1" and Saevecke's time there, from November 4, 2009, can be found at the Ausweichsitz der Verfassungsorgane der Bundesrepublik Deutschland website, http://archiv.ausweichsitz.de/index.php-option=com_content&task=view&id=129&Itemid=39.html.

## 4. Fickle Friends

1. Memo to the CIA deputy director concerning plans for the visit to agency headquarters by Wenger and Meier, February 6, 1963, CREST: 519bded7993294098d5152de.
2. Memo to the CIA deputy director concerning planned visit to agency headquarters by Wenger and Meier.
3. Dispatch from Bonn CIA chief concerning the reaction of Wenger and Meier to suspension of their visit to CIA headquarters, June 5, 1963, CREST: 519bded7993294098d5152ef.
4. Dispatch from CIA Bonn chief concerning German new media revealing Wenger's Nazi past, September 17, 1963. CREST: 519bded7993294098d5152e6.
5. Constantin Goschler and Michael Wala, *"Keine Neue Gestapo": Das Bundesamt für Verfassungsschutz und die NS-Vergangenheit* (Hamburg: Rowohlt Verlag GmbH, 2015), 214.

6. Goschler and Wala, *"Keine Neue Gestapo,"* 214.
7. Secret report on "KGB Exploitation of Hans Felfe," March 1969, CREST: 519cd819993294098d515d32.
8. Secret CIA "damage assessment" report on Heinz Felfe, April 1, 1963, CREST: 519cd819993294098d515d2e.

**5. Secret Agent 9610**

1. Dieter Schenk, *Auf dem rechten Auge blind: Die braunen Wurzeln des BKA* (Cologne: Verlag Kiepenheuer & Witsch, 2001), 123.
2. Schenk, *Auf dem rechten Auge blind*, 165.
3. CIA report on work by "Caravel" (Dickopf) for the agency, March 16, 1950, CREST: 519a6b2f993294098d512230.
4. CIA report on "Project Caravel," March 12, 1954, CREST: 519a6b2f993294098d512217.
5. Memo on unidentified CIA official meeting with "Caravel" at the latter's Wiesbaden home, December 30, 1968, CREST: 519a6b2f993294098d5121bb.
6. Schenk, *Auf dem rechten Auge blind*, 92.
7. Schenk, *Auf dem rechten Auge blind*, 90.
8. Schenk, *Auf dem rechten Auge blind*, 96-97.
9. Schenk, *Auf dem rechten Auge blind*, 98-99.
10. Schenk, *Auf dem rechten Auge blind*, 103.
11. Schenk, *Auf dem rechten Auge blind*, 103.
12. Schenk, *Auf dem rechten Auge blind*, 104.
13. Schenk, *Auf dem rechten Auge blind*, 113-14.
14. Paul C. Blum's letter of recommendation for Dickopf, September 6, 1945, CREST: 519a6b2f993294098d5121eb.
15. CIA Karlsruhe station chief's monthly progress report on "Hathor" (Dickopf), May 25, 1948, CREST: 519a6b2f993294098d512229.
16. Monthly progress report on Dickopf from acting CIA station chief in Karlsruhe, July 31, 1948, CREST: 519a6b2f993294098d512240.
17. CIA Karlsruhe station chief's progress report on Dickopf, December 23, 1948, CREST: 519a6b2f993294098d5121e8.
18. Memo on unidentified CIA case officer's discussion with Dickopf, April 22, 1959, CREST: 519a6b2f993294098d51221a.
19. Memo from an unidentified CIA official on meeting with Dickopf, November 1, 1968, CREST: 519a6b2f993294098d5121bc.
20. The BKA's description of the street renaming can be found at the Bundeskriminalamt's website, "The BKA—Umbenennung Paul-Dickopf-Straße," updated in 2024, https://www.bka.de/DE/DasBKA/Historie/UmbenennungPaulDickopfStrasse/umbenennungPaulDickopfStrasse_node.html.

## 6. A Talk on the Terrace

1. *Report of Initial Contacts with General Gehlen's Organization, by John R. Boker Jr.*, May 1, 1952, CREST: 519cd81f993294098d5168d0, https://nsarchive2.gwu.edu/NSAEBB/NSAEBB146/doc06.pdf.
2. See "America's Seeing Eye Dog on a Leash," a chapter in a secret draft working paper by the CIA titled "Eagle and Swastika: CIA and Nazi War Criminals and Collaborators," dated April 2003, declassified in 2007; CREST: 519697e8993294098d50c2a2.
3. Richard Breitman, Norman J. W. Goda, Timothy Naftali, and Robert Wolfe, *U.S. Intelligence and the Nazis* (New York: Cambridge University Press, 2005), 343–44.
4. Breitman, Goda, Naftali, and Wolfe, *U.S. Intelligence and the Nazis*, 344.
5. Breitman, Goda, Naftali, and Wolfe, *U.S. Intelligence and the Nazis*, 347.
6. See "The Case of Otto Albrecht Alfred von Bolschwing," by Kevin C. Ruffner, a member of the CIA History Staff, in the CIA publication *Studies in Intelligence*, 1998, CREST: 519697e8993294098d50c28e, https://www.cia.gov/readingroom/docs/DOC_0000477271_0.pdf.
7. The exchange between Peter Sichel and CIA's Pullach base is to be found in Ruffner's "Case of Otto Albrecht Alfred von Bolschwing," mentioned earlier.
8. Ruffner, "Case of Otto Albrecht Alfred von Bolschwing."
9. Ruffner, "Case of Otto Albrecht Alfred von Bolschwing."
10. Ruffner, "Case of Otto Albrecht Alfred von Bolschwing."
11. Ruffner, "Case of Otto Albrecht Alfred von Bolschwing." Bolschwing became a U.S. citizen in 1959. The Office of Special Investigations of the U.S. Justice Department launched a criminal case against him in the early 1980s, accusing him of having lied about his Nazi background to gain entry into the United States. With the truth about his role in the Holocaust exposed, Bolschwing voluntarily surrendered his U.S. citizenship but was spared deportation because of his worsening health. He died in 1982 at age seventy-two.

## 7. Toppling the Wall of Silence

1. Eckart Conze, Norbert Frei, Peter Hayes, and Moshe Zimmermann, *Das Amt und die Vergangenheit: Deutsche Diplomaten im Dritten Reich und in der Bundesrepublik* (Munich: Karl Blessing Verlag, 2010), 678–79.
2. Görtemaker and Safferling, *Die Akte Rosenburg*, 222.
3. Conze, Frei, Hayes, and Zimmermann, *Das Amt und die Vergangenheit*, 12.
4. Conze, Frei, Hayes, and Zimmermann, *Das Amt und die Vergangenheit*, 337–38.
5. Conze, Frei, Hayes, and Zimmermann, *Das Amt und die Vergangenheit*, 173.
6. Conze, Frei, Hayes, and Zimmermann, *Das Amt und die Vergangenheit*, 352–53.

7. Conze, Frei, Hayes, and Zimmermann, *Das Amt und die Vergangenheit*, 548–50.
8. Frei and Hayes, "The German Foreign Office and the Past," *Bulletin of the German Historical Institute* (Fall 2011): 55–69.
9. Conze, Frei, Hayes, and Zimmermann, *Das Amt und die Vergangenheit*, 254.
10. Zimmermann, "Secrets and Revelations: The German Foreign Ministry and the Final Solution," *Israel Journal of Foreign Affairs* 5, no. 1 (2011): 115-23.

## 8. The Reckoning

1. See Antwort der Bundesregierung auf die Große Anfrage der Abgeordneten Jan Korte, Sevim Dağdelen, Ulla Jelpke, weiterer Abgeordneter und der Fraktion DIE LINKE; Bundestag document 17/8134, December 14, 2011, https://upgr.bv-opfer-ns-militaerjustiz.de/uploads/Dateien/Presseberichte/1708134.pdf.

## 9. Elusive Perpetrators

1. Frank Bösch and Andreas Wirsching, eds., *Hüter der Ordnung: Die Innenministerien in Bonn und Ost-Berlin nach dem Nationalsozialismus* (Göttingen: Wallstein Verlag), 2018, 122.
2. Richard J. Evans, *The Third Reich at War* (New York: Penguin, 2009), 50.
3. Bösch and Wirsching, *Hüter der Ordnung*, 59.
4. Bösch and Wirsching, *Hüter der Ordnung*, 56.
5. Bösch and Wirsching, *Hüter der Ordnung*, 57.
6. Bösch and Wirsching, *Hüter der Ordnung*, 58–59.
7. Bösch and Wirsching, *Hüter der Ordnung*, 57.
8. Bösch and Wirsching, *Hüter der Ordnung*, 58.
9. Bösch and Wirsching, *Hüter der Ordnung*, 156.
10. Bösch and Wirsching, *Hüter der Ordnung*, 157–58.
11. Bösch and Wirsching, *Hüter der Ordnung*, 158.
12. Bösch and Wirsching, *Hüter der Ordnung*, 159.
13. Tom Bower, *Blind Eye to Murder: Britain, America and the Purging of Nazi Germany—A Pledge Betrayed* (London: Warner Books, 1997), 177.
14. Bower, *Blind Eye to Murder*, 178.
15. Bower, *Blind Eye to Murder*, 176.
16. Bösch and Wirsching, *Hüter der Ordnung*, 160.
17. Bösch and Wirsching, *Hüter der Ordnung*, 160.
18. Bösch and Wirsching, *Hüter der Ordnung*, 149.
19. Bösch and Wirsching, *Hüter der Ordnung*, 151.
20. Bösch and Wirsching, *Hüter der Ordnung*, 151.
21. Bösch and Wirsching, *Hüter der Ordnung*, 143.
22. Bösch and Wirsching, *Hüter der Ordnung*, 144.

23. Bösch and Wirsching, *Hüter der Ordnung*, 144-45.
24. Bösch and Wirsching, *Hüter der Ordnung*, 145.
25. Bösch and Wirsching, *Hüter der Ordnung*, 146.
26. Maren Richter, *Maria Daelen—Ärztin und Gesundheitspolitikerin im 20. Jahrhundert* (Göttingen: Wallstein Verlag, 2020), 11.
27. Richter, *Maria Daelen—Ärztin und Gesundheitspolitikerin im 20. Jahrhundert*, 58.
28. Richter, *Maria Daelen—Ärztin und Gesundheitspolitikerin im 20. Jahrhundert*, 71-79.
29. Richter, *Maria Daelen—Ärztin und Gesundheitspolitikerin im 20. Jahrhundert*, 76.
30. Richter, *Maria Daelen—Ärztin und Gesundheitspolitikerin im 20. Jahrhundert*, 78.
31. Tobias Freimüller, "Mediziner: Operation Volkskörper," in *Hitlers Eliten nach 1945*, ed. Norbert Frei (Munich: Deutscher Taschenbuch Verlag, 2003), 29-31.
32. Bösch and Wirsching, *Hüter der Ordnung*, 733.

## 10. Killers Welcome

1. Patrick Wagner, Imanuel Baumann, Herbert Reinke, and Andrej Stephan, *Schatten der Vergangenheit: Das BKA und seine Gründungsgeneration in der frühen Bundesrepublik* (Cologne: Luchterhand, 2011), 2.
2. Wagner, Baumann, Reinke, and Stephan, *Schatten der Vergangenheit*, 97-98.
3. Wagner, Baumann, Reinke, and Stephan, *Schatten der Vergangenheit*, 98-99.
4. Wagner, Baumann, Reinke, and Stephan, *Schatten der Vergangenheit*, 104-5.
5. Wagner, Baumann, Reinke, and Stephan, *Schatten der Vergangenheit*, 146.
6. Wagner, Baumann, Reinke, and Stephan, *Schatten der Vergangenheit*, 148.
7. Wagner, Baumann, Reinke, and Stephan, *Schatten der Vergangenheit*, 149.
8. Wagner, Baumann, Reinke, and Stephan, *Schatten der Vergangenheit*, 150-51.
9. Wagner, Baumann, Reinke, and Stephan, *Schatten der Vergangenheit*, 153.
10. Wagner, Baumann, Reinke, and Stephan, *Schatten der Vergangenheit*, 108.
11. Schenk, *Auf dem rechten Auge blind*, 188.
12. Schenk, *Auf dem rechten Auge blind*, 190-91.
13. Wagner, Baumann, Reinke, and Stephan, *Schatten der Vergangenheit*, 115-16.
14. Discussions during the 2007 Bundeskriminalamt conferences were chronicled by the BKA in a publication titled *Das BKA Stellt sich seiner Geschichte* (The BKA Confronts Its Past), which can be found at Sonderband2009DasBundeskriminalamtStelltSichSeinerGeschichte.pdf.
15. *Das BKA stellt sich seiner Geschichte* (Cologne: Luchterhand, 2008), 7-21.
16. *Das BKA stellt sich seiner Geschichte*, 95-107.

17. *Das BKA stellt sich seiner Geschichte*, 125-41.
18. *Das BKA stellt sich seiner Geschichte*, 223-24.
19. *Das BKA stellt sich seiner Geschichte*, 230-37.
20. *Das BKA stellt sich seiner Geschichte*, 224-25.
21. *Das BKA stellt sich seiner Geschichte*, 179-84.
22. *Das BKA stellt sich seiner Geschichte*, 215.

**11. The Rosenburg File**

1. Görtemaker and Safferling, *Die Akte Rosenburg*, 11.
2. Görtemaker and Safferling, *Die Akte Rosenburg*, 133.
3. Görtemaker and Safferling, *Die Akte Rosenburg*, 314-15.
4. Görtemaker and Safferling, *Die Akte Rosenburg*, 315.
5. Ingo Müller, *Hitler's Justice: The Courts of the Third Reich* (Cambridge: Harvard University Press, 1991), 211.
6. Görtemaker and Safferling, *Die Akte Rosenburg*, 315.
7. Görtemaker and Safferling, *Die Akte Rosenburg*, 306.
8. Görtemaker and Safferling, *Die Akte Rosenburg*, 307.
9. Görtemaker and Safferling, *Die Akte Rosenburg*, 310-11.
10. Görtemaker and Safferling, *Die Akte Rosenburg*, 354.
11. Müller, *Courts of the Third Reich*, 247.
12. Müller, *Courts of the Third Reich*, 248.
13. Müller, *Courts of the Third Reich*, 246.
14. Görtemaker and Safferling, *Die Akte Rosenburg*, 331.
15. Görtemaker and Safferling, *Die Akte Rosenburg*, 333.
16. Görtemaker and Safferling, *Die Akte Rosenburg*, 333.
17. Görtemaker and Safferling, *Die Akte Rosenburg*, 407.
18. Görtemaker and Safferling, *Die Akte Rosenburg*, 419.
19. Görtemaker and Safferling, *Die Akte Rosenburg*, 87.
20. Görtemaker and Safferling, *Die Akte Rosenburg*, 88.
21. Görtemaker and Safferling, *Die Akte Rosenburg*, 88-89.
22. Görtemaker and Safferling, *Die Akte Rosenburg*, 88.
23. Görtemaker and Safferling, *Die Akte Rosenburg*, 97.
24. When Dehler became federal justice minister, he brought Geiger with him to the Rosenburg, as his personal assistant and section leader on constitutional matters. Geiger used this position as a springboard first to a judgeship on the Federal Court of Justice and then on the Federal Constitutional Court.
25. Görtemaker and Safferling, *Die Akte Rosenburg*, 94.
26. Görtemaker and Safferling, *Die Akte Rosenburg*, 95.
27. Görtemaker and Safferling, *Die Akte Rosenburg*, 101.
28. Görtemaker and Safferling, *Die Akte Rosenburg*, 98-99.

29. Discussions at some of the conferences can be read, in German, on a Justice Ministry website, Die Akte Rosenburg—Das Bundesministerium der Justiz und die NS-Zeit, accessed March 17, 2024, BMJ—Rosenburg-Projekt—Die Akte Rosenburg—Das Bundesministerium der Justiz und die NS-Zeit.
30. In 1956 the Federal Court of Justice handed down a ruling that signaled to judges and prosecutors who had worked for the Nazi regime that they didn't have to worry about prosecution. In the case, the high court struck down the accessory to murder conviction of SS Judge Otto Thorbeck for the 1945 drumhead trial that resulted in the execution of Dietrich Bonhoeffer, Wilhelm Canaris, and other leading resistance figures. The Federal Court of Justice ruled that the Nazi regime had a legitimate right to execute traitors.
31. Remarks by Klaus Kinkel at the Justice Department symposium Die Rosenburg. Das Bundesministerium der Justiz und sein Umgang mit der NS-Vergangenheit, Berlin, April 26, 2012.
32. Remarks by Christoph Safferling to the Leo Baeck Institute at a symposium organized by the German Justice Ministry titled The Rosenburg Files—Former Nazis in the Postwar German Justice Ministry, New York, November 19, 2014.

## 12. A Burial in Chile

1. Martin Cüppers, *Walther Rauff—In deutschen Diensten: von Naziverbrecher zum BND-Spion* (Darmstadt, Germany: WBG, 2013), 72.
2. Cüppers, *Walther Rauff—In deutschen Diensten*, 112.
3. Cüppers, *Walther Rauff—In deutschen Diensten*, 150.
4. Breitman, Goda, Naftali, and Wolfe, *U.S. Intelligence and the Nazis*, 154.
5. Cüppers, *Walther Rauff—In deutschen Diensten*, 172.
6. Cüppers, *Walther Rauff—In deutschen Diensten*, 173.
7. Cüppers, *Walther Rauff—In deutschen Diensten*, 189.
8. Cüppers, *Walther Rauff—In deutschen Diensten*, 194.
9. Breitman, Goda, Naftali, and Wolfe, *U.S. Intelligence and the Nazis*, 153.
10. Cüppers, *Walther Rauff—In deutschen Diensten*, 272.
11. Cüppers, *Walther Rauff—In deutschen Diensten*, 239.
12. Cüppers, *Walther Rauff—In deutschen Diensten*, 275.
13. "Walther Rauff und der Bundesnachrichtendienst," press release about Rauff by the BND, September 23, 2011, https://multimedia.gsb.bund.de/BND/Importer-Downloads/mfg2bnd.pdf.
14. Cüppers, *Walther Rauff—In deutschen Diensten*, 365.
15. Cüppers, *Walther Rauff—In deutschen Diensten*, 377.
16. Gerhard Sälter, *NS Kontinuitäten im BND: Rekrutierung, Diskurse, Vernetzungen* (Berlin: Christoph Links Verlag, 2022), 566.
17. Sälter, *NS Kontinuitäten im BND*, 45–46.

18. Sälter, NS Kontinuitäten im BND, 45–46, 57.
19. Sälter, NS Kontinuitäten im BND, 47.
20. Sälter, NS Kontinuitäten im BND, 56.
21. Sälter, NS Kontinuitäten im BND, 56.
22. Sälter, NS Kontinuitäten im BND, 165–66.
23. Sabrina Nowack, *Sicherheitsrisiko NS-Belastung: Personalüberprüfungen im Bundesnachrichtendienst in den 1960er-Jahren* (Berlin: Christoph Links Verlag, 2016), 169.
24. Sälter, NS Kontinuitäten im BND, 130–37.
25. Sälter, NS Kontinuitäten im BND, 136–37.
26. Sälter, NS Kontinuitäten im BND, 138–39.
27. Sälter, NS Kontinuitäten im BND, 209–10.
28. Sälter, NS Kontinuitäten im BND, 145–46.
29. Sälter, NS Kontinuitäten im BND, 148–55.
30. Sälter, NS Kontinuitäten im BND, 282–85.
31. Sälter, NS Kontinuitäten im BND, 276–79.
32. Sälter, NS Kontinuitäten im BND, 280–81.
33. Felfe's betrayal and how he was finally caught are described in detail in a declassified CIA document titled "KGB Exploitation of Heinz Felfe," March 1, 1969, CREST: 02606327.
34. Peter Carstens, "Eine 'zweite Entnazifizierung,'" *Frankfurter Allgemeine Zeitung*, March 18, 2010.
35. Nowack, *Sicherheitsrisiko NS-Belastung*, 112.
36. Nowack, *Sicherheitsrisiko NS-Belastung*, 368.
37. Nowack, *Sicherheitsrisiko NS-Belastung*, 327.
38. Nowack, *Sicherheitsrisiko NS-Belastung*, 323.
39. Nowack, *Sicherheitsrisiko NS-Belastung*, 328.
40. Nowack, *Sicherheitsrisiko NS-Belastung*, 330.
41. Nowack, *Sicherheitsrisiko NS-Belastung*, 332.
42. Nowack, *Sicherheitsrisiko NS-Belastung*, 308–10.
43. Nowack, *Sicherheitsrisiko NS-Belastung*, 301.
44. Nowack, *Sicherheitsrisiko NS-Belastung*, 303.
45. Nowack, *Sicherheitsrisiko NS-Belastung*, 314–15.
46. Reinhard Gehlen in a conference with Org. 85 on October 23, 1964, Nowack, *Sicherheitsrisiko NS-Belastung*, 317–18.
47. Nowack, *Sicherheitsrisiko NS-Belastung*, 340.
48. Nowack, *Sicherheitsrisiko NS-Belastung*, 417.

## 13. A Tainted Democracy?

1. Volker ter Haseborg, "Ludwig Baumann—desertiert und überlebt," *Hamburger Abendblatt*, January 1, 2013, https://www.abendblatt.de/hamburg/article113167614/Ludwig-Baumann-desertiert-und-ueberlebt.html.
2. Speech by Baumann to the city of Cologne's NS-Dokumentationszentrum, January 23, 2009, "Grußwort Ludwig Baumann," NS-Documentation Center of the City of Cologne, https://museenkoeln.de/ns-dokumentationszentrum/default.aspx?s=1930.
3. Ter Haseborg, "Ludwig Baumann."
4. Dörte Hinrichs and Hans Rubinich, "Fast alle sind vorbestraft, entwürdigt verstorben," *Deutschlandfunk*, August 20, 2009, https://www.deutschlandfunk.de/fast-alle-sind-vorbestraft-entwuerdigt-verstorben-100.html.
5. Dörte Hinrichs, Hans Rubinich, and Hans-Herman Kotte, "Von Verrätern zu Helden," *Frankfurter Rundschau*, January 15, 2019.
6. Speech by Baumann to the city of Cologne's NS-Dokumentationszentrum.
7. Ernst Putzki's letter, read by Sebastian Urbanski at the Bundestag's ceremony, January 27, 2017, to remember victims of the Nazis' euthanasia program, Gedenkstunde des Bundestages für die Opfer des Nationalsozialismus. Addresses given at the memorial ceremony can be found on the Bundestag's website, Deutscher Bundestag, "Bundestag erinnert an die Opfer der 'Euthanasie' im NS-Staat," accessed March 17, 2024, https://www.bundestag.de/dokumente/textarchiv/2017/kw04-de-gedenkstunde-490478.
8. Hartmut Traub's speech about Benjamin Traub, at the Bundestag's memorial ceremony, January 27, 2017, Gedenkstunde des Bundestages für die Opfer des Nationalsozialismus.
9. Sigrid Falkenstein's speech about Anna Lehnkering, at the Bundestag's memorial ceremony, January 27, 2017, Gedenkstunde des Bundestages für die Opfer des Nationalsozialismus.
10. Norbert Lammert's speech at the Bundestag's memorial ceremony, January 27, 2017, Gedenkstunde des Bundestages für die Opfer des Nationalsozialismus.
11. Wagner, Baumann, Reinke, and Stephan, *Schatten der Vergangenheit*, 313-22.
12. Wagner, Baumann, Reinke, and Stephan, *Schatten der Vergangenheit*, 186.
13. Wagner, Baumann, Reinke, and Stephan, *Schatten der Vergangenheit*, 186.
14. Wagner, Baumann, Reinke, and Stephan, *Schatten der Vergangenheit*, 186.
15. Wagner, Baumann, Reinke, and Stephan, *Schatten der Vergangenheit*, 259-60.
16. Wagner, Baumann, Reinke, and Stephan, *Schatten der Vergangenheit*, 163.
17. Wagner, Baumann, Reinke, and Stephan, *Schatten der Vergangenheit*, 163.
18. Wagner, Baumann, Reinke, and Stephan, *Schatten der Vergangenheit*, 163.
19. Wagner, Baumann, Reinke, and Stephan, *Schatten der Vergangenheit*, 166-67.
20. Wagner, Baumann, Reinke, and Stephan, *Schatten der Vergangenheit*, 229-30.

21. Jan Korte's speech, "Entschädigung für Opfer nationalsozialistischer Verfolgung" (Compensation for Victims of National Socialist Persecution), delivered at the Bundestag, December 1, 2006.
22. Klaus-Dietmar Henke, *Geheime Dienste: Die politische Inlandsspionage des BND in der Ära Adenauer* (Berlin: Christoph Links Verlag, 2022), 455–56.
23. Henke, *Geheime Dienste*, 351.
24. Henke, *Geheime Dienste*, 692.
25. Henke, *Geheime Dienste*, 656.
26. Henke, *Geheime Dienste*, 665.
27. Henke, *Geheime Dienste*, 689.

## 14. Redemption

1. Ronen Steinke, *Fritz Bauer: The Jewish Prosecutor Who Brought Eichmann and Auschwitz to Trial* (Bloomington: Indiana University Press, 2020), 13.
2. Friedrich Kiessling and Christoph Safferling, *Staatsschutz im Kalten Krieg: Die Bundesanwaltschaft zwischen NS-Vergangenheit, Spiegel-Affäire und RAF* (Munich: dtv Verlagsgesellschaft, 2021), 377.
3. Kiessling and Safferling, *Staatsschutz im Kalten Krieg*, 382.
4. Steinke, *Fritz Bauer*, 98.
5. Gottfried Oy and Christoph Schneider, *Die Schärfe der Konkretion* (Münster, Germany: Verlag Westfälisches Dampfboot, 2013).
6. Kiessling and Safferling, *Staatsschutz im Kalten Krieg*, 158.
7. Kiessling and Safferling, *Staatsschutz im Kalten Krieg*, 229–31.
8. Kiessling and Safferling, *Staatsschutz im Kalten Krieg*, 231–32.
9. For German speakers, public addresses and writings by Dieter Schenk can be found at his website: dieter-schenk.info.
10. Quotations from Schenk's Essen speech, delivered on November 2, 2017, are taken from a digital copy of the address emailed to me by Schenk.
11. From Schenk's November 2, 2017, address to a meeting of the Schenklengsfeld municipal council, where he was given a bronze medal for his "societal and literary merit." A digital copy of the speech was emailed to me by Schenk.
12. Schenk emailed me a digital copy of the letter to his children, which he wrote on September 14, 2016.
13. Wagner, Baumann, Reinke, and Stephan, *Schatten der Vergangenheit*, 8.
14. From Ralph Giordano's speech on August 8, 2007, at a BKA-organized symposium in Wiesbaden that discussed postwar Nazi continuities within the federal police agency.
15. Giordano was interviewed by the PBS documentary series *American Experience* for a February 8, 2010, program about the World War II Allies' bombing

of Germany. The interview can be found at PBS online, https://www.pbs.org/wgbh/americanexperience/features/bombing-ralph-giordano.
16. From Giordano's speech at a December 6–7, 2011, BKA conference in Wiesbaden marking the sixtieth anniversary of the federal police agency.

## 15. Squandered Opportunities

1. Bösch and Wirsching, *Hüter der Ordnung*, 418–19.
2. Bösch and Wirsching, *Hüter der Ordnung*, 416–17.
3. Bösch and Wirsching, *Hüter der Ordnung*, 427.
4. Bösch and Wirsching, *Hüter der Ordnung*, 430.
5. Bösch and Wirsching, *Hüter der Ordnung*, 433–35.
6. The Social Democrats put up little to no resistance to Adenauer's push to reintegrate former Nazis into the West German civil service. The Social Democrats were in a precarious position. They were so concerned about alienating voters that the party shied away from publicly making a point about their persecution by the Nazis and their resistance to Hitler because this would have drawn a sharp contrast with the majority of Germans who didn't resist. For details, see recent research by German historian Kristina Meyer, Bundeskanzler-Willy-Brandt-Stiftung, https://willy-brandt.de/die-stiftung/organisation/team/dr-kristina-meyer.
7. Görtemacher made the point on November 16, 2016, in Bonn at the Justice Ministry's seventh symposium to discuss the work of the historians and scholars who were commissioned to study the Nazi taint of postwar government ministries and agencies.
8. Email exchange with Professor Gerhard Sälter on May 1, 2023.
9. Email exchange with Sälter on May 1, 2023.
10. Email exchange with Professor Patrick Wagner, April 13, 2023.
11. Email exchange with Professor Norbert Frei, May 5, 2023.
12. Zoom interview with Professor Christoph Safferling, April 5, 2023.
13. Email exchange with Wagner, April 13, 2023.
14. Telephone interview with Professor Klaus-Dieter Henke, March 29, 2023.
15. Telephone interview with Henke, August 2, 2022.
16. The remarks by Conze were made during a discussion at a Justice Ministry conference held at the Wannsee villa, where the Holocaust was plotted. The villa, outside Berlin, is a memorial and educational institute.

## Epilogue

1. For detailed reporting on the rise of this threat, see the excellent five-part 2021 podcast by Katrin Bennhold, Berlin bureau chief of the *New York Times*, titled

*Day X*, https://www.nytimes.com/2021/05/19/podcasts/far-right-german-extremism.html; as well as the 2021 PBS *FRONTLINE* documentary *Germany's Neo-Nazis & the Far Right*, directed by Evan Williams, June 29, 2021, https://www.pbs.org/wgbh/frontline/documentary/germanys-neo-nazis-the-far-right.

2. *Rechtsextremisten in Sicherheitsbehörden*, a situation report on right-wing extremists by the Bundesamt für Verfassungsschutz. The report, released in September 2020, can be found at Rechtsextremisten in Sicherheitsbehörden—Lagebericht (verfassungsschutz.de).

3. Email exchange with Rafael Behr, April 10, 2023.

4. The court decision was announced by the Bundesamt für Verfassungsschutz on March 8, 2022. The press release can be found at Bundesamt für Verfassungsschutz—Presse—Bundesamt für Verfassungsschutz obsiegt vor Verwaltungsgericht Köln gegen die AfD.

5. Markus Balser and Jens Schneider, "Verfassungsschutz stuft 'Flügel' als rechtsextrem ein," *Süddeutsche Zeitung*, March 12, 2020.

6. From the 2022 report on threats to democracy and national security issued by the federal Interior Ministry.

7. Germany's Interior Ministry publishes an annual report, *Verfassungsschutzbericht* (Annual Report on the Protection of the Constitution), on internal threats to the democratic order: from the Right, the Left, spies, and foreign terrorists and criminals. The reports, written in German, can be found online by searching for "Verfassungsschutzbericht."

8. Zoom interview with Dirk Laabs on March 27, 2023.

# Bibliography

Bevers, Jürgen. *Der Mann hinter Adenauer: Hans Globkes Aufstieg vom NS-Juristen zur Grauen Eminenz der Bonner Republik.* Berlin: Christoph Links Verlag, 2009.

Bösch, Frank, and Andreas Wirsching, eds. *Hüter der Ordnung: Die Innenministerien in Bonn und Ost-Berlin nach dem Nationalsozialismus.* Göttingen: Wallstein Verlag, 2018.

Bower, Tom. *Blind Eye to Murder: Britain, America and the Purging of Nazi Germany—A Pledge Betrayed.* London: Warner Books, 1997.

Breitman, Richard, and Norman J. W. Goda. *Hitler's Shadow: Nazi War Criminals, U.S. Intelligence, and the Cold War.* Washington DC: National Archives, 2011.

Breitman, Richard, Norman J. W. Goda, Timothy Naftali, and Robert Wolfe. *U.S. Intelligence and the Nazis.* New York: Cambridge University Press, 2005.

Conze, Eckart, Norbert Frei, Peter Hayes, and Moshe Zimmerman, eds. *Das Amt und die Vergangenheit: Deutsche Diplomaten im Dritten Reich und in der Bundesrepublik.* Munich: Karl Blessing Verlag, 2010.

Creuzberger, Stefan, and Dominik Geppert, eds. *Die Ämter und ihre Vergangenheit: Ministerien und Behörden im geteilten Deutschland 1949-1972.* Bonn: Bundeszentrale für politische Bildung, 2018.

Cüppers, Martin. *Walther Rauff—In deutschen Diensten: von Naziverbrecher zum BND-Spion.* Darmstadt, Germany: WBG, 2013.

*Das Bundeskriminalamt stellt sich seiner Geschichte.* Compilation by the BKA of speeches and panel discussions at the agency's conferences on the Nazi taint on August 8, September 20, and October 31, 2007. Cologne: Luchterhand, 2008.

Evans, Richard J. *The Third Reich at War.* New York: Penguin, 2009.

Foschepoth, Josef. "Postzensur und Telefonüberwachung in der Bundesrepublik Deutschland (1949-1968)." *Zeitschrift für Geschichtswissenschaft*, no. 5 (2009).

Frei, Norbert. *Adenauer's Germany and the Nazi Past: The Politics of Amnesty and Integration.* New York: Columbia University Press, 2002.

———, ed. *Hitlers Eliten nach 1945.* Munich: Deutscher Taschenbuch Verlag, 2003.

Giordani, Ralph. *Die zweite Schuld, oder Von der Last Deutscher zu Sein.* Hamburg: Rasch und Röhring Verlag, 1987.

Görtemaker, Manfred, and Christoph Safferling. *Die Akte Rosenburg: Das Bundesministerium der Justiz und die NS-Zeit.* Munich: Verlag C. H. Beck, 2016.

Goschler, Constantin, and Michael Wala. *"Keine Neue Gestapo": Das Bundesamt für Verfassungsschutz und die NS-Vergangenheit*. Hamburg: Rowohlt Verlag GmbH, 2015.

Henke, Klaus-Dietmar. *Geheime Dienste: Die politische Inlandsspionage des BND in der Ära Adenauer*. Berlin: Christoph Links Verlag, 2022.

Kiessling, Friedrich, and Christoph Safferling, eds. *Staatsschutz im Kalten Krieg: Die Bundesanwaltschaft zwischen NS-Vergangenheit, Spiegel-Affäire und RAF*. Munich: dtv Verlagsgesellschaft, 2021.

Müller, Ingo. *Hitler's Justice: The Courts of the Third Reich*. Cambridge: Harvard University Press, 1991.

Nowack, Sabrina. *Sicherheitsrisiko NS-Belastung: Personalüberprüfungen im Bundesnachrichtendienst in den 1960er-Jahren*. Berlin: Christoph Links Verlag, 2016.

Oy, Gottfried, and Christoph Schneider. *Die Schärfe der Konkretion*. Münster: Verlag Westfälisches Dampfboot, 2013.

Richter, Maren. *"Aber ich habe mich nicht entmutigen lassen": Maria Daelen—Ärztin und Gesundheitspolitikerin im 20 Jahrhundert*. Göttingen: Wallstein Verlag, 2019.

Rückerl, Adalbert. *Die Strafverfolgung von NS-Verbrechen 1945-1978*. Karlsruhe, Germany: C. F. Müller Juristischer Verlag, 1979.

Sälter, Gerhard. *NS-Kontinuitäten im BND: Rekrutierung, Diskurse, Vernetzungen*. Berlin: Christoph Links Verlag, 2022.

Schenk, Dieter. *Auf dem rechten Auge blind: Die braunen Wurzeln des BKA*. Cologne: Verlag Kiepenheuer & Witsch, 2001.

Steinke, Ronen. *Fritz Bauer: The Jewish Prosecutor Who Brought Eichmann and Auschwitz to Trial*. Bloomington: Indiana University Press, 2020.

———. *Fritz Bauer: oder Auschwitz vor Gericht*. Munich: Piper, 2013.

Wagner, Patrick, Imanuel Baumann, Herbert Reinke, and Andrej Stephan, eds. *Schatten der Vergangenheit: Das BKA und seine Gründungsgeneration in der frühen Bundesrepublik*. Cologne: Luchterhand, 2011.

# Index

*Page numbers in italics indicate document scans.*

*"Aber ich habe mich nicht entmutigen lassen"* ("But I Didn't Allow Myself to Be Intimidated") (Richter), 105
Abwehr, 48, 71, 106, 165, 203; Dickopf and, 49, 50, 51, 52, 53, 54
Adenauer, Konrad, xv, xvi, xviii, xx, 20, 91, 92, 107, 109, 116, 119, 145, 192–93, 194, 198, 207, 220; assassination attempt on, 193; Bauer and, 21; Brugger on, 122; civil servants and, 240–41, 242; Cold War and, 238; Dehler and, 143; Dickopf and, 56, 59; dirty tricks and, 17; election of, 13; FDJ and, 199; Gehlen and, 158, 204, 208; Globke and, 11, 12, 14, 16, 17, 21, 22, 203, 204, 208, 245–46; Heinemann and, 11–12; hiring practices and, 144; Kennedy and, 202; Kessler and, 94, 95; KPD and, 200; Massfeller and, 131; Nazi taint and, 121, 168, 181; Ochs and, 196; Oppler and, 236; reintegration and, xix, 267n6; Social Democrats and, 18, 205, 246; Strecker on, 218; on tainted civil servants, xiii; VVN and, 239; war criminals and, 8
Adenauer Decree, 238
AFD. *See* Alternative für Deutschland
Agent 9610, 47
Ahnenerbe (Ancestral Heritage), 119
*Aktion* T4, 193

"Aktion Vulkan" (Operation Volcano), 200–201
Albrecht, Franco, 247, 248, 251
Allende, Salvador, 155
Alternative für Deutschland (AFD), 250, 252
al-Za'im, Husni, Rauff and, 154
Amelunxen, Rudolf, 100
American Experience (PBS), Giordano on, 231
American Legation, 54, 55
Angenfort, Josef, 199
anti-Hitler resistance, 12, 16, 17, 91, 98, 104, 106, 143, 215
antisemitism, 68, 69, 212, 250
Argenton-sur-Creuse, massacre at, 162
Arndt, Adolf, 142
Article 131, 236; Fiebig case and, 176; stipulations of, 7–8
Article 132, 236; civil servants and, 237
Aryanization, 99, 101, 102, 103, 106, 121
Associated Press, xv, xvi, 74, 255n1
Association of Victims of the Nazi Regime (VVN), 238, 239
Atlantic-Express, 141
*Auf dem rechten Augen blind* (Turning a Blind Eye to the Right) (Schenk), xx, 47, 55, 111, 229
Augsburg, Emil, 166–67, 168
Auschwitz, xiii, xvi, 28, 95, 99, 125, 130, 152, 195, 210, 211, 216

Auschwitz Trials, xviii, 216, 217
*Auswärtige Politik Heute* (Foreign Policy Today), 81
authoritarianism, 201, 213, 226, 232, 244

Babi Yar, massacre at, 174
Ballin, Friedrich, 5
BAMAD. *See* Bundesamt für den Militärischen Abschirmdienst
Bamberg, Kristallnacht and, 139
Bamberg Special Court, 140
Bamberg Superior District Court, 140
Barbie, Klaus, xix, 40, 163
Barmbek district, 230, 231
Batista, Fulgencio, 154
Battle of the Bulge, Schreiber and, 163
Batz, Rudolf, 115, 116
Bauer, Fritz, xx, 18, 21, 212, 240; accomplishments of, 216–17; arrest of, 213, 214; career of, 212, 213; described, 209; on economic miracle, 209; flight of, 214; Globke and, 20; Güde and, 220; prosecution by, 210–11; Remer and, 215–16; Waters and, 19
Bauer, Margot, 214
Baumann, Imanuel, 123
Baumann, Ludwig, 181, 182–83, 185; anti-war views of, 184; legacy of, 187–88; peace movement and, 184; rehabilitation of, 187
Baumann, Waltraud, 183
Bavarian state labor court, Zielow and, 174
Bayer, Klaus, xvii, 122
BDC. *See* Berlin Document Center
*Beamtenlaufbahn* code, 241
Bedburg-Hau, asylum in, 190, 192
Beer Hall Putsch, 4
Beethoven, Ludwig van, 209
Begin, Menachem, 194
Behnke, Kurt, 235, 236

Behr, Rafael, 252
Beisner, Wilhelm, Rauff and, 154
Ben-Gurion, David, 20, 205
Bergen-Belsen, 129, 212
Berlin Base, 70, 170
Berlin Document Center (BDC), 70, 71, 102, 128
Berlin Wall, xvi, 87
Bern Police Department, Dickopf and, 53
Bernstorff, Albrecht Graf von, 106
Bertelsmann, xvii
Bertinis, 232
BfV. *See* Bundesamt für Verfassungsschutz
Biden, Joe, 253
Bizone/Bizonia, 96, 142, 143, 235, 236, 237
BKA. *See* Bundeskriminalamt
Blankenhorn, Herbert, report by, 81–82
Bleicher, Max, 238
*Blind Eye to Murder* (Bower), 98
Blum, Paul C., 55
BMI. *See* Federal Interior Ministry
BMJ. *See* Bundesministerium der Justiz
BND. *See* Bundesnachrichtendienst
Boger, Wilhelm, 216
Böhrnsen, Jens, on Baumann, 187
Boker, John R., Jr., Bolschwing and, 68; Gehlen and, 65, 66, 67
Bolschwing, Otto Albrecht Alfred von, 69, 70, 71; Boker and, 68; code name for, 72; fake identity for, 74; political/sociological studies by, 73
Bonhoeffer, Dietrich, 263n30
Bonn, xii, 5, 11, 25, 33, 35, 45, 77; former Nazis in, xi
Bonn American Embassy Club, xii
Bösch, Frank, xvii; research by, 91, 92, 94, 95, 96, 101, 102–3, 104, 105, 108, 236, 244, 246

Botanical Institute, 119
Bower, Tom, 98-99
Brandt, Willy, xvi, 202, 203, 240
Bremen, 179, 188; trial in, 200
British High Commission, 128
Brugger, Siegfried, 122
Brunner, Alois, 40, 80
Bund der Verfolgten des Nazi Regimes (Federation of Victims of the Nazi Regime), 131
Bundesamt für den Militärischen Abschirmdienst (BAMAD), 249, 250
Bundesamt für Verfassungsschutz (Federal Office for the Protection of the Constitution) (BfV), 89, 201, 206, 268n2, 268n4; Wenger and, 37, 38, 39, 40
Bundeskriminalamt (Federal Criminal Police Office) (BKA), xvi, xix, xx, 89, 118, 144, 193, 198, 200, 207, 211, 232, 233, 243, 244; conferences by, 120, 121-22; Dickopf and, 48, 56, 57, 58, 59, 60, 228; exposé on, 47; Freitag and, 114, 116; Gehlen and, 243; inquiry by, 112; Interior Ministry and, 113, 114, 115, 116; Martin and, 119; Michael and, 109, 113; Nazi continuities and, 199; Nazi taint on, 111, 112, 114, 119, 150, 195; Niggemeyer and, 117; Ochs and, 195, 196, 197; Saevecke and, 25, 27, 29, 30, 31, 32, 33, 35, 201; Sch and, 113; Schenk and, 224, 227, 228, 229; secrets of, 122, 229; street renaming and, 258n20; war criminals at, 123-24, 125-26, 224; Ziercke and, 120
Bundesministerium der Justiz (Federal Justice Ministry) (BMJ), xvi, 81, 89, 136, 142, 143, 145, 148, 209, 239, 240, 244, 245, 246, 255n2, 267n16ch15; conferences by, 144, 146, 147; Dreher and, 132, 135, 137; Herrmann and, 108; Kanter and, 130; Massfeller and, 130-31; Merten and, 128-29, 130; Nazi taint on, 9, 127-28, 129, 138; Strauss and, 128; war crimes and, 128; Weitnauer and, 132
Bundesnachrichtendienst (Federal Intelligence Service) (BND), 89, 144, 198, 205, 207, 242; Augsburg and, 167; beginnings of, 159; Clemens and, 42; Crome and, 173, 179; Crüwell and, 165; Felfe and, 170-71, 179, 180; Fiebig and, 176; Gehlen and, 167, 169, 170, 171; Globke and, 15, 203-4; Goertz and, 166; Lermen and, 177; Macke and, 178; Menge and, 178; Nazi taint at, 112, 158-59, 165-66, 168, 169, 178-79; Otto and, 163; Rauff and, 149, 150, 154-55, 156-57; Schreiber and, 164; Six and, 168; Strecker and, 206; Warzecha and, 178; Zietlow and, 174, 175
Bundestag, 7, 78, 87, 88, 181, 185, 187, 188, 189, 190, 192, 193, 202, 216, 221, 223; inquiries by, 219; rehabilitation and, 184
*Bundestelle für Verfolgung von Kriminalbeamten* (Federal Office for the Prosecution of Criminal Investigators), 59
bureaucracies, 7, 40, 88, 165, 190, 210, 245, 253; civil service, 91; filling, 8; postwar, xix, xx; Third Reich, xviii, 12, 15, 141

camp guards, prosecution of, 124, 125
Camp Kornwestheim, 160
Canaris, Wilhelm, 263n30
Carstens, Peter, 172, 182
Castro, Fidel, 154
Catel, Werner, 107, 108
Catholic Center Party, 15, 16, 18
CDU. *See* Christian Democratic Union

Central Council of German Sinti and Roma, 121
Central Council of Jews in Germany, 17, 211
Central Intelligence Agency (CIA), xix, xx, 23, 50, 71; Boker and, 67; Bolschwing and, 69, 72, 73, 74; Bonn government and, 13–14; Clemens and, 42; Dickopf and, 47, 48, 54, 55, 56, 58, 59, 60, 61; Eichmann and, 19–20; Felfe and, 170–71; Gehlen and, 65, 68, 69, 72, 167, 168, 169, 243; Globke and, 13, 14, 15; Saevecke and, 25, 27, 29, 30, 31–32, 201; Schenk and, 112; war criminals and, 66, 149; Wenger and, 37, 38–39, 44
Central Intelligence Group (CIG), 67, 70
Central Legal Defense Agency, 80
Central Office, 57, 80, 212; birth of, 58; BKA and, 113; Dickopf and, 59
chain recruiting, 162
Chancellor's Office, 167, 168, 169–70, 179
Charité Hospital, 105
Charlottenburg police academy, Wenger and, 40
Christian Democratic Union (CDU), 87, 89, 97, 137, 145, 193, 200, 205, 238, 239
Christian Social Union (CSU), 89, 200
CIA. *See* Central Intelligence Agency
CIA Records Search Tool (CREST), 256
CIC. *See* Counterintelligence Corps
CIG. *See* Central Intelligence Group
civil servants: complicity of, 142; experienced, xiii, 8–9; hiring, 8, 236, 240–41, 243; Nazi tainted, xii, xiii, 143, 146; stereotypes by, 196–97; untainted, 237
civil service, 25, 57–58, 89, 91, 94; complexity of, 13; Dickopf and, 48; Dreher and, 135; entering, 15, 100; Nazi taint on, xvi, 119, 128, 132, 146–47, 198, 245, 267n6; postwar, 96, 101, 241; recruiting, 9; war criminals and, 242
civil service law, 235, 237
Clemens, Gerda, 41
Clemens, Hans, 41, 166, 170, 171, 179; Dresden and, 42; Felfe and, 42
Cold War, xi, xii, xv, 34, 37, 77, 87, 125, 179, 201, 202
*Collini Case* (von Schirach), xx
*Commentary on German Racial Legislation* (Globke), 13
Communist Party, 88, 213
Communists, 26, 55, 87, 202, 238
concentration camps, 7, 59, 95, 120, 121, 124, 151, 171, 182
Conference on Jewish Material Claims Against Germany, 194
*Conte Grande*, 154
Conze, Eckart, 246, 267n16
Corbetta, 28; executions in, 29, 31
Counterintelligence Corps (CIC), 67, 153, 158, 170; Otto and, 163
counterpropaganda strategy, xviii
COVID-19, 250, 253
Criminal Code, 133
Crocodile (bar), 217, 219
Crome, Hans-Henning, 174, 176, 177, 178; interviews by, 179; investigation by, 172; recommendations by, 173
Crüwell, Ludwig, 165
CSU. *See* Christian Social Union
Cüppers, Martin, 150, 151, 152; Rauff and, 154, 156

Dachau, 4, 26, 139, 162
Daelen, Felix, 105
Daelen, Maria, 107, 109; Catel and, 108; resistance and, 104, 106; Richter and, 105, 106

Daimler, xvii
*Das Amt und Die Vergangenheit* (The Office and the Past) (Conze, Frei, Hayes, and Zimmermann), xvi, 81, 82, 83, 84; criticism of, 85; release of, 79
*Das letzte Tabu* (The Last Taboo) (Wette and Vogel), 186
Das Reich division, 162
Davis, John, 153
Day X, 247, 253
Dehler, Irma, 139-40
Dehler, Thomas, 127, 137, 141, 220, 240; career of, 138-39; Dreher and, 135; Holocaust and, 139-40; Massfeller and, 131; Weimar democracy and, 138
Demjanjuk, John, 124, 125
denazification, xv, 6-7, 13, 14, 55, 56, 72, 99, 100, 103, 107, 161; judgments of, 97-98
deportation, 80, 97, 103, 104, 120, 128, 130, 152, 179, 225, 228, 231
*Der Angriff* (The Attack), Zietlow and, 174
Der Flügel ("The Wing"), 253
*Der Spiegel*, 80, 107, 108, 207; Dickopf and, 58; exposé by, 32
*Der Staat gegen Fritz Bauer* (The People v. Fritz Bauer) (Kraume), 209
*Der Sturmer*, 139
Deryabin, Petr, 170
Deutsche Bank, xvii
Deutsche Demokratische Partei (German Democratic Party), 138
*Deutsche Polizei* (German Police), 122
*Deutsche Welle*, 218
*Deutschlandfunk*, 186
de Wilde, Martin-Jacobus, 165
Dickopf, Paul, xix, 47, 49, 57, 227-28; arrest of, 51-52; code name for, 48, 54, 55, 56; death of, 60, 63; denazification and, 55; document about, 61, 62, 63; as refugee, 53-54
*Die Akte Rosenburg* (The Rosenburg File) (Kiessling and Safferling), 128, 130, 136, 137, 140, 146, 220
*Die Bertinis* (Giordano), 2322
Die Linke (The Left), 87-88, 201-2
Dienststelle 120 (Office 120), 160-61, 162
Diester, Jörg, 33, 257n12
*Die zweite Schuld, oder Von der Last, Deutscher zu sein* (Second Guilt, or The Burden of Being a German) (Giordano), xvi, 230, 232
Dirección Nacional de Inteligencia (DINA), Rauff and, 155-56
disabilities, 107, 108, 188, 190, 192, 193
Divan, 162, 163, 165
Dorndorf, Alexandra, 251
Dr. Oetker (company), xvii
Dreher, Eduard, 132, 133, 134; EGOWiG and, 137; judgeship for, 135; prosecution of, 136
Dresden Art Academy, 134
Duisburg police, 199
Dulles, Allen, 29, 50; Dickopf and, 54; Kolbe and, 84; Saevecke and, 30
Dullien, Reinhard, 32-33

Eastern Europe Division (CIA), 42
East German Communists, xi, xviii; broadsides by, 131-32
East German Ministry for State Security, 59
East German Ministry of the Interior, 7, 244
EGOWiG. See *Einführungsgesetz zum Ordnungswidrigkeitengesetz*
Ehlich, Hans, 166
Ehrensberger, Otto, 94
Ehrhard, Ludwig, 116

Ehrlinger, Erich, 113
Eichmann, Adolf, xvi, xx, 19–20, 40, 69, 72, 73, 87, 209; capture of, 18, 20, 23, 205, 208, 210, 214; execution of, 21, 206; trial of, 155, 207
*Einfacher Dienst* (Basic Service), 241
*Einfuhrungsgesetz zum Ordnungswidrigkeitengesetz* (Law Accompanying Introduction of the Law on Administrative Offenses) (EGOWiG), 134, 136, 137
Einsatzgruppe A, 115, 166, 177
Einsatzgruppe B, 164, 178; Fiebig and, 175; Filbert and, 113; Gehlen and, 167
Einsatzgruppe C, Zietlow and, 174
Einsatzgruppe H, 174
Einsatzgruppen, xi, 113, 114, 151, 158, 173, 175, 176, 244; mobile murder units, 111; murders by, 4
Einsatzkommando 2, 115, 116
Einsatzkommando 3, 177
Einsatzkommando 9, 175–76
Einsatzkommando Egypt, Rauff and, 151–52
Einsatzkommandos, 28, 111, 113, 114, 117, 118, 126, 152, 158, 175, 178
Einsatzkommando Tilsit, 58, 113
Eisner, Albert D., 74
El-Alamein, 151
Engelsing, Herbert, 12–13, 14
Erhard, Ludwig, 33
Erlen, Heinrich, 112, 117
Essen police, 247; right-wing extremism within, 252
euthanasia, 107, 265n7
Exonerated, 6, 97, 98, 103, 129, 161, 175
extermination camps, 120, 121, 214
"The Face of Terror of the Criminal Bonn State" (brochure), 132

Faeser, Nancy, 250, 251

Falkenstein, Sigrid, 192
"Fallex 62" (military exercise), 32
Far Left, 199
Far Right, 145, 199, 227
FBI, 25
Federal Agriculture Ministry, former Nazis at, 9
Federal Archives, 92
Federal Association of Victims of Nazi Military Justice, 184
Federal Constitutional Court, 198, 217, 262n24
Federal Court of Justice, 212, 217, 262n24, 263n30; Dehler and, 135; Dreher and, 135; Heinrich and, 133; Roma and, 196
Federal Defense Ministry, internal investigation by, 249
Federal Economics Ministry, 89
Federal Finance Ministry, 89
Federal Foreign Office, 77, 78, 79, 81, 83, 89, 120, 144, 206, 243, 246; book about, xvi; hiring practices and, xvii; Merten and, 129; Nazi taint in, 84
Federal Interior Ministry (BMI), xvii, 88, 91, 96, 101, 103, 117, 235, 237, 244, 245; Behnke and, 236; BKA and, 113, 114, 115, 116; culture of, 92; Daelen and, 104, 107; Dickopf and, 48; Freitag and, 116; investigation of, 108; Nazi taint in, 9, 104, 105, 127; personnel continuities and, 89; Rippich and, 102; Rumohr and, 102, 104; Saevecke and, 29; Scheffler and, 100
Federal Office for Administration, Wenger and, 40
Federal Prosecutor's Office, xvi, 159
Federal Transportation Ministry, 89
Felfe, Heinz, 162, 166, 170–71, 180, 207; betrayal by, 264n33; Clemens and, 42; Dresden and, 41; exposure of,

179; Grauer and, 177; investigation of, 171
Fiebig, Konrad, trial of, 175-76
Fifth Rosenburg Symposium, xviii
Filbert, Alfred, 113
"Final Solution of the Jewish Question," 131
Fischer, Joschka, xiii, 78, 144
Fischer-Schweder, Bernhard, 57, 58
Fish-Harnack, Mildred, 12-13
Flemish Nationalist Party, 165
Follower, 6, 97, 98, 134, 161
Forced Sterilization Act, 193
Ford Taurus, 206
Forensic Institute, Martin and, 119
Frank, Hans, 96
Fränkel, Wolfgang, 221, 222, 223
*Frankfurter Allgemeine Zeitung*, 79, 172, 194
*Frankfurter Rundschau*, 135, 216
Frankfurt police, Dickopf and, 49
Free Democrats, 238
Frei, Norbert, xvii, xix, 85, 243
Freie Deutsche Jugend (Free German Youth) (FDJ), 199
Freie Wissenschaftliche Vereinigung (Free Academic Union), 213
Freisler, Roland, 144, 145, 185
Freitag, Gerhard, 114, 115, 116
Frick, Wilhelm, 16
Fritz Bauer Scholarship Prize for Human Rights and Contemporary History, 209-10
*Fritz Bauer* (Steinke), 210
*From the Reich Prosecutor's Office to the Federal Prosecutor's Office* (booklet), 221
Fuczak, Joseph, 222
Führerschule der Sicherheitspolizei (Leadership School for Security Police), Saevecke and, 27-28

gas vans, 149, 151, 155
Gawlik, Hans, 80, 81
Gegen Vergessen—Für Demokratie (Against Forgetting—For Democracy), 146
*Geheime Dienste* (Secret Services) (Henke), 203
Geheime Feldpolizei (Secret Field Police) (GFP), 117, 118, 126, 165, 173
Gehlen, Reinhard, 14, 71, 161, 165, 169, 170, 171, 174, 178, 207-8, 242, 243, 245; Adenauer and, 204, 208; Boker and, 65, 66, 67; counterintelligence and, 65; espionage by, 204, 205; Felfe and, 42, 173; Globke and, 168; Henke and, 203; intelligence operation by, 158; spying by, 159-60, 181; working for, 204
Gehlen Organization, 67, 158, 170, 172, 173; Augsburg and, 166-67; CIA and, 68, 69, 72; Clemens and, 42; code name for, 68; Fiebig and, 175; hiring by, 160, 161-62; Zuber and, 161
Gehrig, Peter, xii, 255n1
Geiger, Willi, 140, 252n24
Geiler, Karl, 142
General Government, 96, 101
genocide, 120, 174, 194, 211
Genoud, François, 49; arrest of, 51-52; Dickopf and, 50, 51, 52, 53
German Civil Servants Association, 103
German Communist Party, 7, 238
*The German Foreign Office under the Nazi Regime*, (Blankenhorn), 82
German Historical Institute, 85
German Intelligence Service, 72
Germanische Leitstelle, 160
Germanization, 96, 100
German Military Intelligence Service, 65
German Security Police, 53

German Tuberculosis Society, 108
*Gesetz zum Schutze des Deutschen Blutes und der Deutschen Ehre* (Law for the Protection of German Blood and German Honor), 16
Gestapo, 9, 17, 26, 39, 53, 56, 116, 140, 154, 157, 158, 161, 164, 168, 169; Daelen and, 106; Dickopf and, 47, 57; Fiebig and, 175; Giordano and, 232; hiring former, 239, 242; Lermen and, 177; Michael and, 111; Otto and, 163; Wenger and, 42; Winker and, 176
Gewerkschaft der Polizei (Union of Police), 122
GFP. *See* Geheime Feldpolizei
Giordano, Lilly, 231
Giordano, Ralph, xvi, 120, 231, 246, 266n14; altercation and, 229–30; death of, 233; hardships for, 232; interview of, 266–67n15; "Second Guilt" and, xix
Globke, Augusta, 21
Globke, Hans, 2–4, 91, 94, 97, 130, 141, 207; Adenauer and, 11, 12, 14, 16, 17, 21, 22, 203, 204, 208, 245–46; criticism of, 206; described, 12, 15, 17, 21; destiny of, 12–13; Eichmann and, 19–20, 21, 23, 205; Gehlen and, 168; Greek Jews and, 18; guidebook by, 11, 17; release of, 13, 16; reservations about, 14
Goebbels, Joseph, 6, 106, 174, 215
Goedicke, Walter, 221–22
Goering, Hermann, 6
Goertz, Reinhard, 166
Goethe, Johann Wolfgang von, 209
Goleniewski, Michal, 170, 171
Görtemaker, Manfred, 146, 267nn6–7; Leo Baeck Institute and, 144; presentation by, 147; research by, 128, 130, 134, 136, 137, 138, 140, 141, 142,

143, 239; Rosenburg project and, 147
Grafeneck killing center, 192
Grand Coalition, 137
Grauer, Gustav, 177
Great Synagogue, destruction of, 94
Greek Jews, deportation of, 128
Greens Party, 78
Greiser, Arthur, 96, 97, 101
Gröning, Oskar, 124–25
Gross, Marko, 248, 249, 252
Güde, Max, 219, 220–21
gypsies, 121, 195

"habitual criminal" law, 135
Hadamar Euthanasia Center, 107, 188, 191
Hamburg, 95, 183, 188; firebombing of, 23
*Hamburger Abendblatt*, 184
Hannibal, 248, 249
Hanning, Reinhold, 125
Hannover, 1960 conference in, 202
Hannover, Heinrich, 200
Harmening, Rudolf, 142
Harnack, Arvid, 12–13
Harnack, Mildred, 12–13
Hauser, Karoline, 135, 136
Hayes, Peter, 85
Health Department, Daelen and, 107; Nazi taint in, 105
Hechelheimer, Bodo, 29
Heidepeter, Wilhelm, 5
Heinemann, Gustav, 100, 132, 230, 238; Adenauer and, 11–12
Heinrich, Hermann, 133, 136
Heinrich XIII, Prince, 250
Helms, Richard, 72
Henke, Klaus-Dietmar, 17, 207; on Adenauer/Globke, 245–46; Gehlen and, 203, 208

Hermann, Franz, 108
Hesse police, 54
Heuberg concentration camp, 213
Heydrich, Reinhard, 150, 151
High Commission on Germany (HICOG), 13
Himmler, Gudrun, cover names for, 159
Himmler, Heinrich, 6, 69, 95, 97, 159
*Historikerkommissionen*, xvii, xx
Hitler, Adolf, xviii, 4, 20, 25, 26, 28, 50, 66, 77, 82, 83, 84, 92; allegiance to, 11; arson attack and, 93; assassination attempt on, 81, 103, 106, 140, 214; death of, 6, 65; Globke and, 16; military courts and, 186; plot against, 14; resistance to, 267n6; rise of, 12, 49, 96, 138, 213, 230, 254; war criminals and, 58
*Hitlers Eliten Nach 1945* (Hitler's Elites after 1945) (Frei), xix–xx
Hitler Youth, 158, 163, 183, 230
Hoherer Dienst (Upper Service), 83, 241; Nazi taint in, 84
Holocaust, xviii, 18, 21, 25, 84, 85, 96, 120, 133, 137, 139-40; complicity in, xi; survivors of, 3-4; vengeance for, 194
*Holocaust* (television series), 156
Hönlinger, Roman, 159
Horstkotte, Hartmuth, 136
Hotel Löwen, 53
Hotel Regina, 28, 153
Hotel Savoy, 165
House of Reuss, 250
Hubener, Otto, 106
human rights, defending, 213
*Hüter der Ordnung* (Guardian of Order) (Bösch and Wirsching), 108, 236

Immigration and Naturalization Service, Bolschwing and, 73

Inner Mission, 97
Innsbruck Special Court, 134, 135-36, 137
Internal Affairs Office, Rumohr and, 104
International Auschwitz Committee, 216
International Criminal Police Organization (Interpol), 48, 60
International Military Tribunal, 6
Irgun, 194
Iron Curtain, 37, 131, 206
Iron Guard, 69, 70
Israeli Intelligence Service, 20
*Israel Journal of Foreign Affairs*, 85

Jacobi, Kurt, 94, 97
Jagow, Dietrich von, 150
Jewish Affairs Department, 69
Jewish Question, 17, 69, 103
Jonckheere, Martin, 165
Jost, Heinz, 166
July 20 conspirators, 214, 215
Jungfer, Otto, 97

Kanter, Ernst, 129, 130
Kappe, Wilhelm, 5
Kardorff-Oheimb, Katharina von, 105
Karle, Michaela, 33, 257n12
Karlsruhe City Hall, 217, 219
Kennedy, John F., 202, 203
Kessler, Erich, 103; Adenauer and, 94, 95; career of, 94-95, 96
KGB. *See* Komitet Gosudarstvennoy Bezopasnosti
Kiepenheuer & Witsch, 229
Kiessling, Friedrich, 220, 223
Kingdom of Württemberg, 82
Kinkel, Klaus, 144, 145
Kirchner, Carl, 221
Klein, Fritz, 161

Knoflach, Josef, 135
Kohl, Helmut, 78, 145, 185
Kohler, Kurt, 159
Kolbe, Fritz, 84
*Kölner Stadtanzeiger*, 40
Komitet Gosudarstvennoy Bezopasnosti (KGB), 171; Clemens and, 41, 42; Grauer and, 177
Korte, Jan, 87, 202
KPD, banning of, 200
Kraków Ghetto, 196
Krapf, Franz, 79
Kraume, Lars, 209
*Kriminalistik* (Criminalistics), 121
*Kriminalkommissar*, 26
Kriminalpolizei (Kripo), 55, 175, 195
Kristallnacht (November 9), 87, 139, 218, 226
Kroll Opera House, 92, 93
Kroppenstedt, Franz, 116
KSK, 249
Kuhn, Friedrich, 139
Kuhn, Hans, 5
Kunze, Johannes, 97

Laabs, Dirk, 253
Lammert, Norbert, 192–93
Landsberg, 166; executions at, 4, 5; protests/counterprotests at, 3–4
Lang, Xavier, 99
Law for the Prevention of Offspring with Hereditary Diseases, 190
Law No. 15, 241
*Lebensraum*, 183, 252
Lehndorff-Steinort, Heinrich Graf von, 106
Lehnkering, Anna, 192, 193
Lehr, Robert, 215
Leo Baeck Institute, 144, 147
Lermen, Dietmar, 157, 177
Lesser Offenders, 6, 97

Lovell, Colonel, 67
Lüpkes, Gerhard, 238

Machiavelli, 245
Macke, Reinhold, 178
Major Offenders, 6, 97
Malmedy, massacre in, 162, 163
Mansfeld, Michael, 205, 206
"The Man with No Name" (Stahle), 39
Marassi prison, 153
Marschner, Erhard, 161
Martin, Anni, 25, 224
Martin, Otto, 119
Marx, Johannes, 239
Massfeller, Franz, 130-31, 132
Max (Soviet handler), Clemens and, 41, 42
McCloy, John J., 5, 83
Meier, Richard, document about, 44, 45; Wenger and, 37, 38
*Mein Kampf* (Hitler), 4
"Memo on German Civil Service Situation," Globke and, 22
"Memorandum for the Director of Central Intelligence," 23
Menge, Waldemar, 178
Mercker, Reinhold, 169
Merkel, Angela, 88, 89
Merten, Max, 18, 20, 128; arrest of, 129; conviction of, 130; denazification of, 129
Messerschmidt, Manfred, 185
Meyer-Buer, Willi, 200
Michael, Eduard, 111, 112, 113, 114
Milan, 28, 152; executions in, 30, 31, 33, 153
Ministries Case, 82
Ministry for All-German Affairs, Felfe and, 41
Morgenthau, Henry, 99
Morgenthau Plan, 99

Mossad, 18, 210
Müller, Ingo, xvi–xvii
*Münchener Post*, 138
Munich District Court, 136
Munich labor court, Zietlow and, 174

National Front, 50
National Socialist Party, 16, 215
National Socialist Student Association, 119
National Socialist Underground (NSU), 87, 211
NATO, 33, 179, 185, 207
"Navel-Gazing 2007" (*Deutsche Polizei*), 122
neo-Nazis, 87, 145, 212, 252
Neuengamme, memorial in, 212
*Nichtigkeitsbeschwerde*, 222
Niggemeyer, Bernhard, 117, 118
Nixon, Richard, 17, 203, 207
Norddeutscher Rundfunk, 232
Nordkreuz, 248–49, 252
North Rhine-Westphalia Ministry for Social Affairs, 100
Notre Dame cathedral, 218
Nowack, Sabrina, 172, 173, 174, 176, 177, 178, 179
*NS-Kontinuitäten im BND* (Nazi Continuities in the BND) (Sälter), 158, 172
NSU. *See* National Socialist Underground
Nuremberg, 3, 6; trials at, 4, 80, 82, 83, 144, 166, 168
Nuremberg Doctors' Trial, 107
Nuremberg Race Laws, 13, 19, 131; Dehler and, 139; Globke and, 16; guidebook for, 11, 15, 17

Oath Keepers, 253
Oberländer, Theodor, 59, 206–7
Ochs, Josef, 193; immigration laws and, 196; Nazi past of, 194–95; Roma and, 197, 198
Oesterhelt, Gerhard, 112, 113, 114, 115, 116
Offenders, 6, 97
Office of National Estimates (CIA), 20, 23
Office of Policy Coordination, 71
Office of Special Investigations, 259n11
Office of Strategic Services (OSS), 49–50, 51, 84; Dickopf and, 50, 53, 54
Office of the Federal Prosecutor, 217
Ohlendorf, Otto, 4, 5
Oklahoma City, bombing in, 253
Oldenburg, Kurt, 181–82
Olivet, Captain, 53
Ollenhauer, Erich, 203
Operation Barbarossa, 150–51
Operation Rusty, 67
Operations Base, 73
Oppler, Kurt, 235, 236, 237
Oradour-sur-Glane, massacre at, 162
Organizational Unit 85 (Org. 85), 179; Schreiber and, 164; Zietlow and, 172
Organization of Jewish Partisans, 194
Ortloff, Siegfried, 203
OSS. *See* Office of Strategic Services
Oster, Hans, 106
Otten, Walter, 179
Otto, Wolfgang, 165; Nazism and, 179; outrages by, 162–63
Oy, Gottfried, 218, 219

Palais Schaumburg, 9
Palm, Stefanie, 91, 92, 95
Parliamentary Council, 143
Party of Democratic Socialism, 88, 202
People's Court, 144, 145
*Persilscheine*, 8, 98
personnel continuities, 89

Peters, Ewald, 116
Petersberg Hotel, 5
Peterson, Georg, 128
Philp, W. R., 66
Pinochet, Augusto, 155–56
Pircher, Maria, 136
Pizzale Loreto square, executions at, 153
Pogede, Adolf Hermann, 186
Pohl, Oswald, 4, 5
Polizeipraxis (Police Practice), 121
propaganda, 85, 87; communist, 199; neo-Nazi, 247
Proud Boys, 253
Prussian Ministry of the Interior, Globke and, 15
public service, 88, 237, 239, 240; Nazis in, 7, 8; return to, 98
Pullach Base, xi, 67, 70, 71, 72, 178
Putlitz, Wolfgang Gans Elder Herr zu, 84
Putzki, Ernst, 190, 193; death of, 188; on Weilmünster, 189

QAnon, 250
*Quereinsteigers*, 237

racism, 17, 105, 121, 131, 138, 142, 226, 239
Rademacher, Franz, 85
Radical Right, 252
Rathgeber, Anton, 135
rat lines, 153
Rauff, Walter: arrest of, 29, 155, 157; Beisner and, 154; career of, 150; code name for, 154; Cüppers and, 154; death of, 156; efficiency of, 151–52; extradition and, 155; gas vans and, 149, 151, 155; Heydrich and, 151; rat lines and, 153; Saevecke and, 28–29
Reagan, Ronald, 145
Realos (Realists), 78

*Rechtsextremisten in Sicherheitsbehörden*, 268n2
Red Army, 106, 186
Red Army Faction, 78
Red Cross, 18, 79, 80
Redenz, Karl Theodor, 81
Red Scare, 199, 201, 204
rehabilitation, 185; blanket, 187; legal, 184
Rehbogen, Johann, 124, 125
Reich Court, 221, 222
Reich Court, Third Criminal Panel of, 222
Reichenberg, 160, 161
Reich Foreign Office, 81, 85
Reich Interior Ministry, 40, 94, 101, 102, 107; Daelen and, 106; Globke and, 12, 14, 19, 97; Kessler and, 95; Scheffler and, 96, 97; Strauss and, 141
Reich Justice Ministry, 8, 222; Massfeller and, 131; Strauss and, 141
Reich Ministry for the Occupied Eastern Territories, Rumohr and, 103, 104
Reich Ministry of Economics, Strauss and, 141
Reichsbahn, Dickopf and, 50
Reichsbanner, 213
Reichsbund der Deutschen Beamten (Reich Union of German Civil Servants), 195
*Reichsbürger* (Citizens of the Reich), 250
*Reichsbürgergesetz* (Reich Citizenship Law), 15
Reichskriminalpolizeiamt (Reich Criminal Police Office) (RKPA), 195; Dickopf and, 47; Ochs and, 197; Saevecke and, 27
Reichsnährstand, xv

Reichssicherheitshauptamt (Reich Security Main Office) (RSHA), 165, 166; Department VII at, 167; Heinrich and, 133; Wenger and, 40, 41
Reichstag, 92, 93, 188; gathering at, 87, 193
Reimers, Paul, 145-46
Reinke, Herbert, 123
Remagen Bridge, 163
Remer, Otto Ernst, 214-15; Bauer and, 215-16
Renz, Ulrich, xv, 255n1
reparations, 129, 194, 201
Revolutionärer Kampf (Revolutionary Struggle), 78
Rhine River, xi, 5, 11, 65, 127
Ribbentrop, Joachim von, 84
Richter, Maren, 104, 108; Daelen and, 105, 106; research by, 105, 107
Richter, Wilhelm, 161
Riga, executions in, 114-15
right-wing extremism, 58, 87, 213, 251; investigating, 249; new breed of, 247; opposing, 146; organization of, 252-53; police department, 248, 252
Rigoll, Dominik, 236; Adenauer Decree and, 238; on Oppler, 237; VVN and, 239
Rippich, Friedrich, 101, 102
Ritter, Karl, 84
Ritter von Lex, Hans, 94, 102, 235
RKPA. See Reichskriminalpolizeiamt
Roemer, Walter, 132, 136
Rögner, Adolf, 216
Roma, 119, 120, 181, 198; compensation claims for, 197; murder of, 121, 195; postwar treatment of, 197; stereotypes of, 197
Rommel, Erwin, 151, 152
Rose, Romani, 121

Rosenburg symposium, 147
Roth, Otto, 239
RSHA. *See* Reichssicherheitshauptamt
Rückerl, Adalbert, 80, 81
Rumohr, Karl von, 102, 103-4

Sachsenhausen, 151
Saevecke, Theodor, xix, 26, 33, 117, 150, 194, 207; arrest of, 29; code name for, 30; conviction of, 33; deployment of, 27-28; destiny of, 28-29; document on, 34, 35; suspension of, 30; war crimes of, 25, 31
Safferling, Christoph, 144, 146, 147-48; civil servants and, 240-41; Leo Baeck Institute and, 144; research by, 128, 130, 134, 136, 137, 138, 140, 141, 142, 143, 220, 223, 239-40, 244, 246; Rosenburg project and, 147
Sälter, Gerhard, 161, 164, 167, 172, 174, 175, 242; chain recruiting and, 162; document review by, 159, 165-66, 168-69; on Gehlen, 158; Otto and, 163
Salz, Josef, 186
Salzgitter, cemetery desecration at, 211
San Vittore prison, 30, 31, 152
Schafheutle, Josef, 135
*Schatten der Vergangenheit* (Shadows of the Past), 112, 116, 123, 197, 199, 200
Scheffler, Gerhard, 100, 101, 102; career of, 96; deportations and, 97
Schenk, Dieter, 47, 49, 111, 228-29; Dickopf and, 50, 52, 53, 54, 55; medal for, 266n11; Niggemeyer and, 117, 118; war criminals and, xx; work of, 224, 225-26, 227, 228
Schenk, Heinz, 224, 226, 228
Schenklengsfeld, 224, 225
Schindler, Oskar, 17, 147

Index 283

Schlegelberger, Franz, 131
Schmid, Carlo, 202
Schmitt, Andre, 249
Schmitt, Rudolf, 136, 137
Schneider, Christoph, 218, 219
Schreiber, Helmut, 163, 164, 165
Schroder, Gerhard, 78
Schulze-Boysen, Harro, 12–13, 14
Schumacher, Hans, 175
Schuster, Armin, 87, 88
Schütz, Carl, 157
Schütze, Horst, 98
Schutzstaffel (SS), xviii, 7, 9, 26, 101, 114, 150, 164, 173; Bolschwing and, 72, 73; Dickopf and, 47, 57; Fiebig and, 175; hiring former, 239, 242; Saevecke and, 28; Schenk and, 112; Wenger and, 39; Zietlow and, 174
SD. *See* Sicherheitsdienst
SDS. *See* Sozialistischer Deutscher Studentenbund
Second Company, 164, 249
Security Group (BKA), 116, 200, 201; Ochs and, 193; reports by, 199; Saevecke and, 33
Security Police, 71, 133; Dickopf and, 49; Martin and, 119
Seelos, Gebhard, 3–4
Shevardnadze, Eduard, 77
Sichel, Peter, 70, 71, 72
Sicherheitsdienst (SD), 9, 26, 71, 150, 158, 160, 161, 164, 171, 173; Augsburg and, 167; Bolschwing and, 68, 69, 72, 73; Dickopf and, 51; Felfe and, 41; Genoud and, 51; hiring former, 239, 242; Otto and, 163; Rumohr and, 103; Saevecke and, 27; Warzecha and, 178; Wenger and, 39, 40; Zietlow and, 174
Sicherheitspolizei, 158

*Sicherheitsrisiko NS-Belastung* (Security Risk Nazi Incrimination) (Nowack), 172
Siebenlist, Wilhelm, 98
Siegfried, legend of, 11
Sima, Hora, 69
Sinti, 119, 120
Six, Franz Alfred, 167–68
Sixth SS Pancer Army, 163
Sobibor, 124, 154
Social Democratic Party (SPD), xvi, 5, 18, 93, 202, 203, 213; Adenauer and, 205; Dickopf and, 54–55; espionage against, 204; Red Scare and, 204; reintegration and, 267n6; SDS and, 219
Socialistische Reichspartei (Socialist Reich Party) (SRP), 215
Sondergerichte (Special Courts), 134, 135, 185, 222
Sonderkommando 1005b, 174, 175
Sonnemann, Günter, 212
Soviet Union, 55; confrontation with, 4–5; opposition to, 11
Sozialistischer Deutscher Studentenbund (Socialist German Student League) (SDS), 219
Spanish Republicans, 218
Spartacus movement, 141
SPD. *See* Social Democratic Party
Spingarn, Stephen, 153
SS. *See* Schutzstaffel
SS *Andrea Dorea*, 74
SS Death's Head units, 162, 163, 173
SS Race and Settlement Main Office, 142, 160
SS-Verfügungstruppe (Dispositional Troops), 162, 173
*Staatsschutz im Kalten Krieg* (Protection of the State during the Cold War), 220

Stähle, Peter, 38, 39
Stammberger, Wolfgang, 223
Stange, Irina, 91, 95
Stangl, Franz, 154
State Criminal Office, 117, 118, 226
State Justice Administrations for the Investigation of National Socialist Crimes, 57
State Secret No.1, 33, 257n12
Stauffenberg, Claus von, 187, 214
Steinke, Ronen, xx, 19, 255n3; on Bauer, 210, 214, 216–17
Stephan, Andrej, 123
sterilization, 107, 109, 181, 190, 192, 193
*Stern*, Wenger and, 39
Stille Hilfe (Silent Assistance), 159
Strategic Services Unit (SSU), 67
Strauss, Elsa, 141–42
Strauss, Hermann, 141–42
Strauss, Walter, 128, 137, 138, 141, 142
Strecker, Reinhard, 205, 217–18; activism of, 223; appearance/character of, 206; obstructionism/harassment for, 223; politics of, 206
Strübing, Johannes, 39
Stuckart, Wilhelm, 15–16, 17
Students for a Democratic Society, 219
Sturmabteilung, 7, 26, 93, 95, 98, 119, 195; Wenger and, 40
Sturmabteilung Jagow, 150
Stutthof, 124
*Süddeutsche Zeitung*, 210
Sudit, Eliser, 194
Swiss Security Service, 51, 53

T4 Euthanasia Program, 107, 190, 192, 193
Tabarr, Akram, 153, 154
Theresienstadt, 139, 142
Thessalonian Jews, 129, 130

Third Criminal Panel, 212, 222
Thorbeck, Otto, 263n30
Todt Organization, 140
Toussis, Andreas, 128, 130
Traub, Benjamin, 183, 189, 190, 191
Traub, Hartmut, 189, 190, 191, 192
treason, 32, 39, 171, 199, 200, 223; conviction for, 187; trials, 185, 186
Treblinka, 154
Trump, Donald, 253
Tulle, massacre at, 162
Tunisian Jews, 152
Turchino Pass, executions at, 153
Two Plus Four Power talks, 77

Ulm, 58; trial in, 113
Unabhängige Historkerkommission (Commission of Independent Historians) (UHK), 150
Undeutsch, Gerhard, 161
*Ungesühnte Nazijustiz* (Unpunished Nazi Jurists) exhibit, 219, 223
United Press International, 255n1
Urbanski, Sebastian, 188
U.S. Army, 67, 69, 72, 160, 173
U.S. Capitol, storming of, 253
U.S. High Commission, Globke and, 12
U.S. Justice Department, 259n11

van Brieland, Erika, 161
Venedey, Hans, 54
Vienna International Airport, 247
Villa Rosenburg, 127–28, 132, 138, 147
Vlamsche National Verbond (Flemish National League), 165
Vogel, Detlef, 146, 147, 186
Vogel, Hans-Jochen, 146
Volksgerichtshof (People's Court), 185
*Volksschädling* law, 135, 136
Volkswagen, xvii

Index 285

von Schirach, Baldur, xx
von Schirach, Ferdinand, xx
von Schulze-Gaevernitz, Gero, 54
Vorbeck, Jürgen, 123
Vorkommando Moskau (Moscow Advanced Command), 167
Vossschmidt, Stefan, 123
VVN. *See* Association of Victims of the Nazi Regime

Waffen-SS, 145, 162, 163, 172, 173, 179
Wagner, Gustav, 154
Wagner, Patrick, 123, 243, 244, 246; on deportation, 120–21
Wannsee conference, 131, 132
Wannsee Institute, 167
Wannsee police, Strauss and, 141
war crimes, 6, 18, 34, 65, 72, 80, 107, 111, 119, 125, 137; committing, 179; prosecution of, 83
War Criminal Prison No.1, 3
war criminals, 47, 57, 87, 125, 153, 156, 198; cases against, 19; civil service and, 242; execution of, 3, 4, 5; exposure of, xx; finding, 124, 125, 129, 179; hiring, 78, 162; justice for, 134, 172; pardons for, 7; prosecution of, 6–7, 124; protesting for, 3–4
War Economy Ordinance, 136
Warlo, Johannes, 217
Warndienst West (Warning Service West), 79
Wartheland, 96, 100, 101, 102
Warzecha, Gerhard, 178
Watergate, 17, 203, 207
Waters, Wayland B., 18, 19, 20
Weilmünster, 188, 189, 190, 191
Weimar constitution, 138
Weiss, Kurt, 166
Weitnauer, Hermann, 132
Weizsäcker, Ernst von, 82, 83

Wels, Otto, 92, 93
Wenger, Erich, 42; allegations against, 43; document about, 44, 45; downfall of, 41; wartime record of, 37–38, 40
Westdeutscher Rundfunk, 232
Westend Hospital, 105
Wette, Wolfram, 185, 186
Wiecher, Hanns J., 206
Wiechmann, Carlo, 220
Wiesenthal, Simon, 80, 81
Wilimzig, Georg, 178
Winker, Paul Helmut, 176
Wirsching, Andreas, xvii, xviii, 102–3; research by, 91, 92, 94, 95, 96, 101, 104, 105, 108, 236, 244
Wolf, Hans, 225, 226
Wolf, Liese, 225
Wolff, Karl, 156
Wolf's Lair, 214
Wolter, Eduard, 40
Wondrak, Hermann, 160–61
Wulkan, Emil, 216
Wuppertal police, Kessler and, 94–95

Zafke, Hubert, 125
Zentrale Rechtsschutzstelle (Central Legal Defense Agency) (ZRS), 79, 81
Zentrale Stelle der Landesjustiz Verwaltungen zur Aufklärung nationalsozialistischer Verbrechen (Central Office of the State Justice Administrations for the Investigation of National Socialist Crimes), 57
Ziegler, Siegfried, code name for, 203
Ziercke, Jörg, 120, 122
Zietlow, Fritz, 171, 172, 173; career of, 174; conviction of, 175; denazification of, 174; investigation of, 175
Zimmermann, Moshe, 85, 86
ZRS. *See* Zentrale Rechtsschutzstelle
Zuber, Ebrulf, 160, 161, 162, 165